A THEORY OF INTERNATIONAL ORGANIZATIONS IN PUBLIC INTERNATIONAL LAW

Grea— ter, lesser, or just different than the sum of their parts? For all their
prom— inence in global affairs, international organizations remain relative
stra— gers from the perspective of international legal theory. Drawing
insig— ts from philosophical discourse, this book moves past binary
mode— ls that would have international organizations be either nothing
over — and above their members or simply analogous to them. Rather than
comp— are international organizations and their members, Chasapis
Tassi— is asks us to understand them both as manifestations of communal
organ— ization and what international law recognizes as 'public' authority.
Theor— izing international organizations as only a branch within a broader
family— of corporate entities, this book allows us to untangle old doctrinal
puzzle— s. These include the extent to which international organizations are
bound— by customary international law and can contribute to its formation, — r whether they enjoy a legal personality that is opposable to
memb— rs and non-members alike.

ORFEA— S CHASAPIS TASSINIS is a Research Fellow at Gonville & Caius
College— and an Affiliated Lecturer at the University of Cambridge, where
he teac— es public international law at the Faculty of Law.

CAMBRIDGE STUDIES IN INTERNATIONAL AND
COMPARATIVE LAW: 193

Established in 1946, this series produces high quality, reflective and innovative scholarship in the field of public international law. It publishes works on international law that are of a theoretical, historical, cross-disciplinary or doctrinal nature. The series also welcomes books providing insights from private international law, comparative law and transnational studies which inform international legal thought and practice more generally.

The series seeks to publish views from diverse legal traditions and perspectives, and of any geographical origin. In this respect it invites studies offering regional perspectives on core *problématiques* of international law, and in the same vein, it appreciates contrasts and debates between diverging approaches. Accordingly, books offering new or less orthodox perspectives are very much welcome. Works of a generalist character are greatly valued and the series is also open to studies on specific areas, institutions or problems. Translations of the most outstanding works published in other languages are also considered.

After seventy years, Cambridge Studies in International and Comparative Law sets the standard for international legal scholarship and will continue to define the discipline as it evolves in the years to come.

Series Editors

Larissa van den Herik

Professor of Public International Law, Grotius Centre for International Legal Studies, Leiden University

Jean d'Aspremont

Professor of International Law, University of Manchester and Sciences Po Law School

A list of books in the series can be found at the end of this volume.

A THEORY OF INTERNATIONAL ORGANIZATIONS IN PUBLIC INTERNATIONAL LAW

ORFEAS CHASAPIS TASSINIS

University of Cambridge

CAMBRIDGE UNIVERSITY PRESS

CAMBRIDGE
UNIVERSITY PRESS

Shaftesbury Road, Cambridge CB2 8EA, United Kingdom

One Liberty Plaza, 20th Floor, New York, NY 10006, USA

477 Williamstown Road, Port Melbourne, VIC 3207, Australia

314–321, 3rd Floor, Plot 3, Splendor Forum, Jasola District Centre, New Delhi – 110025, India

103 Penang Road, #05-06/07, Visioncrest Commercial, Singapore 238467

Cambridge University Press is part of Cambridge University Press & Assessment, a department of the University of Cambridge.

We share the University's mission to contribute to society through the pursuit of education, learning and research at the highest international levels of excellence.

www.cambridge.org
Information on this title: www.cambridge.org/9781009373951

DOI: 10.1017/9781009374002

When citing this work, please include a reference to the DOI 10.1017/9781009374002

First published 2025

A catalogue record for this publication is available from the British Library

A Cataloging-in-Publication data record for this book is available from the Library of Congress

ISBN 978-1-009-37395-1 Hardback

In loving memory of Maria 'Mikrí Latsi

CONTENTS

FIGURES

ACKNOWLEDGEMENTS

There are many people who supported me while writing this book, and to whom I owe my sincere gratitude. I am also thankful to the Cambridge University Press team for making this book possible.

I completed this book as a Research Fellow at Gonville and Caius College at Cambridge, surrounded by many talented academics and good friends. My first thanks go to Lorand Bartels and Sarah Nouwen. As my PhD supervisor, Lorand was present at crucial junctures of developing the ideas behind this book, always prompting me to explore my own curiosity. Next to Lorand, I am deeply grateful to Sarah. For me, Sarah stands as a model of a big-picture thinker who at the same time has the analytical acumen for doctrinal detail and cares about the relationship between the two. She has been incredibly generous to me and shown me more kindness than I could have ever asked for. In the same vein, I thank my good colleagues at the Lauterpacht Centre for International Law with whom I have shared much over the years, including Sandesh Sivakumaran, Surabhi Ranganathan, Rumiana Yotova, Maayan Menashe, and Matilda Gillis. I will always be grateful to all the people who taught me international law at the universities of Thessaloniki, Athens, and New York. Finally, I would like to thank Jan Klabbers for his support ever since serving as my PhD examiner.

My sincere thanks also extend to my college. Caius remains one of those places that truly and unreservedly supports young scholars, making books like this materially possible. I could not be more appreciative of my time with the Fellowship. The same thanks go to the AHRC Doctoral Training Partnership, and the WM Tapp and A Sinclair funds that supported me during my PhD.

Lastly, I thank all those who have stood by me over the past years on a personal level, whether in Cambridge, Athens, or Sifnos. Special thanks go to Anna and Eleftherios, Dimitra, Kalliopi, Anna, Ioannis and Anna-Iasmi, Dafni, Nikos, Afroditi, Ekavi, Ioannis and Athena, Stuart and

Suzan, Carsten, Vedran, Richard, Vasileios, Maria and Ioannis, Theophilos, George, and Nikolaos.

There are no words to express the love I have for my parents, Panos and Evridiki, and my brother, Konstantinos. The same goes for Maria Latsi, who raised me as if I were her own, and to whom I am forever grateful.

TABLE OF CASES

International Court of Justice and Permanent Court of International Justice

Other International Jurisdictions

National Jurisdictions

TABLE OF INSTRUMENTS

ABBREVIATIONS

AJIL	American Journal of International Law
BYIL	British Yearbook of International Law
CJIL	Chinese Journal of International Law
CJTL	Columbia Journal of Transnational Law
CUP	Cambridge University Press
ECHR	European Convention of Human Rights
ECtHR	European Court of Human Rights
EJIL	European Journal of International Law
EPO	European Patent Organization
EU	European Union
GAL	Global Administrative Law
HUP	Harvard University Press
ICC	International Criminal Court
ICCPR	International Covenant on Civil and Political Rights
ICESCR	International Covenant on Economic Social and Cultural Rights
ICJ	International Court of Justice
ICRC	International Committee of the Red Cross
ICTR	International Criminal Tribunal for Rwanda
ILA	International Law Association
ILC	International Law Commission
ILO	International Labour Organization
ILOAT	International Labour Organization Administrative Tribunal
IMF	International Monetary Fund
IOLR	International Organizations Law Review
JICJ	Journal of International Criminal Justice
OUP	Oxford University Press
PCIJ	Permanent Court of International Justice
PUP	Princeton University Press
QIL	Questions of International Law
TRIPS	Agreement on Trade-Related Aspects of Intellectual Property Rights
UN	United Nations
VCLT 1969	Vienna Convention on the Law of Treaties

VCLT 1986	Vienna Convention on the Law of Treaties between States and International Organizations or between International Organizations
WHO	World Health Organization
WTO	World Trade Organization
YILC	Yearbook of the International Law Commission

~

Introduction

This book addresses two interrelated problems regarding the legal nature of international organizations in public international law. The first problem concerns whether and why these institutions can be thought of as legally distinct from their members. The second problem pertains to the content of international organizations' legal personality, meaning their capacities, rights, and obligations, assuming that they are legally distinct from their members. To address these two problems, this book embarks on a philosophical investigation of the nature of corporate existence itself. It argues that we cannot adequately theorize the existence of any corporate entity, including international organizations, without first making up our minds as to how and why the existence of its members is possible to begin with. Thus, this book revisits deeply entrenched doctrinal assumptions about international organizations as well as their members, including, most prominently, states. Rather than dwell on how international organizations may compare to or differ from their members, this book draws emphasis on the fact that all these entities represent potentialities of communal planning and organization. The outcome is a legal theory of 'institutional genealogy'. I coin this term to signify that both international organizations and their members ultimately rise from the same root: the capacity of an organized community of human beings to self-describe.

Why engage with theory to begin with? For some time now, international organizations have been seen as a field lacking in sustained theoretical reflection and riddled with paradoxes. As two authorities have suggested in that regard: 'international organizations law is one of those fields of international law where theorization by lawyers has been kept to a minimum ... it is not even clear what a theory of international organizations law would be a theory of.[1] Yet the field has been

[1] Jan Klabbers and Guy Fiti Sinclair, 'On Theorizing International Organizations Law: Editors' Introduction' (2020) 31(2) EJIL 489, 494. See also Jan Klabbers, *An Introduction to International Organizations Law* (4th edn, CUP 2022) 3. Notably, Henry

1

increasingly content with an image of doctrinal ambiguity – sometimes expending more effort in theorizing the ambiguity rather than the institutions themselves. Indeed, much of contemporary scholarship has rationalized the field's puzzles either as built-in uncertainties that can be properly resolved only through normative fiat, or, for the more critical variant, as problems that are better looked at from the 'outside', without engaging with them at a doctrinal level. Another strand has steered towards developing, much needed in their own regard, political economy accounts of international organizations, usually in terms of global governance, but with less interest in updating doctrine.

Without firm theoretical grounding, however, clear answers on key doctrinal problems surrounding international organizations remain elusive.[2] Almost eighty years after the International Court of Justice's (ICJ) Advisory Opinion in the *Reparation for Injuries Suffered in the Service of the United Nations* – often hailed as a milestone for the evolution of international organizations law[3] – the discipline still appears to lack 'a

---

Schermers and Niels Blokker also introduce their classic treatise on international institutional law with the aphorism that 'theoretical reflection in the field of international organizations has been limited': Henry G Schermers and Niels M Blokker, *International Institutional Law* (5th edn, Martinus Nijhoff 2011) 9. See also Anne Peters, 'Constitutional Theories of International Organisations: Beyond the West' (2021) 20(4) CJIL 649, 676, calling for a refocusing on theory. Studies of regional international organizations often focus more on describing particular features of these institutions rather than theorizing the field in more abstract terms: see eg Marco Odello and Francesco Seatzu (eds), *Latin American and Caribbean International Institutional Law* (Springer 2015). For the main Chinese textbooks' approach to theorizing international organizations, see Yifeng Chen, 'International Institutions as Forms and Fora: Rao Geping and the Law of International Organizations in China' (2023) 34(4) EJIL 855, 864–871. For the relative underdevelopment of Third World approaches to theorizing international organizations law, see Kehinde Folake Olaoye, 'Samuel Kwadwo Boaten Asante and the United Nations Centre on Transnational Corporations (1975–1992)' (2023) 34(2) EJIL 291, 308–315. Cf Ernest Toochi Aniche, 'Beyond Neo-functionalism: Africa in Search of a New Theory of Regional Integration' in Ernest Toochi Aniche, Ikenna Mike Alumona, and Inocent Moyo (eds), *Regionalism, Security and Development in Africa* (Routledge 2021).

[2] See eg Catherine Brölmann, 'A Flat Earth? International Organizations in the System of International Law' 70 Nordic Journal of International Law 319, suggesting that there are inherent tensions in accommodating international organizations as independent actors that exist in parallel to their members in the international legal system; see also Edward Chukwuemeke Okeke, *Jurisdictional Immunities of States and International Organizations* (OUP 2018) 2, on the controversies and confusion surrounding the immunities of international organizations.

[3] See eg Thomas D Grant and Rowan Nicholson, 'The Early United Nations Advisory Opinions (1948–62)' in Eirik Bjorge and Cameron Miles (eds), *Landmark Cases in Public International Law* (Hart 2017).

convincing theory on the international legal personality of international organizations',[4] as well as any 'plausible theory of obligation' for these institutions.[5] It thus remains unclear whether international organizations can contribute to the formation of norms of customary international law directly, rather than merely as fora in which states can express their views.[6] Furthermore, questions of whether international organizations are bound by the same customary norms as states – so crucial when one considers the ever-expansive field of activities of international organizations and the near total lack of treaty obligations – have largely escaped analytical closure. Pressing problems of applying the law in relation to international organizations thus endure: is the International Monetary Fund (IMF) bound by human rights law? Is there a right to head-of-state immunity before the International Criminal Court (ICC)? Which laws, if any, were applicable to the United Nations (UN) in relation to the cholera outbreak in Haiti in the 2010s?

Questions such as these cannot be answered on the basis of normative choice, however well-intended, nor does political economy speak directly to them, at least in a practically meaningful way. Instead, they present real, and sometimes pressing, legal questions that beg for some resolution within the confines of the discipline.[7]

Most sustained doctrinal approaches to these problems have been taken over by a binary mindset about the legal nature of international organizations. International organizations, so we have been told, can be conceptualized either as mere treaty arrangements between states, sometimes also known as the 'contractual' view, or as independent legal subjects, sometimes also known as the 'constitutional' view. Taken

---

[4] Klabbers, *Introduction to International Organizations Law* (n 1) 2.

[5] Jan Klabbers, 'The Paradox of International Institutional Law' (2008) 5 IOLR 1, 15. For one of the earliest academic expositions of this problem, see Mahnoush H Arsanjani, 'Claims against International Organizations: Quis Custodiet Ipsos Custodes' (1981) 7 Yale Journal of World Public Order 131, 174.

[6] See eg Lorenzo Gasbarri, 'Beyond the Either/Or Paradigm in the Formation of Customary International Law by International Organizations' in Jean d' Aspremont and Sufyan Droubi (eds), *International Organizations and the Formation of Customary International Law* (Manchester University Press 2020) 102; Kristina Daugirdas, 'International Organizations and the Creation of Customary International Law' (2018) 31 EJIL 201.

[7] Jan Klabbers, 'Theorizing International Organizations' in Anne Orford and Florian Hoffmann (eds), *The Oxford Handbook of the Theory of International Law* (OUP 2016) 618. See also Jan Klabbers, 'The EJIL Foreword: The Transformation of International Organizations Law' (2015) 26 EJIL 9–15.

together, these two views are commonly taken to reflect an 'all-embracing dichotomy' that pervades theorizing these institutions for doctrinal purposes.[8]

The theory developed in this book overcomes this dichotomy. This book argues that, at closer inspection, both these antithetical models rest on certain obscure, and ultimately misplaced, initial assumptions about the state. Constructing the state in the image of the so-called natural person, the field has tended to misleadingly analogize, either explicitly or implicitly, the problem of theorizing international organizations to that of corporate entities in domestic law. Drawing inspiration from philosophical discourse on collective entities, this book advances an alternative theoretical foundation that moves away from this analogy and its problems. Rather than trying to compare and contrast international organizations with states or analyse the former as reducible to the latter, this book shifts our focus back to continuity in the exercise of public power as the key in theorizing both institutions.

Given the increased popularity of more critical approaches among international lawyers, this move to legal theory is worth explaining on its own terms.[9] Certainly, the search for doctrinal answers does not negate the presence of an 'outside' world with its own dynamics, and indeed normative as well as distributional contestation.[10] It also does not mean that there will no longer be more or less powerful actors, trying to achieve their aims through international institutions. All such observations are valuable in their own regard and have rightly given rise to a distinct body of scholarship. What this book suggests, however, is that law still has its own role to play in all this. In turn, legal reasoning derives its authority and persuasiveness from being attentive to coherence and scrutinizing one's operating assumptions. In this epistemological point of departure, law and legal reasoning are not simply derivative or

---

[8] Jean d'Aspremont, 'The Law of International Organizations and the Art of Reconciliation: From Dichotomies to Dialectics' (2014) 11 IOLR 428, 430.

[9] For the rise and trajectory of critical approaches to international law, as well as the difficulty (and possible futility) of neatly categorizing them, see Fleur Johns, 'Critical International Legal Theory' in Jeffrey L Dunnoff and Mark A Pollack (eds), *International Legal Theory* (CUP 2022).

[10] See, for example, BS Chimni, 'International Institutions Today: An Imperial Global State in the Making' (2004) 15 EJIL 1; BS Chimni, 'International Organizations: 1945–Present', in Jacob Katz Cogan et al (eds), *The Oxford Handbook of International Organizations* (OUP 2016) 123–129; Antony Anghie, 'Time Present and Time Past: Globalization, International Financial Institutions, and the Third World' (2000) 32 NYUJILP 243.

epiphenomenal to other domains of knowledge or existence; a legal theory is thought of as being a possible and worthwhile endeavour. And, while there can be reasonable differences of opinion on what is the 'right' answer to a certain legal question, a potential disagreement need not as such threaten the whole disciplinary edifice, as indeed is not the case when two historians or two economists disagree on a given point. In short, this book proceeds on the basis that there are more and less convincing ways of thinking analytically about international organizations, and a meaningful choice can be made between them within the confines of the law.

At the same time, we have to recognize that theories do not originate out of nowhere. They are all about, and ultimately as good as, their starting assumptions. Assumptions shape the form that problems, as well as solutions, take – the paths taken, as well as those left untrodden. They orient us, sometimes in subtle and imperceptible ways, from the smallest of issues to the broadest of outlooks. Thus, if we are to overcome current doctrinal puzzles, we need to draw out in the open existing assumptions and openly interrogate them. Consequently, part of theory building is understanding where we come from and how our numerous assumptions operate, both on their own terms and in relation to one another.

When it comes to international organizations, the field's operating theoretical frameworks can be described on at least two levels of abstraction.

At the first level we find certain general constructions that condition much of doctrinal legal analysis. Such is for instance the aforementioned binary of the 'treaty' and 'subject' conceptions of international organizations. These represent particular takes on the *objet théorétique*, namely in this case the notion that an international organization *is* essentially a treaty or that it *is* a self-constituted autonomous subject. In terms of concrete legal consequences, these two models translate roughly as follows: international organizations are either mere treaty arrangements between states or independent legal actors. A host of ancillary positions on doctrinal matters then draws support from these conceptualizations. For example, if international organizations are seen as independent legal actors in their own regard, then their legal personality can be understood to be opposable to non-members, whereas if they are thought of as mere contractual arrangements, they will enjoy a legal existence, if any, only vis-à-vis their members.

Beyond these doctrinally oriented outlooks, there is a meta-theoretical level that is worth keeping in mind. Although terminology varies, this includes popular notions such as 'functionalism' and 'constitutionalism'. Functionalism, simply put, refers to the idea that international organizations are agents of their members tasked with carrying out certain functions.[11] Constitutionalism is generally identified with the idea that international organizations represent objective cessions of state sovereignty and the creation of altogether new political entities.[12] Although theories such as functionalism and constitutionalism, along with more focused outlooks such as Global Administrative Law (GAL) or

---

[11] For functionalism, see generally Klabbers, 'Theorizing International Organizations' (n 7). Michel Virally was one of the first international lawyers to overtly theorize international organizations around the idea of the functions which they perform. See Michel Virally, 'La Notion de Fonction Dans La Théorie de l'organisation Internationale', in Suzanne Bastid and others (eds), *Mélanges offerts à Charles Rousseau: La communauté internationale* (Pédone 1974). On the functionalist origins of regional integration in Latin America, see Gordon Mace, 'Regional Integration in Latin America: A Long and Winding Road' 1988 43(3) International Journal 404. The idea that international governance is at its core functional, meaning that states use international organizations to reduce the costs of solving collective action problems, is well established in international relations. See Robert Keohane, *After Hegemony: Cooperation and Discord in the World Political Economy* (PUP 1984); Barbara Koremenos, Charles Lipson, and Duncan Snidal. 'The Rational Design of International Institutions' (2001) 55(4) International Organization 761. For a 'postfunctionalist' approach to international organizations in international relations, see Liesbet Hooghe, Tobias Lenz, and Gary Marks, *A Theory of International Organization* (OUP 2019). See also Michael Barnett and Martha Finnemore, *Rules for the World: International Organizations in Global Politics* (CUP 2004).

[12] On the 'constitutionalization' of international organizations, see Anne Peters, 'Constitutionalisation', in Jean d'Aspremont and Sahib Singh (eds), *Concepts for International Law: Contributions to Disciplinary Thought* (Edward Elgar, 2019). On the parallel development of functionalism and constitutionalism, see Anne Peters, 'International Organizations and International Law', in Jacob Katz Cogan, Ian Hurd, and Ian Johnstone (eds), *The Oxford Handbook of International Organizations* (OUP 2017). On Third World approaches to the development of international organizations law, see Olaoye (n 1). For a historical interpretation, and critique, of the idea that international organizations are supposed to represent limitations of state sovereignty, see Arnulf Becker Lorca, *Mestizo International Law: A Global Intellectual History 1842–1933* (CUP 2015) 179–199. On thinking about the evolution of international organizations in terms of gradual layering rather than radical changes in different modes of governance, see Guy Fiti Sinclair, *To Reform the World: International Organizations and the Making of Modern States* (OUP 2017). For the particular contribution of Latin America's regional practices to the development of international organizations, see Tom Long and Carsten-Andreas Schultz, 'Republican Internationalism: The Nineteenth-Century Roots of Latin American Contributions to International Order' (2022) 35(5) Cambridge Review of International Affairs 639, 644. On the development of regional integration in Africa, see Samuel Osagie Odobo, 'Conceptualising and Historicising African Regionalism in the Context of Pan-Africanism' in Ernest Toochi Aniche, Ikenna Mike Alumona, and Inocent Moyo (eds), *Regionalism, Security and Development in Africa* (Routledge 2021).

International Public Authority that draw on concepts of administration and public law, do not necessarily aim at solving particular doctrinal problems as such, this level often informs legal imagination and serves as normative backdrop for choices at the analytical level.[13] For example, a 'functional' approach is often associated with a 'private law paradigm' and a 'contractual' understanding of international organizations. In turn, this is often linked to a theory of 'derivative' (or granted) personality, which is usually understood in a relative manner, meaning that it is not opposable to non-members. Conversely, a 'constitutional' approach tends to be identified with public law and a 'subject' conception of international organizations. In such a framework, international organizations are often supposed to possess an 'inherent' legal personality that is opposable *erga omnes*. Thus, even though outlooks such as functionalism or constitutionalism can be understood as normative theories, they also lend themselves to doctrinal transplantation, normally along the same binary lines that the more analytical 'treaty' and 'subject' conceptions do.[14]

---

[13] Indicatively on Global Administrative Law, see Benedict Kingsbury, Nico Krisch, and Richard B Stewart, 'The Emergence of Global Administrative Law' (2005) 68 Law and Contemporary Problems 15; on International Public Authority, see Armin von Bogdandy and others (eds), *The Exercise of Public Authority by International Institutions: Advancing International Institutional Law* (Springer 2010). For scholarship that openly engages with most contemporary theoretical approaches, see José Alvarez, *International Organizations as Law-Makers* (OUP 2005). On approaches balancing between functionalism and constitutionalism, see Evelyne Lagrange, *Functionalism According to Paul Reuter* (2020) 31(2) EJIL 543.

[14] A word of caution is warranted regarding the often-overlapping vocabularies of international lawyers and international relations scholars, who might both employ terms such as 'functionalism', 'constitution', 'contract', 'public authority', as well as 'autonomy', among others. Sometimes the use of such terms may unveil common themes, as for example with the idea of 'functionalism' (see n 9). It may even be the case that developments in one field broadly correspond to those in the other, as for example when both international lawyers and international relations scholars started picking up on the idea that international organizations may sometimes produce negative externalities: see Arsanjani (n 5) and Barnett and Finnemore (n 11), respectively. Historical research may also challenge popular conceptions of international organizations' relation to states (see eg Sinclair (12)) in a manner not too dissimilar from what this book intends on doing from the point of view of legal theory. Such overlaps and parallel developments are by no means accidental. Yet each discipline has its own logic of inquiry, constrains, conditions for persuasiveness, variations in themes, as well as path-dependencies. To give one example: many international lawyers appear to dwell on the distinction between the constituent instrument of an international organization as a contract as opposed to a constitution, whereas many international relations scholars casually analyse constitutions *as* contracts and vice versa without putting so much weight on either categorization.

The work at hand breaks with such binaries when thinking analytically about international organizations. Questioning their fundamental assumptions, it argues that *both* the 'treaty' and the 'subject' conception, as they are normally construed, offer insufficient, and ultimately flawed, ways of theorizing these institutions. Indeed, viewing anything and everything through the lens of this dipole, we have obscured from ourselves more productive lines of inquiry, leaving a host of more practical questions in doctrinal limbo. To this end, this book delivers a critique to both the 'treaty' and 'subject' conceptions before moving on to suggest an alternative framework.

The critique I raise is twofold.

The first limb of my critique is that the treaty/subject binary speaks only to part of the problem of theorizing international organizations – it is thus incomplete. Indeed, the binary provides a way to imagine the relationship between an organization and its members. It suggests that organizations are either 'open', transparent entities that amount to little more than elaborate contractual arrangements, or 'closed', opaque legal subjects that enjoy their own separate existence. However, as presently configured, this binary provides few insights into international organizations' legal nature, *assuming* that they are structurally distinct legal entities. Most importantly, this question encompasses the conceptual relation between these institutions and states as species of legal actors, and the resulting content of their legal personality. This is a key relation that we need to investigate if we are to reason analytically about whether international organizations can contribute to the formation of customary international law in their own name, or the extent that custom applies to their activities in the same manner that it does to states.

The second limb of my critique is that the treaty/subject binary also faces difficulties with respect to the phenomenon that it is primarily geared to address, namely the relationship between an organization and its members. At closer inspection, both ends of the binary turn out to not cohere with well-accepted premises of public international law or with their own findings. Although analytically less demanding, the 'treaty'

An investigation of who is 'right' or 'wrong' in this respect seems somewhat meaningless in the abstract. Rather what matters is to appreciate the research question posed each time and the framing it corresponds to. Generally, while this book will flag such lateral moves and use of terms whenever this illuminates a potentially deeper thematic connection, it will refrain from drawing direct comparisons across disciplines just for the sake of comparison.

conception finds itself in tension with the notion that these institutions enjoy a separate legal existence. This seems hard to square with practice suggesting that international organizations, at least in a minimal sense, do rise as entities above their founding treaty arrangements. This includes the basic notion that international organizations can have acts attributed to *them* (as opposed to their members) or that *they* and *their* officials may enjoy certain privileges and immunities. However, the more popular 'subject' conception also produces an unsatisfactory account of the legal personality of those institutions and their distinct will. Properly construed, this line of thought cannot buttress analytically the much acclaimed 'objectivity' of international organizations' legal personality. It often ends up sourcing it in a presumed 'rule of incorporation' or other positive rule of international law, whose customary status remains uncertain. At the same time, the accompanying notion that international organizations enjoy a *volonté distincte* that is supposed to elevate them into something more than mere contractual arrangements remains notoriously nebulous, and of almost 'metaphysical' import.[15]

At this point you might legitimately wonder: can it really be that our operating models have been that off their target? To put things into better perspective, we need to bear in mind that neither the 'treaty' nor the 'subject' conceptions are themselves fully fledged theories, at least in the sense contemplated here. Rather than being holistic frames of reference, they generally emerge from looking closely at how particular puzzles, including the very idea of legal personality, have been reasoned through in international legal discourse based on their expressed or inferred underlying assumptions. The two conceptions are, in a sense, 'bottom-up' theories that exhibit all the virtues and flaws that this type of theory making tends to exhibit: intuitive in some respects, but patchy and inconsistent in others. Still, the binary has developed a certain path-dependency, creating overall a problematic picture. Beyond that, identifying the two analytical models with otherwise fixed normative, 'top-down' outlooks, such as constitutionalism or functionalism, risks giving them the appearance of a conceptual rigidity that they do not necessarily enjoy.

Indeed, many scholarly authorities never lost sight of the somewhat makeshift and, ultimately, unsatisfactory, character of our current theoretical models. The remedy to this predicament has largely been to employ the models insofar as they make sense, but then adopt pragmatic, or in

---

[15] Catherine Brölmann, *The Institutional Veil in Public International Law: International Organisations and the Law of Treaties* (Hart Oxford 2007) 21.

some cases outright normative, positions when the models' logic appears to run out. This sensibility is largely responsible for why, even if our models are far from perfect, the field outwardly maintains an image of operating coherence. Thus, all too often, scholars have expressed genuine hesitation before drawing all the necessary conclusions that would follow naturally from adopting their models when their better judgement points to another direction. Consider, for example, the imbalance that ascribing equal weight to the practice of international organizations and states would create for the identification of custom following the 'subject' conception, especially given how the former outnumber the latter. Yet even when scholars have quietly 'bent' the rules to allow for more sensible solutions, this has rarely been justified by relying on an alternative holistic framework or revisiting the discipline's chief theoretical premises. In sum, while few have been really satisfied with the field's theories, this has not led to a sustained analytical interrogation of the underlying models, let alone to moving past them.

To surpass this conundrum, we first need to let go of the dominant piecemeal approach, however appealing it may seem in tackling individual questions. Thus, we must reconstruct, as faithfully and as comprehensively as possible, the treaty/subject conceptions, if only to then closely interrogate them. And, for this interrogation to be fruitful, it must take at face value the assumptions of either side of the binary. Take for instance the potent idea that international law might feature a customary rule of incorporation for international organizations. If this rule cannot be shown to exist in customary international law, the whole line of thought should be questioned, rather than being adopted as reflecting the doctrine's best available 'rationalization'.[16] Instead, to overcome the limits of our current constructions, we need to follow them faithfully up to their breaking points and appreciate why they may come up short. Thus, in lieu of asking whether the existence of a rule of incorporation is the best rationalization that doctrine currently has to offer, which it probably is, this book will be investigating how we got to the point where such a hypothesis became necessary in the first place.

Next to aiming for a more holistic approach, we also need to discern and, if necessary, critique the immanent logic of current models. In this respect, as counterintuitive as it may seem at first, this book suggests that the two antithetical ways of conceptualizing international organizations

---

[16] Cf Fernando Bordin, *The Analogy between States and International Organizations: Legal Reasoning and the Development of the Law of International Organizations* (CUP 2018) 63.

turn out to share a common conceptual framework. *Both* the treaty and the subject conception tend to understand the underlying problem of corporate existence of international organizations in the same manner, even as they offer different solutions to it. Despite appearances, both conceptualizations take off from similar crude assumptions about the state – the entity that after all is supposed to form the most common building block of international organizations. These assumptions point to a 'billiard ball', and at its core anthropomorphic, understanding of the state as a fundamental, irreducible, and inherently unitary entity.[17]

This model of the state should be familiar to most international lawyers as a mental shortcut that we often employ for explaining some of international laws' most fundamental concepts either to ourselves or to others. In essence, this conception analytically approximates the state to a closed off and unitary entity modelled after the individual human being. In turn, this suggests that the problem of international organizations resembles, at a fundamental level, a familiar problem of domestic law, namely the relationship between 'natural' and 'moral' persons. This book argues that, even though intuitive in certain respects, this exegesis unnecessarily pushes analytical thinking into a corner from where it cannot convincingly extract itself.

Anthropomorphic models of the state distort the theorizing effort with respect to international organizations. When it comes to the structural relationship between international organizations and their members, these models suggest that international organizations are by default nonentities. This premise leaves two equally unsatisfying avenues for theorizing the legal distinctiveness of these institutions. The first, as just seen, is to argue that the system of international law has developed a rule of incorporation that specifically recognizes international organizations as entities distinct from their members, much in line with how the problem would be tackled in many domestic jurisdictions. The alternative is to argue that international law has itself undergone a 'radical extension of its definition' so that other entities can now essentially enjoy the same legal status as states based on their objective existence in social reality.[18] Aside from their conceptual complexities, both these propositions have

---

[17] The 'billiard ball' metaphor, often employed in international relations, is usually attributed to Arnold Wolfers, *Discord and Collaboration: Essays on International Politics* (Johns Hopkins Press 1962).

[18] Finn Seyersted, 'Objective International Personality of Intergovernmental Organizations: Do Their Capacities Really Depend upon the Conventions Establishing Them?' (1964) 34 Nordic Journal of International Law 3, 93.

been notoriously hard to prove in positive law, leaving the field without a full analytical justification for its existential premise, namely the separate legal personality of international organizations.

When it comes to the conceptual relationship between states and international organizations as species of legal actors – a key topic that has mostly been neglected by scholarship thus far – the analogy between states and individuals leads to a confusing conundrum. Anthropomorphic interpretations of the state's legal personality suggest that international organizations are either 'artificial' or 'fictional', and thus somehow less 'real' than states, or that they too should be theorized as 'organic' or 'soulful' entities, and thus on par with states. Trapped between the opposite ends of this crude binary, the discipline has been left with unappealing avenues for theorizing these institutions. We must either accept that there is a hardwired category difference between states and international organizations or analyse the latter as if they were essentially just another state.

Moving past this framework, this book revisits the problem of theorizing international organizations from first principles. It suggests that international lawyers have to tackle a classic philosophical problem before making any headway: when, if ever, can we talk of a corporate entity that is not merely the aggregate of its members? Furthermore, if we accept that there can be genuine or 'real' corporate entities, what is their conceptual relationship to their members? The premise that surfaces for tackling these questions is that problems of existence are meaningful only when posed in relative terms: a thing's existence *in relation* to something else. In turn, this suggests that we must interrogate the 'conditions of existence' not just of the composite entity whose existence we seek to investigate, but also that out of which it is supposed to emerge, its 'atoms' so to speak. When it comes to corporate entities, this line of reasoning requires that we look at the members' existence as much as that of the corporate entity itself. Zeroing in on these questions, the book advances a philosophically inspired argument about the personality of international organizations and their relationship to the personality of their members, including most prominently states.

The result is a theory that presents a radical departure from the explicit or implicit assumptions of most current approaches but coheres better with practice and can also help resolve key doctrinal ambiguities. This book argues that the problem of theorizing international organizations is fundamentally *not* similar to the problem of theorizing corporate entities made out of 'natural' or 'soulful' human beings. The answer to our problems is neither that international organizations are 'artificial' and somehow intrinsically different to states, nor that they too are 'natural' or 'soulful', and thus similar enough to states to be counted as such. Instead, I argue that *both* entities should be understood as artificial. Couched in these terms, the key to fully grasping their conceptual relationship does not lie with some sort of comparison between the two or by understanding one as made out of the other. Rather, it is to show that, even if international organizations indeed emerge as wholes distinct from their parts, their existence emanates from a reshuffling and reconfiguration of what remains at its root public power that formally derives its authority from a collective, usually organized as a state, with all the conditions and consequences that international law attaches to the exercise of that power.

Reframing the problem underlying international organizations law in this way allows for a more nuanced and convincing theoretical account of these institutions. It suggests that there is no innate difference between international organizations and states, without falling into the pitfalls of current approaches. Ultimately, this book argues that states and international organizations are variations on the same theme along a single spectrum, rather than phenomena that are fundamentally distinct or fundamentally similar by way of an abstract comparison.[19]

The closest domestic law proxy to the theory advanced here is that of sub-state autonomous public actors such as statutory or public authorities that possess their own legal personality. These actors may be legally distinct and functionally independent from the central government or the state stricto sensu, yet operate in the space of public law and public obligations. The closest construction within international law is that of a confederation – a distinct legal entity, whose existence is anchored in an international agreement rather than a national constitution, while the states that make it up retain their international legal personality. Hence, international organizations may not themselves be states in the sense of fulfilling the classic Montevideo criteria for statehood,[20] but, as my

---

[19] There are several works in neighbouring disciplines that, in one form or another, pick on the same idea that there is a fundamental conceptual continuity between governance at the state and international levels. For international relations, see Hooghe, Lenz, and Marks (n 11); Michael Zürn, *A Theory of Global Governance: Authority, Legitimacy & Contestation* (OUP 2018); for organization theory, see Göran Ahrne and Nils Brunsson, *Meta-organizations* (Edward Elgar 2011). For a more historical approach by an international lawyer, see Sinclair (n 12).

[20] See generally James Crawford, *The Creation of States in International Law* (2nd edn, OUP 2007) 45–62.

argument goes, they should be analysed as entities that belong to the same broader category of legal subjects as states as far as international law is concerned. In other words, there is plenty of analytical space to accommodate international organizations in the spectrum between fully fledged autonomous entities and mere contractual arrangements, as well as between states and non-state actors, without equating them with either opposite end of these spectrums.

How does this translate in practice? Crucially, for the purposes of doctrinal problems such as those identified earlier, this means that international organizations enjoy, by virtue of being (re-)organizations of the same capacity that underpins the existence of states in international law, a legal existence that is opposable to other states without the need of recognition. Similarly, the legal distinctiveness of international organizations is not to be sought in some rule of incorporation or otherwise a change in the definition of international law, nor is their distinct will to be traced back to some decision-making procedure by majority. Rather, it is because their existence is rooted in the capacity of a community to self-describe through institutions that international organizations enjoy their legal distinctiveness, much in the same manner that it happens with states. This common root between international organizations, states, and a variety of other entities that are nested products of this self-description, including sub- and supra- state entities with their own legal personality, then implies that there is no fixed category distinction between them in the eyes of the legal system. Thus, international organizations can contribute to the formation of customary international law directly and in their own name, with the important caveat that their practice is not to be weighed separately from that of their members in terms of its representativeness. Finally, this view means that the corpus of customary international law that is applicable to states also applies to international organizations, while the treaty obligations of their members in their 'individual' capacities do not directly bind the organization and vice versa. Equally important, customary international law applies to states and international organizations to the same extent, and not just to the extent that these entities may or may not be analogous. International organizations may not be like states in terms of them having no territory or nationals of their own, but that part of international law is all the same binding upon them. Most importantly, international organizations are bound to respect such norms when interacting with states, even when they themselves are not beneficiaries of those norms in the strict sense.

Chapter 1 outlines how this book understands the problem of theorizing international organizations in public international law. It breaks down the problem into two related but distinct aspects: the structural relationship between these institutions and their members and the conceptual relationship between these institutions and states as species of legal entities. The first relationship relates to the idea that international organizations enjoy a 'distinct will' from their members and hence differ from other forms of interstate cooperation, as well as to the opposability of their legal personality to non-members. The second relationship concerns whether a range of propositions that are usually associated with states, especially those relating to the creation and application of customary norms, can be extended to international organizations, assuming that the latter exist as legally distinct entities from their members. The chapter then turns to questions of methodology. It discusses the basic epistemological restrictions and goals that attach to doctrinal legal theory as understood in this book.

Chapters 2 and 3 explore the limitations of current theoretical constructions in addressing the aforementioned two key aspects of international organizations law.

Chapter 2 challenges current approaches aimed at conceptualizing international organizations in relation to states as species of legal actors. First, it suggests that neither the popular notion that international organizations enjoy a legal personality nor the notion that they are autonomous entities can provide a conclusive answer as to how these institutions relate to states. This chapter demonstrates that the dominant understanding of legal personality as a formal predicate with no inherent status – that is as a shorthand expression for a set of specific rights and obligations that an entity enjoys – makes it analytically impossible to securely infer from this concept *additional* substantive rights and obligations. Likewise, if legal personality merely denotes a right-and-duty-bearing-entity in international law – to be sure, only one among many such entities – it does not seem convincing to pick out international organizations as being capable of contributing to the formation of international law solely on that basis. The chapter provides a similar response to views that seek to draw an analogy between states and international organizations based on the idea that they are both autonomous actors. Just because two actors are autonomous does not ipso facto mean that they have identical substantive rights, obligations, or capacities. This chapter concludes by challenging the notion that international organizations should be analysed as states because they are just *façon de parler* for their member states acting together. It argues that this view oversimplifies the membership roster of international organizations that may include entities other than states, while it also finds itself in tension with the notion that these institutions enjoy a distinct legal existence to begin with.

Chapter 3 turns to the problem of how current approaches theorize the analytical distinctiveness of international organizations from their members. First, this chapter revisits the prevalent theories about the legal personality of international organizations. Tracing their roots in domestic law, this chapter explains why these familiar constructions of corporate personality do not translate well in the international legal order. The chapter explains how basing our accounts of the legal personality of international organizations on corporate law theories produces two equally unsatisfying theories. Either international law must be shown to feature a separate rule explicitly recognizing the legal personality of international organizations – a proposition that is notoriously hard to prove in positive law – or international organizations must be shown to be 'natural' persons on par with states – a proposition that seems in tension with the idea of sovereign equality.

Next, this chapter explains how the notion of the volonté distincte, traditionally considered key in demonstrating that international organizations are not just an aggregate of their members, has proved problematic to pin down. It argues that the dominant criterion used in the literature to detect the existence of such a will, namely the existence of a majority-decision-making procedure within the organization, exhibits serious flaws. In the final analysis, the chapter shows that any decision-making procedure, including deciding by majority, can theoretically be traced back to an initial unanimous agreement on it by the organization's members. This means that there is no hard-and-fast analytical distinction between majority-based and other forms of decision-making when it comes to international organizations, making this criterion incapable of serving as the objective benchmark for the independent will of these institutions that it is commonly thought to be.

Chapter 4 moves on to investigate the underlying assumptions with which the discipline has tended to theorize international organizations. It suggests that the heart of the problem lies in the theoretical model of the state that most international organizations law scholars have, implicitly or explicitly, adopted in their analyses. In this respect, most approaches seem to follow a seemingly outdated anthropomorphic construction of the state as a natural person, akin to the individual human being in domestic law, even if understood only as a legal fiction. This chapter explains how such an approach may derail theorizing international organizations. Admitting international organizations in the international legal order under this framework rests on either proving a change in law allowing for the emergence of international organizations with legal personality (usually theorized as a rule of incorporation) or by arguing that international organizations are effectively 'natural' persons themselves, on par with states. This chapter concludes by suggesting that the problem of theorizing international organizations should be viewed in an altogether different framework. States should not be conceptualized as 'natural' human beings, even if only for the purposes of international law. Rather, they, too, should be understood as corporate persons.

Chapters 5 and 6 begin to unravel the field's theoretical conundrum by looking at the problem of corporate existence as such from a philosophical perspective.

Chapter 5 lays the foundations for this discussion. It explores the idea that some entities enjoy a 'real' existence of their own as opposed to being mere shorthand expressions for their members acting in tandem. Popular intuitions regarding this question seem conflicted: we are both accustomed to thinking that the sum is greater than its parts, as well as viewing an entity as really nothing over and above its parts. Navigating between these two rough ontological instincts, this chapter moves toward a better understanding of what it means for an entity to be non-redundant to begin with. First, it discusses the old idea that only causally active entities can be thought to be real. Next, it introduces the notion of 'grounding', a non-causal way of understanding independent existence and the relations that underpin it. Following the discussion of causation and grounding, this chapter turns to how we should understand the problem of separate or 'real' existence with respect to international organizations. It suggests that this question is inherently relative, meaning that it makes sense only when considered in relation to other entities – in this case most prominently states – that are already admitted as non-redundant. This chapter concludes by suggesting that the key to resolving this problem is to first uncover the rationale that international law employs in buttressing states as 'real' entities and then examine whether it can be equally applied to international organizations.

Chapter 6 zeroes in on the problem of the existence of corporate entities specifically with respect to human beings, the framing that contemporary scholarship has generally employed as a blueprint when thinking analytically about states and international organizations. This

chapter looks at the two main schools of thought regarding this philosophical problem. According to the first, human beings are naturally
irreducible 'soulful' or organic entities. Following this line of argument,
any corporate entity made up of such entities will ultimately be reducible
to them and not enjoy a separate existence of its own. According to the
second school, individuals themselves are miniature organizations of
sorts: they are not naturally irreducible, but they themselves consist of
several parts that come together into one. Per this school of thought, the
problems that underpin corporate existence are not qualitatively different
from those that underpin individual existence. Accordingly, the same
rationale that can make human beings rise as entities above and beyond
their parts as individuals can philosophically buttress the non-redundant
existence of corporate entities.

Chapter 7 argues that international lawyers should view the problem
of theorizing the corporate existence of international organizations vis-à-
vis states along the lines of the second school of thought, whereby the
fundamentality of the members of a corporate entity is not taken for
granted to begin with. Although it may be disputed in philosophy
whether individuals are metaphysically irreducible entities, there can be
little doubt that states are not such entities. This alternative way of
conceptualizing the problem of theorizing international organizations,
with states themselves being understood as constructed entities, provides
a more nuanced way of approaching key problems of international
organizations law. It explains why, in the final analysis, it is the same
capacity to constitute a state that lies behind the emergence of international organizations. Thus, it dismisses the idea that the legal personality of international organizations needs to be anchored in a rule of
incorporation or a successful comparison between them and states based
on some abstract criteria. Rather than searching for new rules of incorporation or comparing and contrasting states and international organizations for all intents and purposes, scholars should instead think of both
entities as manifestations of public authority that inherently admits
gradation. In this regard, this chapter explains how international law
too understands the state as a unitary yet artificial entity. Looking at cases
of sub- and supra- state institutions, including federal states as well as
confederations, this chapter argues that international law is far more
flexible in the forms of community organization it allows than international organizations scholars typically assume. Likewise, international
organizations should be understood as an inbuilt offshoot of a community's capacity to self-describe. This chapter argues that it is ultimately

this 'genealogical' connection with the state that defines the legal nature of international organizations rather than any fundamental abstract similarity or difference between the two actors.

Chapter 8 employs the insights developed in Chapter 7 to inform how we should understand international organizations as such, as well as the notion that these institutions may be legally distinct from their members. Revisiting the problem of defining international organizations, this chapter accounts for entities other than states taking part in the founding and functioning of these institutions. It also suggests that the analytical import of such a definition may be much more limited than it may initially be assumed. Since international organizations do not form a separate class of entities characterized by a notion of 'organizationhood', the practical value of any definition is largely confined to clarifying the ordinary meaning of the term 'international organization' for the purposes of treaty interpretation. Moreover, once we have conceptualized international organizations as members of a family of entities that includes states, we can let go of trying to analytically prove their distinct will through the existence of a specific decision-making procedure. Instead, distinct will should be analysed in conventional terms, much in the same terms that are used for states and any other state-like entities. Finally, the opposability of international organizations' legal personality vis-à-vis non-members may rest on the same basis as that of their members; if the state's legal personality is treated by international law as objective, the same reasoning should apply to international organizations.

Chapter 9 zeroes in on the relationship between international organizations and customary international law. Parting with rough anthropomorphic conceptions of the state, this chapter recasts this problem as one of pinning down the correct level of abstraction at which international law is supposed to operate in that regard. It argues that international organizations should be construed neither as mechanistic, soulless entities, nor as if they were just another state. Instead, the practice of international organization should count towards the formation of international custom, with the caveat that it should not be weighed separately from that of its members when assessing its representativeness. Thus, if an organization with three member states as well as those states engage in some practice, then (1) the practice of all four entities counts and (2) between the four of them, they would still be producing only three states' worth of practice. When it comes to applying customary international law, the genealogical connection with states suggests that international organizations are in principle bound by the same norms, even though the rights and duties that they derive from them in a given factual situation may differ considerably compared to those of states. For example, international organizations may not derive concrete rights from customary norms on territorial integrity but are bound by them regardless and have to respect these norms in their interaction with states.

1

Prolegomena to a Legal Theory of International Organizations

1.1 Theorizing International Organizations as a Twofold Problem

A theory's purpose is nothing more than to 'know and describe its object', that is to unveil its true identity.[1] But how can one 'describe', let alone come to 'know', an abstract concept, for example an international organization? Theorizing itself seems to be based on a metaphor: just like physical objects, abstract concepts can be 'described' and eventually become 'known' to us. The metaphor works well enough but requires caution. This is not some detached scientific measurement about an entity that is supposed to objectively exist somewhere 'out there'. Rather, it is, if anything, an investigation centred on the inquirer's needs: to theorize is to understand something in terms that are meaningful *to us*. When theorizing international organizations as lawyers, we are trying to puzzle out the features of something for the sake of our interaction with it in a predefined context, in this case public international law, that is populated by other, no less abstract concepts such as 'custom' or 'statehood'. Rather than seeking absolute knowledge, it is this interaction with a concept that conditions the types of things we would be interested in knowing about it as well as the ultimate limits of that knowledge. Theorizing in that sense is inherently practical. It is born out of the actual need for an ever more accurate conceptual map to help fill gaps in our understanding and guide us forward when new questions arise.

Up to relatively recently in the discipline's history, the need for theories regarding international organizations focused almost exclusively on the relationship between these institutions and their members. The discipline's major preoccupation has been, and arguably still is, how to delimit international organizations' agency and functions vis-à-vis their members. By contrast, questions regarding the interaction between these

---

[1] Hans Kelsen, *Pure Theory of Law* (Max Knight tr, The Law Book Exchange Ltd 2005) 1.

institutions and the 'outside' world took much longer to inform theoretical inquiry.[2] Indeed, as perceived creatures of international law acting within given mandates, international organizations were initially thought of being almost incapable of committing wrongful acts in the first place.[3] While this framing has certainly lost much of its appeal, the interaction of international organizations with entities apart from their members largely remains uncharted territory.

This book argues that these two angles – the membership relationship and as the relationship with the outside world – are fundamentally connected, yet they also pose distinct questions that cannot be collapsed to each other. At a fundamental level, the membership relation concerns whether and why international organizations exist or not as legally separate entities from their component parts. The relationship with the outside world raises a distinct set of questions. Here the problem revolves around the legal nature proper of these institutions: assuming that these entities exist separately from their parts, what more can be said about the content of their legal personality? Do they enjoy the same position, as in the same capacities, rights, and obligations, with states in the international legal order, are they sui generis entities, or something in between?

This twofold approach already shifts focus from how the field generally goes about defining these institutions. Such definitions are important to look at, as they form a standard feature of most studies of the subject that necessarily presupposes some theoretical reflection.

Most definitions of international organizations are solely preoccupied with the legal distinctiveness of an organization from its members. To the extent that they are concerned with these institutions' legal nature, it is mainly to set them apart from entities such as NGOs and multinational corporations.[4] Such definitions normally proceed on the basis of four

---

[2] See generally Jan Klabbers, 'Theorizing International Organizations' in Anne Orford and Florian Hoffmann (eds), *The Oxford Handbook of the Theory of International Law* (OUP 2016).

[3] See ILC, 'Report by Mr. R. Ago, Chairman of the Sub-Committee on State Responsibility' (1963) UN Doc A/CN.4/152, 229.

[4] Robin Churchill and Geir Ulfstein, 'Autonomous and Institutional Arrangements in Multilateral Environmental Agreements: A Little-Noticed Phenomenon in International Law' (2000) 94 AJIL 623, 632; Catherine Brölmann, *The Institutional Veil in Public International Law: International Organisations and the Law of Treaties* (Hart Oxford 2007) 13–24; Jan Klabbers, *An Introduction to International Organizations Law* (4th edn, CUP 2022) 6–14; Henry G Schermers and Niels M Blokker, *International Institutional Law* (5th edn, Martinus Nijhoff 2011) 30–49. See also ILC, 'First Report on

definitional elements. The first element is the organizations' interstate basis: international organizations are generally thought to be the creation of states and/or other international organizations of an intergovernmental nature. In this respect, many studies tend to downplay, or at the very least not dwell upon, the idea that international organizations may be created and membered by entities other than states and international organizations, including by sub-state entities with their own legal personality and non-self-governing territories.[5] The second element is that international organizations should be based on an international agreement that normally takes the form of a treaty.[6] Thirdly, international organizations must display some degree of autonomy from their members. This is often analysed in the literature as requiring the organization to possess 'at least one organ with a will of its own'.[7] Finally, legal personality figures in some definitions as a separate criterion for the existence of an international organization, whereas in others it is considered a quality that is attributed by international law only after the other three conditions are met, including the organization already having a will that is distinct from its member states.[8]

Relations between States and Inter-governmental Organizations, by Mr. Abdullah El-Erian, Special Rapporteur' (1963) UN Doc A/CN.4/161 and Add.1, 166 (para 48).

[5] See eg Klabbers (n 4) 9–10, referring only to examples of states and international organizations as members. Similarly, Brölmann (n 4) 17; Phillippe Sands and Pierre Klein, *Bowett's Law of International Institutions* (6th edn, Sweet & Maxwell 2009) 16; Lorenzo Gasbarri, *The Concept of an International Organization in Public International Law* (OUP 2021) 5–6, referring only to member states. Cf Chittharanjan F Amerasinghe, *Principles of the Institutional Law of International Organizations* (2nd edn, CUP 2005) 10, 105, referring in passing to state-like entities as members of the UN; Schermers and Blokker (n 4) 66–71, admitting a wide range of entities as members but also suggesting that 'in principle, parts of states cannot be independent parties to the treaty embodying the constitution of an international organization'.

[6] Cf Finn Seyersted, 'Objective International Personality of Intergovernmental Organizations: Do Their Capacities Really Depend upon the Conventions Establishing Them?' (1964) 34 Nordic Journal of International Law 47, 48–55, suggesting that an international agreement is not strictly necessary for the establishment of international organizations, and that the latter are, legally speaking, in a similar position to states, in the sense that international law does not question the circumstances of their existence but merely whether they exist as a matter of fact or not.

[7] Schermers and Blokker (n 4) 30–49. Similarly, Klabbers suggests that an international organization must 'possess at least one organ which has a will distinct from the will of its member states'; Klabbers (n 4) 12–14; see also Brölmann (n 4) 20–21. Cf Amerasinghe, who does not provide a definition of international organizations, only a series of characteristics that distinguish international governmental organizations from other organizations. He does not include among these characteristics the presence of a distinct will. Amerasinghe (n 5) 10.

[8] See Brölmann (n 4) 19–22. Some authors provide only a definition of international organizations with legal personality. See eg Ian Brownlie, *Principles of Public*

Yet despite the apparent general agreement on these three plus one elements – interstate basis, existence of an international agreement, some degree of autonomy, and legal personality – the essential features of the legal nature proper of international organizations remain obscure. This problem goes beyond efforts to define international organizations. Apart from the aphorism that whatever they are, international organizations have something to do with states, the legal nature proper of these institutions remains surprisingly elusive in terms of more sustained theoretical thinking. The latter too has almost exclusively focused on the membership relation as *the* key to theorizing these institutions.

This relation has normally been understood in binary terms: international organizations can be conceptualized either as independent entities or as mere assemblages of their members. For example, Catherine Brölmann has described the legal image of international organizations as 'open structures that are vehicles for states' versus their legal image as 'closed structures that are independent legal actors'.[9] Fernando Bordin for his part has coined the terms 'treaty conception' – according to which international organizations represent elaborate treaty transactions between states – and 'subject conception' of international organizations – following which these institutions are independent legal persons under a purported rule of general international law.[10] In his monograph Lorenzo Gasbarri describes the binary as one of 'functionalist' and 'constitutionalist' conceptualizations of international organizations, whereby the latter's institutional veil is characterized by 'crystalline transparency' or 'an impermeable opacity', respectively.[11] In the first case the relationship at the foundation of international

---

International Law (7th edn, OUP 2008) 649. Others provide a separate definition for international organizations with legal personality and for those without. See eg Nigel White, *The Law of International Organisations* (3rd edn, Manchester University Press 2016) 9. Cf Angelo Golia and Anne Peters, 'The Concept of International Organization' in Jan Klabbers (ed), *The Cambridge Companion to International Organizations Law* (CUP 2022) 29–30, who add two more elements to the traditional definition of international organizations: the idea that an organization must 'fulfil tasks of global public interest or of global public relevance which could not be accomplished by any state alone' and the notion that international organizations must feature some kind of a permanent infrastructure, including a 'seat, a functioning infrastructure and budgetary means'.

[9] See Brölmann (n 4) 1.

[10] Fernando Bordin, *The Analogy between States and International Organizations: Legal Reasoning and the Development of the Law of International Organizations* (CUP 2018) 52.

[11] Gasbarri (n 5) 18, 33. Gasbarri ends up rejecting both these conceptualizations as instituting 'false dichotomies'.

organizations is thought to be 'contractual' and in the second 'constitutional'.[12] More broadly, Jean d'Aspremont refers to the 'all-embracing dichotomy' between 'contractualism' and 'constitutionalism', the first emanating from the notion that international organizations are essentially treaties and the second from the notion that they represent autonomous legal actors.[13]

These two conceptions – which following Bordin I will chiefly refer to as the 'treaty' and 'subject' conceptions – are generally thought to reflect different normative and, crucially for this study, analytical images of international organizations.[14] Accordingly, a host of doctrinal issues are approached in terms of adopting either one of the two mindsets. Thus, questions such as the foundation of the organization's legal personality in general international law or in the will of its members,[15] the opposability of the organization's legal personality to non-members,[16] whether the organization's powers are 'attributed' or 'inherent',[17] and whether their constituent instruments should be interpreted as treaties or as constitutions (whatever that may signify)[18] are frequently discussed through the medium of the treaty/subject models. All in all, d'Aspremont lists no

---

[12] ibid.

[13] Jean d'Aspremont, 'The Law of International Organizations and the Art of Reconciliation: From Dichotomies to Dialectics' (2014) 11 IOLR 428, 430; see also Christiane Ahlborn, 'The Rules of International Organizations and the Law of International Responsibility' (2012) 8 IOLR 397.

[14] From a normative standpoint, the constitutional view, frequently associated with the broader idea of constitutionalism in international law, implies that a greater degree of public control and scrutiny should be exercised over international organizations. The contractual view is thought to borrow normative inspiration from concepts of domestic private law. See generally Jan Klabbers, 'Constitutionalism Lite' (2004) 1 IOLR 31. The critique raised in this book with respect to both the contractual and the constitutional understanding of international organizations concerns these as *analytical* models rather than as normative frameworks. Questioning the analytical persuasiveness of a doctrinal model does not imply that there are no fundamental political and normative tensions at the heart of international organizations as institutions of governance.

[15] Brölmann (n 4) 78–90.

[16] Seyersted (n 6) 1; Hugo J Hahn, 'Euratom: The Conception of an International Personality' (1958) 71 Harvard Law Review 1001.

[17] See eg Klabbers (n 4) 50–68; Schermers and Blokker (n 4) 155–189.

[18] For one of the first distinctions between the constituent instrument as a *traité-contrat and as a traité-loi*, see Andrea Rapisardi-Mirabelli, 'La Théorie Générale des Unions Internationales' (1925) 7 Collected Courses of the Hague Academy of International Law 345–352. For an overview of the literature on the constituent instrument as a treaty versus the constituent instrument as a constitution, see Ahlborn (n 13) 407–410. On how constitutional interpretation can be distinguished from traditional treaty interpretation, see Amerasinghe (n 5) 59.

fewer than eighteen areas of persistent theoretical disagreement concerning international organizations law, ranging from an organization's creation to its functioning, and its potential dissolution, where contradicting solutions emerge on the lines of the contractual or the constitutional frameworks. If anything, this list demonstrates the prevalence of these two models in thinking about international organizations.[19] It has even been argued that the paradigmatic tensions between these two conceptions of international organizations are themselves constitutive of the field, and thus inherent in any serious theoretical approach.[20]

As enticing as this binary framing can be in its analytical simplicity, it is incomplete when compared to how theorizing international organizations is understood in this book. As a whole, this binary framing is mostly preoccupied with the admittedly important problem of conceptualizing the structural relationship between international organizations and their members, and all the supplementary positions that are thought to result from such a conceptualization. Yet this approach does not explain much about the other dimension of international organizations' existence, namely their legal nature, *assuming that they are legally distinct from their members*. In this respect, picking a side on the binary conceptions represents only the start of the inquiry, and even then, it is only part of a bigger puzzle. Thus, properly construed, the binary does not really speak to the relationship between states and international organizations as species of legal actors or yield many safe insights into the content of their legal personality. Theorizing international organizations in that sense remains an irreducibly twofold problem.

To go back to our metaphor about theorizing, the first question we need to ask is: are international organizations 'a' thing to begin with? The second question is, assuming that they are a thing, what kind of a thing are they?

When asking whether international organizations are 'a' thing, the question is whether and to what extent they should be understood as entities that are distinct from their members from the perspective of international law. Answers to this problem range from the notion that international organizations are totally independent holistic actors to the idea that they are merely aggregates of their members. When asking 'what kind' of a thing they are, I am inquiring into those general features that international organizations might possess, in the event that they do truly exist as legally distinct entities. The chief question here concerns whether

---

[19] See d'Aspremont (n 13) 436–437.
[20] ibid 429–430.

Distinct legal person

State ——————————————————————————— Non-state actor

Aggregate of individual actors

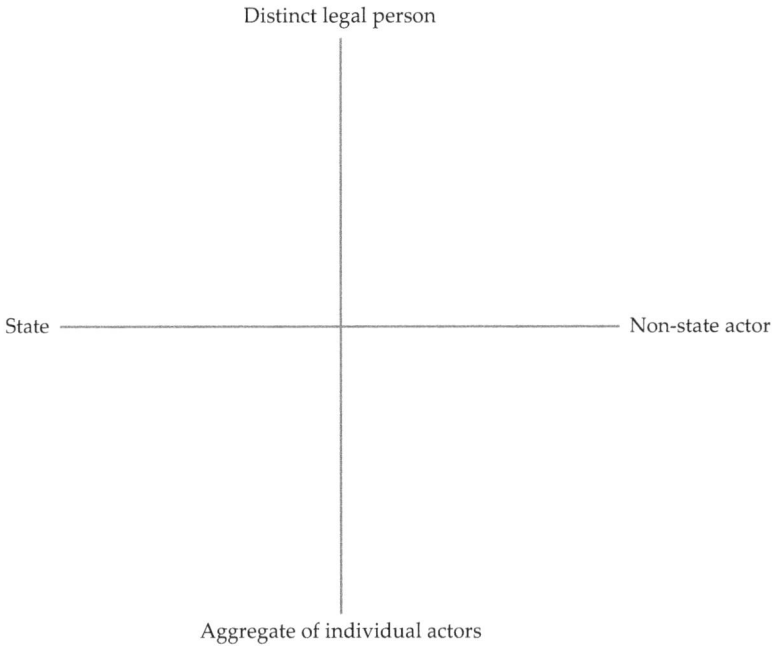

Figure 1.1 Mapping the legal nature of international organizations: Two sets of analytical opposites

and how international organizations relate conceptually to states as species of independent legal actors in terms of capacities, rights, and obligations under customary international law. Current answers to this problem range from the notion that international organizations should be analysed as non-state actors, to the idea that they should be analysed as if they were another independent state. This whole framing for theorizing international organizations can be outlined as shown in Figure 1.1.

Here, the vertical axis represents the structural relationship between an international organization and its members ranging from total independence (and thus distinct legal personality) to total assimilation (and thus another name for a group of states acting together). The horizontal axis represents the conceptual relationship between international organizations with states as species of legal subjects, ranging from a complete analogy with states (and thus analyzing them as if they were another state) to an identification as non-state actors (and thus sui generis with respect to states).

As this book develops its theoretical argument, it will explain that these two axes are closely intertwined and more productively dealt with when viewed together, while maintaining that they represent conceptually different questions. With respect to the problem of legal distinctiveness, the book will show that, owing to an implicit analogy with the problem of corporate entities in domestic law, current theories grasp the problem in a manner that rests on some form of legislative intervention before international organizations can be admitted as legal persons – a proposition that is not only currently untenable in law, but also unnecessary. Instead, this book will offer an alternative conceptualization of the problem whereby the independent existence of international organizations is sourced in the same power that underpins the independent existence of states in international law. With respect to the problem of their legal nature, this book will explain why, from an analytical perspective, the state/non-state binary is unnecessarily crude. It will argue that international organizations fundamentally differ from other non-state actors, but also that they cannot be treated as if they were another independent state for all intents and purposes.

1.2   Meta-theoretical Framework

We have already taken the first step towards crafting a legal theory of international organizations; the problem of the 'nature' of international organizations has been shown to possess not one, but two dimensions of analysis: one pertaining to their relationship with their members, and another pertaining to their legal nature stricto sensu, including how they relate to states as species of legal actors. Before diving more into this bifurcation of the problem, some observations on the theorizing exercise as such are necessary. These concern (1) what counts as a successful theory within the confines of this book's inquiry; (2) what are the ground rules for getting there; (3) certain concrete methodological commitments that this book undertakes specifically regarding theorizing international organizations.

Evidently the question of what counts as 'success' in theorizing is of great interest to this book, as it not only advances a new theory but also critiques both halves of the existing binary way of theorizing international organizations. A successful theory as understood here is one that is capable of generating a series of ancillary propositions on doctrinal problems that are consistent with each other and cohere with the broader framework of public international law. Thus, a theory should ideally go beyond just 'making sense'. Indeed, the treaty/subject conceptions, while potentially flawed in certain respects, still have potentially profound insights to offer, and parts of them seem intuitive. This is not so by chance. Indeed, our folk philosophical theories about groups in general tend to follow this binary. All groups can be conceptualized either as another name for complex interactions of individuals or as entities distinct from the latter. Nevertheless, however appealing, the simplicity of this construction can be deceptive: it makes sense, but at a level of abstraction that may ultimately take away rather than add nuance to our accounts. Instead, the aim here is to work towards a 'cognitive whole that produces substantiated (well-justified) solutions to given juridical problems',[21] adding 'to the law's precision and coherence, by analyzing legal concepts and rules through clarification of their connection with other concepts and rules'.[22]

Aiming for a theory that is internally consistent does not mean that a single conceptual paradigm must dominate the whole discourse of international organizations law. In this respect, we must distinguish the case of necessary logical/analytical inconsistency from the case where there is a circumscribed and internally justified difference in the use of a term. This is especially relevant, since most far-reaching theoretical contributions to the subject in recent years have sought to combine the treaty/subject binary, arguing that international organizations should be understood both as treaties and as subjects depending on the circumstances. Gasbarri, for example, conceptualizes international organizations as 'dual entities', their constituent instruments being 'treaties and constitutions simultaneously'.[23] Brölmann's seminal work has also theorized international organizations beyond the crude treaty/subject binary, suggesting that they are neither exclusively open entities, as the contractual view would have them, nor closed ones, as the constitutional view implies, but 'transparent'.[24] In both cases, the ensuing theoretical image is something akin to the famous rabbit-duck illusion: there is both a duck and a rabbit in the picture but you cannot see both of them at once. Such ideas – essentially perspectival responses to the uncompromising rigidity of the treaty/subject binary – are certainly possible and not ipso facto internally inconsistent.

---

[21] Aulis Aarnio, 'Paradigms in Legal Dogmatics: Toward a Theory of Change and Progress in Legal Science' in Aleksander Peczenik, Lars Lindahl, and Bert Van Roermund (eds), *Theory of Legal Science* (Lund 1983) 28.

[22] Robert Alexy and Aleksander Peczenik, 'The Concept of Coherence and Its Significance for Discursive Rationality' (1990) 3 Ratio Juris 130.

[23] Gasbarri (n 5) 9–10, 108.

[24] Brölmann (n 4) 1, 253.

There are, however, limits as to how far one can go down this path, especially if the theorizing task is understood as it is here. Some questions admit neither variated answers nor perspectival evaluation. For example: either international organizations enjoy a legal personality that is opposable to non-member states without the need for recognition or they do not. From an analytical perspective, there is simply no third possibility. Similarly, either their practice counts in the first instance towards the formation of customary international law or it does not, and so on. Thus, while 'dual legality' approaches may be more or less successful in re-imagining some aspects of the treaty/subject binary, they face their own limitations.[25]

Moreover, when a theory develops carve-outs to its field of application or to general international law, these must be explained and justified in some analytically comprehensive way. For example, if we theorize international organizations in the image of the state, then we should also be able to explain whether their practice counts equally as that of states for the formation of custom, and, if not, explain why not. Likewise, if we assume that the default position of international organizations being merely treaty arrangements between states is overcome through a rule of incorporation or other norm of international law, then we need to be able to show the existence of such a rule, and so on. Limitations to the field of application of a theory should be justifiable by reference to other operative principles or rules, while conditioning of a theory to such principles or rules needs to also argue for their existence in positive law.

In that sense, the requirement of internal consistency is bound to a specific field of inquiry, in this case international law. However, this does not preclude seeking inspiration for theory building outside international law altogether. Concepts such as 'contract' and 'constitution' already hint at this. This is neither surprising nor suspicious. At all times, legal doctrine rests upon core analytical and ontological assumptions about the nature of law and its institutions, even if these are not always spelled

---

[25] This much seems clear to Brölmann, for whom describing the layered nature of international organizations 'aims briefly to point at certain systemic conditions of international law which, within the positivist paradigm, could hamper the reconceptualization of organizations'. Catherine Brölmann, 'A Flat Earth? International Organizations in the System of International Law' 70 Nordic Journal of International Law 319. Cf Lorenzo Gasbarri, 'Beyond the Either/Or Paradigm in the Formation of Customary International Law by International Organizations' in Jean d' Aspremont and Sufyan Droubi (eds), *International Organizations and the Formation of Customary International Law* (Manchester University Press 2020); Lorenzo Gasbarri, 'The Dual Legality of the Rules of International Organizations' (2017) 14 IOLR 87.

out.[26] Accordingly, thorough analysis of so-called black-letter rules and puzzles may prove inseparable from the wider theoretical and philosophical questions regarding the subject of legal regulation and be thus supplemented by the corresponding conceptual structures.[27] In that sense, when it comes to theory building, 'the tasks of the doctrinal writer and the legal philosopher are not radically far apart'.[28]

Doctrinal legal theory, as understood here, may thus draw resources from within and outside a specific legal system, or even outside law altogether. A doctrinal legal theory may proceed by utilizing concepts already found within a given legal system (for example, the concept of a treaty or a state) or legal concepts located outside that particular legal system (for example, the concept of the contract or the constitution) or, finally, by referring to non-legal concepts altogether (for example, the concept of corporate entities in philosophical discourse).[29]

That being said, an important caveat is in order: while from a methodological point of view doctrinal legal theory can draw inspiration from any available pool of concepts, the insights provided must be in the final analysis rendered into terms that a particular legal system (in this case public international law) can process, if that theory is to serve a doctrinal purpose as envisaged in this book.

To give one example of a theoretical breakthrough in international organizations discourse that has so far not yielded a comprehensive in-doctrine revolution, we can turn to the project of GAL. The latter has sought to approach the problems of global governance, including international organizations, from an entirely new angle. It has analysed international organizations as entities exercising 'global administration', deducing a series of principles emanating from this characterization that are mostly inspired by US administrative law. In doing so, GAL represents a rupture from the mainstream study of international organizations, which it does not consider particularly helpful in tackling the pressing problems of transparency, accountability, and participation.[30]

---

[26] Aarnio (n 21) 28–30.

[27] Aleksander Peczenik, *Scienta Juris, Legal Doctrine as Knowledge of Law and as a Source of Law* (Springer 2005) 31.

[28] Sean Coyle, 'Two Concepts of Legal Analysis' in Sean Coyle and George Pavlakos (eds), *Jurisprudence of Legal Science: A Debate about the Nature of Legal Theory* (Hart 2005) 20.

[29] Cf John Dewey, 'The Historic Background of Corporate Legal Personality' (1926) 35 Yale Law Journal 655, 656.

[30] Benedict Kingsbury, Nico Krisch, and Richard B Stewart, 'The Emergence of Global Administrative Law' (2005) 68 Law and Contemporary Problems 15; See also Benedict

GAL's core assumption about global governance, namely that it approximates administration, could perhaps give rise to an alternative doctrinal legal theory of international organizations. However, thus far, the GAL project appears to not have taken any sustained interest in reconceptualizing international organizations for the purposes of international legal doctrine, nor has it sought to systemically address problems such as legal personality or participation in the formation of customary international law from an analytical perspective.[31]

On the contrary, a doctrinal legal theory of international organizations as envisaged here should develop a set of systematically related propositions which are expressed, or at least are readily expressible, in the vernacular of doctrinal discourse. Unlike GAL and other theories operating at that level, the aim here is to tackle existing analytical problems from the perspective of public international law, even if inspiration for this may be sought outside the discipline. In short, doctrinal legal theory may have no fixed starting point, but has a defined purpose and end goal: to develop a theoretical understanding that enables, justifies, and articulates new analytical input to persistent doctrinal puzzles and gaps within international law's internal logical framework.

How can such a theoretical understanding be developed? The requisite methodology for tackling similar problems in legal theory is often sought in some sort of abductive line of reasoning.[32] This entails forming an interpretative hypothesis that can best explain the available observations that one seeks to capture in theoretical terms, and then testing that hypothesis against contrary evidence. Legal theory then takes the form of an 'inference to the best explanation', in the sense that: '[i]n making this inference one infers, from the fact that a certain hypothesis would explain the evidence, to the truth of that hypothesis.'[33] Methodologically, theory building may thus rely heavily on putting forward a certain interpretative assumption and then testing this assumption against the existing evidence or practice that the theory seeks to capture. In this

---

Kingsbury and Lorenzo Casini, 'Global Administrative Law Dimensions of International Organizations Law' (2009) 6 IOLR 319.

[31] d'Aspremont (n 13) 449.

[32] Generally, on the rise of abductive reasoning in social sciences and the humanities, see Willis F Overton, 'Evolving Scientific Paradigms: Retrospective and Prospective', in Luciano L'Abate (ed), *Paradigms in Theory Construction* (Springer 2012) 31–66.

[33] Gilbert H Harman, 'The Inference to the Best Explanation' (1965) 74 The Philosophical Review 88, 89.

respect, as John Gardner suggests, theorists such as Bentham, Hart, and Kelsen can be viewed as 'all other philosophers, [who] are offering an interpretation of their subject matter that plays up the true and important and plays down the true but unimportant'.[34]

Of course, what constitutes a 'better' explanation and which properties of an entity are 'important' or 'unimportant' will depend on one's meta-theoretical commitments. For a legal theory that rests on a positivist methodology, that is, a theory that seeks to ascertain what the law is rather than what it ought to be, this demands not relying on purely moral justificatory grounds for founding its conclusions. Ultimately, the success of a legal theory rests on the degree of analytical insight it can provide into the juridical and societal relationships that it seeks to capture and not on its moral desirability per se.[35]

Major debates in jurisprudence, including debates about the nature of law itself as a set of binding norms, have often revolved around furnishing the best possible interpretative assumption about law, and then testing that assumption against a series of legal or societal facts that are considered commonplace about law, in order to examine whether the assumption indeed corresponds to them.[36] To give one textbook example, at the first half of the nineteenth century, John Austin developed his 'sanctions theory' which hypothesized that laws are like commands.[37] For Austin, a command was an expression of a wish coupled with the threat of a sanction. Accordingly, the law itself was simply the expression of the wish of a sovereign coupled with a threat that the sovereign's dominance in a society made credible. About a hundred years after Austin's theory, HLA Hart successfully criticized the sanction theory of law by showing that not all laws can be analysed as commands by the sovereign in the sense of criminal or administrative law. Among other things, Hart argued that some laws are power-conferring rules that do not impose any obligation on legal subjects, for example laws which grant power to officials or private persons or laws conferring contractual capacity. Evidently, Austin's theory had missed

---

[34] John Gardner, 'Legal Positivism: Five-and-a-half Myths' (2001) 46 The American Journal of Jurisprudence 199, 206.

[35] Coyle (n 28) 16–17.

[36] See Jeremy Waldron, 'Planning for Legality' (2011) 109 Michigan Law Review 883, 883–885.

[37] John Austin, *The Providence of Jurisprudence Determined* (Wilfrid Rumble ed, first published 1832, CUP 2009).

something important about the nature of law and the entities that fall under it. Hart went on to advance his own theory of law by describing it as originating in a social practice among the officials of a legal system, resolving some problems of previous theories, while perhaps creating some new ones.[38] The purpose here is not to delve deeper into these particular theories but to show how legal theory normally goes about theorizing the object of its study through a process of trial and error, example and counterexample, seeking to capture as accurately as possible a certain practice.

But what happens when the object that a theory seeks to capture lacks a generally agreed description? International organizations' discourse can also be thought to operate on the back of certain basic interpretative hypotheses about its object of study – the familiar treaty and subject models – with the caveat that there has been much less overt theorizing and focused discussion about the legal nature of these institutions in general. Instead, the bulk of theorizing has been distributed among studies of particular aspects of the law (for example, powers, legal personality, responsibility, interpretation of constituent instruments, and so on), which most commonly proceed on the basis of either the contractual or the constitutional hypothesis regarding the legal nature of international organizations.[39] Even though less developed by comparison, approaches on these institutions' legal nature stricto sensu have also been generally caught between a seemingly uncompromising binary between state and non-state.

Such cross-cutting radically antithetical interpretations pose a major methodological hurdle in developing a holistic legal theory of international organizations. Indeed, while the first international organizations date back to the mid to late nineteenth century, the givens of international organizations *law* are quite scarce. As already pointed out, the field lacks a commonly accepted theory of personality, a theory of obligation, as well as a theory of participation in the formation of customary international law. d'Aspremont's list of eighteen areas of disagreement that I mention in the Introduction serves well to prove this point, even as it mostly covers what are here considered membership-focused problems. This suggests that it may be extremely difficult to pin

---

[38] HLA Hart, *The Concept of Law* (3rd edn, OUP 2012) 26–49.
[39] See eg Brölmann (n 25) 320; Gasbarri, 'The Dual Legality of the Rules of International Organizations' (n 25) 91.

down with certainty the practice that a legal theory of international organizations would ideally seek to capture.[40]

The danger is then that of a legal theory that rests on aphorisms and circular arguments, leading to statements like the following: international organizations do not contribute directly to the formation of customary law because they are merely contractual arrangements between states; international organizations are merely contractual arrangements between states, and this is evidenced by the fact that they do not contribute to the formation of customary law in their own name. In other words, the absence of a stable analytical framework that can help to test the validity of a theory may also seriously undermine the persuasiveness of such a theory. At the same time, this sustains the notion that the matter cannot really be resolved within the law but needs some extra-legal commitments for it to be overcome.

The strategy employed in this book for getting out of this impasse is to bring into the discussion less disputed but more general propositions. The conjecture here is that progress can be made by exploring the conceptual and analytical continuities between international organizations and other legal institutions recognized by international law, while also providing the resources to articulate central ways in which the phenomenon of international organizations may go beyond concepts such as statehood, treaties, and non-state actors in international law. As will be shown, this move benefits from delving into ideas and classifications drawn from other domains of scholarship, such as philosophy and logic.

Owing to the disputed nature of many propositions of the law of international organizations, this study will not take *any* conclusions for granted regarding the nature of these institutions or their position within the international legal order – including ones such as the 'objective' legal personality of international organizations, a proposition that might be well accepted in scholarship but often rests on obscure analytical foundations. In a similar vein, I will generally not employ arguments from practice to derive analytical conclusions, even as the theory proposed in the end will indeed be shown to be compatible with practice. Judicial decisions and especially their scholarly interpretation, including staples such as the *Reparation for Injuries* Advisory Opinion, will be consulted with scepticism when called for. This might seem to be an overzealous

---

[40] d'Aspremont (n 13) 436–437.

approach, but it is employed more so as to challenge existing theoretical approaches to justify their conclusions from first principles rather than dispute the common sense they often exhibit.

1.3   Conclusion

This chapter introduced the two chief theoretical puzzles that a comprehensive legal theory of international organizations should be able to address: conceptualizing the relationship between international organizations and their members, and conceptualizing the relationship between international organizations and states as species of legal subjects. The first problem pertains to the legal existence of such institutions, or in other words whether they are indeed something over and above their members. The problem of their legal nature stricto sensu entails answering what exactly international organizations are, assuming that they are something over and above their members. In posing these questions, the aim is to produce a series of systemically related and mutually supportive propositions about the legal nature of international organizations in public international law. These propositions should help advance an enhanced understanding of the legal phenomenon as such, throwing new light to existing analytical puzzles and conceptual challenges as viewed from within the international legal system.

2

Situating International Organizations in Relation to States as Species of Legal Actors

2.1 Assumptions behind the Problem

'International organizations are definitely not states';[1] 'international organizations are analogous to states'.[2] One may be excused to find both these views equally intuitive in the abstract. In fact, not only is the problem of how international organizations relate analytically to states *as species* of legal actors underdeveloped, it is also sometimes altogether absent from current theoretical thinking. Yet a number of important questions, including the existence and extent of rights and obligations for international organizations under customary international law, as well as their capacity to contribute to the formation of that law, arguably rest on the conceptual relationship between these institutions and states on the one hand, and non-state actors on the other. Accordingly, this chapter argues that whether and when international organizations should be treated as states, as non-state actors, or as something entirely different, is a question worth asking in its own right. It is one that cannot be answered solely by reference to the idea that international organizations enjoy a legal personality of their own or the notion that they are comparable to states because both are supposed to be legally autonomous. It is also not a problem that can be resolved simply by adopting a position on the treaty/subject binary discussed in Chapter 1. In the final analysis, the latter only bears upon the structural relationship between an international organization and its members, and its degree of autonomy from them. It thus provides very few solid insights as to the content of the legal personality of international organizations from the perspective of general international law.

---

[1] Allain Pellet, 'International Organizations Are Definitely Not States' in Maurizio Ragazzi (ed), *Responsibility of International Organizations: Essays in Memory of Sir Ian Brownlie* (Martinus Nijhoff 2013).

[2] Fernando Bordin, *The Analogy between States and International Organizations: Legal Reasoning and the Development of the Law of International Organizations* (CUP 2018).

The problem of the conceptual relationship between states and international organizations as presented here carries with it a set of assumptions about international law as such. These are neither novel nor particularly controversial, but they are worth articulating in advance.

The first assumption is that only a specific sub-class of entities among those commonly referred to as 'subjects' or 'legal persons' can contribute directly and in their own name to the formation of customary international law. This includes most prominently states, leaving to the side for the time being the question of how to evaluate the practice of international organizations. By contrast, although certain non-state actors, such as the International Committee of the Red Cross (ICRC), may play a significant role in that respect, for example, by identifying and publishing state practice in relation to specific fields of law, they are generally incapable of directly contributing to the formation of customary international law in their own name. This much has already been accepted by the International Law Commission (ILC) in its current project on the identification of customary international law.[3] Moreover, this position has been endorsed by the International Law Association (ILA) in its 2000 report on the formation of customary international law.[4] This premise, well accepted in international legal doctrine, is maintained throughout the following discussion.

The second assumption is that certain substantive norms that apply by virtue of customary international law to states are not by default directly applicable to non-state actors, again leaving to the side for the time being the problem of how to categorize international organizations. This does not mean that only states can be addressees of international legal norms. Indeed, current scholarly consensus suggests that any entity can be the subject of a right and/or obligation in international law and be thus considered to enjoy its own 'legal personality' in that sense. But defined in this way, legal personality becomes a formal rather than a status concept. It merely denotes the existence of some rights and obligations; it is not a predicate from which a fixed set of rights and obligations is immediately derived. Thus, in the case of entities other than states, the

---

[3] ILC, 'Draft Conclusions on the Identification of Customary International Law, with Commentaries' (2018) UN Doc A/73/10, 130, Draft Conclusion 4(2).

[4] Committee on Formation of Customary (General) International Law, 'Statement of Principles Applicable to the Formation of General Customary International Law' in International Law Association London Conference Final Report of the Committee (International Law Association, London 2000) 1, 32, Principle 16.

formal conception of legal personality does not operate as a status that generates certain particular capacities, justifying the idea that legal personality has no 'inherent content'.[5] As Roland Portmann explains in this respect, 'there is no rationale for identifying the consequences attached to international personality with the rights, duties, and capacities of states'.[6]

This means that the default position of international law regarding non-state actors is essentially that of a blank slate. Norms of customary international law *may* develop with respect to a non-state actor, and some states *may* agree, for example, in a treaty, to endow it with certain rights and obligations. Nevertheless, when this form of legislative intervention is lacking, non-state actors cannot be said to automatically bear the same rights and obligations as states.[7] In that scenario, the only way to extend application of these rules to such other actors would be to identify a separate, and presumably new, customary legal norm that specifically addresses the non-state actor in question.[8] In turn, this also signifies that 'non-state actors' do not comprise of a homogenous analytical category: certain rights may develop for armed groups but not for corporations, and so on. In essence, the denomination reflects a compromise analytical scheme that negatively defines what is not a state.[9] In other words, classifying an entity as a non-state actor does not mean that all non-state actors are the same in terms of their rights, obligations, or capacities.

This last set of remarks prompts a final observation about the concept of legal personality in international law. This entails a distinction between the content of legal personality (meaning the rights and duties that an entity may enjoy by virtue of it belonging to a specific category of legal persons), its effect (meaning the extent to which these rights and

---

[5] Catherine Brölmann, *The Institutional Veil in Public International Law: International Organisations and the Law of Treaties* (Hart Oxford 2007) 78. Such aphorisms have led some prominent authors to advocate in favour of even abandoning the concept of legal personality in international law altogether. See eg Rosalyn Higgins, *Problems and Process: International Law and How We Use It* (OUP 1994) 49; Emmanuel Roucounas, 'The Users of International Law', in Mahnoush H Arsanjani and others (eds), *Looking to the Future: Essays on International Law in Honor of W. Michael Reisman* (Brill–Nijhoff 2011) 217.

[6] Roland Portmann, *Legal Personality in International Law* (CUP 2010) 274.

[7] See also, with respect to international organizations: Nigel D White, *The Law of International Organisations* (3rd edn, Manchester University Press 2016) 116–118.

[8] Portmann (n 6) 272–273.

[9] See Philip Alston, 'The "Not-a-Cat" Syndrome: Can the International Human Rights Regime Accommodate Non-State Actors?' in Philip Alston (ed), *Non-State Actors and Human Rights* (OUP 2005).

duties are opposable to other legal persons), and the way of identifying it (meaning whether the test for attribution of that legal personality is subjective or objective).[10] In the case of the state, for example, it is generally accepted that once an entity fulfils the criteria for statehood, it automatically enjoys all the rights and duties normally attached to states, and that these are, in principle, applicable vis-à-vis all other states, whether the state in question is recognized by them or not.[11]

Things are less straightforward with non-state actors. To be certain, the status of some non-state actors also requires no ad hoc recognition by states in that sense. For example, the fundamental human rights of individuals under customary international law do not rest upon any particular state recognizing the status of the concerned individuals as human beings: attribution of such status is effected directly by interpreting and applying the relevant norms of international law.[12] Yet two clarifications should qualify this absence of a need for recognition.

First, as just mentioned, even though an individual's status operates in that sense in an objective fashion, that is without any need for recognition, this alone does not provide any ground for extending to individual human beings the same rights and duties that states have. This reasoning extends to any other entities that may also happen to have certain rights and duties under international law, as for instance armed groups or, under certain circumstances, corporations.

Second, a distinction needs to be drawn between the cases where a norm of customary international law that is universally applicable among states grants certain rights to an entity and where a non-state entity owes its rights and duties (and thus the content and extent of its legal personality) to the existence of a treaty. In the latter case, the relative effect of treaty provisions means that the entity endowed with some rights and obligations under the said treaty does not really legally 'exist' as such in the eyes of entities towards which those rights and obligations are not

---

[10] For a similar distinction, see Brölmann (n 5) 78–94.

[11] Here the working assumption follows the so-called declaratory theory of recognition for the establishment of statehood, namely the notion that recognition by other states is not necessary for the ascription of such a status under general international law, and that the respective rules of customary international law, such as non-intervention, apply regardless of the presence of recognition. See James Crawford, *The Creation of States in International Law* (2nd edn, OUP 2005) 17–28. For a more detailed discussion of this assumption and its consequences with regard to theorizing international organizations, see text to n 88 in Chapter 7, text to n 42 in Chapter 8.

[12] See also Portmann (n 6) 272–273.

opposable. For example, according to certain authors, bilateral investment treaties may be thought to grant direct rights to investors.[13] One could thus argue that in that limited sense, investors may be thought to have some measure of legal personality vis-à-vis the host state.[14] However, it does not follow that this personality extends towards third states. In this case, the legal importance of any type of recognition may seem at best operating within the framework of article 35 of the Vienna Convention on the Law of Treaties (VCLT 1969),[15] and its stringent requirements, and at worst as being a legally meaningless act. Of course, this does not imply that the entity may not be legally visible in a different capacity depending on the context: for example, someone qualifying as an investor under one treaty may still be seen as an individual human being for the purposes of human rights law, customary or treaty-based.

In sum, while the state/non-state binary may seem rather crude, it introduces well enough the problem explored here: an examination of whether and when certain rights, obligations, and capacities that are normally associated with states also attach to international organizations or whether the latter should be analysed as non-state actors with all the consequences identified herein.

2.2   A Question Worth Asking in Its Own Regard: Should International Organizations Be Analysed as State or as Non-state Actors?

Contrary to the question of whether international organizations should be analysed as unitary entities or as mere groupings of their members, the question of whether these institutions should be treated as states or as non-state actors in the aforementioned sense has received only sparse

---

[13] See eg Zachary Douglas, *The International Law of Investment Claims* (CUP 2009) 10–39.

[14] See eg Patrick Dumberry and Erik Labelle-Eastaugh, 'Non-State Actors in International Investment Law: The Legal Personality of Corporations and NGOs in the Context of Investor-State Arbitration' in Jean d'Aspremont (ed), *Multiple Perspectives on Non-state Actors in International Law* (Routledge-Cavendish 2011).

[15] Vienna Convention on the Law of Treaties (adopted 23 May 1969, entered into force 27 January 1980) 1155 UNTS 331, art 35 ('Treaties providing for obligations for third States'): 'An obligation arises for a third State from a provision of a treaty if the parties to the treaty intend the provision to be the means of establishing the obligation and the third State expressly accepts that obligation in writing.' See also Vienna Convention on the Law of Treaties between States and International Organizations or between International Organizations (adopted 21 March 1986, not yet in force) UN publication, Sales No E.94.V.5, art 35.

scholarly attention. Despite some more recent works arguing that international organizations should indeed be analysed as states in a variety of contexts – ranging from questions of international responsibility to the application of customary international law[16] – the broader literature has remained ambivalent. If anything, the more popular view seems to conceptualize international organizations as anything but states. Allain Pellet's aphorism that international organizations 'are definitely not states'[17] is certainly not contradicted by how many international organizations present themselves. For instance, the UN's website explains that the organization is 'neither a State nor a Government'.[18] Even in broader epistemological terms, international lawyers tend to think of international organizations as non-state actors, as shown by the place normally reserved for international organizations in journals, collected volumes, and books on *non*-state actors in international law.[19] None of this is necessarily conclusive regarding the *legal* treatment that international organizations should have in international law. That being said, it can be equally misleading to dismiss it merely as semantics. What is at issue here from an analytical perspective is not whether these two kinds of entities are identical – there are obvious differences across as well as within each kind. Rather, it is whether there is a category gap between states and international organizations such that would justify diverse treatment in the eyes of international law.

The idea that there may indeed be such a category gap between states and international organizations can be traced at least as far back as the 1949 *Reparation for Injuries* Advisory Opinion. Famously in that case, the International Court of Justice (ICJ) had to tackle the question of whether the UN had a right to ask for reparations for damage suffered by one of its agents. While the Court recognized the UN's legal personality, it also signalled against a complete analytical equation between international organizations and states. As the Court held:

---

[16] See eg Kristina Daugirdas, 'How and Why International Law Binds International Organizations' (2016) 57 Harvard International Law Journal 325; Bordin (n 2).
[17] Pellet (n 1).
[18] UN, 'About UN Membership', <www.un.org/en/about-us/about-un-membership> accessed 9 February 2025.
[19] See eg the editorial note in the first issue of the journal 'Non-state actors and International Law' where the editors argued in favor of including international organizations among non-state actors, and thus within the subject area of their journal. Malgosia Fitzmaurice, Peter Muchlinski, and Milena Szuniewicz, 'From the Editors' (2001) 1 Non-St. Actors & IL 1.

> ... the Court has come to the conclusion that the Organization is an
> international person. That is not the same thing as saying that it is a State,
> which it certainly is not, or that its legal personality and rights and duties
> are the same as those of a State. Still less it is the same thing that it is "a
> super-State", whatever that expression may mean.[20]

This idea that international organizations are not states, not unpreced-
ented in international jurisprudence,[21] was confirmed in the subsequent
case law of the Court.[22]

At the time, the Court's conclusion in *Reparation for Injuries* solved a
divisive problem, namely whether the UN enjoyed a distinct legal existence
from its members and could thus ask for reparation in its own name. But
the Court's affirmative answer on this matter came hand in hand with
seemingly unhinging the concept of legal personality from the same status
function that it performs with regard to states. The recognition of the UN's
legal personality is essentially confined to admitting the organization's
capacity of holding rights and duties in its own name. It does not really
provide by itself a definitive answer as to the existence of specific rights and
duties, let alone as to the ipso facto existence of all the rights and duties
normally associated with statehood. In this context, instead of presenting
merely a question of semantics, the placement of international organizations on the 'non-state' side of the state/non-state binary would seem in
the first instance to carry concrete consequences for a host of legal issues.

Arguably, the most important of these is the question of rights and
obligations under customary international law. If legal personality alone
gives 'no answer ... to the question of what rights and duties individual
organizations have',[23] a position that seems to be consistent with current
doctrine, then presumably we cannot simply extend the customary
norms that apply to states to international organizations just by invoking
their legal personality. Instead of asking whether there is a reason not to
apply the same norms to states and international organizations, this
approach suggests that we should be looking for positive reason before

---

[20] *Reparation for Injuries Suffered in the Service of the United Nations* (Advisory Opinion)
[1949] ICJ Rep 174, 179.
[21] *Jurisdiction of the European Commission of the Danube between Galatz and Braila*
(Advisory Opinion) [1927] PCIJ Rep Series B No 14, 64 (stating that 'the European
Commission is not a state, but an international institution with a special purpose').
[22] *Interpretation of the Agreement of 25 March 1951 between the WHO and Egypt* (Advisory
Opinion) [1980] ICJ Rep 73, 89.
[23] Henry G Schermers and Niels M Blokker, *International Institutional Law* (5th edn,
Martinus Nijhoff 2011) 993.

we can draw that connection. As per standard customary law doctrine, this normally translates to the need to establish new and separate norms addressing specifically international organizations. Following this view to its necessary conclusions, we would need to adduce specific evidence establishing the relevant practice and opinio juris regarding these institutions.

Two examples can showcase how this theoretical conundrum may play out in practice. The first concerns the privileges and immunities that international organizations may themselves enjoy under customary international law. Tackling this question, Sir Michael Wood – later to become the ILC's Special Rapporteur on the identification of customary international law – argued in a 2013 publication that we need to inquire as to whether there is a general practice supporting the emergence of such a rule *specifically* with respect to international organizations.[24] This framing of the question already assumes that whatever they are, international organizations are not states, and thus existing norms on state immunities cannot be extrapolated to them by pure deduction. This idea of an intrinsic and not just descriptive difference between states and international organizations persists in spite of these institutions' presumed interstate basis. The opposite view, according to Wood, represents a 'somewhat simplistic view' of international organizations that does not correspond to 'a real understanding of their legal nature'.[25] According to him, 'recourse even by analogy to the legal position of sovereigns [is] wholly unnecessary and illogical',[26] thus suggesting that the search for separate and more specific norms is the only way forward.

The second example presents the reverse problem: whether immunities enjoyed by states under customary international law can be binding on, and thus opposable against, international organizations. In the *Al Bashir* case, the ICC answered this question in the negative.[27] When examining whether it had to respect customary head-of-state immunity

---

[24] Michael Wood, 'Do International Organizations Enjoy Immunity under Customary International Law?' (2013) 10 IOLR 287.

[25] ibid 294.

[26] ibid 295. Citing Robert Y Jennings's Foreword in Pieter HF Bekker, *The Legal Position of Intergovernmental Organizations: A Functional Necessity of Their Legal Status and Immunities* (Brill 1994) vii. For an equally sceptical view of this analogy, see José Alvarez, 'Book Review: "International Organizations and Their Exercise of Sovereign Powers" by Dan Sarooshi' (2007) 101 AJIL 674.

[27] *The Prosecutor v Omar Hassan Ahmad Al-Bashir* (Judgment) ICC-02/05-01/09 OA2 (6 May 2019) [1]–[2], [114]–[117]. Note that this presents a different question from the potential non-applicability of functional immunities under customary international law to 'subordinate' state officials for violations of international criminal law before national courts: see Claus Kreß, Peter Frank, and Christoph Barthe, 'Functional

of a former head of state of a non-member state, the ICC looked for a separate new norm that applied specifically to international courts instead of just applying the existing norms.[28] The reason for looking for these separate new norms was, according to the court, the 'fundamentally different nature' of international as opposed to domestic, meaning state, courts.[29] This implied distinction between the two types of subjects suggested the non-automatic application of the same corpus of norms to both, unless it was supported by separate evidence of practice and opinio juris to that effect. On the basis of the failure to find that kind of evidence in the case before it, the ICC, itself an international organization, essentially held that the duty to respect the customary rule of head-of-state immunity did not create any binding obligations for it.

We may be tempted to look at these examples as isolated within their factual contexts, but the underlying principles that they speak to are important to flesh out. The core idea here is that, given their distinct legal nature, states' rights and obligations do not normally extend to international organizations. As a matter of principle, this essentially suggests that '[d]ifferent rules of public international law apply to States and international organizations' as the UN Secretariat has claimed on at least one occasion.[30] Although seldom expressed in so many words, the same kind of thinking can be found in other organizations as well, as, for example, the International Bank for Reconstruction and Development arguing that 'general international law' (presumably including customary law) is not binding on it or any other international organizations in the absence of explicit norms to that effect.[31]

It is worth situating this discussion within the overarching argument that this book puts forward. Indeed, one may be inclined to agree or disagree with conclusions such as the ones reached by Wood or the ICC. In fact, this book will eventually suggest that international organizations

---

Immunity of Foreign State Officials before National Courts: A Legal Opinion by Germany's Federal Public Prosecutor General' (2021) 19(3) JICJ 697.

[28] ibid para 116.

[29] ibid.

[30] Comments of the United Nations Secretariat on behalf of the United Nations System Organizations on European Data Protection Board 'Guidelines 2/2020 on Articles 46 (2) (a) and 46 (3) (b) of Regulation 2016/679 for Transfers of Personal Data between EEA and Non-EEA Public Authorities and Bodies' (15 December 2020), para 27, <https://edpb .europa.eu/sites/default/files/webform/public_consultation_reply/2020.05.14_letter_to_ edpb_chair_with_un_comments_on_guidelines_2–2020.pdf> accessed 9 February 2025.

[31] Sabine Schlemmer-Schulte, 'International Bank for Reconstruction and Development (IBRD)' *Max Planck Encyclopedia of International Law* (OUP 2011) para 102.

and states are not of a 'fundamentally different nature' and that the application of the same norms of customary international law to the latter is indeed both necessary and logical, just in a manner that requires greater nuance than our current approaches can afford. Yet it is also essential to appreciate that even at this preliminary level of analysis, the 'all-embracing' treaty/subject dichotomy does not appear to be that all-embracing after all in practice. Arguments such as those put forward by Wood or the ICC are *not* premised on the notion that international organizations do not enjoy a legal personality or on the notion that they are somehow not legally autonomous. Rather they are premised, either explicitly or implicitly, on an interpretation of the meaning and content of that personality. In either case, this matter was not, and this book argues rightly so, resolved by simply choosing whether to view international organizations as contractual arrangements or as legal subjects in their own regard. Both Wood and the ICC accept the latter premise and still go on to argue that new and more specific norms of customary international law are needed before the same law that applies to states can be extended to international organizations.

Our operating paradigms thus reveal themselves as partial: even within the 'subject' conception of international organizations, there exists considerable latitude. Conversely put, one cannot collapse the question of the content of the legal personality of international organizations to the fact that they enjoy such a personality to begin with. Suggesting that international organizations are legal subjects does not signify by itself that they are states, not even that they are similar to states in any meaningful way for the types of questions examined here. The following pages expand on this point by looking at how various scholars have unsuccessfully tried to reduce the question of international organizations' legal nature to that of whether they enjoy or not a separate legal existence from their members.

2.3   Current Approaches to the Nature of International Organizations' Legal Personality and Their Limitations

2.3.1   The Formal Conceptions of Legal Personality and Subjecthood

One popular approach to mapping the legal nature of international organizations vis-à-vis states is to assume that the idea of legal personality can carry that load in full. Taking off from the premise that international organizations are subjects of international law, capable of enjoying rights and obligations on their own account, this line of argument usually unfolds as follows: (1) international organizations are subjects of international law; (2) subjects of international law are bound by customary international law; (3) X is a norm of customary international law; (4) international organizations are bound by legal norm X.[32] Such analyses are often accompanied by references to international case law. Most prominently, this includes the ICJ's dictum in its 1956 *WHO-Egypt* Advisory Opinion that '[i]nternational organizations are subjects of international law and, as such, are bound by any obligations incumbent upon them under general rules of international law'.[33] Other references typically include the dictum of International Criminal Tribunal for Rwanda (ICTR) in the *Rwamakuba* case that 'the United Nations, as an international subject, is bound to respect rules of customary international law, including those rules that relate to the protection of human rights'.[34] On this basis, this view goes on to argue that international organizations have the same rights and obligations as states when it comes to customary international law as long as their activities call for their application – recognizing, for example, that international organizations do not possess territory in the same manner that states do or feature nationals of their own.[35]

Although fairly intuitive in its conclusions, this line of reasoning is ultimately unpersuasive. It bypasses the presumed category gap between states and international organizations only by subsuming both entities under the broadest possible category of 'legal persons' or 'legal subjects'. This creates an illusion of homogeneity where none really exists. This approach may appeal to domestic legal imagination, where the idea of legal personhood normally performs such a status function, wherefrom capacities, rights, and obligations normally flow ipso facto. However, as already explained, this does not reflect how terms such as 'legal person' or 'legal subject' operate in the international legal order. As far as the

---

[32] See eg Phillippe Sands and Pierre Klein, *Bowett's Law of International Institutions* (6th edn, Sweet & Maxwell 2009) 766–767; Eyal Benvenisti, *The Law of Global Governance* (Brill 2014) 100; see also Guglielmo Verdirame, *The UN and Human Rights; Who Guards the Guardians?* (CUP 2011) 70–71.

[33] *Interpretation of the Agreement of 25 March 1951 between the WHO and Egypt* (n 22) 89–90.

[34] See *The Prosecutor v André Rwamakuba* (Decision) ICTR-98-44C-T (31 January 2007) [48].

[35] Sands and Klein (n 32) 767.

latter is concerned, legal personality and subjecthood denote an entity as a point of attribution for rights, obligations, or capacities. In that sense, legal personality indeed does not have any inherent content. This means that whether international organizations may enjoy a legal personality of their own or not presents a different question from the scope of their rights and obligations in international law.[36] This is consistent with broader practice regarding non-state actors – regarding whom the recognition of legal personality is normally not presumed to imply the application of the whole corpus of custom.

It also makes analytical sense: the question of whether an entity has the capacity to enjoy rights and obligations does not answer the question of which rights and obligations it actually possesses. If the concept of legal personality is understood as a formal predicate with no inherent content but merely denotes that an entity enjoys *some* rights and/or obligations, then it seems analytically impossible to securely infer from this concept *additional* substantive rights and obligations. Similarly, if legal personality just signifies a right-and-duty-bearing-entity in international law – to be certain only one among many such entities – it does not seem convincing to pick out international organizations as being capable of contributing to the formation of international law solely on that basis. Thus, the more meaningful question is not whether international organizations are subjects of international law or legal persons, but rather what type of subject or legal person they might be. This is the question that Wood and the ICC are essentially tackling.

Existing ICJ case law does not overturn this conclusion. To begin with, the *WHO-Egypt* Advisory Opinion does not resolve the problem as it is sometimes thought. The Court proposed that international organizations are bound by these 'general rules of international law' that are 'incumbent upon them'.[37] However, it did not explain which rules are in fact

---

[36] Similarly, see Schermers and Blokker (n 23) 993: '[T]he fact that an international organization is an international person does not mean that it is in the same position as a state in the context of international relations. To be an international person means only *to be capable* of bearing rights and duties. No answer is given to the question of what rights and duties individual organizations have.' (Citing other authors who share this view.) See also Portman (n 6) 173ff; Brölmann (n 5) 1, who describes international organizations as 'the most conspicuous non-state actors in international law'. For a more reserved view on the topic, see Richard Collins, 'Non-state Actors in International Institutional Law' in Jean d'Aspremont (ed), *Participants in the International Legal System* (Routledge 2011).

[37] *Interpretation of the Agreement of 25 March 1951 between the WHO and Egypt* (n 22) 89–90.

'incumbent upon' these institutions. Rather the Court made a general statement to the effect that international organizations are indeed capable of being bound by general rules of international law, presumably including those of customary law.[38] This conclusion, entirely consistent with the earlier approach of the Court in *Reparation of Injuries*, is in line with what has been said thus far about the operation of legal personality in international law.

By contrast, the ICTR in *Rwamakuba* does indeed depart from what has been said so far by suggesting that a part of customary international law, in that case human rights, applies automatically to an international organization by virtue of the latter having a legal personality of its own.[39] For this proposition, the Appeals Chamber cited the *WHO-Egypt* as well as the *Reparation for Injuries* Advisory Opinion. Yet as we have seen, the first of these opinions is not conclusive on the matter, and the latter could, if anything, be thought to support the exact opposite conclusion by suggesting, as we have seen, that while the UN is a legal person, '[t]hat is not the same thing as saying that it is a State, which it certainly is not, or that its legal personality and rights and duties are the same as those of a State'.[40] That being said, the point here is not whether a decision such as the one in *Rwamakuba* is consistent or not with the 'canon' of the *Reparation for Injuries* Advisory Opinion or any other judicial pronouncement, but rather whether it is persuasively reasoned in itself. Indeed, sometimes this 'canon' is itself not entirely free of contradictions and less-than-persuasive points. Instead, the focus should be on careful analysis of the respective reasoning. In the case of *Rwamakuba*, this seems neither right nor wrong in the abstract, but rather incomplete.

2.3.2 Legal Personality and Subjecthood beyond Their Formal Conceptions

The critique against the idea that international organizations should be analytically equated to states because they both enjoy legal personality

---

[38] See also Jan Klabbers, 'The Paradox of International Institutional Law' (2008) 5 IOLR 1, 14–15.

[39] It should be borne in mind that this was just one among many arguments relied upon by the Appeals Chamber, including the UN's own commitment that the ICTR and the ICTY 'must fully respect internationally recognized standards regarding the rights of the accused at all stages of its proceedings': *The Prosecutor v André Rwamakuba* (n 34) [48]–[49].

[40] *Reparation for Injuries Suffered in the Service of the United Nations* (n 20) 179.

stands even if we accept some wiggle room, as we generally should, and recognize that certain corollary secondary rights and obligations are immanent to the concept.

This includes claiming, for example, that the right to ask for reparations logically follows from the possession of a certain right in the first place, as the ICJ held in *Reparation for Injuries*.[41] Nevertheless, this goes back to a much older, and more fundamental, idea, dating at least as far back as the Permanent Court of International Justice's (PCIJ) *Factory at Chorzów* case, not to an equation of international organizations and states. In the *Factory at Chorzów* case, the PCIJ held that 'the breach of an engagement involves an obligation to make reparation in an adequate form. Reparation therefore is the indispensable complement of a failure to apply a convention and there is no necessity for this to be stated in the convention itself'.[42] Although the case related to whether a right to reparation needed to be enshrined separately in a convention, the more general principle, accepted by the International Law Commission (ILC) in its work on state responsibility,[43] is that substantive rights and obligations may entail necessary legal consequences that go beyond their substantive core. Properly construed, this includes corollary claim-rights and duties, such as the obligation to make reparations following the breach of an international obligation.

Yet accepting this logical proposition about the content of rights and duties, and thus legal personality, does not mean that the said legal persons are automatically equated with states from the perspective of general international law. This may seem clearer in the context of the *Reparation for Injuries* Advisory Opinion.[44] There the Court held that

---

[41] See *Reparation for Injuries Suffered in the Service of the United Nations* (n 20) 184, where the Court held that 'it is a principle of international law that the breach of an engagement involves an obligation to make reparation in an adequate form'.

[42] *Case Concerning the Factory at Chorzów (Germany v Poland)* (Judgment) [1927] PCIJ Rep Series A No 9, 21.

[43] ILC, 'Draft Articles on Responsibility of States for Internationally Wrongful Acts, with Commentaries' (2001) II/2 YILC 31, 91, paras 1–4 (art 31 and commentary thereto) citing the aforementioned *Case Concerning the Factory at Chorzów* (n 42).

[44] As is well known, this case related to the UN asking reparation from Israel for the assassination of Count Folke Bernadotte, the UN Mediator in Palestine, and other members of the UN Mission to Palestine. See Yuen-li Liang, 'Notes on Legal Questions concerning the United Nations Reparation for Injuries Suffered in the Service of the United Nations' 43 AJIL 460.

the UN had a right to ask, and members a corresponding obligation to provide, every assistance in any action undertaken by it or to accept and carry out the decisions of the Security Council.[45] Leaving to the side for the moment the question of why, if the UN's legal personality is ultimately sourced in rights and obligations that are conventional in nature, it would still be opposable to a non-member, the idea that once the UN is recognized as 'a subject of international law, and thus capable of possessing international rights and duties', then it also 'has the capacity to maintain its rights by bringing international claims' hardly seems objectionable.[46] In that sense, even when narrowly construed as the existence of some ad hoc rights and obligations, legal personality should be understood to encompass all of the claim-rights and duties that are the logical corollary of those rights and obligations, such as the right to bring claims to maintain them or seek reparations.[47] At the same time, however, the existence of corollary rights and duties does not open the door to the argument that an entity also enjoys an open-ended number of non-corollary rights and duties. To put this into a more practical perspective: even if the UN has a right to ask for assistance from its member states, and bring claims against them in that regard, this alone does not by itself support the notion that the UN bears particular obligations under customary law, for example, to respect the right to health of the people in Haiti.[48]

---

[45] *Reparation for Injuries Suffered in the Service of the United Nations* (n 20) 178, 183.

[46] ibid 179.

[47] Leaving to the side the question of whether the addressees of international legal norms are also the true holders of the respective rights. On this point, see Bart L Smit Duijzentkunst, 'The Concept of Rights in International Law' (Doctoral dissertation, University of Cambridge 2015). The more general idea that is alluded to here can be condensed in the legal maxim *quando lex aliquid alicui concedit concedere videtur et id sine quo res ipsa esse non potest* ('when the law bestows anything upon anyone, it is deemed to bestow also that without which the thing itself cannot be'). See *Applicability of Article VI, Section 22, of the Convention on the Privileges and Immunities of the United Nations* (Advisory Opinion) [1989] ICJ Rep 177 (Separate Opinion Judge Shahabudeen) 220.

[48] See also Rowan Nicholson, *Statehood and the State-Like in International Law* (OUP 2019) 205, who points out that the Court 'did not identify any relevant substantive rights borne by the United Nations that might be breached by a non-member state'; Chittharanjan F Amerasinghe, *Principles of the Institutional Law of International Organizations* (2nd edn, CUP 2005) 392–393, arguing that 'a non-member state does not owe specific duties to the organization under [international] law'.

Broader constructions of legal personality that stop short of an analytical assimilation to states seem equally unhelpful. This includes understandings of legal personality as an entitlement to 'participate' in a given legal system,[49] or the capacity to make claims for injuries suffered and be held internationally responsible.[50] This approach too seems to infer the existence of one capacity or attribute from the presence of another. Again, this is not to say that some legal attributes may not be the necessary corollary of an entity enjoying a recognized capacity under international law. For example, if we accept that international organizations can be held responsible for their internationally wrongful acts or that they have the capacity to sign treaties, it seems plausible to argue that basic rules governing attribution of conduct or the expression of consent need not be identified anew for international organizations, or that in any event they should develop along analogous lines, as some authors have reasonably argued.[51] However, having the capacity to undertake international obligations or be held responsible for one's violations and make international claims tell us nothing about the nature and extent of those rights or obligations, let alone that these are the same as those of states.[52] Neither does it tell us much about an entity's capacity to contribute specifically to the formation of international custom or about the opposability of its rights and obligations to third parties and vice versa.[53] Once more, the result is not a conclusion that is necessarily wrong, but one that does not naturally follow from its premises.

2.3.3   The Analogy between States and International Organizations

Less obvious but equally serious complications arise with the idea that there exists some deeper analogy between international organizations

---

[49] Brölmann (n 5) 68–69.

[50] Portmann (n 6) 275.

[51] See eg Bordin (n 2).

[52] See also Crawford (n 11) 43 ('That an entity has rights and obligations under international law or may be responsible for conduct that is internationally wrongful does not make it a state', referring specifically to international organizations).

[53] See eg ILC, 'Draft Articles on the Responsibility of International Organizations, with Commentaries' (2011) II/2 YILC 2, 46, para 3: '[n]othing in the draft articles should be read as implying the existence or otherwise of any particular primary rule binding on international organizations'.

and states such that would make them enjoy a functionally equivalent position in the international legal system wherever possible. This idea revolves around the notion that international organizations share an important 'relevant similarity' with states, usually conceptualized in terms of their legal autonomy, that may negate the potential category gap between the two kinds of entities. If the dominant view suggests that international organizations are 'neither sovereign nor equal',[54] this line of thinking either suggests that international organizations are sovereign too,[55] or that they at least enjoy a trait, such as legal autonomy, that plays an analytical role similar to sovereignty.[56] Accordingly, and contrary to the formal conception of legal personality, the legal personality of international organizations should be thought to approximate that of states in that it performs a status function. Consequently, capacities as well as rights and obligations can be immediately inferred simply by designating an entity as an international organization. And, because this status function is thought to rest in both the case of states and international organizations on a shared trait, the capacities, rights, and obligations thus derived are essentially similar, with the caveat that there are some factual differences between the two sets of actors (again, for example, the absence of territory or a population for international organizations). Within this framework, these differences are not determinative of legal status. They are assessed in a quantitative manner, bringing, for example, international organizations to a similar legal position to that of a land-locked state vis-à-vis the law of the sea.[57]

---

[54] ILC, 'Sixth Report on the Question of Treaties Concluded between States and International Organizations or between Two or More International Organizations by Mr. Paul Reuter, Special Rapporteur – Draft Articles with Commentaries (Continued)' (1977) UN Doc A/CN.4/298, 120, para 6. See also *Judgments of the Administrative Tribunal of the International Labour Organization upon Complaints Made against UNESCO* (Advisory Opinion) [1956] ICJ Rep 77, 97: '[A]rguments, deduced from the sovereignty of States, which might have been invoked in favour of a restrictive interpretation of provisions governing the jurisdiction of a tribunal adjudicating between States are not relevant to a situation in which a tribunal is called upon to adjudicate upon a complaint of an official against an international organization'; *M v Organisation des Nations Unies et l' État Belge (Ministre des Affaires Étrangères)*, Civil Tribunal (Brussels) (11 May 1966) 45 ILR 446, at 453 ('The United Nations is not a sovereign power. It has neither territory or population').

[55] Finn Seyersted, *Common Law of International Organizations* (Brill 2008) 43ff.

[56] Bordin (n 2) 77.

[57] For an example of such analysis, see Daugirdas (n 16) 367, where the author compares international organizations to landlocked states with respect to the law of the sea.

Although present as an implicit assumption throughout the discourse, two scholars in particular have developed more comprehensive theoretical accounts of this idea: Finn Seyersted and Fernando Bordin. Seyersted, who is justly considered a pioneer in the field of international organizations law, first published his work in the 1960s.[58] His scholarship was shaped by the idea that international organizations were proper subjects of international law, not too different from states, and thus enjoyed their own 'inherent' powers as opposed to being viewed as always acting on the basis of an authorization from their members. In a similar vein, Bordin's seminal work suggests that international organizations should be conceptualized as subjects of international law that are analogous to states, for a variety of purposes, but most prominently for matters pertaining to the law of treaties and international responsibility.[59] While there are differences between Seyersted and Bordin in terms of both focus and approach, their common insight is that international organizations should be conceptualized as legal subjects because they enjoy legal autonomy. In turn, this legal autonomy may justify similar treatment with states in the eyes of international law in a range of different contexts. Nevertheless, careful scrutiny reveals that these arguments too cannot settle the overarching problem of whether international organizations and states belong to the same class of legal persons.

In his work, Seyersted sought to bypass the apparent differences between states and international organizations by focusing instead on the attributes that they share in common. The existence of those shared characteristics was taken to signify that an entity belonged to a more abstract class of legal subjects, which Seyersted collectively termed 'self-governing' or 'sovereign'. The idea was then that for this class of legal subjects, legal personality performed a status function, and thus additional attributes would flow from designating an entity as 'self-governing' or 'sovereign'. Thus, instead of overtly modelling international organizations after the state, Seyersted modelled international organizations, states, *and* other international subjects such as the Holy See or insurgent groups, after the theoretical construction of the 'self-

---

[58] See Finn Seyersted, 'Objective International Personality of Intergovernmental Organizations: Do Their Capacities Really Depend upon the Conventions Establishing Them?' (1964) 34 Nordic Journal of International Law 3; Finn Seyersted, 'The Legal Nature of International Organizations' (1982) 51 Nordic Journal of International Law 203.

[59] Bordin (n 2) 76.

governing' or 'sovereign' actor. This self-governing actor was construed as a self-referring locus of authority, 'not subject to the jurisdiction of any other organized community'.[60] The common attribute of all self-governing actors is that they enjoyed some amount of 'organic jurisdiction', meaning that they are governed by their own 'public law' and enjoyed a legal monopoly over relations with their organs and officials.[61]

This allowed Seyersted to suggest that international organizations enjoy a legal personality whose content was similar to states and other 'self-governing' entities, such as the Holy See or insurgents. In that way, his theory drew a working distinction between these actors and other actors such as corporations or non-governmental organizations, entities that we might still classify as legal persons if we understand legal personality to bear no inherent content. At the same time, his analogy operated at the more abstract level of the 'self-governing' actor classification, hence not risking the more controversial move of directly equating the international organization with the state at the conceptual level – a position that would have been on its face contrary to the *Reparation for Injuries* Advisory Opinion. From that point, Seyersted drew a normative and analytical parallel between international organizations and other 'self-governing' actors, understanding legal personality in international law as a status from which specific capacities, such as treaty-making or the capacity to send and receive diplomatic representatives, would flow automatically.[62]

Seyersted's account has justly been referred to as the closest the discipline ever got to developing its own legal theory of international organizations.[63] It exhibits, however, two important limitations when examined in the context of the questions investigated here. First,

---

[60] Seyersted, 'Objective International Personality' (n 58) 47–48.
[61] Seyersted (n 55) 82.
[62] From which other rights and duties would presumably flow, although Seyersted refrained from claiming that the rights and duties of all these entities were necessarily the same. See Seyersted (n 55) 396. As he briefly explained:

> [t]he rights and duties of different types of sovereign communities under international law may vary because of their different nature. However, when the difference in nature do not require different legal rules, the rules which have been developed in relations between States may usually be applied by analogy to other sovereign communities, to the extent that their activities call for the application of such rules.

[63] Jan Klabbers, 'On Seyersted and His Common Law of International Organizations' (2008) 5 IOLR 381, 384.

Seyersted's original theory does not really settle the question of whether, and to what extent, international organizations should be analysed as states regarding more specific propositions normally associated with states, such as capacity to contribute to the formation of customary international law. Second, the foundational premise of his theory remains problematic when viewed from the perspective of positive law.

To begin with, the theory's greatest strength – bypassing the problem of the seemingly implausible equation between international organizations and states by proposing an altogether new category of 'self-governing' subjects – is also one of its enduring limitations with respect to how international organizations relate to states as species of legal subjects. By questioning the distinction between the different categories of legal subjects and severing any strong analytical tie between an organization and its members (exemplified by the way in which he treated constituent instruments as beyond the reach of international law), Seyersted's approach made conceptual progress on several fronts. For example, his theory was able to rationalize the treaty-making capacity of international organizations, as well as the extent of their powers, which he understood to be 'inherent' and not merely implied. But by the same token, the theory left more specific questions regarding the legal nature of international organizations beyond definite analytical conclusion. Following Seyersted's account, international organizations could be thought to be, strictly speaking, non-state actors even as they belonged to the more abstract category of self-governing actors.

The questions that prompted our inquiry thus remain: are international organizations bound by the norms of customary international law that are binding on states? Does their practice count equally to that of states for the formation of customary international law? If the answer to these questions is affirmative simply on the basis that international organizations are 'self-governing' or autonomous, we again risk conflating two different questions: whether an entity enjoys a distinct legal existence, even of a more substantive content than standard theory on legal personality would allow, and what type of entity it is, assuming that it enjoys such an existence. But again, in the *Al Bashir* case, the ICC did not dispute that it was a legally autonomous or a 'self-governing' actor; the court was in fact exercising that autonomy in issuing its decision. Rather, it asked the different question of whether a separate norm of customary law needed to be identified specifically extending head-of-state immunity to the courts of international organizations, such as itself.

Conceptualizing the court as a self-governing actor seems to have no bearing upon this question. Indeed, as already explained, international legal theory never really endorsed an understanding of legal personality whereby the legal rights, duties, and capacities identified with it are automatically considered as being identical to those of states. Supplanting legal personality for legal autonomy would seem to make little difference from an analytical perspective in that regard.[64] In sum, while such a theory can provide novel insights, for example, with respect to the powers of international organizations, it runs into many of the same limitations as previous constructions of legal personality with respect to broader problems regarding the legal nature of these institutions.

What is more, while certainly theoretically conceivable, such a departure from this understanding of legal personality was conditioned on a change in positive law that was ultimately left unproven. As Seyesrted explained, his theory suggested 'a radical extension of the definition of international law'.[65] According to him, it was on account of this radical extension that the international legal system could now accommodate international organizations as self-governing actors. Even if Seyersted shunned away from a straight analogy between international organizations and states, it could be argued that if a radical change to the system could have led to international organizations being recognized as 'self-governing actors', then another such change could occur that would essentially recognize for international organizations a functionally similar position to states, thus bridging the apparent gap between the notions of being a legally autonomous entity and the notion that an entity can be analysed in similar terms as the state. The problem with this line of thinking is that there is scant evidence to support such a radical change in terms of positive law. As Bordin has convincingly argued, it is indeed very difficult to prove such a change *in law*, and Seyersted himself produced little evidence in terms of practice or opinio juris in that regard.[66]

Yet Bordin's own answer to the problem seems equally unsatisfying when viewed in the context of the present inquiry.[67] In his work, Bordin

---

[64] Portmann (n 6) 274.

[65] Seyersted, 'Objective International Personality' (n 58) 93.

[66] Bordin (n 2) 62. See also Klabbers (n 63) 382; William T Worster, 'Relative International Legal Personality of Non-State Actors' (2016) 42 Brooklyn Journal of International Law 207, 215.

[67] As Bordin suggests in this respect:

> [r]easoning by analogy is not to be conflated with arguments about the existence of customary rules as traditionally understood, that is, it is not a substitute for general practice accompanied by a sense of legal obligation.

theorizes the existence of 'an implicit rule of incorporation in contemporary international law'.[68] This rule of incorporation is understood as 'a structural rule of international law' that admits international organizations' membership in the international community.[69] This echoes how domestic law sometimes frames the problem of corporate existence, where a rule of positive law may extend the status of a legal person to an entity that would otherwise be just an intricate contractual arrangement. Likewise, this argument suggests that because of a putative implicit rule of incorporation, international organizations can be analysed as proper subjects of international law.[70]

This theory, however, runs much into the same complications as Seyersted's when it comes to the foundation of its claims in established international law. It too recognizes that the development of such a rule of incorporation would require nothing short of 'radical and structural' change in international law, and that it thus poses a serious epistemological challenge from the perspective of positive law.[71] Still Bordin maintains that the presupposition of such a rule of incorporation affords a 'better *rationalization*' over its theoretical alternative, namely the 'treaty conception' of international organizations.[72]

This lack of clear grounding in positive law may not be crucial for the main argument that Bordin advances in his book, and the ensuing analogy seems compelling within certain *de lege ferenda* contexts – chiefly in the work of the ILC.[73] Indeed, the two ILC projects that Bordin persuasively zeroes in on – the law of treaties and responsibility of international organizations – are oriented more towards structural concepts such as autonomy (implying, for example, that an autonomous actor can only be bound by a treaty pursuant to its consent), and less towards exploring the deeper similarities between states and

---

But it provides, in its own context and on its own terms, a justification for making propositions about the content of the law in situations of uncertainty. (Bordin (n 2) 238.)

[68] ibid 77, 83, 85.

[69] ibid 62. See also Lorenzo Gasbarri, *The Concept of an International Organization in Public International Law* (OUP 2021) 106 ('[Legal] personality is conferred ... by member states on the basis of a norm of international law').

[70] See also Bordin (n 2) 198, where he compares the situation with 'domestic systems have developed highly developed regimes for the creation and operation of corporate bodies'.

[71] ibid 62–63, 86. See also Henner Gött, *The Law of Interaction between International Organizations* (Springer 2020) 450.

[72] Bordin (n 2) 63 (emphasis in the original).

[73] ibid 37–38.

international organizations with regard to their nature as species of legal subjects in the manner contemplated here. At the same time, the ILC's work in those projects was itself largely suggestive of progressive development rather than codification, thus limiting the need to trace propositions back to positive law.

The argument for a rule of incorporation works less well when considered through the lens of positive law and the questions considered here. In that regard, either one is of the opinion that, analytically speaking, the emergence of a separate norm is necessary before the international legal system can accommodate international organizations or one is not. If one thinks that such a norm is necessary and then goes on to analyse its content, then the way forward should be to examine whether such a norm actually exists in positive law or not, not whether it would be more rational to assume that it does. This may be unproblematic with respect to the inquiry that Bordin undertakes in his book,[74] yet it presents insurmountable obstacles for the questions tackled in this book. Indeed, if we remove the premise that 'a radical extension of the definition of international law' has taken place from Seyersted's syllogism, or the idea that there is an implicit rule of incorporation in international law from Bordin's analysis, we are back to treating legal autonomy as a status concept effectively similar to statehood. In doing so, we collapse the problem of the content and nature of international organizations' legal personality to that of its existence, essentially suggesting that legal subjectivity or autonomy can by themselves justify the analytical equation between international organizations and states.

Bordin offers his own intricate account for assuming this position. Arguing that the problem should be viewed in a systemic context, he suggests that 'the rule of incorporation implicit in contemporary international law does not – and could not, without more – authorise States to create body corporates operating outside the overarching legal system under which States operate individually'.[75] Although appealing, Bordin's argument here begs further interrogation. Given the uncertainty surrounding the existence and content of a possible rule of incorporation in positive law, the argument might seem to infer an 'is' from an 'ought'. In other words, it is almost as if there *should* be a

---

[74] ibid.
[75] ibid 83.

rule of incorporation, and this rule *should* extend the same rules to states and their creations.

Crucially, however, even if we were to assume that such a rule of incorporation existed, it is not evident where to go from there based on systemic reasoning alone. To begin with, states are behind the creation of all sorts of legal subjects in international law, and these, as we have seen, do not ipso facto share the rights and obligations normally associated with statehood.[76] Furthermore, the argument that obligations of member states 'when they operate individually' also bind international organizations does not sit well with the general acceptance that international organizations are not automatically bound by the treaty commitments of their member states – this legal separation being the cornerstone of the 'subject' conception. Indeed, if one follows this rationale faithfully, then there is no analytical reason to discriminate between conventional and customary law, leaving one wondering what is after all the meaning of 'independent' legal personality. Moreover, it somewhat simplifies questions surrounding the membership of international organizations, reductively assuming that all international organizations are made up of states or of other international organizations, when the latter in practice may feature a variety of other entities, including non-self-governing territories and/or other sui generis non-state entities among their members.[77]

Finally, at a more abstract level, the implicit analogy between international organizations and corporate bodies of domestic law[78] may not be as far reaching as one may initially assume. It is by no means a foregone conclusion that in all legal systems, the entirety of the law that applies to so-called natural persons applies to corporate ones. For example, the question of whether corporations can be held criminally liable is a difficult and divisive normative problem, and one that has found varied solutions across different domestic legal orders.[79] Critically,

---

[76] For example, the ICJ held in its *Kosovo* Advisory Opinion that '... the scope of the principle of territorial integrity is confined to the sphere of relations between states'. Accordingly, the Court found that principle did not bind as such non-state actors, including the respective individuals in the case of that Opinion: *Accordance with International Law of the Unilateral Declaration of Independence in Respect of Kosovo* (Advisory Opinion) [2010] ICJ Rep 403, 437.

[77] See indicatively Schermers and Blokker (n 23) 66–71.

[78] Bordin (n 2) 198.

[79] For a comparative study of civil and common law jurisdictions in that regard, see Mark Pieth and Ivory Radha (eds), *Corporate Criminal Liability: Emergence, Convergence, and Risk* (Springer 2011).

the problem is generally understood as different from the idea that a corporate body can be admitted as a legal person in a given jurisdiction. For example, legislative approaches to whether corporations can be held criminally liable differ even among jurisdictions that accept them as distinct legal entities.

Indicative of this is that even when the ILC arguably adopted the 'subject' conception of international organizations in its work on responsibility of international organizations, this did not really help illuminate the extent to which customary law that governs interstate relations should also apply to these institutions.[80] Even as the ILC explicitly carved out from the scope of its work the existence of primary rules binding on international organizations,[81] the few times where the issue could not be avoided are quite telling in that regard. Questions such as whether international organizations enjoy the right of self-defence or whether the prohibition of the use of force is owed to them proved quite controversial in the relevant ILC sessions. They were certainly not resolved merely by adhering to a 'subject' conception of international organizations.[82]

---

[80] On the ILC's approach, see also Bordin (n 2) 58.

[81] ILC (n 53) 46, para 3.

[82] On self-defence, see Gaja's fourth report, suggesting that it would be 'odd' if an international organization could not lawfully respond to an armed attack; ILC 'Fourth Report on Responsibility of International Organizations, by Mr. Giorgio Gaja, Special Rapporteur' (2006) UN Doc A/CN.4/564 and Add. 1–2, 107, para 15. During the ensuing discussions, various members of the ILC, including Sir Ian Brownlie, argued that international organizations did not enjoy the same right of self-defence as states did in customary international law; ILC, 'Yearbook of the International Law Commission 2006 Volume 1: Summary Records of the Meetings of the Fifty-Eight Session 1 May–9 June and 3 July–11 August 2006' (2006) UN Doc A/CN.4/SER.A/2006, 70, para 20 (Brownlie), 71 para 27 (Rao); ILC, 'Yearbook of the International Law Commission 2009 Volume 1: Summary Records of the Meetings of the Sixty-First Session 4 May–5 June and 6 July–7 August 2009' (2009) UN Doc A/CN.4/SER.A/2009, 22, para 59 (Vasciannie), 18, para 23 (Melescanu), 15, para 23 (Al Marri), 24–25, para 12 (Kamto), 25, para 20 (Comissário Afonso), 79, para 19 (Hmoud). See also comments by the WHO: 'a circumstance such as self-defence is by its very nature only applicable to the actions of a State' ILC, 'Yearbook of the International Law Commission 2006 Volume 1' (ibid), 64, para 33. For the members that sided with Gaja's approach see ILC, 'Yearbook of the International Law Commission 2009 Volume 1' (ibid), 19, para 36 (Dugard); see also ILC, 'Yearbook of the International Law Commission 2009 Volume 1' (ibid), 8, para 30, and ILC, 'Yearbook of the International Law Commission 2006 Volume 1' (ibid), 65, para 4 (Escarameia), 65, para 11 (Mansfield). The final text of the draft articles remains equivocal: '[T]he wrongfulness of an act of an international organization is precluded *if and to the extent* that the act constitutes a lawful measure of self-defence under international law' (emphasis added). Similar conceptual problems arose with respect to

Finally, if we assume that the argument from analogy is successful, we are led to the counter-intuitive overgeneration of fully fledged legal subjects in the international legal order. If we posit that international organizations count analytically as just another state on the basis that they enjoy some relevant similarity, then there appears no built-in limiting principle in those theories[83] to safeguard against the rather odd conclusion that both states and international organizations equally count as different entities when, for example, assessing their contribution to the formation of customary international law, or when assessing the emergence of a *jus cogens* norm. Indeed, when thinking about the formation of customary international law, the standard inquiry usually entails a survey of state practice, but it is rarely thought that a corresponding survey of international organizations' practice is also necessary, not even of those organizations whose mandate seems relevant to the customary rule in question.[84] As Sean Murphy observes, '[p]resumably, it cannot mean that to establish a general practice accepted as law, it is necessary to establish that the practice is "sufficiently widespread and representative" . . . among both states and all of the thousands of international organizations, since no one approaches customary international

whether the prohibition of the use of force was owed to international organizations in the context of draft article 53 on countermeasures. The commentary to that article also reflects the difficult parameters of the question that go beyond just admitting the legal personality of international organizations: 'the use of force could be considered a countermeasure taken against an international organization only if the prohibition to use force is owed to that organization. This occurs if the organization is considered to be a component of the international community to which the obligation is owed' ILC, 'Yearbook of the International Law Commission 2006 Volume 1' (ibid), 74, para 33.

[83] The only apparent limiting principle would be a narrow construction of the notion of the 'relevant similarity' on the basis of which the analogy is being argued. As already explained, such a narrow construction may indeed generate insights regarding certain domains, such as the law of treaties or responsibility. As Bordin (n 2) 81, explains in this regard, 'it can be similarly proposed that the secondary rules laying down the conditions and consequences of the internationally wrongful acts of States extend to international organizations, insofar as the latter are also legally autonomous entities which may breach obligations assumed on the international plane'. While an analogy at this level of abstraction can be relatively uncontroversial, any venturing beyond this is bound to run into the same difficulties as the broader conception of legal personality discussed earlier, namely that it would have to rely on some sort of inductive reasoning when it comes to identifying which primary rules that are binding on states are also binding on international organizations.

[84] For the idea that international organizations can only contribute to the formation of rules that are relevant to their mandate and/or are specific to international organizations, see ILC (n 3) 131, para 5, Commentary to Draft Conclusion 4.

law in that way'.[85] Another indication for this is article 53 of VCLT 1969, which refers to jus cogens as a norm that is 'accepted and recognized by the international community of *States* as a whole', without mentioning international organizations.[86] In a similar fashion, article 85 of the Vienna Convention on the Law of Treaties between States and International Organizations or between International Organizations (VCLT 1986) provides that only instruments of ratification deposited by states will count towards its entry into force, thus excluding international organizations that have acceded to the treaty.[87] Even if these examples do not provide absolute evidence towards the resolution of the theoretical debate, they pose standing challenges for an unproblematized 'subject' conception of international organizations that formally analogizes these institutions to states. This suggests that even as an interpretative hypothesis, the notion that international organizations are analytically just another independent state is unconvincing.

All in all, while arguments from analogy may yield valuable insights, it is far from evident how they would apply consistently in practice for the range of questions examined here. The chief problem appears to be that for the analogy to take hold in positive law, a change in the latter appears to be necessary – a change that even proponents of the analogy find hard to showcase. But even if such a change were to take place, too much would still be up for interpretation. A postulated 'rule of incorporation' might provisionally answer the question of whether international organizations possess an independent legal existence, but it is far from clear where to go from there. In short, just because both international organizations and states are in some sense autonomous, and thus *could* merit similar treatment *in some* respects, it does not follow that they *are* treated

---

[85] See eg Sean D Murphy, 'Identification of Customary International Law and Other Topics: The Sixty-Seventh Session of the International Law Commission' 109 AJIL (2015) 822, 830–831; Kristina Daugirdas, 'International Organizations and the Creation of Customary International Law' (2018) 31 EJIL 201, 228. Daugirdas argues that a comprehensive survey of the practice and opinio juris will, in most cases, not be necessary, as only a small fraction of rules of customary international law is relevant for international organizations. Still, this does not settle the problem as a matter of principle, nor does it speak to the respective problem with jus cogens norms.

[86] VCLT 1986 (n 15) art 53 (emphasis added). See also ILC, 'Second Report on *jus cogens* by Dire Tladi, Special Rapporteur' (2017) UN Doc A/CN.4/706, 30–39, emphasizing that it is still the recognition and acceptance by the international community of *states* that is relevant in the identification of peremptory norms.

[87] VCLT 1986 (n 15) art 85, which also includes Namibia, represented by the United Nations Council for Namibia.

similarly *in all* their aspects as a matter of positive international law. Ultimately, this is a question that cannot be answered simply by subscribing to the 'subject' conception of international organizations. Consequently, theorizing international organizations cannot be reduced to a theory of them having an independent legal personality, or even a theory of them being legally autonomous actors.

2.3.4   *International Organizations as Merely Another Name for a Group of States Acting in Tandem*

One may be tempted to overcome this conundrum by instead adopting a 'treaty' conception of international organizations. This would suggest that international organizations are ultimately just another name for their members acting in tandem through a treaty. This view has rightly been criticized for being in tension with another fundamental idea of international organizations law, namely that international organizations are something different than the sum of their members and, in some sense at least, legal persons in their own regard.

The idea that international organizations are just another name for a group of states acting together, and thus qualify as states for the purposes of applying customary international law, was present during discussions of the draft VCLT 1986 in the ILC. When discussing the application of specific norms of international law to the activities of international organizations, the question arose as to whether these institutions were bound by the prohibition of the use of force. The Commission's Special Rapporteur argued that since the GA Resolution on the Definition of Aggression[88] provided that the term 'state' included the concept of 'a group of states', it should also be the case that international organizations were included in the definition and thus bound by the prohibition.[89]

The first thing to note here is that this approach, premised as it is on a substitution of the organization by its members, oversimplifies the complexities surrounding the membership of these institutions.[90] Indeed, many organizations, including the UN and the World Trade

---

[88] UNGA Res 3314 (14 December 1974) annex, Definition of Aggression.

[89] ILC, 'Yearbook of the International Law Commission 1979 Volume 1: Summary Records of the Meetings of the Thirty-First Session 14 May–3 August 1979' (1979) UN Doc A/CN.4/SER.A/1979, 69, 74, para 38.

[90] To this effect, see comments by Šahonović who asked whether an international organization could be 'completely assimilated with groups of States' without, however, providing further context: ILC, 'Yearbook of the International Law Commission 1980 Volume 1:

Organization (WTO), have featured, or continue to feature, among their membership entities that are not considered states in international law. This has historically encompassed sub-state entities, such as Hong Kong for the WTO, or non-self-governing territories for the UN.[91] Although many theoretical approaches tend to gloss over this practice, the conclusion should be that, out of the gate, the attempt to reduce international organization to 'groups of states' can only refer to a subset of these institutions.

Setting to the side how this argument may not work at all depending on a particular organization's membership, analysing international organizations as agglomerations of states suggests a legal image of organizations as an aggregate actor.[92] Regardless of whether one agrees with this approach, it is important to underline how this understanding conditions how other aspects of international organizations should be theorized. For example, staying on the course of the reductionist approach employed when drafting article 52, the ILC's commentary also put forward the idea that international organizations could be *directly* bound by the UN Charter, even though they are not parties to it, as potential basis for holding that international organizations were bound by the prohibition of the use of force enshrined in article 2(4) of the Charter.[93] This seems consistent with the analysis of organizations as groups of states: indeed, if international organizations are merely the sum of their parts, it makes sense to posit that they have the same obligations as those states that make them up, including their treaty obligations, at least when these are binding on all of its members. On the other hand, this represents an apparent conflict with the independent legal

Summary Records of the Meetings of the Thirty-Second Session 5 May–15 July 1980' (1980) UN Doc A/CN.4/SER.A/1980, 44, 48, para 35.

[91] See indicatively Schermers and Blokker (n 23) 66–71.

[92] It is worth noting that, in the end, the ILC's commentary did not offer a consistent treatment of the question of whether international organizations were bound by the prohibition of aggression. On one hand, the commentary to article 52 (coercion of a State or of an international organization by the threat or use of force) followed the Special Rapporteur's rationale, noting that '[h]owever the expression "group of States" is defined, it covers an international organization': ILC (n 53) 56, para 6 (Commentary to art 52); see also 56, para 2 (Commentary to art 53). Other parts of the commentary did not follow this rationale. For example, the commentary to article 75 stated that the Commission refrained from making any pronouncement on whether the prohibition of the use of force applies to international organizations, leaving it open to further discussion by the states and international organizations whether the term 'aggressor State' could cover international organizations: ILC (n 53) 70, para 2 (Commentary to art 75).

[93] ibid 56, para 7 (Commentary to art 52).

personality of international organizations and the relative effect of treaty obligations (the *pacta tertiis* rule) as enshrined in article 34 VCLT 1986.[94] The latter suggests that international organizations enjoy a distinct legal existence from that of their members, meaning that presumably they are not just another name for a group of states.[95]

Thus, the analytical conundrum faced by the ILC when drafting the VCLT 1986 can be summarized as follows. If international organizations can be reduced to a group of states, then it becomes difficult to analytically make sense of their separate legal personality; on the other hand, if they cannot be reduced to a group of states, how can they be bound by the same obligations as states, such as the prohibition of the use of force? Once again, we are put in an unenviable position between two potentially sensible intuitions in apparent conflict: the idea that international organizations are legal persons being in tension with the idea that international law's background customary norms should equally apply to them.

Overlooking this conundrum, several authors have followed a reductionist approach to theorizing international organizations. At the same time, they have usually offered no analytical explanation as to how this reductionist approach coalesces with other aspects of the law where non-reductionist images of these institutions exist. For instance, Christian Tomuschat suggests that international organizations may be characterized:

> as common agencies operated by States for the fulfilment of certain common tasks. Now, if States acting individually have been subjected to certain rules thought to be indispensable for maintaining orderly relations within the international community, there is no justification for exempting international organizations from the scope *ratione personae* of such rules.[96]

---

[94] See also Brölmann (n 5) 239, questioning the equation of international organizations with 'groups of states': '[h]owever, in a legal sense this is not necessarily so. Rather, it expresses a functionalist, "open" view of organisations as vehicles for states, which precisely does not proceed from the organisation as an independent moral person.'

[95] More recent studies of the ILC do little to lift this lingering ambiguity over the legal nature of international organizations as state or non-state actors. For example, the Commission's draft conclusions on the identification and evidence of customary international law deal with international organizations separately from non-state actors but also not on par with states. Draft conclusion 4 reads: '[i]n certain cases, the practice of international organizations also contributes to the formation, or expression, or creation, of rules of customary international law,' while the commentary states that '[i]nternational organizations are not states'. See ILC (n 3) 130–131, Draft Conclusion 4 and Commentary thereto.

[96] Tomuschat's analysis also invites the question of which rules of customary international law are indeed 'indispensable for maintaining orderly relations within the international community'. Christian Tomuschat, 'International Law: Ensuring the Survival of Mankind on the Eve of a New Century: General Course on Public International Law (Volume 281)' in

Henry Schermers also provided, among other grounds, an essentially reductionist justification as to why international organizations should be considered bound by customary international law. He suggested that they are so bound because their 'member States were bound by international customary law when they created the organization and thus may be presumed to have created the organization as being so bound'.[97] Although in some ways sensible, such reductionist rationales create analytical complications further down the road. If international organizations are to be understood as mere groups of states, one might ask whether they should also be bound by the treaties of their member states, and what would the meaning of their independent legal personality be in that context.[98] Jan Klabbers points his finger exactly at this problem:

> Yet, the question presents itself: if states can only be bound through their consent, why should it be different for other actors, such as international organizations? One possible answer might be that they are composed of states, and that typically, if all member states are bound, this binding force extends to organizations, but that stumbles across the formidable objection that it would make nonsense of the 'distinct will' of international organizations: if truly distinct from its member states, then they cannot be seen (save in highly unique circumstances perhaps) to have taken over their member states' individual organizations [sic] – and if so, it would seem plausible to argue (owing from the same distinct will) that the member states as such are no longer under those obligations.[99]

In simple terms, if the legal personality (however the latter is understood) of international organizations is recognized as denoting some form of independent existence, it may seem contradictory to analyse these institutions as another name for a group of states.

The tension between independent legal personality and a transitive rationale goes beyond the problem of the rights and obligations of international organizations. This can be exemplified by the International Law Association's (ILA) work on the formation of

---

Collected Courses of the Hague Academy of International Law (Brill, 1999) 134–135. For discussion of a similar rationale with respect to the capacity of international organizations to contribute to the formation of customary international law, see Bordin (n 2) 123.

[97] Henry G Schermers, 'The Legal Bases of International Organization Action' in René-Jean Dupuy (ed), *A Handbook on International Organizations* (2nd edn, Martinus Nijhof 1998) 402.

[98] Indeed, most authors have refrained from adopting a reductionist approach when it comes to treaty obligations, perhaps owing to the prevalent approach to the question of personality. Still, the opposite view remains popular among some international lawyers. For a brief summary of those, see Daugirdas (n 16) 325.

[99] Footnotes omitted. Klabbers (n 38) 16.

international custom. The ILA Report notes with respect to the practice of international courts and tribunals: '[s]ome authors regard the decisions of international courts and tribunals as a sort of delegated State practice. But this is misleading. ... the purpose of international courts and tribunals is to act *independently* of those appointing them.'[100] On that basis, the ILA Report suggested that the practice of international courts and tribunals does not count towards the formation of new norms of customary international law. Framing the problem as having to choose between independent international courts and courts that can contribute to the formation of customary international law, the ILA opted for the first option. Regardless of whether one agrees with that conclusion, the reality of the problem must be recognized.

All in all, the view that international organizations are just another name for their member states acting together could potentially provide some insights into the problem of whether they should be analysed as states or non-state actors. However, it does not properly account for the fact that many international organizations feature entities other than states among their members. Beyond that, the answers that this approach offers come at a seemingly high price, essentially by admitting international organizations as 'state-non-actors'. This approach risks collapsing organizations to their members. This alone is not enough to discredit this approach from an analytical point of view – after all it might be the case that international organizations are nothing over and above their member states – but adopting it should come in conscience of its consequences or with an argument that negates them.

2.4   Conclusion

Surveying current theoretical approaches to international organizations, a bigger picture emerges. To begin with, the idea of legal personality is not the safe analytical refuge that it is sometimes assumed to be. Furthermore, while more sophisticated approaches have emerged, namely the treaty/subject framework, these have generally been less 'all-embracing' than commonly thought. Approaches operating within this binary are mostly preoccupied with the question of whether and to what extent international organizations are independent legal entities in relation to their members. Less sustained theoretical attention has been

---

[100] Emphasis in the original. 'Statement of Principles Applicable to the Formation of General Customary International Law' (n 4) Principle 10 and commentary thereto.

paid to the question of what happens after it has been established that international organizations enjoy a separate legal existence.

The temptation at this point is to import solutions from the problem of legal distinctiveness and assume that they can do all the work for the problem of the legal nature proper as well. Alternatively, it is to ignore completely the problem of legal distinctiveness and analyse international organizations as another name for their members acting in tandem. Both of these strategies seem unappealing without further explanation; the first because it gravitates towards assumptions that are difficult to prove in positive law, and the second because it disregards the varied membership of international organizations and, when pushed to its analytical extreme, tends to negate their independent existence, rendering the question of how they relate to states as actors less relevant to begin with.

In sum, when an organization is recognized to have a legal personality different from that of its members, the question arises as to how that personality relates to states as species of legal actors. This inquiry seems largely defined by seemingly rigid binaries between aggregate/holistic and state/non-state actors. The challenge then for theories operating within the two analytical binaries can be summarized as follows: as soon as an international organization is recognized as being something different than a mere aggregate of its members (which is often the starting assumption of the doctrine), then it is perceived as being a non-state actor, whose legal personality seems to be by default a blank slate in the eyes of international law, barring of course the emergence of new and specific customary norms or a more general rule of positive law that analytically approximates these institutions to states.

The Problem of Analytically Distinguishing International Organizations from Their Members

3.1 The Hallmarks of Separate Existence: Legal Personality and Distinct Will

So far, this book has explored the puzzles surrounding the legal nature of international organizations *assuming* that they enjoy a separate legal existence from their members. This assumption invites the question: why should international organizations be analysed as distinct objects of legal concern to begin with, as opposed to (presumably quite elaborate) treaty arrangements between certain states acting together in a coordinated manner? Even if the independent legal existence of these institutions is by now a well-accepted scholarly proposition, the analytical foundation for this remains open to scrutiny.

Most approaches to this problem involve two concepts: an 'objective' legal personality, meaning one that is opposable vis-à-vis third parties, and a distinct will, which is a more nebulous notion supposed to denote some form of autonomy of the organization from its members in its decision-making. These two concepts are often thought to convey different dimensions of separateness between an organization and its members. Legal personality concerns whether an international organization is treated as a distinct legal entity from the perspective of the international legal order. Distinct will can be thought to reflect some autonomy at the institutional level that allows the organization's behaviour to be distinguished in a meaningful way from that of its members.

Both notions of separateness are generally considered fundamental for showing the existence in law of international organizations as entities over and above their members.[1] Nevertheless, the relationship between

---

[1] See Rosalyn Higgins, 'The Legal Consequences for Member States of the Non-Fulfilment by International Organizations of Their Obligations toward Third Parties' [1995] Yearbook of the Institute of International Law 251, 254 ('an international association lacking legal personality, and possessing no *volonté distincte*, remains the creature of the state's members who are thus liable for its acts').

them is often unclear. Distinct will as evidence of an organization's autonomy is commonly rehearsed as a definitional element of international organizations.[2] By contrast, legal personality sometimes forms part of definitions, whereas other times it is considered a consequence of the other three conditions having been met (interstate basis, existence of an agreement, and distinct will).[3] Thus, for some, 'without autonomy, independent legal personality is difficult to conceive'.[4] For others, the relationship between the concepts cannot be ordered in a linear fashion: 'autonomy is both a postulate and an effect of legal personality ... legal personality is thus a cause, but also a consequence of the *fact* of autonomy'.[5] As so often in this field, such approaches may seem at the same time reasonable and paradoxical: autonomy is a condition for legal personality which then creates the legal space for autonomy.

Leaving this Escherian image to the side for the time being, it is important to trace the first principles that should guide this investigation. To begin with, there is no predefined way in which legal personality and distinct will or factual autonomy are supposed to function in a given legal system. Thus, the idea of legal distinctiveness may apply to entities that exhibit no amount of factual autonomy in any real sense of the word (consider for example various one-person limited liability companies across domestic jurisdictions). Conversely, as a matter of principle, the factual autonomy or otherwise real capacity for distinct will of an entity or person may still not be enough to make it ipso facto a *legal* person in a given legal system. The latter seems especially true in legal systems, such as international law, which also feature a formal conception of legal personhood that is not itself generally attached to any factual

---

[2] Henry G Schermers and Niels M Blokker, *International Institutional Law* (5th edn, Martinus Nijhoff 2011) 29–47; Jan Klabbers, *An Introduction to International Organizations Law* (4th edn, CUP 2022) 12–14; Catherine Brölmann, *Institutional Veil in Public International Law: International Organisations and the Law of Treaties* (Hart Oxford 2007) 20–21. Cf Lorenzo Gasbarri, *The Concept of an International Organization in Public International Law* (OUP 2021) 106 ('it is not necessary to make a reference to autonomous will and legal personality for the purposes of definition. Indeed, they are both inherent features of the duality of their legal systems'). See also Chittharanjan F Amerasinghe, *Principles of the Institutional Law of International Organizations* (2nd edn, CUP 2005) 10.

[3] Brölmann (n 2) 19–22; Nigel White, *The Law of International Organisations* (3rd edn, Manchester University Press 2016) 9.

[4] Brölmann (n 2) 76.

[5] Emphasis in the original. Guglielmo Verdirame, *The UN and Human Rights: Who Guards the Guardians?* (CUP 2011) 59.

precondition of autonomy.[6] The point here is that the coupling of autonomy to legal personality or the meaning thereof should not be taken as a matter of course.

Nor should we take for granted the analytical justification for arguing that international organizations exhibit a distinct will or an objective legal personality of their own. As the following pages argue, upon closer inspection, both these notions rest on shaky foundations. Our chief theories on legal personality fail to produce a generalizable conclusion that does not rest on the emergence of a new rule of customary international law, evidence for which remains elusive. At the same time, the distinct will requirement too remains highly elusive, lacking any convincing criterion for its identification. That being said, in critiquing our dominant accounts about legal personality and distinct will, the following pages do not seek to revive any old-fashioned reductionism about international organizations. Rather, the aim is to derive intellectual value from exposing the limitations of current approaches which, however practical or intuitive in certain respects, lead to impractical or counterintuitive outcomes in others.

3.2   Revisiting the Dominant Theories on the Legal Personality of International Organizations

3.2.1   *Theorizing the Legal Personality of Corporate Entities in Domestic Law*

If we are to overcome the limits of our current theories on the legal personality of international organizations, we need to understand the analytical constructions that loom in their background. In this respect, common references to international organizations as entities 'analogous to bodies corporate of domestic law',[7] a 'rule of incorporation',[8] or a 'contractual relationship' between an organization and its members[9] correspond to domestic law approaches to the problem of corporate

---

[6] With the exception of states, for which both 'formal' and 'actual' independence need to be present to some extent. For the complicated relation between these two notions when it comes to applying the criteria for statehood in international law, see James Crawford, *The Creation of States in International Law* (2nd edn, OUP 2007) 88–89.

[7] See Sir John Fischer Williams, 'The Status of the League of Nations in International Law' (1926) 34 ILA Rep Conf 675, 677. For similar analogies, see Arnold D McNair, 'The Functions and Differing Legal Character of Treaties' (1930) 11 BYIL 100, 111.

[8] Fernando L Bordin, *The Analogy between States and International Organizations: Legal Reasoning and the Development of the Law of International Organizations* (CUP 2018) 77.

[9] Gasbarri (n 2) 17.

existence.[10] However, theories surrounding the latter are more sophisticated than the current discourse tends to acknowledge. This sophistication should be uncovered if we are to make sense of the dilemmas posed by current theories that have been conditioned by the domestic law framing, and appreciate why ultimately they all lead down a path of reasoning that is very hard to follow when it comes to international organizations.

The first thing to note in that regard is that the discipline's accepted bifurcation of the problem of corporate existence for international organizations, meaning the contradistinction between international organizations as contractual arrangements and proper bodies corporate, actually represents an analytical simplification of the problem. In fact, studying more closely the problem of corporate existence in domestic law shows that the available analytical constructions are not two, but three. One according to which corporate entities are 'real', another that describes them as 'fictional', and a final one that conceptualizes them as a nexus of contracts between natural persons.[11] The important nuance to be recovered from this tripartite reconstruction of the problem is that the so prevalent 'either/or' way of thinking about the legal personality of international organizations is by no means the complete picture, while the often presumed conceptual continuities between domestic and international law on this matter are more dubious than what they may seem at first.

The Real Entity theory of corporate existence was famously advanced in the context of the unification of the German state by Otto von Gierke. Gierke's classic theory understood associations and groups of individuals as potentially separate entities over and above their members, both in an ontological as well as a legal sense. The theory was developed in the context of drafting the German civil code in the second half of the nineteenth century. It was generally aimed at preserving certain German medieval institutions, such as fellowships and townships, that predated the existence of the then newly unified German state. With his theory, Gierke attempted to counter the eliminative approach of theorists

---

[10] See also *Attorney General v Nissan* [1969] UKHL 3 (Lord Pearce), suggesting that '[t]he United Nations is not a super-State nor even a sovereign State. It is a unique legal person or corporation'.

[11] For a brief summary of the respective theories, see David Rönnegard, *The Fallacy of Corporate Moral Agency* (Springer 2015) 105–107; see also Peter A French, 'The Corporation as a Moral Person' (1979) 16 American Philosophical Law Quarterly 207.

such as Friedrich Karl von Savigny. The latter maintained that the only true subjects were the individual and the state, with nothing standing in between unless explicitly recognized and permitted by law as a legal fiction. In practice this was to be achieved by putting in place a rule of incorporation.[12] Against this, Gierke argued that the personality of particular social groups with historic ties was ontologically 'objective'. By this, Gierke meant that their legal existence derived directly from social reality and without the need for recognition by the state through legislation, most prominently without the need for a rule of incorporation to that effect. Gierke's theory did not suggest that *all* types of associations enjoyed such objective social and thus according to him, legal personality. However, Gierke was one of the first modern thinkers to imply that, at least for certain categories of group entities, attribution of legal personality by the state was not necessary, and, in any event, an act of recognition by the state was merely declaratory and not constitutive.[13]

By contrast, the Fiction theory conceived corporate persons as created through the recognition of the law, and not enjoying a separate existence from their members in any deeper ontological sense. According to this theory, as generally attributed to Savigny, the corporate person was merely an abstract creation of the law, an artificial legal entity that exists purely because the law wills it into existence on an 'as if' basis. Incorporation was thus conceptualized as a monopoly of the state: only the state could grant legal personality to corporate entities, having adopted a rule of incorporation for that purpose.[14] Corporations themselves required 'no souls, no state of minds, and no missions' to be recognized by the law;[15] they were theorized as purely fictitious entities as far as the latter was concerned.

---

[12] David Runciman, *Pluralism and the Personality of the State* (CUP 1997) 93–94.

[13] Janne E Nijman, *The Concept of International Legal Personality: An Inquiry into the History and Theory of International Law* (TMC Asser Press 2004). Gierke's theory was eventually taken up by jurist and historian Frederic Maitland and introduced to the Anglo-Saxon world, where Gierke's ideas were employed to theorize the status of the corporation in the domestic legal systems of the UK and the US. See Miriam Theresa Rooney, 'Maitland and the Corporate Revolution' (1951) 26 New York University Law Review 24.

[14] Ron Harris, 'The Transplantation of the Legal Discourse on Corporate Personality Theories: From German Codification to English Pluralism and American Big Business' (2006) 63 Washington and Lee Law Review 1421, 1424.

[15] ibid 1429.

Finally, the Nexus of Contracts theory, advanced in the United States in the late nineteenth to early twentieth century, theorized the corporate person as a mesh of contractual obligations between its members that does not necessarily rest upon recognition by the state, but is fully reducible to physical persons and their interactions.[16] Essentially, this theory would have corporate persons treated literally as aggregates of their members. Thus, the name of the corporate person would serve only as a shorthand expression that covers the underlying natural persons and their relations.[17] This theory rationalized corporate law as administering a complex web of relations employing pre-existing concepts of private law such as contract, agency, and trust.[18] Following this view, when the possibility of incorporation is present in the law, it should be conceptualized merely as a more expedient way of obtaining the same legal situation that could have been achieved independently through the careful and copious drafting of private contracts.

Certainly this short exposition of these three theories too represents a simplification of their rich history and contexts.[19] What is relevant, however, to keep from this tripartite construction of the problem is that the either/or framework of thinking about corporate existence that is so prevalent in the discourse about international organizations tends to (1) obfuscate key overlaps between seemingly antithetical notions of corporate legal personality; (2) conceal divergences between views that would seem to lie on the same end of the binary.

Indeed, despite their antitheses, the Real Entity and the Fiction theories suggested a roughly similar *structural* image for the corporate legal person. Even as they disagreed on how legal personality was to take effect in a given legal order, both these theories painted the legal image of a unitary and opaque corporate person, whose members were not legally visible outside the legal person. In other words, both these theories were non-reductionist from a purely legal perspective insofar as they supported the notion that a corporate legal entity could qualify as

---

[16] The theory is sometimes alternatively referred to as the 'Legal Aggregate Theory'. See French (n 11) 209.

[17] ibid 209.

[18] Marc Moore, *Corporate Governance in the Shadow of the State* (Hart 2013) 63.

[19] See eg John Dewey, 'The Historic Background of Corporate Legal Personality' (1926) 35 Yale Law Journal 655; Mark M Hager, 'Bodies Politic: The Progressive History of Organizational "Real Entity" Theory' (1988) 50 University of Pittsburgh Law Review 575, 612. For a more modern presentation of the problem, see Eva Micheler, *Company Law: A Real Entity Theory* (OUP 2021) 2–22.

a non-eliminable legal subject. By contrast, the Nexus of Contracts theory interpreted the corporate entity as an aggregate of legal relationships that was in reality legally redundant.

If the Real Entity and the Fiction theories painted the same structural image for associations, they had diverse *ontological* underpinnings: the former supported the notion of an organic corporate entity that enjoys a group mind, while the latter made no such metaphysical commitment. The Fiction theory either denied any autonomous social or metaphysical existence to corporate entities or remained agnostic towards it. Thus, the Fiction theory found itself on the same ontological page as the Nexus of Contracts theory when it came to non-state corporate persons, in that they both were open to some form of reductionism regarding associations of individuals other than the state, even if the Fiction theory then went on to make up for this through legal fiction. By contrast, the Real Entity theory maintained that certain groups enjoyed a separate ontological existence from their members, a fact that the law could, and according to that theory should, take note of rather than constitute from scratch through legislative intervention.

Of the three theories, the Real Entity made the strongest and more explicit ontological commitment regarding group entities. Yet it should be noted that this theory was based on a particular take on the ontology of the collective, namely that such groups could enjoy a separate organic or metaphysical existence that qualified them as legal persons in their own right. This view on the ontology of the collective was in turn seemingly founded on the rough assumption that groups possess a group 'mind' or a 'soul', and a collective conscience that could qualify them as persons in their own right.[20] Eventually, however, the idea of a group mind that operated beyond the level of the coordinated dispositions of the group's individual members was thought as being philosophically

---

[20] As Frederic Maitland notes in his introduction of Gierke's work:

> [the] German Fellowship is no fiction, no symbol, no piece of the State's machinery, no collective name for individuals, but a living organism and a real person, with body and members and a will of its own. Itself can will, itself can act; it wills and acts by the men who are its organs as a man wills and acts by brain, mouth and hand. It is not a fictitious person . . . .

Otto von Gierke, *Political Theories of the Middle Age* (Frederic W Maitland tr, CUP 1900). See also Janne E Nijman, 'Non-State Actors and the International Rule of Law' in Cedric Ryngaert and Math Noortmann (eds), *Non-State Actor Dynamics in International Law* (Routledge 2016) 113.

indefensible.[21] But, regardless of whether one agrees or not with this critique, it is important to discern the underlying analytical foundation that such a theory would have to rely on in order to succeed: the notion that corporate entities enjoy a legal personality *because* they are real must ultimately be tied to some extra-legal argument, namely that these entities do indeed enjoy a 'real' existence outside the law.

3.2.2 Limitations of the Standard Account of the Legal Personality of International Organizations

Appreciating the nuances surrounding the three aforementioned theories can help illuminate key argumentative path-dependencies in the discourse on the legal personality of international organizations, as well as potential blind spots. Indeed, apart from the widely borrowed vocabulary, current discourse on international organizations echoes deeper structural elements of the debates surrounding corporate existence in domestic law.

These continuities exhibit themselves most prominently on two fronts: the relationship between distinct will and legal personality, and the relationship between legal personality and the background legal order. Both these inquiries are closely interrelated. The first concerns whether distinct will, conceived as some form of irreducibility of the organization's corporate existence, is necessary *before* its legal personality can be recognized in international law. The second concerns whether that legal personality is indeed accorded by the legal system as such, and thus can be presumed to have an 'objective' legal effect, or whether it just reflects the intra-se dispositions of an organization's members, and is thus only relative in effect.

Yet the appearance of continuities can also be misleading, given that the circumstances in domestic and international law differ significantly. The danger here is that focusing on the continuities risks missing some of international law's particular features, while at the same time inheriting unnecessary limitations of domestic debates.

Consider for instance the debate on the foundation and scope of international organizations' legal personality. Differing views on this

---

[21] Christian List and Philip Pettit, *Group Agency: The Possibility, Design, and Status of Corporate Agents* (OUP 2011) 9. On the political context of corporate realism, see Runciman (n 12) 34ff; Nijman (n 13) 30.

issue have led to the respective 'subjective' and 'objective' theories of legal personality.[22] The subjective theory has generally been associated with constitutive recognition, a wilful act that either creates the organization or, in the case of non-members, accepts its existence, and thus has only a 'relative' effect. By contrast, the objective theory treats legal personality as ultimately resting on the operation of the legal system as such, rather than the volitions of individual members and the recognizing non-members. It is thus presumed to lead to a legal person whose existence is in theory opposable erga omnes regardless of recognition.[23]

Famously, the *Reparation for Injuries* Advisory Opinion offered little guidance in resolving this debate. According to one popular view, the Court's reasoning in that case was circular because it inferred the UN's legal personality from certain capacities such as the capacity to enter into international agreements or make international claims, while also maintaining that a condition for the exercise of these capacities was the existence of legal personality.[24] At the same time, the analysis behind the opposability of the UN's legal personality to a non-member was not very precise – apparently inferring a power to create such an entity from the fact that the states in question represented the 'vast' majority of the international community.[25] The rationale would also seem hard to extrapolate to many other organizations that cannot boast near universal membership, and for whom the question of the opposability of their legal personality would presumably be more pressing. In general, as Jan Klabbers has rightly suggested, the Court's opinion can accommodate 'diametrically opposed theories' on the concept of international legal personality.[26]

---

[22] Klabbers (n 2) 48–49; Brölmann (n 2) 77.

[23] Phillippe Sands and Pierre Klein, *Bowett's Law of International Institutions* (6th edn, Sweet & Maxwell 2009) 476–480; Amerasinghe (n 2) 79.

[24] *Reparation for Injuries Suffered in the Service of the United Nations* (Advisory Opinion) [1949] ICJ Rep 174, 178–179. For the critique of circularity, see eg Ian Brownlie, *Principles of Public International Law* (7th edn, OUP 2008) 57; Sands and Klein (n 23) 476; Andrew Clapham, *Human Rights Obligations of Non-State Actors* (OUP 2006) 117.

[25] '[T]he Court's opinion is that fifty States, representing the vast majority of the members of the international community, had the power, in conformity with international law, to bring into being an entity possessing objective international personality, and not merely personality recognized by them alone, together with capacity to bring international claims': *Reparation for Injuries Suffered in the Service of the United Nations* (n 24) 185.

[26] Klabbers (n 2) 46.

Regardless of the ambiguities present in the Court's opinion, eventually the 'objective' theory became increasingly prevalent.[27] The most elaborate justification supporting the objective theory was provided by Finn Seyersted, who came very close to proposing a version of the Real Entity theory for international organizations. As discussed in Chapter 2, Seyersted supported the notion that international organizations enjoy a legal personality that is analytically equivalent to that of states and other 'self-governing' entities, such as the Holy See or insurgents. What Seyersted identified in common between all these entities was that they existed objectively once a set of factual conditions were met. Hence, international law's recognition of them was merely declaratory as opposed to constitutive.[28] This allowed linking international organizations to other 'self-governing' actors, most prominently the state, and understanding legal personality in international law as performing a status function from which certain inherent capacities would flow. At the same time, because these capacities were derived directly from general international law as opposed to the intentions of an organization's members, those entities' status could be theorized to be opposable vis-à-vis members and non-members alike.

Seyersted's theory was structured around the insight that for states and certain other subjects of international law such as the Holy See, it did not matter 'how' these had been established but simply that they 'existed'. Extending this principle to international organizations, he argued that their constituent instrument had the same analytical relevance to their existence and capacities that a national constitution had to a state: it was evidence of a social fact of organization that international law took note

---

[27] Brölmann (n 2) 90. Cf Switzerland's recognition of the UN's legal personality before it became a member, enshrined in Agreement on Privileges and Immunities of the United Nations Concluded between the Swiss Federal Council and the Secretary General of the United Nations on 19 April 1946 <https://www.ungeneva.org/sites/default/files/2021-02/Accord-P-I-1946-E.pdf> accessed 9 February 2025, art 1: '([t]he Swiss Federal Council recognises the international personality and legal capacity of the United Nations . . .'. See also the recognition of the legal personality of the ILO and the BIS in respective treaties between these organizations and Switzerland. For the USSR's non-recognition of the EEC, see Schermers and Blokker (n 2) 1142. For non-recognition by national courts, see *ECOWAS v Bank of Credit and Commerce International*, French Court of Appeals, Paris (13 January 1993) 113 ILR 473. For the importance of recognition in earlier case law, see, among others, *United Nations v B*, Civil Tribunal (Brussels) (27 March 1957) 19 ILR 1957, 489.

[28] Finn Seyersted, 'Objective International Personality of Intergovernmental Organizations: Do Their Capacities Really Depend upon the Conventions Establishing Them/?' (1964) 34 Nordic Journal of International Law 3, 47.

of.[29] Accordingly, Seyersted's view was premised on a strict separation between the internal law of the organization (including its constituent instrument) and public international law: it was not 'the provision of the constitution or the intention of its framers which establish the international personality of a State or an intergovernmental organization, but the objective fact of its existence'.[30] This would then source international organizations' legal personality directly into social reality, without needing the structural support of an international constitutive treaty or a rule of incorporation.

Arguably, Seyersted embedded an ontological claim – an argument about social facts and social reality – in his analytical construction. Thus, in a way, Seyersted was a pluralist when it came to the legal subjects of international law, even if this stance did not rest upon an overt ontological stance on corporate personhood as Gierke's theory did. International organizations were better analysed as closed and self-referring systems of authority – that is, as 'self-governing' actors and not simply as intricate contractual arrangements between their members. If one follows this line of thinking, international law's involvement in admitting the legal personality of these institutions could indeed be understood as a subsequent recognition of fact in a declaratory manner.[31]

While there have been doubts as to whether Seyersted's theory went that far,[32] it should be noted that it only works if it actually goes that far.

---

[29] According to Seyersted, for states, these factual conditions were 'territory, population and a sovereign government', whereas for international organizations, these were:

> International organs (i.e. organs established by two or more sovereign States), which are not all subject to the authority of any one State or other organized community (but only to that of the participating States acting jointly through their representatives on such organs), which perform 'sovereign' and/or international acts in their own name and which are not authorized by all their acts to assume obligations (merely) on behalf of the several participating States. (ibid 46–47, citations omitted)

[30] ibid 45.

[31] As Seyersted characteristically noted,

> States may come into existence in two ways, either through an understanding between the inhabitants of a territory, or through imposition by a group which assumes power over the inhabitants. Thus, an agreement between all the 'members' is not necessary. It is not the acts by which a State is created, but the objective facts which result from them which constitute the relevant criteria for the existence of a State. (Finn Seyersted, *Common Law of International Organizations* (Brill 2008) 43.)

[32] Brölmann (n 2) 87.

Responding to arguments that would have international organizations occupy a similar position to unincorporated associations in domestic law, Seyersted suggested the correct analogy was with those domestic legal systems that accept the general legal personality of groups *without* explicit legislative provisions or rules of incorporation.[33] Echoing the Real Entity theory, Seyersted suggested that looking for such a rule of incorporation was not only unnecessary but also futile, since it presupposed some kind of centralized legislative power, which had, according to him, no counterpart in international law.[34] At the same time, however, this domestic law conceptualization of the problem, coupled with the dismissal of the need for a rule of incorporation, implied that some argument for international organizations' independent existence in social reality had to be put forward.

This construction ultimately rests on some form of corporate realism that begs clarification. It is one thing to argue that the existence of international organizations may correspond to social facts and can be part of an 'objective reality', it is quite another to argue that it does so in a concrete instance. While other international lawyers have employed similar ideas in that respect,[35] the fact remains that no principled theory comparable to Gierke's has been advanced by international lawyers to fulfil that role.[36] The only possible exception, the notion of the distinct

---

[33] Seyersted (n 28) 95; Seyersted (n 31) 58–59.

[34] Seyersted (n 31) 58.

[35] See eg Verdirame (n 5) 60

> international organisations can, and do, operate as discrete institutional agents rather than as the long arm of their most powerful member states; their true social and political nature is much more than the sum of the wills of their member states ... their legal personality is not a mere legal fiction, which, while perhaps convenient or even necessary, bears little relation to reality

Rosalyn Higgins, *Problems and Process: International Law and How We Use It* (OUP 1994) 48 ('the objective legal reality of international personality. ... is not a matter of recognition. It is a matter of objective reality'). See also James D Fry, 'Rights, Functions, and International Legal Personality of International Organizations' (2018) 36 Boston University International Law Journal 221, 234; David J Bederman, 'The Souls of International Organizations: Legal Personality and the Lighthouse at Cape Spartel' (1996) 36 Vanderbilt Journal of Transnational Law 275, 371.

[36] In this respect, it is worth noting that Gierke himself viewed administrative unions – the proto-international organizations of his time – as contractual arrangements between states and not as 'real' entities resembling those associations of domestic law for which he developed his theory. Otto von Gierke, *Community in Historical Perspective* (Antony Black ed, Mary Fisher tr, CUP 1990) 164–167.

will of the organization, is not really an argument about social reality in the aforementioned sense, but rather a more limited notion about decision-making aimed at distinguishing between an organization and its members in practice. Even as such, the notion is notoriously under-explored and, as we shall examine in Section 3.3, not very persuasive.

The theory's coherence with the broader context of public international law is also not self-explanatory. Granted, social facts may – in one form or another – be thought of as elements behind international law's recognition of states' legal personality. However, the same cannot be said about the majority of other actors, for whom their ontological relationship with social reality is typically of little relevance to international law, and certainly does not lead by itself to claims of personhood in Seyersted's sense, meaning personhood wherefrom inherent capacities are supposed to flow. Indeed, one can construe exceptions to this rule, such as the Holy See, but these may be best explained on the basis of ad hoc rules.[37] Moreover, if the test is truly self-referential, it would again lead to an over-generation of legal subjects with no apparent limiting principle. It is perhaps for these reasons that, as we have seen, Seyersted complemented his theory on international organizations with a plea for a 'radical extension of the definition of international law'[38] that would make space for these other 'self-governing' entities. The limits of such an approach are, however, hard to miss. At best this is an appeal for a sweeping change in the law rather than a sustained argument that this change is already part of positive law.[39]

Perhaps sceptical of Seyersted's more far-reaching claims, but also reluctant to accept a reductionist view of international organizations, many scholars have sought to retain the conclusions of Seyersted's theory without its premises. This has led to a variation of Seyersted's theory whereby the legal personality of international organizations is considered 'objective' because it is accorded by reference to general international law once a number of criteria have been met.[40] Legal personality can thus be

---

[37] Generally, see John R Morss, 'The International Legal Status of the Vatican/Holy See Complex' (2015) 26(4) EJIL 927. For the legal personality of armed groups see Katharine Fortin, *The Accountability of Armed Groups under Human Rights Law* (OUP 2017) 152ff.

[38] Seyersted (n 28) 93.

[39] Jan Klabbers, 'On Seyersted and His Common Law of International Organizations' (2008) 5 IOLR 381, 387.

[40] For an early exposition of this position, see Manuel Rama-Montaldo, 'International Legal Personality and Implied Powers of International Organizations' (1970) 44 BYIL 111, 112. See also Brölmann (n 2) 83; Schermers and Blokker (n 2) 989; White (n 3) 113–114.

thought of as 'objective' rather than 'subjective' in the sense that it emanates directly from general international law and not from the members' will. This view goes on to suggest that the organization's legal personality is opposable vis-à-vis non-members without the need of recognition by them. Quite importantly, this view departs from the classic Fiction theory by not assuming that a rule of incorporation justifies the legal personality of international organizations, while at the same time disavowing notions that the latter can be analysed simply as a web of treaty obligations.

Even as it reaches a sensible conclusion without having to rest on a rule of incorporation or a 'radical extension' of the definition of international law, this version of the objective theory runs into complications of its own. Crucially, it ends up conflating different analytical questions, namely the question of whether there is an objective test for attributing legal personality and the question of whether that personality is itself objective in the sense of being opposable to non-members.[41] Yet an objective test for attribution is not the same as the objective legal effect that personality may have. Granted, an *erga omnes* legal effect does not necessarily entail the imposition of obligations by the constituent instrument on third parties.[42] However, it still consists in the admission of the organization as a separate legal actor without the requirement of any ad hoc recognition. This would cover scenarios such as the injury of an organization's official by a non-member state and the respective invocation of responsibility, as the ICJ had to consider in *Reparation for Injuries*. To put into the context of that case, why would Israel, at the time not a member of the UN, have an obligation towards the international organization not to harm its agents if the UN's legal personality is sourced in treaty rights and obligations?

Now, the test for whether an international treaty has been concluded may be thought to be 'objective' in the sense that the relevant test may be derived from some generally applicable customary norms. However, this certainly does not make the treaty in any sense 'objective' or in any manner opposable towards third parties. In the same sense, the fact that the test for attribution of international legal personality to an

---

[41] Cf Rowan Nicholson, *Statehood and the State-Like in International Law* (OUP 2019) 204; Brölmann (n 2) 78–90, who also draws this distinction but seems to treat these two questions as one when it comes to establishing the opposability of an organization's legal personality to non-member states.

[42] Seyersted (n 28) 95–96.

international organization may be 'objective' rather than subjective (and is thus to be verified by reference to an objective set of criteria) does not automatically mean that the organization's legal existence as a distinct focal point for rights and obligations is itself 'objective' or opposable to non-members. Thus, the question remains as to whether an organization is a mere agglomeration of its members based on a nexus of contractual obligations or a separate corporate person that for some reason enjoys a legal existence that is opposable erga omnes.

Indeed, under the current analytical framework, this possibility only seems viable based on a Seyerstedian construction, supposing that its problems can be overcome, or in a version of the Fiction theory. The transplantation of the latter to international law, however, remains a dubious proposition, and the status of a putative rule of incorporation in positive law has been questioned by the scholar who articulated this theory in the first place.[43] An alternative whereby a customary norm according 'objective' legal personality has to be identified in relation to each and every international organization individually raises perhaps even greater problems.[44] It would also probably restrict the erga omnes effect to organizations with universal or near-universal membership, and thus those in the least need of it. In the few cases apart from *Reparation for Injuries* where this problem has arisen in practice, the matter turned to whether there was a specific rule of customary international law about international organizations supervening the more general rule on the relative effect of treaties.[45] A predictable negative finding necessarily

---

[43] Bordin (n 8) 62–63.

[44] For this idea see Arangio-Ruiz in ILC, 'Yearbook of the International Law Commission 1985 Volume 1: Summary Records of the Meetings of the Thirty-Seventh Session 6 May– 26 July 1985' (1985) UN Doc A/CN.4/SER.A/1985, 291, para 16 ('As to the question whether or not there was a general rule of international law which attributed personality to some organizations, he would be inclined to say that custom or an unwritten rule took shape for each organization when it had achieved some degree of independence and, in particular, some degree of universality').

[45] See *ECOWAS v Bank of Credit and Commerce International* (n 27), where French Courts did not give legal effect to the legal personality of ECOWAS. The *International Tin Council v Amalgamet Inc.* case is sometimes mentioned as an example where courts of a non-member accepted the existence of an international organization without the need for recognition, but that case concerned whether the International Tin Council enjoyed privileges and immunities under the US International Organizations Immunities Act, which it did not, since the latter applies by its own wording only to international organizations to which the US is a member. See *International Tin Council v Amalgamet Inc* (1988) 524 NYS2d 971.

leads to not attributing any effect to the legal personality of an organization vis-à-vis non-members.

Where does that leave us? The field's operating assumption about international organizations enjoying separate legal personality from their members rests on uncertain theoretical foundations. If we assume that there is currently no rule of incorporation guaranteeing the legal personality – and thus no legislatively sanctioned analytical separation between an organization and its members – then we are hard-pressed to find another basis for justifying that conclusion. A more coherent theory within this overarching framework would have to rely on at least two premises. First, international organizations possessing some form of corporate existence that is directly sourced in social facts. Second, presumably, a 'radical extension of the definition of international law' or some equivalent notion that allows the system to register the existence of such new entities. Given the difficulties inherent in these two propositions, it is ultimately unclear whether we can really accommodate the notion of international organizations having their own 'objective' legal personality in the way typically contemplated in the literature.

3.3   Revisiting the 'Distinct Will' Requirement

Even as it forms a key part of most definitions of international organizations, the requirement that an organization exhibits a distinct will of its own, or a volonté distincte, remains an obscure notion. Most importantly for the purposes of our previous discussion, distinct will could be conceptualized as a condition for an international organization to be elevated as something truly 'over and above' its members, instead of being merely an agglomeration of other subjects of the law without its own personality.

Although scholars rarely delve deep into the question of what the indicia of an organization's volonté distincte are, most definitions turn to what can be seen as a roughly causal test. This reflects the idea that international organizations enjoy a separate existence from their members when they can make at least some decisions independently of them.[46] The

---

[46] Cf Niels Blokker, according to whom

> [i]t is irrelevant for this purpose whether these decisions are taken unanimously, by majority vote, by consensus, or by any other means. What is relevant is that the decisions emanate not from any *ad hoc* grouping of states, but from a body upon which powers have been bestowed to adopt such decisions, a body that is therefore more than the sum of its members.

background assumption seems to be that if all the decisions of an international organization are fully accounted for in terms of the conduct of its members (including most prominently their voting), then the organization '[b]ecomes indistinguishable from other forms of cooperation'.[47] In principle, such an entity would not be much different than groupings such as coalitions of the willing or the G20.

In this regard, the most common benchmark employed to theorize an organization's volonté distincte is whether it possesses at least one organ with the power to impose its will upon at least one member without its concurrent vote – essentially the potential for some decisions to be reached without the members' consensus. For example, Klabbers traces autonomy back to the capacity of an organization to take binding decisions against the will of one or more members.[48] Seyersted on his part defined international organizations as 'international organs . . . which are not authorized by all their acts to assume obligations (merely) on behalf of the several participating communities', reasoning that '[i]f they are so authorized, they are joint organs of the participating States, rather than distinct legal entities'.[49] Similarly, Paul Reuter traced the 'volonté propre' of an international organization to its ability to adopt decisions without following a rule of unanimity.[50] Tarcisio Gazzini further suggests that 'the degree of autonomy enjoyed by international organizations ultimately depends on the possibility of adopting decisions by majority'.[51] The latent premise here is that in order to become a candidate for international legal personality, an international organization must somehow demonstrate a capacity for action that may not be reduced to the intentions of its members.

It is worth scrutinizing this line of reasoning further, as it (1) seems to play a key role in structuring popular scholarly understandings of

(Niels M Blokker, 'International Organizations and Their Members' (2004) 1(1) IOLR 139, 154; White (n 3) 9.)

[47] Klabbers(n 2) 13. See also Tarcisio Gazzini, 'Personality of International Organizations' in Jan Klabbers and Asa Wallendahl (eds), *Research Handbook on the Law of International Organizations* (Edward Elgar 2011) 35.

[48] Klabbers (n 2) 12.

[49] Seyersted, *Common Law of International Organizations* (n 31) 392.

[50] Paul Reuter, 'Principes de droit Internationale' (1961) 103 Collected Courses of International Law 517.

[51] Tarcisio Gazzini, 'The Relationship between International Legal Personality and the Autonomy of International Organizations' in Richard Collins and Nigel D White (eds), *International Organizations and the Idea of Autonomy: Institutional Independence in the International Legal Order* (Routledge 2011) 205.

international organizations' distinct legal existence; and (2) echoes arguments encountered across disciplines dealing with the problem of corporate existence.

Abstracting from the problem of international organizations, the principle at work here seems to be that if corporate entities are not themselves causally necessary in our explanations of what is going on in the world, then there is little to distinguish them from their members just acting in concert, and thus nothing to entrench them ontologically. When transposed to international law, this line of thought seeks to compensate for the prevalence of methodological statism in legal discourse. Methodological statism in that regard refers to an outlook that would analyse everything related to international organizations in terms of what states do, through concepts such as agency, authorization, and consent (usually this outlook is facilitated by the aforementioned questionable tendency to conceptually reduce international organizations' membership only to states as opposed to other actors). In this respect, decision-making by majority would seem to suggest that there are, at the very least, some situations of discontinuity between the intentions of international organizations and (at least some of) their members (some members voted Y, but the organization did X), thus seemingly escaping the aforementioned methodological statism.

While superficially intuitive, such an understanding of distinct will faces serious challenges, both conceptual and practical. To begin with, it would mean that many international organizations would fail to meet the requirements laid down by the literature. As Klabbers readily admits, '[t]here, are after all, precious few organizations that can take binding decisions against the will of one or more member states; ... From such an angle then, few organizations possess a distinct will'.[52] The dominant interpretation of the distinct will requirement would also probably negate by default, rather counter-intuitively, all two-member organizations, for which the conceptual line between consensus and majority is elusive.

---

[52] Jan Klabbers, *Advanced Introduction to the Law of International Organizations Law* (Edward Elgar 2015) 9. See also Brölmann (n 2) 21; and Verdirame (n 5) 33, who argues that the test 'set[s] the bar too high'. According to a 2015 survey that compiled voting rules from 266 international organizations, 118 of them (45 per cent) featured majoritarian voting, 92 decision my unanimity (35 per cent), 47 weighed voting (18 per cent), and 9 featured no voting rules at all (3 per cent): Daniel J Blake and Autumn Lockwood Payton, 'Balancing Design Objectives: Analyzing New Data on Voting Rules in Intergovernmental Organization' (2015) 10 Review of International Organization 377, 387.

This would run contrary to the jurisprudence of the ICJ, which has, on at least one occasion, accepted the legal personality of a two-member organization that reached its decisions by consensus.[53] The Court has also generally shied away from this reasoning when determining the existence of an international organization's legal personality.[54] Granted, this tension with practice is by no means conclusive – it could be after all that the practice itself is misguided and should be revisited. But the dissonance between theory and practice seems striking enough at this point to give room for some pause.

The test also runs into conceptual difficulties. The following example may help illustrate some of these. Suppose that three states sign a treaty creating an international organization featuring two organs: one organ that decides by majority voting and another that decides by the unanimous vote of its members. Should the decisions of the organization be attributed to it or to its members, assuming the lack of a regulative fiction or a rule of incorporation in that regard?[55] As we just saw, an objection regarding those decisions taken by unanimous vote is that these can be

---

[53] The 'Comisión Administradora del Río Uruguay' (Administrative Commission of the River Uruguay) set up by Argentina and Uruguay and tasked with promoting the development and management of the Uruguay River. See *Case Concerning Pulp Mills on the River Uruguay (Argentina v Uruguay)* (Judgment) [2010] ICJ Rep 14, 53.

[54] For example, the decision-making-by-majority test for distinct will was not applied by the Court when it found that the Global Mechanism of the United Nations Convention to Combat Desertification did not enjoy a legal personality of its own. *Judgment No. 2867 of the Administrative Tribunal of the International Labour Organization upon a Complaint Filed against the International Fund for Agricultural Development* (Advisory Opinion) [2012] ICJ Rep 10, 36. This problem is different from having an entity whose decisions are subject to subsequent approval by individual governments. For example, the Administering Authority for Nauru was deemed not to enjoy a legal personality of its own by the ICJ, given that 'the Administrator was at all times appointed by the Australian Government and was accordingly under the instructions of that Government. His "ordinances, proclamations and regulations" were subject to confirmation or rejection by the Governor-General of Australia'. See *Case Concerning Certain Phosphate Lands in Nauru (Nauru v Australia)* (Preliminary Objections – Judgment) [1992] ICJ Rep 240, 256–258. Decision-making capacity was one of the factors taken into consideration by the ICJ in *Reparation for Injuries*, but this was not explicitly tied to decision-making by majority, and, most importantly, it was interpreted not as a condition of legal personality, but rather as evidence of the members' intention to endow the organization with it. *Reparation for Injuries Suffered in the Service of the United Nations* (n 24) 178–179. See also text to n 101 in Chapter 7.

[55] Note that this problem is not resolved by having recourse to the rules of international law concerning the attribution of acts to international organizations. The question here is what makes an international organization a distinct entity from its member states in the first place.

reduced to members' individual behaviours. Therefore, this argument goes, there is no need to postulate the organization as a separate entity, and the latter becomes indistinguishable from 'collective organs where a common will emerges and is attributed to all States which have the organ in common'.[56] But why can something similar not be said about those decisions taken by majority voting? Indeed, even if an organization appears to have such a decision-making power in spite of some of its members, this could be explained by virtue of those members consenting beforehand to that particular decision-making procedure when acceding to the organization. In other words, if one goes down the road of methodological statism – the starting framework within which the test seeks to prove that at least certain international organizations can be thought of as non-reducible – then there is little reason to stop at the voting stage. If we accept that a member has consented in advance to be bound by decisions taken by the majority, then we can still engage in a reductionist analysis, just a more elaborate one. The same rationale could put into question any reliance on a specific decision-making procedure as the hallmark of separate existence: even the most complex or original procedure could be considered to emanate from individual dispositions at an earlier point in the process.

One may counter that it is precisely at the moment of signing this founding treaty that a new entity comes to life, and that, *from the perspective* of that entity, its existence and its will is indeed separate from that of its members. However, the question then becomes whether and why we should care about how things appear to be from the internal perspective of that entity. Here we should remind ourselves that the causal view of international organizations' distinct will has been developed to supply an objective ontological benchmark in the context of international law, so that we may not confuse international organizations with joint organs and groups of states. If all that matters is how things appear from the perspective of the organization, then trying to pin down the separate will to a specific objectively observable procedure, majority-driven or not, may seem unnecessary to begin with. And of course, an adequate explanation would still be pending as to why we should prioritize viewing things from the perspective of the organization. At this point we lapse into the familiar problems of our objective

---

[56] ILC, 'First Report on Relations between States and Inter-governmental Organizations, by Mr. Abdullah El-Erian, Special Rapporteur' (1963) UN Doc A/CN.4/161 and Add.1, 159, 165, para 48.

personality theories: we could remedy this by assuming the existence of a rule of incorporation, with all the problems and limitations that have been identified regarding such a move.

Furthermore, when decision-making procedures differ among organs, the dominant account runs into another complication. Even if we were to endorse the criterion of an organization possessing an organ that can issue binding decisions against the will of at least one of its members, it remains uncertain as to what we should make of organs that may still require unanimous vote in order to reach a decision or these that may not require unanimity but still manage to meet it. Should these decisions count as that of the organization or of its members? Indeed, the insistence that the organization has 'at least' one organ that can take decisions against the will of at least one of its members seems hard to pin down. It is almost as if this is the minimum breath of life that is necessary before the organization can become fully alive and unitary in our eyes. Yet one could question this approach: staying faithful to the test's logic, we would then have to apply it across the different organs of the organization and instances of decision-making, instead of assuming that they all cohere into a single whole to begin with.

Finally, the criterion leaves much to be desired in broader terms of conceptualizing the idea of distinct existence as something more than a mere formality. To the extent that distinctiveness is understood as independence, the criterion focuses on formal decision-making at the level of organs, obscuring the problem as it may occur in the implementation of these decisions. Contrast, for example, an organization that decides by unanimous vote to set up an international criminal tribunal but leaves it to the discretion of its secretariat how to implement this and another organization that reaches the same decision by majority vote, but then has to provide follow-up approvals for every single step taken to make this happen, down to the level of what items will appear on the menu of the canteen that will service the new court. The comparison in terms of which organization is more or less independent from its members is anything but straightforward. The idea here is that the line between decision-making and implementation can be hard to trace in practice. Thus, concentrating only on the former may itself turn out to be highly artificial.

All in all, despite being superficially intuitive, the prevalent test for the presence of a distinct will does not erect a theoretical bulwark against reducing international organizations to their members as it is often assumed. It also provides few solid insights into how we should think about independence, whether we conceive it as a condition for legal personality or as a consequence thereof. That leaves the theories and definitions of international organizations that rely on the test in an awkward position: they either have to go back to some version of the Fiction theory, looking for customary rules that implement the distinction between an organization and its members vis-à-vis the outside world, or come up with an alternative test.

3.4 Conclusion

This chapter has argued that both key notions commonly employed to separate an organization from its members, namely its legal personality and its volonté distincte, demand further interrogation. As currently construed, the notion of an objective legal personality is ultimately based upon proving either that a rule of incorporation has evolved in the system of international law or that the latter has undergone a radical extension of its definition. Both assumptions seem problematic when viewed from the perspective of positive law. At the same time, the prevalent understanding of the volonté distincte as resting on the presence of majority decision-making procedure within an international organization does not seem to offer a workable abstract benchmark for deciding whether the organization is indeed irreducible to its members.

Common Assumptions about the State When Theorizing International Organizations

4.1 Moving Past the Analytical Dead-End

While the four corners of theorizing international organizations are relatively easy to identify, it is more challenging to move anywhere beyond that. When should an entity be thought of as an aggregate of its members and when as an international organization? How do international organizations relate to states in the international legal system? If anything, Chapters 1–3 have argued that these problems cannot be properly conceptualized in terms of the familiar 'all-embracing dichotomies', which at closer inspection turn out to be neither 'all-embracing' nor confined to only two analytical images.

If existing solutions are analytically the best that they can be but still exhibit serious limitations, how can we move past them? Instead of trying to find a solution that better fits the current framework according to its own terms, the following pages question whether these are the right terms to begin with. The argument is that, while there is something wrong with current efforts to theorize international organizations, this ultimately boils down to how the problem has been construed in the first place. Crucially, this involves the dominant models about not only international organizations but also those concerning the state. The commonplace moves that underpin this problematic conditioning will be shown to be (1) employing a rough atomistic image of the state akin to a natural person, even if only for analytical purposes, often complemented by (2) drawing an ensuing working analogy with how domestic private law tends to conceptualize the problem of corporate existence. After explaining the origins and underlying rationales behind these moves, this chapter will explain how they lie behind many of the field's conundrums.

That a common set of assumptions underpins much of our current theorizing efforts may not be obvious at first glance. Indeed, international organizations' discourse features a rich syncretic vocabulary that may seem to defy neat categorization in terms of a single overarching framework. 'Functionalism', 'constitutionalism', 'global administrative law', or 'international public authority' represent only some ways in which lawyers and non-lawyers have sought to imagine these institutions. Without taking anything away from the diversity of these outlooks, the focus here will be on the underlying *analytical* assumptions insofar as questions of positive law are concerned. These turn out to be much more streamlined than may be initially assumed. This set of starting assumptions – perhaps not shared by all scholars in the field but potent enough to shape the discourse – will be argued to have misleadingly imposed an uncompromising initial framing, no matter how many layers of theory are then applied over it.

While these assumptions may not always be explicit, they reveal themselves more clearly once we reverse engineer the theorizing problem from the devised solutions. The first shared assumption is essentially hidden in plain sight: coming up with benchmarks to analytically distinguish international organizations from their members only makes sense if one accepts that a challenge to escape group reductionism lies at the foundation of the discipline to begin with. In other words, regardless of where one stands on the 'treaty/subject' binary, the debates we have so far explored exhibit a common analytical baseline, namely that *by default* international organizations are 'nothing over and above' their members.[1]

Differences of opinion as to where to go from there should not obscure this shared starting point. While the treaty conception understands this starting point as insurmountable, and thus analyzes international organizations as treaties, the subject conception devises ways to move past it, arguing that international organizations may indeed rise 'over and above' their members from the perspective of the international legal order, provided certain circumstances are met. Simply put, both outlooks see an obstacle to the admission of international organizations in the international legal system. The difference is that the second outlook suggests that the obstacle can be, or already has been, overcome.

The main arguments for achieving this should be familiar by now. Some have linked the emergence of international organizations as distinct legal entities to 'a radical extension of the definition of

---

[1] For the origins of that view in late nineteenth-century legal thought, see Jochen von Bernstorff, '*Autorité oblige*: The Rise and Fall of Hans Kelsen's Legal Concept of International Institutions' 31(2) EJIL 2020, 497, 500.

international law'.[2] Others have spoken of a 'structural change' that occurred in the international community at some point in the development of the discipline.[3] More recent scholarship has theorized this in terms of a new customary rule that recognized the legal personality of international organizations – as we have seen sometimes conceptualized as a rule of incorporation.[4] Regardless of individual variations, the common denominator underpinning such positions is that *some* change in law, however that change is construed, needs to have taken place before international organizations can be thought of as distinct legal entities in the eyes of international law.

This framing may seem appealing at first, especially as it broadly corresponds to popular understandings of the field's historical evolution. In its general outline, this suggests a move from proto-international organizations of the nineteenth century that were thought to be hardly distinguishable from treaties, towards complex forms of governance through a sequence of evolutionary frog leaps in the late 1910s and then the late 1940s – roughly coinciding with the establishment of the League of Nations and the UN.[5] In an almost Darwinian manner, international organizations are often thought to have evolved from inanimate assemblages to protozoan and then highly complex institutions, as international life and the international legal system underwent fundamental changes.[6]

---

[2] Finn Seyersted, 'Objective International Personality of Intergovernmental Organizations: Do Their Capacities Really Depend upon the Conventions Establishing Them?' (1964) 34 Nordic Journal of International Law 3, 93.

[3] ILC, 'Third Report on the Question of Treaties Concluded between States and International Organizations or between Two or More International Organizations by Mr. Paul Reuter, Special Rapporteur – Draft Articles with Commentaries' (1974) UN Doc A/CN.4/279 and Corr.1 (E. only), 135, 150, para 20.

[4] See eg Fernando Bordin, *The Analogy between States and International Organizations: Legal Reasoning and Development of the Law of International Organizations* (CUP 2018) 54 ('[i]nternational law thus contains, as is common in domestic legal systems, a rule of incorporation for international organizations'), 198 ('just as domestic systems have developed highly developed regimes for the creation and operation of corporate bodies, the international rule of incorporation may evolve over time so as to establish more detailed and demanding requirements for the creation and operation of international organizations').

[5] Jan Klabbers, 'The Emergence of Functionalism in International Institutional Law: Colonial Inspirations' (2014) 25 EJIL 645, 649–650.

[6] Regardless of this narrative's inaccuracies, its staying power has endured. For a critical account, see ibid.

Most importantly, this narrative has also influenced contemporary accounts of the field's doctrinal trajectory.[7] The latter is often conceptualized as a series of doctrinal breakthroughs that largely mirror the field's perceived historical development. Thus, first came the gradual acceptance by scholars that states were not the only subjects of the international legal order.[8] This was accompanied by the emergence of the International Labour Organization (ILO) and the League of Nations, along with the recognition that the latter enjoyed a legal status that was distinct from its members.[9] This was followed by arguments that took the League's status as a basis of comparison for other international organizations.[10] At the last, and current, stage of evolution came *Reparation for Injuries*, which famously recognized the UN's legal personality.[11] The reception of that opinion and the eventual expansion of its rationale to practically all international organizations represents the closing of the first 'doctrinal circle' in theorizing the separate legal personality of these institutions, even as critical details have remained elusive.[12]

The simplified but popular narrative of progressive advancement towards legal recognition through a series of doctrinal leaps reveals

---

[7] See eg David J Bederman, 'The Souls of International Organizations: Legal Personality and the Lighthouse at Cape Spartel' (1996) 36 Vanderbilt Journal of Transnational Law 275–276. See also Richard Collins, 'Non-state Actors in International Institutional Law' in Jean d' Aspremont (ed), *Participants in the International Legal System* (Routledge 2011) 1071; Catherine Brölmann, *The Institutional Veil in Public International Law: International Organisations and the Law of Treaties* (Hart Oxford 2007) 39–94; Jan Klabbers, *An Introduction to International Organizations Law* (4th edn, CUP 2022) 16–23; Robert Kolb, 'History of International Organizations or Institutions', *Max Planck Encyclopedia of International Law* (2011) <https://opil.ouplaw.com/view/10 .1093/law:epil/9780199231690/law-9780199231690-e501> accessed 5 February 2025; Eyal Benvenisti, *The Law of Global Governance* (Brill 2014) 27–36; Chittharanjan F Amerasinghe, *Principles of the Institutional Law of International Organizations* (2nd edn, CUP 2005) 1–6; See also José Alvarez, *International Organizations as Law-Makers* (OUP 2005) 19–20.

[8] See eg Brölmann (n 7) 46; Bederman (n 7) 335. For the state-only conception of international legal personality, see Roland Portmann, *Legal Personality in International Law* (CUP 2010) 42–79.

[9] See eg Lassa Oppenheim, *International Law: A Treatise*, vol 1 (3rd edn, Longmans, Green & Co 1920) 269. Cf Klabbers (n 5) 649.

[10] See Bederman (n 7) 348–349. See also Richard Collins, 'The League of Nations and the Emergence of International Administration: Finding the Origins of International Institutional Law' (2019) 71 Revista Española de Derecho Internacional 285.

[11] Andrea Bianchi, 'The Fight for Inclusion: Non-State Actors and International Law' in Ulrich Fastenrath and others (eds), *From Bilateralism to Community Interest: Essays in Honour of Bruno Simma* (OUP 2011) 41.

[12] Amerasinghe (n 7) 87; Bederman (n 7) 349; Brölmann (n 7) 74–75.

something so obvious that is hardly ever questioned. This is the idea that not just the political but also the original *analytical* environment posed a barrier to international organizations becoming entities of their own, and that, therefore, a series of developments or 'turning points' were in fact decisive in ensuring that the legal system opened up to admit such new entities.[13] Hence, our 'folk' histories of the field's evolution are often structured around the notion of changes in the international legal system. However, we seldom pause to ask whether these changes really needed to take place from an analytical point of view. Instead, we tend to take this for granted and then try to work things out from within that framework.

But is it actually correct to suggest that international law had to undergo such a change *as a matter of law*? We cannot answer this question before we get a clear grasp of the assumptions that made such a change seem necessary in the eyes of those advocating for, and occasionally against, it. This will pave the way for arguing that the problem of accommodating international organizations into the contemporary international legal system *has never been* at its basis analytical. It has never been analytical in the sense that no new or separate norms were ever needed to admit those institutions as distinct legal entities. Likewise, no structural change or redefinition of the international legal system needed to have occurred at a definite historical moment in the past, be it the League of Nations or the UN (without taking away anything from the broader political significance that attached to the emergence of these two institutions). Instead, the analytical possibility for such institutions was there all along, even if for some other (extra-legal) reasons it was not picked up immediately or it was initially met with hesitancy by part of the discipline.

4.2   The Heart of the Problem: Theorizing the Corporate Existence of the Members of International Organizations

4.2.1   *Anthropomorphism in Theorizing the State for the Purposes of International Law*

It is now time to ask: what have been the implicit assumptions that necessitated a discourse of leaps in terms of positive law in the first

---

[13] For alternative accounts to this mainstream understanding of the evolution of international organizations, see Guy Fiti Sinclair, *To Reform the World: International Organizations and the Making of Modern States* (OUP 2017); Arnulf Becker Lorca, *Mestizo International Law: A Global Intellectual History 1842–1933* (CUP 2015) 179–199.

place? Perhaps counterintuitively, the problem lies with latent understandings of the state when theorizing international organizations, rather than with the latter as such. In this respect, an unrefined understanding of the state's legal personality seems to have taken hold within international legal scholarship, with downstream consequences for how the possibility of international organizations' emergence and existence have been conceptualized. This unrefined understanding has many scholars view the state as roughly analogous to the natural person of domestic law, if only for the purposes of legal analysis. In its broad outline, this model aligns with the also popular 'billiard ball' metaphor that treats the state as an opaque, closed-off, unitary, and irreducible unit of legal analysis.[14] In turn, such background assumptions about the state's naturalness and fundamentality, whether explicit or implicit, have created an almost impossible analytical situation for international organizations. Within this framework, the latter have to be conceptualized either as artificial, and thus somehow less real entities, or as natural ones, and thus somehow equivalent to states. Ultimately, this framing warps the analysis surrounding international organizations as well as states, asking the discipline to prove propositions that it does not have to, while leaving others beyond its reach.

It may seem puzzling to suggest that such a rough, perhaps even outdated, set of ideas about the state's legal personality would have any influence on the doctrine of international organizations as it stands today. Indeed, the idea that the state enjoys some kind of metaphysical or natural existence, or that it is somehow ontologically fundamental, has lost its purchase with most contemporary international lawyers – for roughly the same reasons that Gierke's corporate realism also lost its appeal in the domestic legal context.[15] Imagining the state as an organic entity that enjoys its own soul and/or body and mind was eventually thought of as being epistemically defenceless: one could neither prove nor disprove these notions. It was also gradually understood to threaten the core tenet of ethical individualism, that is, the notion of the inherent moral worth of each individual human being. Thus, many prominent

---

[14] For the 'billiard ball' metaphor, see Arnold Wolfers, *Discord and Collaboration: Essays on International Politics* (Johns Hopkins Press 1962).

[15] For the origins of this view in German public law, where the 'historical and organic view of the state dominated', see Portmann (n 8) 52. For the gradual demise of this view after 1918, see Catherine Brölmann and Janne E Nijman, 'Personality' in Sahib Singh and Jean d'Aspremont (eds), *Concepts for International Law: Contributions to Disciplinary Thought* (Edward Elgar 2019) 678, 683.

international legal scholars promoted a 'fictional' understanding of human associations, the state included, and their avowed demystification.[16] In this context, the individual was taken by many as the true ontological focal point remaining once all fiction was set aside.[17] Catherine Brölmann concisely summarizes this intellectual development, observing that '[t]he *legal* identity of the state was no longer linked to a pre-existing metaphysical identity but seen as a fictional and conventional understanding'.[18]

Crucially, however, this change in philosophical thinking about corporate entities, including the state, was never really pushed to its full analytical conclusions by international lawyers, who generally steered clear of any sort of 'anarchic individualism'.[19] The state may have been

---

[16] Various authors understood this fictional character in different ways, and it is impossible to lump them all together. Janne Nijman summarizes this general outlook by suggesting that scholars such as Brierly, Kelsen, Lauterpacht, Scelle, and Politis:

> ... basically denied the existence of anything like a real collective entity and reduced it to the level of individual actions. ... The individual was in their eyes the *true* or *real*, primary and original subject of international law. For the abovementioned authors, only individuals have consciousness, will, and personality required to bear the moral obligation to obey (international) law and to further justice through law and institutions. Hence '[r]*eal* personality can only attach to individuals*, not to states nor to any other social actor. If attributed by the legal system to such actor it was a pure fiction.

Janne E Nijman, 'Non-State Actors and the International Rule of Law' in Cedric Ryngaert and Math Noortmann (eds), *Non-State Actor Dynamics in International Law* (Routledge 2016) 111 (citations omitted).

[17] Hersch Lauterpacht would note in this respect that '... upon final analysis, it is difficult to escape the conclusion that unless legal duties are accepted as resting upon the individual being, they do not in practice and, to some extent, in law obligate anyone': Hersch Lauterpacht, 'The Subjects of the Law of Nations', reprinted in Fleur Johns, *International Legal Personality* (Routledge 2010) 173. Hans Kelsen on his part denied the state as an organic or even a social reality and would claim that rights and duties conferred upon corporate entities were in reality given to individuals, if only indirectly: Hans Kelsen, *General Theory of Law and State* (HUP 1945) 181–188. For Kelsen, the term 'legal person' did not designate the human being but merely a point of attribution for rights and duties: Janne E Nijman, *The Concept of International Legal Personality: An Inquiry into the History and Theory of International Law* (TMC Asser Press 2004) 191. Georges Scelle also maintained that the corporate personality of the state was merely a fiction, and thus an inadequate instrument for scientific analysis: Georges Scelle, *Précis de Droit Des Gens: Principes et Systématique*, vol II (CNRS 1932) 73ff.

[18] Brölmann (n 7) 38.

[19] As Hans Aufricht rightly observed in 1943, 'Scelle's argumentation against the "state" as a legal entity would, consistently applied, lead ultimately to an anarchic individualism.' See

demystified by being analyzed by many as nothing 'over and above' the sum of its parts except for the intervention of a legal fiction; however, this line of reasoning was generally exhausted in the moral domain, rather than employed to dismantle the state altogether as a locus of rights and duties.[20] In other words, whatever its philosophical significance, the emerged reductionist stance towards the state did not really alter how many international lawyers conceptualized the analytical foundations of the law and the ensuing rough analogy between the state and the individual human being. Thus, the analogy, even if not taken literally, has had an enduring impact. In many respects, the discipline still appears to operate at least *as if* the state is analogous to the natural person.[21]

But before exploring the analogy's legacy in contemporary legal thinking, we should pause to appreciate the problem that it was devised to address in the first place.

Indeed, international law faces a reductionist challenge with states that is conceptually quite similar to the one that it faces with international organizations. Of all institutions in international law, it is states that certainly need to be theorized as entities 'over and above' their parts, if they are to serve as distinct objects of legal concern, let alone the system's most common points of reference. As Nehal Bhuta suggests in this respect, '[t]he status of a state as both legal and moral subject rest[s] upon a strong ontology of the sources of its unity, boundedness, and agency'.[22] If those are taken away and the state is analyzed from a legal perspective as literally the mere assemblage of some individual human beings, then that is as good as saying that it does not exist: *it* cannot

---

Hans Aufricht, 'Personality in International Law' reprinted in Fleur Johns (ed), *International Legal Personality* (Routledge 2010) 50. For similar comments by Klabbers on Kelsen's understanding of corporate existence, see Jan Klabbers, 'The Concept of Legal Personality' (2005) 11 Jus Gentium 35, 48.

[20] Portmann (n 8) 131.

[21] For one of the earliest modern studies of how this analogy influenced international legal discourse, see Edwin DeWitt Dickinson, 'The Analogy between Natural Persons and International Persons in the Law of Nations' (1917) 26 Yale Law Journal 564. See also Jean d'Aspremont, 'The International Law of Statehood and Recognition: A Post-Colonial Invention' in Thierry Garcia (ed), *La Reconnaissance du Statut d'Etat à des Entités Contestées* (Pedone, 2018) where he argues that even though international lawyers frequently deny the anthropomorphic charge, such arguments have persisted in international legal thinking for centuries.

[22] Nehal Bhuta, 'State Theory, State Order, State System – Jus Gentium and the Constitution of Public Power' in Stefan Kadelbach, Thomas Kleinlein, and David Roth-Isgkeit (eds), *System, Order, and International Law: The Early History of International Legal Thought from Machiavelli to Hegel* (OUP) 406.

assume obligations, *it* cannot be held responsible, *it* cannot authorize individuals to act as its representatives, and so on. The analogy between the state and the natural person provides a model for overcoming this challenge by approximating the abstraction of the state to the closely lived reality of the individual human being. Therefore, the analogy is aimed at an existential problem of international law, while also being fairly intuitive in its broad outline – one need only think how casually the analogy is utilized when teaching international law.

It is little wonder then that the discipline remains 'replete with anthropomorphic moves' when theorizing the state.[23] In this respect, epithets such as 'original' or 'natural' are still frequently employed to describe the state's legal subjecthood.[24] For instance, the *Max Planck Encyclopaedia* entry on the subjects of international law suggests that states are 'original' subjects in the sense that they are 'born' instead of being 'created'.[25] As another classic study on statehood puts it, 'States are natural-born . . . and are not relative subjects of international law created by existing States as, for example, international organizations.'[26] From this point, the analogy with domestic law almost suggests itself: as an original subject, the state is 'presumably pre-existing the legal order in which it operates, comparable to the individual in municipal law'.[27] The analogy with the individual then serves as a basis for constructing the legal image of the state as a commensurably naturally or inherently unitary and irreducible entity.[28]

---

[23] See Jean d'Aspremont, 'The International Law of Statehood: Craftmanship for the Elucidation and Regulation of Births and Deaths in International Law' (2014) 29 Connecticut Journal of International Law 201, 212.

[24] Portmann (n 8) 81; Christian Walter, 'Subjects of International Law', *Max Planck Encyclopedia of International Law* (2007) <https://opil.ouplaw.com/view/10.1093/law:epil/9780199231690/law-9780199231690-e1476>, accessed 5 February 2025; Brölmann (n 7) 37. See also Bordin (n 4) 116–118; Robert Kolb, *Theory of International Law* (Hart 2016) 185–187.

[25] Walter (n 24). See also Kolb (n 24) 186; Christian Dominicé, 'La Société Internationale à La Recherché de Son Équilibre' (2006) 370 Collected Courses of International Law 144–147, who distinguishes between original, created, and recognized subjects. On the theological connotations of such an 'original' personality for the state, see Hermann Kantorowicz, 'The Concept of the State' (1931) 35 Economica 1, 9–12.

[26] Stefan Talmon, 'The Constitutive versus the Declaratory Theory of Recognition: *Tertium Non Datur*?', (2004) 75(1) BYIL 101, 101–102, 125 (further analogizing the creation of a state to 'the birth of a child').

[27] Brölmann (n 7) 37. See also Bordin (n 4) 116–118; Tom Sparks, 'State' in Sahib Singh and Jean d' Aspremont (eds), *Concepts for International Law: Contributions to Disciplinary Thought* (Edward Elgar 2019) 838, 841–842.

[28] For similar observations regarding international relations' theories about international organizations, see David C Ellis, 'Theorizing International Organizations: The

Such an anthropomorphic conception of the state, whether we take it literally or not, is bound to influence our doctrinal models. If anything, it makes further analogies with domestic law appear themselves more natural. Consider for example how often criminal law concepts are recruited to frame issues such as justification and excuse[29] or coercion.[30] Yet, regardless of whether the analogy's underlying logic is truly adhered to at a philosophical level (one may presume that it is often not), it brings with it a whole lot of conceptual baggage that we should be conscious of.[31] Indeed, it makes little doctrinal difference if we philosophically distance ourselves from the notion of the state as enjoying its own metaphysical existence but then still theorize it as such, if only for the purposes of international law.[32] In practice, many *doctrinal* models of the state continue to largely echo a notion of the human being as a fundamental, natural, intrinsic, organic, and non-reducible entity for a variety of different contexts.

4.2.2 The Anthropomorphic Premise in Theorizing International Organizations

Certainly, modelling the state after the individual human being, even when adopted on an 'as if' basis, has some explanatory value. As already mentioned, it rationalizes the state's unity and agency as in some sense independent from the underlying substratum of individual human beings, while also opening up avenues of reasoning present in private law.[33] Nevertheless, it may also conceal questionable metaphysical

---

Organizational Turn in International Organization Theory' (2010) 1 Journal of International Organizations Studies 11.

[29] Federica Paddeu, *Justification and Excuse in International Law* (CUP 2018) 1–20.

[30] Marko Milanovic, 'Revisiting Coercion as an Element of Prohibited Intervention in International Law' (2023) 117(1) AJIL 601.

[31] See eg ibid 618–619.

[32] For rival non-metaphysical ways of theorizing the state, see James Crawford, *The Creation of States in International Law* (2nd edn, OUP 2006) 6ff; Portmann (n 8) 131ff; Aufricht (n 19) 37. However, crucially, these theories have not necessarily supplied a dominant alternative *legal* image of the state in international law in general, let alone one for the purposes of theorizing international organizations.

[33] See eg Lauterpacht's influential study that drew on models from private law to make arguments about the interpretation and development of international law: Hersch Lauterpacht, *Private Law Sources and Analogies in International Law* (Longmans, Green & Co Ltd 1927).

propositions, namely the obscure notion that the state is somehow a 'natural' and 'intrinsic' entity, and that it shares with human beings not only unity of agency but also an analogous ontological position.

Such notions are often considered a harmless relic of the past that does not have an impact on the doctrine as it stands today: who after all really believes that states are 'born' or that they have a soul/mind of their own? Yet, regardless of whether all this is taken at face value or not, scholars too often proceed to analyse international organizations as if states were individual human beings.

To begin with, many scholars explicitly analogize the state to the individual human being for doctrinal purposes when theorizing international organizations. As Brölmann observes: '[o]n the international plane the natural person could be said to have its counterpart in the state, the primary subject of international law, whereas legal or corporate persons ... would be the secondary subjects of international law with "derived" personality.'[34] Elsewhere Brölmann explains that the contradiction between states as natural and international organizations as artificial legal persons has led to a 'mechanistic, functionalist view of international organizations that has persisted even when international organizations came to be recognized as independent actors'.[35] Jan Klabbers also describes the dominant functionalist approach towards international organizations as stemming from the assumption that international organizations are the creations of other entities, whereas states

---

[34] Footnotes omitted. Brölmann (n 7) 57–58. Brölmann also notes that '[T]his was the starting point for any discussion on legal personality of organisations, notwithstanding a by that time articulate critique of the concept of legal person and of the state as a legal person'. See also Reinhold Reuterswärd, 'The Legal Nature of International Organizations' (1980) 49 Nordic Journal of International Law 14, who argues that '[t]hose who assert that international organizations are subjects of international law usually think of them as international counterparts to juristic persons in municipal law', giving examples from the German-speaking literature on this topic; and Arnold D McNair, 'The Functions and Differing Legal Character of Treaties' (1930) 11 BYIL 100, 111, who analogizes international organizations to corporations of private law.

[35] Catherine Brölmann, 'Capturing the Juridical Will of International Organisations' in Jean d'Aspremont and Droubi Sufyan (eds), *International Organizations and Non-State Actors in the Formation of Customary International Law* (Manchester University Press 2020) 47. The idea that international organizations do indeed act as independent actors is well established in the neighbouring field of international relations; See Michael Barnett and Martha Finnemore, *Rules for the World: International Organizations in Global Politics* (CUP 2004). However, this observation has had much less success in transforming analytical models for the purposes of public international law.

are 'somehow organically existing'.[36] Confirming Klabbers' observation, it is common for scholars to refer to international organizations as analogous to 'corporations of private law'.[37] Quite tellingly, a classic study of the subject describes sovereign states as 'natural persons', and international organizations as civil law corporations. It argues that just as a corporation 'cannot marry and is not subject to military service', so international organizations cannot exercise all the rights and duties that states have.[38]

More subtle evidence that a rough anthropomorphic conception of the state has been at work can also be found in the way that international lawyers seek to address specific problems of international organizations law. In this respect, as we have seen, many scholars implicitly or explicitly draw inspiration from domestic law on the relations of private individuals. This is done, for example, when theorizing the existence of a rule of incorporation and drawing analogies with corporate bodies of domestic law,[39] or insisting that the correct analogy lies with 'those systems of municipal law which take the opposite approach by recognizing the general juridical personality of associations without legislative provisions and/or incorporation'.[40] Similarly, others analogize organizations without legal personality as 'unincorporated associations or partnerships of national law'.[41] Almost naturally, many scholars proceed on the familiar notion that if the state is like an individual in the

---

[36] Klabbers expresses scepticism about this distinction. See Jan Klabbers, 'Autonomy, Constitutionalism and Virtue in International Institutional Law' in Richard Collins and Nigel D White (eds), *International Organizations and the Idea of Autonomy: Institutional Independence in the International Legal Order* (Routledge 2011) 122. The presumed difference between international organizations and states is also evocatively captured by the Frankenstein analogy, a favourite in the field. See among others, Andrew Guzman who has described international organizations as a form of 'artificial life' akin to the monster created by Dr Frankenstein 'in an attempt to improve on a world only populated by humans'. Andrew Guzman, 'International Organizations and the Frankenstein Problem' (2013) 24 EJIL 999, 100.

[37] McNair (n 34) 111.

[38] Ignaz Seidl-Hohenveldern, *Corporations in and under International Law* (Grotius 1987) 74.

[39] See eg Bordin (n 4) 10, 85, and 198. Although Bordin suggests that he 'does not seek to draw analogies between rules of international law and company law', he also adds that the terminology of 'corporate entity', 'corporate body', and 'rule of incorporation' is 'helpful for capturing and tackling problems that both systems share'.

[40] Seyersted (n 2) 94–95. See also Finn Seyersted, 'The Legal Nature of International Organizations' (1982) 51 Nordisk Tidsskrift International Ret 203, 204–205.

[41] Amerasinghe (n 7) 69.

international legal order, then it makes sense to conceptualize international organizations as the respective corporate legal person of private law.[42]

Crucially, this underlying analytical conditioning of the problem prevails regardless of whether one subscribes to a so-called constitutional or contractual understanding of these institutions. Therefore, the aphorism that '[t]he constitutional view relies on the public dimension of international institutions, while the contractual view is based on the analogy with private national enterprises'[43] seems inaccurate when viewed from an analytical perspective, even if it may capture well elements of more normative debates. Instead, most international lawyers have tended to conceptualize international organizations for doctrinal purposes via private law concepts: either as corporations of private law or as mere contractual arrangements. By contrast, ideas of public law have supplied mostly normative inspiration rather than alternative analytical models.[44]

All in all, rather than being a relic of the past or analytically toothless, the atomistic conceptualization of the state as a 'natural' individual human being and an irreducible point of reference remains the conceptual context in which some of the most problematic aspects of international organizations' law have been theorized. Ultimately, however, this anthropomorphic premise about the state leaves only narrow, and ultimately unnecessarily stringent, theorizing paths for international

---

[42] See Bederman (n 7) 353–358 outlining how the League of Nations was conceptualized as a corporate body in municipal law. See also Clarence Wilfred Jenks, 'The Legal Personality of International Organizations' (1945) 22 BYIL 267, 271; Klabbers (n 19) 60 ('[i]t is potentially accurate to state that the law on personality has been dominated by corporate law concerns'); Nikolaos Voulgaris, according to whom '[t]he dictum of the ICJ in the Reparation for Injuries case was therefore a watershed. With the personality of International Organisations taken for granted, legal scholarship in the UN era addresses the issue by drawing parallels between International Organisations and corporations possessing personality under national laws.' Nikolaos Voulgaris, *Allocating International Responsibility between Member States and International Organizations* (Hart 2019) 56.

[43] Lorenzo Gasbarri, 'The Dual Legality of the Rules of International Organizations' (2017) 14 IOLR 87, 95.

[44] See eg Benedict Kingsbury, Nico Krisch, and Richard B Stewart, 'The Emergence of Global Administrative Law' (2005) 68 Law and Contemporary Problems 15; Dan Sarooshi, 'The Role of Domestic Public Law Analogies in the Law of International Organizations' (2008) 5 IOLR 237. See also the collected volume by Armin von Bogdandy and others (eds), *The Exercise of Public Authority by International Institutions: Advancing International Institutional Law* (Springer 2010).

organizations. It does erect a 'prison of our own choosing'[45] that conditions how we understand issues such as international organizations' legal personality, their functions in relation to their members, as well as their relationship to states as species of legal actors.

4.3   How an Anthropomorphic Image of the State Distorts the Theorizing of International Organizations as Entities Distinct from Their Members

4.3.1   Ascription of Legal Personality

Conceptions of the state as analogous to private individuals of domestic law suggest that states cannot grant a distinct legal personality to organizations on their own or that, even if they can, this personality will only have a relative ambit and not affect non-members without prior recognition.[46] In other words, the default position here seems to be that international organizations cannot rise as entities over and above their members vis-à-vis non-members if they only owe their status as distinct legal persons to their members. Given the underlying analogy between the state and the natural person, this position initially makes sense. Indeed, it would seem counterintuitive for most lawyers to accept that two individuals can create a corporate entity, bestow it with a legal status on their own, and have that arrangement to be legally opposable to third parties. A similar conceptualization of the problem for international organizations appears almost self-evident: their status must be shown to be something more than a direct ascription by their member states, or otherwise it should be dealt with as an *inter partes* predicate.

Setting up the discipline's conceptual starting point in this manner also points to possible avenues for moving past it. These are the theories of legal personality that have been discussed in Chapter 3. Such theories seek to overcome a default position of relative personality by arguing that (1) international law has evolved in such a way that it now contains a rule of incorporation that ascribes an objective status to such arrangements

---

[45] Rosalyn Higgins, *Problems and Process: International Law and How We Use It* (OUP 1994) 49.

[46] See eg Brölmann (n 7) 88–89, who suggests that the relative personality of international organizations is in line with the 'will theory' on the foundation of the legal personality of international organizations. See also Jan Klabbers, who argues that the will theory must resort to recognition by non-members in order to yield an organization with objective legal personality: Klabbers (n 7) 47–48.

regarding international organizations; and/or (2) international organizations owe their status directly to international law rather than to the will of their member states; and/or (3) that international organizations obtain their status essentially by being themselves 'real' entities akin to states, that is, by being autonomous or self-governing actors. The problems that these theories run into have been discussed in Chapter 3. What is worth keeping in mind here is how the solutions mirror how the problem is perceived, whether the latter is stated explicitly or not.

4.3.2   International Organizations' Distinct Will

As seen in Chapter 3, mainstream approaches to the problem of distinct will suggest that if all the decisions of international organizations can be traced back to the attitudes and decisions of their members, then these institutions are simply another name for the latter acting in tandem. The latent anthropomorphic premise here is that states should be dealt with as 'natural' agents, again akin to the position that humans roughly occupy in domestic legal settings.Within this framework, states are fundamental entities, below and beyond which no cause is traced in the legal system unless otherwise stipulated. In the same manner in which in a domestic legal setting we would legally attribute a murder to the murderer rather than to his arm,[47] the rough analogy with the natural person suggests that states subsume the causal contributions of sub-state actors and assume the authorship of acts that are appropriately connected to them, as the law provides. For example, in a legal context, we do not claim that the state's head of state *caused* her state to sign this treaty. Instead, we treat the state as an entity that incorporates certain kinds of causes and re-describes them as parts of a process. Accordingly, a head of state signing a treaty *counts as* the state signing the treaty.

Thus, in international law, attributing a particular conduct to a state is often taken to mark the end goal of our causal inquiries. Much in the same way that in domestic law we would normally not attribute a murder to the weapon but to the individual wielding it, in international law we would not be satisfied with attributing a use of force to a missile hitting a

---

[47] As Hart and Honoré summarise the principle underlying this position: '[a] deliberate human act is therefore most often a barrier and a goal in tracing back causes in such inquiries: it is often something *through* which we do not trace the cause of a later event and something to which we do trace the cause through intervening causes of other kinds'; HLA Hart and Tony Honoré, *Causation in the Law* (2nd edn, OUP 1985) 44.

target or to an individual pushing the launch button. Rather we try to link that launch back to a state. And, assuming that we could link a respective use of force back to a state, normally through our rules on attribution, we then stop looking for the underlying causes (much like in domestic law we would attribute the firing of a gun to a person rather than to the finger pulling the trigger).[48]

Understanding the role of the state in this manner as both the default limit and goal of our causal inquiries tasks the discipline with showing that international organizations can leave their own causal mark on the world.[49] In terms of the domestic analogy, international organizations must be shown to be neither the arm nor the weapon.[50] They need to interpose themselves in the causal chain of events that links their members to a course of action. If the causal contributions of members cannot simply be brushed aside, then the aim here is to show that at least some of the decisions of international organizations do not rely on such contributions from individual members, but instead exhibit their own causal efficacy.

Viewed under this light, the purpose of the volonté distincte requirement is to carve out a space, even the tiniest one, wherein the agency of the members does not take over that of the international organization. Thus, without such distinct will, international organizations are presumed to be mere mirrors of members' attitudes, and not distinguishable from classic forms of interstate cooperation. When that is the case, they slide back to the assumed default contractual image of these institutions. Once more, the aim here is not to rehearse the difficulties with implementing this line of reasoning, but rather to flag the conceptual framework within which this exercise becomes necessary.

---

[48] ibid 41.

[49] It is only the *default* limit and goal because the same conduct may be cognizable from the perspective of another branch of international law, for example international criminal law, for the purposes of which we would indeed go below the level of the state. Without such special rules, however, such conduct seems prima facie indifferent to international law. See, for example, *Accordance with International Law of the Unilateral Declaration of Independence in Respect of Kosovo* (Advisory Opinion) [2010] ICJ Rep 403, 437, where, without a link between a state and the purported violation of Serbia's territorial integrity (a principle which the Court found to be applicable only in interstate relations), the acts of the authors of Kosovo's unilateral declaration of independence were deemed indifferent from the perspective of general international law.

[50] See also Guglielmo Verdirame, *The UN and Human Rights: Who Guards the Guardians?* (CUP 2011) 60 (arguing that international organizations are not merely the 'long arm of their most powerful states').

4.4 How an Anthropomorphic Image of the State Distorts the Theorizing of International Organizations in Terms of Their Conceptual Relationship with States

4.4.1 The 'Either/Or' Framing of the Conceptual Relationship between International Organizations and States

To begin with, an anthropomorphic understanding of the state may create the impression that 'state-ness' is itself an intrinsic or 'natural' property, and thus it cannot be transferred to 'artificial' or 'mechanistic' entities. In this regard, the natural versus artificial framing seems to dominate legal imagination: corporate entities are supposed to be 'abstract' and 'created' entities, whereas human individuals inherently natural, minded, and/or soulful beings. Construed in this way, the anthropomorphic premise suggests a hardwired qualitative difference between states and international organizations. States are 'born', 'natural', and/or 'organic' legal subjects, whereas international organizations are 'created' and 'artificial' ones.

This implies a default category distinction between states and international organizations, underpinning different classification and treatment for the purposes of the law. The latter may then serve to preclude automatically extending propositions about the content of the law concerning the former to the latter. This is the type of distinction between states and international organization that could justify seeking separate norms to be identified specifically in relation to the latter, as for example the ICC did with head-of-state immunity in *Al Bashir*.[51] In that sense, the anthropomorphic premise creates the space for assuming an intrinsic qualitative distinction between states and international organizations. This leaves two possible avenues for theorizing the legal nature of international organizations: either go around the anthropomorphic premise or go over it – in other words, either admit international organizations as entities inherently different to states or simply extend the anthropomorphic imagery to them as well.

4.4.2 Going around the Anthropomorphic Premise: The Problem of the Blank Slate

Going around the anthropomorphic premise suggests that, while the state indeed occupies a special systemic position, international law is

---

[51] *The Prosecutor v Omar Hassan Ahmad Al Bashir* (Judgment) ICC-02/05-01/09 OA2 (6 May 2019) [1]–[2], [114]–[117].

open to other entities joining the system, with the caveat that these entities' subjecthood does not automatically equate them to states. In this vein, the state's unique nature as a legal subject is understood as a barrier to entry for other entities such as international organizations not to the system of international law in general, but only to the club of 'original' or 'primary' legal subjects, or, perhaps more intuitively, to the club of 'state' subjects, hence the popular qualifier of international organizations as 'non-state' actors to get around this restriction. This designation as non-state thus creates a new default legal–ontological position regarding international organizations that is premised on these institutions being qualitatively different from states.

This implies a conceptual detachment between them and the state, echoing the mechanistic versus natural actor distinction that authors such as Brölmann have been referring to.[52] Within this framework, the conceptual admission of international organizations leans on the creation of an altogether new category which presumably does not offend the state-centred sensibilities of the anthropomorphic premise. This solution leads to a compromise on the treatment of the category problem regarding international organizations. If the function and creation of international organizations can indeed be conceptualized as independent of their members, and if the legal personality of states is analogized to that of individual human beings with intrinsic and natural connotations, then the picture of international organizations' legal nature truly is that of *non*-state actors.

The non-state actors view avoids offending the anthropomorphic premise, but the price of this theory is that it yields only limited insights with respect to the category problem. Yes, the legal order can accommodate international organizations under certain conditions, but the nature of their legal personality is by definition different from that of states. One may assume that similar substantive norms may develop with respect to those entities, but the default picture is that they do not automatically have the same rights and duties, as they belong to different conceptual categories of legal subjects. Thus, putative new norms that may develop will be at best specific to international organizations. Before that happens, international organizations are, analytically speaking, essentially a blank slate in the eyes of general international law.

---

[52] Brölmann (n 35) 47. See also Catherine Brölmann, 'A Flat Earth? International Organizations in the System of International Law' (2001) 70 Nordic Journal of International Law 319, 340, suggesting that 'states and organizations are not easily interchangeable as legal entities, because they are not the same *typus*'.

Following this account, the things that we know about the legal personality of non-state actors should also hold true here. For example, as a matter of principle, non-state actors are generally thought of as being incapable of contributing directly and in their own name to the formation of customary international law. As far as the content and effect of their personality are concerned, this view leads to a formal and ultimately relative construction of legal personality, where, as already discussed in Chapters 1–3, legal personality denotes merely the existence of some rights and obligations in relation to some other actors. Pushed to its extreme, the consequences of this analytical construction may – as with the view that reduces international organizations to aggregates of states – also be construed to negate the existence of international organizations as a species of legal entities, but from the exact opposite direction. International organizations do exist, but they are all unique in terms of their rights and duties.[53]

4.4.3 Going over the Top of the Anthropomorphic Premise: The Problems of Unverified Premises and Overgeneration

An alternative tactic is to 'go over the top' of the presumed human-like status of the state, essentially claiming that international organizations too should be conceptualized in anthropomorphic terms. This line of thinking denies that a meaningful distinction can be drawn between international organizations and states in the first place. Crucially, this is not achieved by questioning anthropomorphic assumptions regarding the state, but by extending them to international organizations. This view goes over the top, so to speak, of the problem: if states are 'natural' or 'organic' irreducible entities, then international organizations, and potentially other subjects as well, may qualify for that status. To paraphrase David Bederman, this strand of thought has sought to demonstrate that international organizations too have a 'soul'[54] or that

---

[53] As Rama-Montaldo suggested in this respect, a formal conception of legal personality for international organizations 'leads to a pluralistic law of international organizations, and tends to reduce the possibility of a general theory's being built upon them'. Manuel Rama-Montaldo, 'International Legal Personality and Implied Powers of International Organizations' (1970) 44 BYIL 111, 113.

[54] Bederman himself does not make that point, but his reference to the 'souls' of international organizations captures well the anthropomorphic metaphors many scholars are susceptible to when theorizing international organizations. See Bederman (n 7) 376 ('The entire debate about the status of intergovernmental organizations [has been] reduced to a

they too are 'organic' entities, and, in a sense, competitors to their member states,[55] instead of being 'spiritless mechanism[s]'.[56] Such qualities then qualify them to partake in the rights and obligations that states have. This line of reasoning would suggest that international organizations are entities both 'over and above' their members, but also occupy an analogous analytical position as their members within the international legal system. Similarly, to the 'going around' tactic, this account also does not justify this conclusion on account of these institutions being made up of states. Rather, it reasons that international organizations are comparable to states in some legally relevant sense. The presumed similarities are then isolated and treated as hallmarks of the type of entity that a state is.

'Going over' the anthropomorphic comes with its own limitations and path-dependencies. To begin with, we might ask, why focus on the presumed similarities and not on the differences? Certainly, arguments from analogy are not unwarranted when these are focused on a specific relevant similarity.[57] For example, the shared capacity of states and international organizations to conclude treaties may suggest comparable legal treatment of both entities with respect to treaty law. However, why would it also imply the application of the same substantive rules to both types of entities or the capacity to contribute to the formation of customary international law? As we have already discussed, the answer to such questions seems unpersuasive if it rests on an inductive basis, and incomplete if it posits a change in law – such as a change in the very definition of international law or the emergence of a rule of incorporation – that it cannot substantiate.

As already alluded to, a further limitation of modelling international organizations after states is the side effect of overpopulating the legal order with legal subjects of a supposedly identical analytical footprint. For example, if international organizations too have a soul, one would expect that they can contribute *on an equal footing* to custom's formation. This echoes the classic problem of domestic legal theories that admit

---

moral inquiry for which international lawyers were professionally and epistemically unsuited: do international institutions have souls?').

[55] See Klabbers (n 5) 666, who describes the alternative to functionalism as the view that international organizations are 'organic creatures in their own right, as competitors to their member states, rather than as the latter's creations and instruments'.

[56] Brölmann (n 35) 50.

[57] See Bordin (n 4) 19ff; Christiane Ahlborn, 'The Use of Analogies in Drafting the Articles on the Responsibility of International Organizations – An Appraisal of the "Copy-Paste Approach"' (2012) 9 IOLR 53, 61–66.

the 'real' personality of the corporation: if they are true persons and not the offspring of a legislative fiction, should not they be allowed to vote as well? If international organizations are truly like states, we should then be surveying both state *and* international organizations' practice when assessing the emergence of a new norm, making sure that the practice is representative of both. Accordingly, we would also expect their acceptance and recognition to be taken into account as well when identifying norms of peremptory character. Arguably, both propositions would disrupt in counterintuitive ways the subject ecology of the international legal system.

4.5   A Better Problem for International Organizations Law?

All in all, as the talk of 'natural' versus 'artificial', and 'individual' versus 'corporate' legal persons shows, the elemental problem of international organizations law has not been only to show that these institutions are entities 'over and above' their members. Rather, it has been to show that these institutions are entities 'over and above' their members *in a legal system that is presumed to operate as if states enjoy a naturally distinct and irreducible existence, akin to that of the individual human being.*

Couched in these terms, the problem fundamentally mirrors the question of whether corporate entities can enjoy a real existence vis-à-vis their individual members in the context of many domestic legal systems. This is the problem of how it is possible to theorize non-reducible corporate entities given popular ontological assumptions about the irreducible status of individual human beings. In a similar manner, the main preoccupation of the discipline with respect to international organizations has been how to theorize these institutions as non-reducible corporate entities given that their members, often presumed to consist only of states, are themselves thought of as being somehow ontologically fundamental, at least for the purposes of international law. Under this account, the legal personality of the state forms a default barrier against recognizing a distinct legal existence for international organizations, a barrier that can only be overcome by a change in positive law.

This chapter promised a better problem for international institutional law rather than a better solution to the problem as it is currently configured. The better problem is this: how to theorize international organizations as entities 'over and above' their members *in a system that already recognizes the state as an artificial legal person.* In other words, this description of the problem drops the anthropomorphic limb of current doctrinal conception of the state, regardless of whether this notion is admitted merely on a fictional basis or not. Stripping away our understanding of the state from its latent metaphysical or naturalistic connotations, a clearer path for theorizing international organizations can emerge. This path suggests that international organizations, even in their most developed form, are an inherent possibility of the system. In a nutshell, the argument is this: any system of law based on the notion of the state as a person also encompasses the notion of international organizations as distinct legal entities with a similar legal footprint to that of the state without the need for any changes in positive law to that effect. Following this account, the state's legal personality is not an analytical barrier that needs to be overcome by a change in law but the key to unlock a better theory about international organizations.

What does it mean that theory building about international organizations should proceed from the premise that the state itself is a corporate legal person rather than a 'natural' one? Answering this question, Chapters 5 and 6 take a step back before moving two steps forward, looking at the problem of corporate existence as such in its more abstract philosophical dimension. The overarching argument will be that the exact same problems that riddle international organizations' existence are those that underpin the corporate existence of states. International law's solution to the latter problem entails a solution to the former.

4.6 Conclusion

This chapter has shown that the discipline's default position is that international organizations are 'nothing over and above' their members, and that accordingly some change in law is thought as necessary before they can be admitted as legally distinct entities. The assumption behind this position is that states are themselves somehow in-doctrine natural entities, roughly comparable to individual human beings of domestic law. This premise implies that international organizations are made-up entities, and that the relationship between them and states is akin to that of an individual human being and a corporation. The problem then is how to show that these institutions can be entities 'over and above' their member states in a legal system that is presumed to operate as if those members enjoy a distinct and irreducible, 'natural' or 'metaphysical' existence akin to that of the individual human being.

In contrast to this picture, this chapter has suggested an alternative starting premise. States should not be conceptualized as 'natural' human beings, even if only for the purposes of international law. Rather, they too should be understood as corporate persons. The problem of international organizations law can then be conceptualized in the following terms: whether international organizations are entities 'over and above' their members in a legal system that already recognizes the state as an artificial legal person. The remainder of this book explains what this proposition means, and how it may help resolve some of the most persistent conundrums of international organizations law. It will be shown that, in the final analysis, international law does not need special rules or doctrines to accommodate international organizations as distinct legal entities, rather a proper configuration of those currently available.

Looking for 'Real' Entities

Insights from Philosophical Discourse

5.1 The Place of Philosophy in the Present Inquiry

Our common intuitions about groups in general, not just international organizations, vary considerably. Both the idea that the whole can be different from the sum of its parts and the idea that a group is nothing over and above its members may appear equally intuitive in the abstract. It should thus come as no surprise that international lawyers have not been alone in trying to make sense of this conundrum. Classic philosophy, philosophy of science, action theory, social ontology, as well as many other bodies of scholarship have all tackled similar problems in one form or another. Broader questions regarding creation, independent existence, and identity – not just about groups but for all sorts of entities, including chairs, tables, and human beings themselves – have been posed by thinkers since time immemorial. Exploring key ideas developed in these respective areas can help put into perspective problems that international lawyers face with regard to international organizations, and eventually overcome them.

I should note from the outset that the ambition of this interdisciplinary detour is not to address an audience of philosophers, let alone to resolve fundamental puzzles regarding corporate existence for all intents and purposes. Moreover, the purpose here is not to present the reader with a magical solution imported from another discipline, as if these problems had crystal-clear answers to begin with that only needed to be transposed to legal analysis. Instead, the aim is to clarify which theoretical constructions are available and explain why some provide a better framework over others for analysing international law's exposed theoretical problems with respect to international organizations. The aim is to refine our understanding of existing challenges and eventually surpass them working with the ideas that we already recognize and accept from the domain of legal knowledge. In the end, the solution comes from within the discipline but it only arrives after the problem has been put into the correct perspective.

5.2   The Idea of Reductionism between Conflicting Intuitions

As already discussed in Chapters 1–4, an existential condition for international organizations' law is a theory that convincingly separates these institutions from their members. But what does it mean for a group, or for that matter any entity, to exist or to be redundant in the first place? When asking this question, philosophers are generally trying to uncover whether talk of such an entity is purely metaphorical. If it is purely metaphorical, then we are justified to assume that the entity in question is somehow less fundamental or real; that it is merely a shorthand expression for something else that we employ to save the time and energy that a full explanation would entail. On the other hand, if talking about such an entity is somehow non-metaphorical, we tend to assume that this entity is 'real', meaning that it enjoys an independent existence from the entities that make it up. A successful reductionist claim then rests on showing that an entity can be removed from our vocabulary without any loss of meaning.

Reductionism is a popular way of thinking about groups as well as other entities. With respect to groups of human beings, from humble playgroups all the way to states and international organizations, reductionism may seem to stem from a rather sensible intuition: 'nothing happens in society save in virtue of something that human beings do or have done'.[1] Reductionist thinking can question the ontological status of other entities as well: the classic aphorism that an entity is 'nothing over and above its parts' speaks to that tendency. We may thus quip, for example, that a ship is 'nothing over and above' the wooden planks that make it up, or that a wall is just a set of bricks stacked on top of each other.

Reductionism may seem intuitive in some ways and counterintuitive in others. Next to the notion that an entity is 'nothing over and above its parts', we are also inclined to think that sometimes the 'whole is greater than the sum of its parts'. For instance, when an old wooden plank of a ship is replaced with a newer one, we tend to resist the notion that this results in a new ship. The logic behind this seems to be that the ship is

---

[1] Roy Bhaskar, *The Possibility of Naturalism: A Philosophical Critique of the Contemporary Human Sciences* (3rd edn, Routledge 1998) 192.

not *just* a set of its parts, for if it were merely just that, then a change in those parts would result in the change of the set, and thus to a 'new' ship.[2] Similarly, at the same time that we might celebrate the role of individual human beings as the originators of everything that happens in a society, we might be more sceptical about the aphorism that 'there is no such thing as society'.[3]

Our conflicting intuitions surrounding the idea of reductionism provide fertile ground for philosophical investigation. Reductionism strikes at the core of what it means for a thing to be, and how its relationship to other entities is to be understood. The following pages will investigate these themes but assume an agnostic position when it comes to the 'real' or non-reducible existence of any particular kind of entity. Reference to entities as if they were irreducible will be made for the sake of philosophical exposition, without adhering to any particular set of starting assumptions about either individuals or groups, or indeed any other entities.

5.3   Exploring the Notion of Non-redundant Entities

How can one establish that an entity is non-redundant? One may distinguish between two ways of thinking about this problem.[4] The first is to show that an entity is non-identical to the entities out of which it is made: to show that I am not identical with my bodily parts, a clock is not

---

[2] The puzzle that can be traced back to ancient historian Plutarch. In his *Lives*, Plutarch recounted the story of Theseus' famous ship that was on display in Athens for many centuries. Over the years, as one by one the ship's wooden planks wore down due to old age, they were replaced by new ones. This prompted Plutarch to question whether the ship would remain the same if all its planks were eventually replaced by new ones. Revisiting the puzzle, Thomas Hobbes offered his own twist, asking what would happen if, as the original planks were removed, they were gathered up and used to build a second ship identical to the first one. Which of the two, if any, would then be the famous Ship of Theseus? See Plutarch, *Lives: Theseus and Romulus, Lycurgus and Numa, Solon and Publicola* (Bernadotte Perrin tr, HUP 1967) 49. For Hobbes' version, see Thomas Hobbes, *Elements of Philosophy: The First Section, Concerning Body* (R&W Leybourn 1656) 100. Generally, on the puzzle, see Michael C Rea, 'The Problem of Material Constitution' (1995) 104 The Philosophical Review 525.

[3] This quote belongs to Margaret Thatcher from an interview that she gave to Douglas Keay for the *Woman's Own* Magazine in 1987. In the original version of her comment, Thatcher asked, 'Who is society? There is no such thing!', but this was later popularized as 'there is no such thing as society'. See Margaret Thatcher 'Interview for *Woman's Own*', 23 September 1987, <www.margaretthatcher.org/document/106689> accessed 5 February 2025.

[4] See eg Dave Elder-Vass, *The Causal Power of Social Structures: Emergence, Structure and Agency* (CUP 2010).

identical to its mechanical components, an orchestra is not identical to its members, and so forth. The second is to show that an entity is non-identical to the entities that it is made of, *plus the relations that obtain between them*. To refute this kind of reductionist claim, one would have to show that a human being or a clock is distinct not only from the sum of their parts but also from the interactions between those parts. For example, with respect to putative group entities such as an orchestra, proving that it exists in a non-metaphorical sense would entail showing that there is something more to it than its members playing simultaneously and in a coordinated manner.

International lawyers tend to understand the reductionist challenge with respect to international organizations in the second manner. Showing that international organizations are basically complex forms of cooperation between states is generally not considered a persuasive answer to the default reductionist thesis about these institutions. On the contrary, it is the impression of international organizations being nothing but 'members plus relations' that the discipline seeks to overcome through the notion of distinct will. Absent such distinct will, international organizations are thought to be 'indistinguishable from other forms of cooperation',[5] and thus, in principle, not capable of enjoying an existence of their own in the eyes of international law. Indeed, the starting assumption seems to be that when two or more states enter into an agreement, however complex, this seems to leave no analytical residue that would need to be covered by introducing the notion of an international organization. Something additional needs to be happening before an international organization becomes 'distinguishable' from other forms of cooperation.

Nevertheless, this construction of the problem also obscures part of its complexity when viewed in more abstract philosophical terms. That complexity stems from the fact that, arguably, relations can obtain not only *between* but also *within* entities. Take for example the idea of a human being. One could analyse it as a set of bodily parts and their relations. They could thus conclude that the notion of a human being is just metaphorical shorthand for other things and therefore ontologically redundant. But then again, the notion of bodily parts can be broken down into cells which then can be broken down to even smaller entities, all the way down to elementary particles of physics and their interactions.

---

[5] Jan Klabbers, *An Introduction to International Organizations Law* (4th edn, CUP 2022) 13.

Yet when we think about entities, we generally tend to assume that at least some of them are non-redundant. For those entities we disregard the fact that they can be broken down into more elementary elements; we adopt an ontological benchmark and subsume certain relationships under it. For example, if we adopt the ontological benchmark of the human being, we may then analyse some relations as *internal* to it and thus hidden from our ontological view.[6] It is this rationale that permits us to attribute the firing of a gun to a human being and not to the finger that pulls the trigger. In that case, we do not take the human being out of the picture by analysing it as just a set of 'bodily parts plus relations'. Instead, we consider it as being in some sense an irreducible or fundamental entity.

The question of which ontological benchmarks we should adopt presents an interesting philosophical question – for example, why would smaller mean more fundamental? – that this book has the luxury to leave unanswered. Instead, the question here should concern where *international law* draws the line that separates the internal from the external and thus creates its own 'real' entities. Equally crucial is the question of *how and why* international law draws that line. This book's critique so far has been that methodological statism draws the line at the level of the state because it considers that the latter enjoys a 'natural' existence akin to that of an organic entity or because it is in any event somehow inherently fundamental to the system.

5.4   The 'Mark of Being': Philosophical Underpinnings of the Search for a Criterion of Existence for International Organizations

What does it take then for an entity to count as something over and above its parts, plus the relations that obtain between them? As we have seen, many international lawyers answer this question with respect to international organizations by requiring that the latter are not merely loci where state wills are expressed. Standard theory asks that in *some* way, at least *some* decisions of an international organization must be made in a manner that is not completely determined by the attitudes of its members. To put it differently, if the existence of international organizations has to make some difference in the international legal order, it has

---

[6] HLA Hart and Tony Honoré, *Causation in the Law* (2nd edn, OUP 1985) 42–44.

to produce something that is not fully explained by the contribution of its members, an act that would have otherwise not taken place. This is often traced back to the capacity of an organization to make decisions against the will of at least one of its members, to serve as a 'cause' for members doing something rather than being the arena where members' attitudes are expressed.

A rich philosophical tradition lies behind the notion of exerting an influence in the world as a benchmark for independent existence. At its core, this criterion echoes the so-called Eleatic principle according to which 'to be is to be causally active'.[7] Inspired by Plato's *Sophist*,[8] the Eleatic principle is often employed as a general test that all sorts of entities must pass in order to gain admission to our ontology.[9]

The Eleatic principle has been extensively employed to question the reality of corporate entities, on the basis that they would seem to be causally idle.[10] As philosopher Dennis Armstrong has suggested in that regard: '[A] general argument is given against postulating any of these (additional) entities. They all lack causal power: they do not act. ... [w]e have no good reason to postulate anything which has no effect on the spatio-temporal world.'[11] As he further clarifies, 'everything that exists must make a difference to the causal power of something'.[12] Based on this understanding of the Eleatic principle, another philosopher has noted specifically regarding social entities that '[i]f this principle is

---

[7] The Eleatic principle, as echoed by many standard approaches to theorizing international organizations, can be understood as follows: to be is to make a causal difference *within the system* in which an entity operates, meaning in the case of international organizations, to make a causal difference with respect to states' rights and obligations.

[8] The principle owes its name to the 'mark of being' offered by the Eleatic stranger in Plato's dialogue: 'I suggest that anything has real being that is so constituted as to possess any sort of power either to affect anything else or to be affected, in however small a degree, by the most insignificant agent, though it be only once. I am proposing as a mark to distinguish real things that they are nothing but power.' For a translation of the relevant passages and discussion, see Paul Seligman, *On Being and Not-Being: An Introduction to Plato's Sophist* (Martinus Nijhoff 1974) 30.

[9] See eg David M Armstrong, *A Theory of Universals: Universals and Scientific Realism*, vol II (CUP 1980) 45ff. For a thorough discussion of the limitations of the Eleatic principle, see Mark Colyvan, *The Indispensability of Mathematics* (OUP 2001) 39–66.

[10] Tobias Hansson Wahlberg, 'Why the Social Sciences Are Irreducible' (2019) 196 Synthese 4961.

[11] Armstrong (n 9) 5. On a general critique of how the Eleatic principle has been employed by Armstrong, see Graham Oddie, 'Armstrong on the Eleatic Principle and Abstract Entities' (1982) 41 Philosophical Studies: An International Journal for Philosophy in the Analytic Tradition 285, 295.

[12] David M Armstrong, *A World of States of Affairs* (CUP 1997) 41.

accepted, then, in order to defend the reality of ontologically irreducible social objects, one will have to show that such objects have causal abilities beyond those of the interrelated individuals'.[13] International lawyers' mainstream understanding of the distinct will requirement corresponds closely to this idea.

In Chapter 3, I examined why the test commonly employed by international lawyers in this regard ultimately faces complications when transposed to international organizations. Here, however, it is more important to understand the problem of distinct will in its abstract dimension. A large part of the discipline suggests that for international organizations to be 'real', they have to exert some power over their members that would not have existed but for the existence of the organization – hence the idea that this occurs when the organization is able to reach decisions without the ad hoc agreement of all of its members. Based on the existence of such distinct will, this view concludes that at least some international organizations are in fact distinguishable from other forms of interstate cooperation, even though a consistent application of the criterion does not yield very promising results.[14]

In turn, this causal rationale for fulfilling the distinct will desideratum broadly corresponds to the counterfactual theory of causation, especially popular among lawyers. According to this theory, 'a cause [i]s something that makes a difference, and the difference it makes must be a difference from what would have happened without it. Had it been absent, its effects – some of them, at least, and usually all – would have been absent as well'.[15] Thus, international lawyers seem to be asking: Had it not been for international organization X, would the same thing have happened from the perspective of the law? If the answer is negative, then an organization can be considered to be a non-reducible, and thus in some sense 'independent', entity. If the answer is affirmative, then the organization should be considered as a mere contractual arrangement.

---

[13] Wahlberg (n 10) 4983.

[14] Jan Klabbers, *Advanced Introduction to the Law of International Organizations* (Edward Elgar 2015) 9.

[15] This counterfactual theory of causation was famously developed by David Lewis in David Lewis, 'Causation' (1973) 70 Journal of Philosophy 556. Peter Menzies and Helen Beebee, 'Counterfactual Theories of Causation', in Edward N Zalta (ed), *The Stanford Encyclopedia of Philosophy* (2019) <https://plato.stanford.edu/archives/win2019/entries/causation-counterfactual/> accessed 5 February 2025; Laurie A Paul, 'Counterfactual Theories' in Helen Beebee, Christopher Hitchcock, and Peter Menzies (eds), *The Oxford Handbook of Causation* (OUP 2009).

5.5   Introducing the Notion of Non-causal Dependence

What is missing from this exposition of the problem is that, arguably, dependency relations that are non-causal may also obtain between different entities. Consider for instance the following two sentences that seem to denote a causal connection between different entities: the table broke down because I put a heavy statue on top of it; the house burned down because of a gas explosion. It seems rather straightforward that in these cases 'because' conveys a causal form of dependency. However, things seem less clear with examples such as: the table broke down because its feet could not hold that much weight; the statue is heavy because it weighs 50 kg; the house burned down because its doors, windows, walls, and roof burned down.

The second set of examples do not sit well with our general intuitions about what counts as causation, even if they could all be considered 'counterfactual' in some sense. Indeed, we often tend to think that a house's burning doors, windows, walls, and roof did not 'cause' it to burn down, at least not in the same way that a gas explosion may have done; and that the statue weighing 50 kg does not 'cause' it to be heavy in the same way that my putting it on top of a table may cause it to collapse. Yet we would still recognize that the house burning down and the statue being heavy are somehow dependent on the doors, windows, walls, and roof burning down, and the statue's weight, respectively.

Such distinctions between different varieties of 'because' are especially relevant when thinking about so-called socially constructed notions as well.[16] Consider for instance the idea of murder. Let's assume that there is a generally accepted norm in place to the effect that when someone kills another person with deliberately premeditated malice aforethought, he counts as a murderer. Now, we could say that X is a murderer *because* he killed Y with deliberately premeditated malice aforethought. We could also say that he is a murderer *because* there is a norm in place describing what counts as murder to begin with. Finally, we could say that Y was murdered *because* X stabbed him to the heart. All of these uses of 'because' are correct in a way, but to say that they denote the same kind of relation oversimplifies matters at the risk of confusion.

---

[16] See generally John R Searle, *The Construction of Social Reality* (Penguin 1996) pp 27ff; Brian Epstein, *The Ant Trap: Rebuilding the Foundation of the Social Sciences* (OUP 2015) pp 74ff. The example of murder is taken from Epstein.

In philosophy this difference between causation and the relations just described is generally exemplified by using the words 'in virtue of' instead of 'because', which is more narrowly associated with causal relationships.[17] Following this logic, a house can be said to have burned down *in virtue of* the doors, windows, walls, and roof burning down; a statue being heavy *in virtue of* weighing 50 kg; someone being counted as a murderer *in virtue of* a norm to that effect, and so on. In philosophical terms, the notion of one proposition holding true in virtue of another is often known as 'grounding'.[18]

Even from this small set of examples, it should be apparent that grounding itself can convey a variety of different relationships. Much work has been carried out by philosophers to systematize the different types of relationships that make a grounding-type relation obtain. Yet what is important for the purposes of the present inquiry is that grounding, or the different relationships that the term seeks to capture, is distinct from the notion of physical causation, while still denoting some form of dependence of one proposition to another.[19]

The distinction between the two is particularly important to appreciate when it comes to exploring relations between 'higher-' and 'lower-' level entities. Consider for instance two everyday states of affairs: my alarm clock going off at 8:00 a.m. and me waking up. Each of these can be examined at different levels of analysis. Instead of saying that the clock's alarm went off, we might say that the inner mechanical parts of the clock interacted in such and such ways so as to make a loud ringing noise. Instead of saying that I woke up, one might say that my brain went from one chemical state to another. The inner mechanical workings of the

---

[17] Kit Fine, 'Guide to Ground' in Fabrice Correia and Benjamin Schneider (eds), *Metaphysical Grounding: Understanding the Structure of Reality* (CUP 2012) 37.

[18] ibid 37; Paul Audi, 'Grounding: Toward a Theory of the *In-Virtue-Of* Relation' (2012) 12 The Journal of Philosophy 685; Ricki Bliss and Kelly Trogdon, 'Metaphysical Grounding', in Edward N Zalta (ed), *The Stanford Encyclopedia of Philosophy* (2016) <https://plato.stanford.edu/entries/grounding/> accessed 5 February 2025.

[19] For an analysis of why grounding is different from physical causation, see Jonathan Schaffer, 'Grounding in the Image of Causation' (2016) 173 Philosophical Studies 94, 94–95. See also Gideon Rosen, 'Metaphysical Dependence: Grounding and Reduction' in Bob Hale and Aviv Hoffmann (eds), *Modality: Metaphysics, Logic, and Epistemology* (OUP 2010) 109. See eg Fine (n 17) 38, who distinguishes between natural, normative, and metaphysical grounding. Some philosophers refer to the metaphysical, natural, and normative grounding relationships as being essentially of the same kind, whereas others see metaphysical grounding forming a separate category. These potential distinctions bear no consequences for the more elementary type of syllogism advanced here.

clock and the inner chemical workings of my brain represent different levels of analysis. Theoretically we could delve even deeper than this, again drilling down to the very elementary particles of physics that make up the mechanical parts of the clock or my brain.

Now assume that these two states of affairs, namely the alarm ringing and me waking up, are connected in such a way that the alarm ringing causes me to wake up.[20] In principle, no matter how we analyse the relationship between a clock and its parts or between me and the physical state of my brain, the nature of the causal relationship between the two states of affairs remains unaffected. The relationship between the clock and its mechanical parts remains one of dependency – the clock would not function without them – but, arguably, of a different kind.[21] Accordingly, in this case we can schematize causation with a horizontal arrow, obtaining *between* different states of affairs, whereas forms of non-causal dependency as vertical ones obtaining *within* them (Figure 5.1).[22]

Dependency relations such as the ones depicted by the vertical arrows in Figure 5.1 may come in many varieties. One of them is identity. Identity denotes a strong form of ontological dependence that essentially admits no fluctuation. Thus, if we assume that the vertical arrows in Figure 5.1 convey identity relations, this would mean that any change at any level would break the identity chain and lead to the creation of a different entity. For example, if we assume that at a given moment in time a house is *identical* to its specific roof, walls, doors, and windows, and then, at a later moment I replace a window, then the original house and the one with the replaced window could be thought of as different houses, them being identical to a different set of roofs, walls, doors, and

---

[20] The point of reference throughout is 'states of affairs' or 'events' rather than 'facts', leaving open the question of individuating facts from a general philosophical perspective. Some philosophers argue that facts are individuated by the propositions that they express, meaning that 'the clock going off' is a different fact to 'the clock's mechanical parts interacted in such and such ways so as to make a loud ringing noise'. Others advance the so-called worldly conception of facts where facts are 'individuated by their constituents and the manner in which those are individuated'. See Paul Audi, 'A Clarification and Defense of the Notion of Grounding' in Fabrice Correia and Benjamin Schneider (eds), *Metaphysical Grounding: Understanding the Structure of Reality* (CUP 2012) 103.

[21] In this sense, as philosopher Jonathan Schaffer notes, '[g]rounding is something like metaphysical causation. Roughly speaking, just as causation links the world across time, grounding links the world across levels'. Jonathan Schaffer, 'Grounding, Transitivity, and Contrastivity' in Fabrice Correia and Benjamin Schneider (eds), *Metaphysical Grounding: Understanding the Structure of Reality* (CUP 2012) 122. See also Jonathan Schaffer, 'On What Grounds What' in David Chalmers, David Manley, and Ryan Wasserman (eds), *Metaphysics: New Essays on the Foundation of Ontology* (OUP 2009) 347–383.

[22] Similarly, Elder-Vass (n 4) 53.

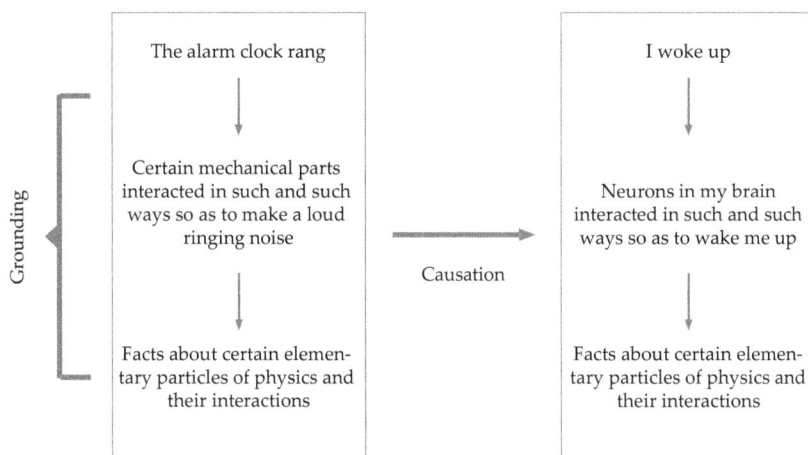

Figure 5.1   The distinction between 'vertical' and 'horizontal' forms of dependence

windows.[23] Similarly, if we assume that I am literally identical with my bodily parts and the latter with the underlying cells, and so on, then any change at any level, say cutting my hair, would put the old identity relation into question.[24]

We can, however, imagine looser and less demanding kinds of ontological dependence. Relationships such as composition and constitution do not entail necessarily any strict identity between higher- and lower-level entities, nor are they causal in the classic sense.[25] Composition refers to the dependence relationship that may obtain between something and its parts (consider for example the relationship between a book and its individual pages). Constitution, not to be confused with the meaning of the word in law or political science, refers to the relationship between something that the stuff that it is made of (consider for example the relationship between a book and paper). These relationships may be employed to describe how, even if a higher-level entity can be thought as being non-identical to the lower-level entities that make it up, it still derives important properties from them. For example, the weight of the book will still depend on the combined weight of its pages; its chemical

[23] For the problem of change in relation to the problem of identity, see Andre Gallois, 'Identity over Time', in Edward N Zalta (ed), *The Stanford Encyclopedia of Philosophy* (2016) <https://plato.stanford.edu/entries/identity-time/> accessed 5 February 2025.

[24] For an exposition of this problem, see Eric T Olson, *The Human Animal: Personal Identity without Psychology* (OUP 1997) 37–42.

[25] Simon J Evnine, 'Constitution and Composition: Three Approaches to Their Relation' (2011) 27 Protosociology 212.

Causation

| Facts about certain elementary particles of physics and their interactions | Certain mechanical parts interacted in such and such ways so as to make a loud ringing noise | The alarm clock went off | I woke up | My brain went from sleeping to being awake | Facts about certain elementary particles of physics and their interactions |

Sentences involving ontologically redundant entities?

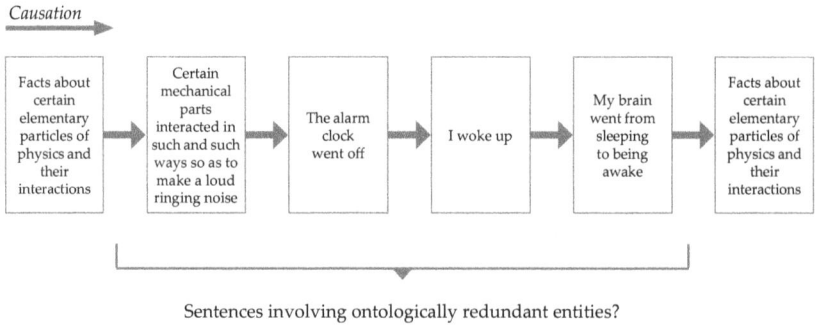

Figure 5.2   What would the world look like without admitting any non-causal forms of dependence?

composition will still depend upon the material that it is made of, for example paper, and so on.[26]

It may appear that by introducing the notion of non-causal forms of dependence, this book has pulled a rabbit out of the philosopher's hat, so to speak. That I have assumed that a higher-level entity can in certain circumstances really be distinct from the lower-level entities that make it up – the very thing that international lawyers are trying to prove with respect to international organizations. In response to this, I should clarify that this assumption has been entirely provisional. It was crafted solely for the purposes of exposition of alternative ways of imagining certain kinds of ontological relationships that may be missing from our register. The examples themselves are not meant to present bulletproof philosophical arguments, not even arguments from so-called common sense. It may be, after all, that in some deep philosophical sense, every time something changes in my physiological sub-structure, we have a new me, and every time something changes in the material structure of my house, we have a new house. For all we know at this point, the accurate version of Figure 5.1 could be as shown in Figure 5.2.

5.6   Existence as a Problem of Starting Assumptions

Having introduced the notion of non-causal dependence, we can return to the question of when higher-level entities should be considered non-redundant. As one would suspect, this is a huge area of philosophical

---

[26] See Kathrin Koslicki, 'Constitution and Similarity' (2004) 117 Philosophical Studies 327, 333.

investigation. Yet once more, it is more important to appreciate what this question entails rather than answering it for all intents and purposes. Two thoughts are key in this respect. The first is that the question of existence is meaningful only when asked with respect to one entity in relation to another. The second thought is the notion that what counts as real may be subject-relative: different things may count as real in different contexts.

The first thought is inspired by the work of philosopher and logician Willard Quine. Quine famously suggested that ontological questions framed in absolute terms are pointless. According to him, only onto-logical questions that concern the existence of something in relation to something else can be meaningfully addressed.[27] This relative under-standing of the problem of existence may help put our puzzle into better perspective. Whenever we inquire whether something is non-redundant, we do so to determine its relation to other entities that we already assume to be non-redundant. Thus, instead of asking whether 'the clock is real' in the abstract, we should be asking whether it is real *in relation* to its mechanical parts. But the latter question is meaningfully posed only if we assume that these parts are themselves 'real' and non-redundant to begin with (otherwise we would be asking whether the clock is just metaphor-ical shorthand for something else that is itself a metaphorical shorthand for yet another entity).

The problem here, as far as we are concerned, is not whether we should accept the mechanical parts as real or not, but the *why* of it. One may consider these mechanical parts as themselves being a meta-phorical shorthand for what goes on at the level of subatomic physics, and hence reject both the notion of a clock and its mechanical parts as equally redundant. But the inquiry as a whole only makes sense if one assumes that something, at some level, is real to begin with. In turn, this

---

[27] Willard V Quine, 'Ontological Relativity and Other Essays' (Columbia University Press 1969) esp. 55–57. The idea behind this aphorism is that '[w]e cannot know what something is without knowing how it is marked off from other things. Identity is thus a piece with ontology. . .'. Elsewhere Quine would express this idea with the precept 'No entity without identity'. What Quine meant by this is that we should not posit entities without having adopted beforehand clear criteria for individuating those entities. Peter Hylton and Gary Kemp, 'Willard Van Orman Quine', in Edward N Zalta (ed), *The Stanford Encyclopedia of Philosophy* (2020) <https://plato.stanford.edu/archives/spr2020/entries/quine/> accessed 5 February 2025. See also Mark A Seabright and Lance B Kurke 'Organizational Ontology and the Moral Status of the Corporation' (1997) 7 Business Ethics Quarterly 91.

assumption has to be followed by a justificatory rationale, which ought to be applied consistently. To give a simple example from our discipline: if we assume that states are non-reducible entities because they have a mind and soul of their own, but international organizations are thought to lack such attributes, then it makes sense to consider the former as fundamental and the latter as ontologically redundant.[28]

What should then be our rationale for counting any entities as real? While it may seem impossible to answer that question in the abstract, once more it is important to uncover the nuance embedded in the question. In this respect, as another philosopher, Keith Campbell, has explained, the 'search for a criterion for the real must be understood as a search for a criterion *for us to count something as real*'.[29] Much like theorizing an entity, what counts as real *for us* depends on who is asking the question, and for what purpose. Thus, the question of what is real is relative in the sense that it is not only better posed for one entity in relation to another entity but also that different things may count as real within different contexts.[30] As another scholar has put it, specifically with respect to law:

> [I]n contrast to the context-free project of philosophers ... the conceptual framework and methodology of the legal project provide contextualizing devices that render finite the number of factors whose possible involvement is subject to investigation; that individuate (at a level of modal fragility to serve law's purposes) the specified factor whose influence is being examined ... and that individuate the phenomenon (again, at a level of specificity to serve law's purposes) in relation to which that influence is judged.[31]

---

[28] This is, for example, apparently why Otto von Gierke seemed to dismiss earlier international organizations as being mere contractual arrangements. Cited in David J Bederman, 'The Souls of International Organizations: Legal Personality and the Lighthouse at Cape Spartel' (1996) 36 Vanderbilt Journal of Transnational Law 275, 355.

[29] Keith Campbell, 'Selective Realism in the Philosophy of Physics' (1994) 77 The Monist 27–28.

[30] This is different from the idea of global relativism, according to which 'everything is relative'. Someone may not be a relativist and still accept that the meaning of a word may be different depending on the context, for example when used in legal discourse. For an introduction to (and a refutation of) the notion of global relativism, see Adam J Carter, 'Global Relativism' in Adam J Carter (ed), *Metaepistemology and Relativism* (Palgrave MacMillan 2016).

[31] Jane Stapleton, 'Causation in the Law' in Helen Beebee, Christopher Hitchcock, and Peter Menzies (eds), *The Oxford Handbook of Causation* (OUP 2009) 750.

Combining this interpretation of Quine and Campbell's insights can offer a better understanding of the question that led us to this point. Thus, when we ask whether 'international organizations are real for the purposes of international law', we ask whether we should count them as real in relation to other entities, most prominently states, *that we already accept as real*. In other words, we assume that these members are real for the purposes of international law and explore the ontological relationship between them and a putative higher-level entity.[32] Finally, this question is not context-free: asking whether an entity is real in relation to another entity that we already accept as real prompts us to investigate the criterion that we have employed in order to buttress the notion that the other entity is actually real within that particular context.

5.7 The Limits of Causal Powers as a Mark of Independent Being

What has been discussed so far can help us understand the limits of causation as a mark of independent being. Consider again David Lewis' counterfactual understanding of causation, whereby for something to amount to a cause, it must make a difference from what would have happened without it – the famous but-for test which is implicit in many contemporary analyses of international organizations' volonté distincte. One salient criticism of Lewis' theory was that it ended up capturing too much in terms of causation, as patterns of counterfactual dependence would seem to apply with equal force to factual patters of non-causal determination.[33] Thus, according to Lewis' test, we would say that the alarm clock going off is the cause of me waking up, since had the alarm not rung, I would have continued sleeping. However, following this

---

[32] By contrast, philosophers may be interested in whether an entity is real outside of any particular context. They may disagree over whether entities exist naturally or not, whether there are fundamental entities or not, or whether there is a conceptual element to all entities or not. In each of these cases, their criterion for counting something as real may be different and they may disagree over which is the correct criterion to begin with. See eg Jonathan Schaffer, 'Is There a Fundamental Level?' (2003) 37 Noûs 498; Kit Fine, 'Things and Their Parts' (1999) 23 Midwest Studies in Philosophy 61. Accordingly, some philosophers take the task of ontology to describe not only what exists but also what exists in the most fundamental sense; see eg Rosen (n 20) 112. Others take social ontology to be the study of building relations between different types of entities; see Brian Epstein, 'A Framework for Social Ontology' (2016) 46 Philosophy of the Social Sciences 147, 149.

[33] Jaegwon Kim, 'Causation, Nomic Subsumption, and the Concept of Event' (1973) 70 The Journal of Philosophy 217.

counterfactual rationale, we can also identify other factual patterns as amounting to a cause: for example, a specific mechanical part of the alarm striking a metallic bell inside of it, my ability to hear, the electrical grid powering the alarm clock, the workers maintaining the electrical grid, and so on. Similarly, in the case of a murder, we could identify as the counterfactual cause the finger pulling the trigger, the victim's loss of blood, a low enough atmospheric pressure that permits a bullet to fly through the air, and so on.

In response to these concerns, Lewis sought to clarify his theory by insisting that causal relations obtain only between events that are 'wholly distinct', or between separate 'boxes' in terms of our analysis.[34] Lewis then explained that for an event to be distinct from another, the two events must not be identical, nor should one be part of another, or be implied by it.[35] For example, in the case of the alarm clock and me waking up, we could think that the inner mechanical components are part of the clock and my finger is part of me.

In abstract philosophical terms, Lewis' solution represents a classic chicken and egg problem, which echoes the main challenge with Quine's approach to the problem of ontology: should we first draw the lines of individuation between things and events and then describe the relations that occur between them as causal, or should we first investigate which relations are genuinely causal and then proceed to individuate things and events on the basis of these relations? Rather than resolving this philosophical puzzle, the more modest point to keep in mind here is that talk of causation makes little sense without having individuated the relata that causation is supposed to connect. In turn, this individuation is premised on identifying 'vertical' forms of dependence – determining for example when an event is part of another as opposed to an altogether different one – and separating them from causal or 'horizontal' forms of dependence, within and for the purposes of a specific frame of reference. These will then form the demarcation lines along which entities or events may be candidates for standing in causal relations.[36]

---

[34] David Lewis, 'Events' reprinted in David Lewis (ed), *Philosophical Papers: Volume II* (OUP 1986) 256. Crucially for Lewis, two events may be not distinct and yet be non-identical. As he put it: 'I and my nose are not identical, but neither are we distinct.'

[35] Menzies and Beebee (n 15).

[36] There are many theories in philosophy about what kinds of entities may serve as causal relata, including events, but also states of affairs, facts, and situations. See Peter Menzies, 'A Unified Account of Causal Relata' (1989) 67 Australasian Journal of Philosophy 59; Douglas Ehring, 'Causal Relata' in Helen Beebee, Christopher Hitchcock, and Peter

Again, one may argue that criteria for individuating causal relata may be defined in a deeper metaphysical sense and that there is a way of separating one thing from another on account of its intrinsic properties. Many philosophers view the task of ontology as coming up with definitive criteria in this respect. But again, even if such a general ontological account were possible,[37] we would not be concerned with it at this point. Rather, our inquiry takes place within a framework of inquiry that already incorporates its own rationale for individuating entities and thus separates causal from non-causal forms of dependence.

Causation employed in this sense is context-sensitive: in another world or for the purposes of a different inquiry, the clock may be viewed as an extension of the electrical grid that powers it, making it true that it is the electrical-grid-plus-clock that wakes me up. This basic point is especially true when it comes to law: a doctor may determine the cause of death to be loss of blood, whereas a judge may determine that the cause of death was being fired upon with a gun, even if they may be referring to the same person getting killed. International law is no different in this respect. It also features a criterion for individuating actions and entities on the basis of which causal relations may obtain. The key is uncovering what this rationale consists of and then examine whether it can be extended to the individuation of another kind of entity, namely international organizations.

5.8 Conclusion

This chapter introduced the problem of reductionism in its more abstract philosophical dimension. It explained that our search for the 'real' should take place within a particular context that follows its own criteria of individuation. Although the question of abstract ontological fundamentality is central to philosophy, it is not as central to international legal theory. Accordingly, our task when exploring the non-reducibility of international organizations to their members does not rest on drilling

---

Menzies (eds), *The Oxford Handbook of Causation* (OUP 2009). For a summary see Jonathan Schaffer, 'The Metaphysics of Causation', in Edward N Zalta (ed), *The Stanford Encyclopedia of Philosophy* (2016) <https://plato.stanford.edu/archives/fall2016/entries/causation-metaphysics/> accessed 5 February 2025. Regardless of the theory that one adopts, the individuating of the different relata is crucial to any theory of causation.

[37] For a sceptical response to that possibility, see Edward J Lowe, 'Individuation' in Michael J Loux and Dean W Zimmerman (eds), *The Oxford Handbook of Metaphysics* (OUP 2005).

ontologically until we hit rock bottom – if such a thing actually exists. Rather it turns to uncovering relational facts that obtain between international organizations and their members, most prominently states, *assuming* that these members form non-reducible points of reference for the level of reality that we are zooming in. Thus, the eventual goal is not to prove that states are themselves 'real' in a deep philosophical sense; instead, it is to uncover the most plausible theory that could support this assumption within the context of public international law and see whether that theory has anything to say about entities such as international organizations.

Corporate Existence as a Problem of Starting Assumptions about Members' Existence

6.1 Personal Identity in Philosophical Discourse

6.1.1 The Close Relationship between Individual and Group Existence

If questions of existence are meaningful only when posed in a relative manner, then one way to start thinking about the existence of corporate entities is to first explore the presumed existence of their building blocks. Thus, when investigating whether groups can rise as entities distinct from the human beings that make them up – a problem which has in many ways been employed as the blueprint for theorizing international organizations – we should first examine what is supposed to make their members themselves irreducible entities to begin with.

As this chapter demonstrates, the supporting reasoning regarding the 'real' existence of human beings as members of corporate entities leads to two fundamentally different ways of configuring the latter's existence. The first one understands human beings as organic or soulful natural entities; the other understands them as organizations of a miniature size or artificial entities. The first understanding poses an essentially insurmountable barrier to the possibility of corporate existence; the second is more accommodating. Rather than suggesting which stance is more persuasive from a philosophical perspective, this chapter carefully extracts from the aforementioned discussion a more refined way of thinking about the problem of corporate existence in general. With respect to international organizations, this way of thinking affords a more nuanced understanding than the discipline's current dichotomies afford, turning our attention to properly theorizing the state.

6.1.2 Personal Identity of Human Beings

The idea that human beings – the entities that are supposed to form the ultimate foundation of corporate entities – are themselves distinct from their parts hardly seems objectionable to begin with. Yet, at closer glance, it may seem difficult to pin down what it is exactly that makes humans 'real' entities in the first place. The problem was famously immortalized by ancient playwright Epirchamus of Syracuse in one of his comedies. Drawing inspiration from Heraclitus' famous saying that 'no man ever steps in the same river twice', Epirchamus told the tale of an ingenious debtor who tried to break free of a contract claiming that he was no longer the same man as the one who agreed to it in the first place.[1] When the creditor expressed his irritation, the debtor gave back the following response: 'if you add a pebble to a collection of pebbles', he said, 'then you no longer have the same collection of pebbles'. The debtor then continued:

> Now consider mankind in the same way. One man grows, and another again shrinks; and they are all undergoing change the whole time. But a thing which naturally changes and never remains in the same state must ever be different from that which has thus changed. And even so you and I were one pair of men yesterday, are another to-day, and again will be another tomorrow, and we will never remain ourselves, by this same argument.[2]

Accordingly, the debtor concluded he was not the same person as the one who took on the debt and was therefore not responsible for its payment. Upon hearing this, the frustrated creditor struck the debtor. When the debtor threatened to take him to court for this unprovoked attack, the lender coolly expressed his sympathy. He nevertheless responded that, according to the debtor's own rationale, he was no longer the same person who had hit him.[3]

Epirchamus' script rests on hyperbole to flag a problem that rarely surfaces in everyday life.[4] Generally, we do not live our lives like Epirchamus' debtor and we expect others to not conduct themselves like

---

[1] For a more detailed exposition of the puzzle and its origins, see Vincent Descombes, *Puzzling Identities* (HUP 2016) 43ff. See also David Sedley, 'The Stoic Criterion of Identity' (1982) 27 Phronesis 255.

[2] Diogenes Laertius, *Lives of the Eminent Philosophers*, vol I (Drew Hicks tr, HUP 1925) 287.

[3] Ryan Wasserman, 'Material Constitution' in Edward N Zalta (ed), *The Stanford Encyclopedia of Philosophy* (2018) <https://plato.stanford.edu/archives/fall2018/entries/material-constitution/> accessed 5 February 2025.

[4] There are various thought experiments that can undermine the confidence of our common intuitions in that regard. John Locke, for example, asked us to imagine the case of a prince whose entire memories and consciousness were transferred inside the body of a cobbler. At the same time, all of the cobbler's memories and consciousness were transferred to the body of the prince. Who should we then count as the prince and who as the cobbler?

that either.[5] On the whole, we usually think that human beings can survive at least some changes in their bodily and mental composition, and that we are capable of exhibiting some degree of unity of agency through time. For example, when I cut my hair, I do not conclude that I am now a different human being. In philosophy, the proposition that human beings can survive such changes is generally known as 'personal identity' or 'identity through time'.[6]

6.1.3 Personal Identity of Corporate Entities: Mixed Intuitions

The question of which theory is the best to base our view that *we* are non-reducible entities has been the subject of endless philosophical debates.[7] Yet the main puzzle has been to explain how and why we acquire our personal identity rather than whether we enjoy one. By comparison, when confronting the problem of corporate entities, our ontological intuitions seem to run out faster: can such entities really be thought as distinct from their members to begin with? While we might have laughed with the excuse presented by Epirchamus' debtor, can we really say that a group of two people remains the same after one of them is replaced by another?

According to Locke, the person goes where the consciousness goes. John Locke, *An Essay Concerning Human Understanding* (Tegg & Son 1836) 229.

[5] As Hart and Honoré noted,

> [our] sense of respect for ourselves and others as distinct persons would be much weakened, if not dissolved, if we could not think of ourselves as separate authors of the changes we make in the world. If we had to share the authorship of such changes with numerous prior agents, of whom it could be said that, had they not acted as they did, we should not have been able to bring about the change, we could no longer think of ourselves as separate authors in the way we now do. (HLA Hart and Tony Honoré, *Causation in the Law* (2nd edn, OUP 1985) lxxx–lxxxi.)

[6] See, generally, Christine M Korsgaard, 'Personal Identity and the Unity of Agency: A Kantian Response to Parfit' (1981) 18(2) Philosophy and Public Affairs 101–132; Michael E Bratman, *Intentions, Plans, and Practical Reason* (CUP 1999).

[7] For relatively more recent scholarship on this puzzle, see Derek Parfit, *Persons and Reasons* (OUP 1984); Carol Rovane, *The Bounds of Agency: An Essay in Revisionary Metaphysics* (PUP 1998); Richard Swinburne, *The Evolution of the Soul* (Clarendon Press 1997). See also the collected volume by John Belof and John R Smythies (eds), *The Case for Dualism* (University of Virginial Press 1989); Paul F Snowdon, *Persons, Animals, Ourselves* (OUP 2014); Peter van Inwagen, 'Materialism and the Psychological-Continuity Account of Personal Identity' (1997) 11 Philosophical Perspectives 305.

Take for instance the following example of a hypothetical 'modern Greek literature reading group'. If the reading group has two members, Nick and Sarah, and then Sarah leaves and John joins as her replacement, is it still the same group? What if Nick also leaves the group and is replaced by Catherine or by no one at all? If only one or no members at all remain, would we say that the reading group ceases to exist? Can the reading group's existence be extended into the past so that an order for new books that Nick and Sarah made when they were members bind the group as such, whose members are now Catherine and John? And can Catherine and John make a decision that will still be binding for the reading group of the future, regardless of whether they are still its members? These are questions that are in certain respects similar to those that we may ask about human beings, even though our intuitions in the case of corporate entities appear more complex. Contrary to what most of us would accept with respect to human beings, it is not a given that a book club can exist as an entity over and above its parts to begin with.

6.2   Two Ways of Thinking about the Problem of Corporate Existence

How should we think then of the problem of existence with respect to entities such as our modern Greek literature reading group? One way to navigate this labyrinth of a philosophical problem[8] is to go back to our

---

[8] For this problem from the perspective of social ontology, see eg Dave Elder-Vass, *The Causal Power of Social Structures: Emergence, Structure and Agency* (CUP 2010); Paul Sheehy, *The Reality of Social Groups* (Ashgate 2006); Hans Bernard Schmid, *Plural Action: Essays in Philosophy and Social Science* (Springer 2009); Tobias Hansson Wahlberg, 'Why the Social Sciences Are Irreducible' (2019) 196 Synthese 4961; Brian Epstein, *The Ant Trap: Rebuilding the Foundation of the Social Sciences* (OUP 2015). For approaches in terms of metaphysics, see eg Gabriel Uzquiano, 'Groups towards a Theory of Plural Embodiment' (2019) 115 The Journal of Philosophy 423; Katherine Ritchie, 'The Metaphysics of Social Groups' (2015) 10 Philosophical Compass 310, 316; Nick Effingham, 'The Metaphysics of Groups' (2010) 149 Philosophical Studies 251. For questions of agency and personhood in relation to groups, see eg Deborah P Tollefsen, *Groups as Agents* (Polity 2015); David Copp, 'What Collectives Are: Agency, Individualism and Legal Theory' (1984) 23 Dialogue 249; Christian List and Philip Pettit, *Group Agency: The Possibility, Design, and Status of Corporate Agents* (OUP 2011); Raimo Tuomela, *The Philosophy of Sociality: The Shared Point of View* (OUP 2007); Peter A French, *Collective and Corporate Responsibility* (Columbia University Press 1984); Margaret Gilbert, *On Social Facts* (PUP 1989); Rovane (n 7); Frank Hindriks, 'The Status Account of Corporate Agents' in Hans B Schmid, Katinka

overarching framework for approaching the problem of existence: questions of existence are meaningfully addressed when posed in a relative fashion, the key then being uncovering the underlying rationale for accepting why the building blocks of any entity are themselves not redundant in the first place. In other words, if the question regarding corporate existence is whether these entities are 'real' in relation to the individuals that make them up, then that question only makes sense if those individuals are thought of as real to begin with.

Indeed, philosophers grappling with the question of corporate existence generally admit the notion of individual existence but they accept it for different reasons. In turn, their rationale for endorsing the notion of individual existence influences the way in which they approach the problem of corporate entities. Given the diversity of approaches to the problem of individual existence, I group thinkers into two broad outlooks: those that consider individuals as naturally irreducible entities and those that do not.

The first group understands individuals as naturally occurring irreducible entities, whose ontological existence is taken as a given and is thus non-negotiable. To put it in terms of our previous analysis, every individual forms *by default* an opaque 'box' of their own, whose contents we need not delve into to resolve the puzzle of corporate existence. This means that these theories take individuals as the fundamental particles of our social ontology. They consider them as a priori unitary entities, existing in some deeper sense. The question then becomes whether a supra-individual entity can emerge out of the interrelation of these boxes, or, otherwise, how entities made up of such entities can count as individuals in their own regard. Throughout the rest of this book, I will call this first way of thinking about the problem as the 'individual vs organization' view of corporate existence because it axiomatically assumes the existence of individuals as irreducible points of reference.

The second view looks at the problem of corporate existence as not categorically different to that of individual existence. Whereas the 'individual vs organization' view looks at individuals as opaque boxes and non-negotiable ontological benchmarks, this view looks at the existence of individuals as something that also needs to be explained. As one commentator puts it: 'there is no *special problem* about collective actions

Schulte-Ostermann, and Nikos Psarros (eds), *Concepts of Sharedness: Essays on Collective Intentionality* (Ontos 2008) 119; Hans Kribbe, *Corporate Personality: A Theory of Political Association* (Doctoral dissertation, London School of Economics 2014).

which is not encountered in the analysis of individual actions and vice versa'.[9] According to this view, it is not as if individuals are empirically observable entities than collectives are abstractions: 'we cannot "see" persons any more that we can see groups: Both are realities that extend beyond the range of human perception. Both are abstractions from and summaries of our observations of more limited aspects of reality'.[10]

Affording no ontological benefit of doubt to individuals, this way of looking at the problem suggests that the same human faculty that can give rise to an individual can also create a group entity, the difference between the two being one of degree or scale rather than quality. According to this line of thought, the non-metaphysical 'glue' that holds an individual together, whatever that is, can also bring into existence a genuine group entity or at least one that is as genuinely real as the individual. For the remainder of this book, I will call this the 'organization vs organization' view of corporate existence, because by opening up the black box of the individual, it effectively treats it as a sort of miniature organization in itself.

In the following pages, I outline the basic contours of the 'individual vs organization' and the 'organization vs organization' viewpoints regarding corporate existence. At this point I should clarify that these two viewpoints represent a practical way of capturing broader strands of literature on corporate entities, not definite perspectives in which thinkers should be categorized on this deep and complex issue. Many writers exhibit

---

[9] Katinka Schulte-Ostermann, 'Agent Causation and Collective Agency' in Hans B Schmid, Katinka Schulte-Ostermann, and Nikos Psarros (eds), *Concepts of Sharedness: Essays on Collective Intentionality* (Ontos Verlag 2008) 205. See also Roger Scruton arguing that 'if you divide things finely enough, everything is composed of problematic parts', suggesting that the common objections facing the existence of corporate entities are, if anything, the same that arise with respect to individual human beings. Roger Scruton, 'Corporate Persons' (1989) 63 Proceedings of the Aristotelian Society: Supplementary Volumes 239, 252. Scruton in fact argued that in some respects, the existence of corporate entities was less problematic than that of individual human beings:

> [t]hose features which confer personality – the decision-making process, and the channels of accountability – also establish the identity of the institution. These are institutional facts, and also constitutive of the institution which displays them. The usual paradoxes of personal identity – which between the first and third-person perspectives, and a further tension (real or imagined) within the third-between the personal and animal natures of the embodied agent – do not and cannot arise.

[10] Charles K Warriner, 'Groups Are Real: A Reaffirmation' (1956) 21 American Sociological Review 549, 552.

variations in how they use terms such as 'person' or 'agent' or 'meta-physical', making it difficult to classify them neatly. Moreover, several authors are not always explicit about their own theoretical underpin-nings, featuring unspoken or uninterrogated assumptions.[11] Yet in its broad outline, the distinction should help map the main arguments sur-rounding this problem that are replicated across debates in different disciplines, including the one that international lawyers have been having with respect to international organizations. Ultimately, this book withholds judgement on which framework is best for looking at the problem of human beings in relation to corporate entities in the abstract. Instead, it explains what it means to understand the problem of international organ-izations in a system that already recognizes the corporate existence of states, rather than one where international organizations are to be com-pared to states that are considered equivalent to natural human beings.

6.3   Corporate (Non-)Existence within the 'Individual vs Organization' Framework

The 'individual vs organization' view proceeds from the assumption that individuals themselves are opaque and fixed building blocks from which corporate entities are to be theorized. A set of heterogeneous assumptions tend to lie behind this ontological reification of the individual. Most often these coalesce around two key notions: the idea that individuals are real because they enjoy some kind of spiritual or metaphysical existence,[12] and/or the idea that individuals are real because they enjoy an organic

---

[11] In that respect, one of the most popular approaches that has unclear theoretical underpin-nings is that of List and Pettit (n 8), who although seemingly opposed to the notion of a Cartesian Ego, 'retain a form of metaphysical and normative individualism on which human beings qualify as natural persons': Carol Rovane, 'Group Agency and Individualism' (2014) 74 Erkenntnis 1663. Another prominent account that can be seen as being somewhat unclear on these matters is Deborah Tollefsen's: '[a]ccording to the ontological individualist, groups are composed of individual human beings and do not exist as entities "over and above" these individuals. Most theorists agree with ontological individualism, and I am no exception. Groups are composed of individuals and they act via the actions of individuals. But this doesn't support the idea that groups don't exist': Tollefsen (n 8) 4.

[12] This idea can be traced back to the famous French philosopher of the 1600s, René Descartes. Descartes distinguished between two kinds of substance: 'mental' and 'corpor-eal' or physical substance. He seemed to ground personal identity on the subsisting identity of an underlying mental substance, an immaterial 'Ego' doing all the thinking rather than on the continuity of physical facts about a person's body or brain. Descartes thus seemed to believe that a *meta*-physical basis lay at the foundation of our existence, a

existence.[13] All such accounts of individuals' distinctiveness suggest that they are somehow more real or fundamental than corporate entities, and intrinsically so. The result of this construction is that individuals are 'natural' entities or persons and are thus to be distinguished from corporate entities that exist only on an 'artificial' basis, if at all.[14]

Once the individual is cemented as the elementary building block, most philosophers either reject the notion of corporate entities altogether[15] or concentrate their efforts on explaining how we may suitably interrelate through joint individual commitments and shared goals so as to give rise to the appearance of such entities, which remain nonentities in any deeper ontological sense.[16]

soul or *res cogitans*. Thus, according to the dualist approach, there is something special about the immaterial stuff that we are made of that makes us naturally and intrinsically capable of independent being. See generally René Descartes, *Meditations on First Philosophy* (John Cottingham tr, CUP 1996). For the distinction that Descartes drew between material and immaterial substance, see Edward Slowik, 'Descartes and Individual Corporeal Substance' (2001) 9 British Journal of the History of Philosophy 1; Marleen Rozemond, 'Real Distinction, Separability, and Corporeal Substance in Descartes' (2011) 35 Midwest Studies in Philosophy 240.

[13] See eg David Rönnegard, *The Fallacy of Corporate Moral Agency* (Springer 2015) 28, who criticizes accounts of corporate agency for not addressing the 'metaphysical' level of existence. This distinction between soulful individuals and soulless corporate entities may be traced back at least as far back as 1246 AD, when Pope Innocent IV argued that a corporate entity could not be condemned because it was lacking a soul, nor decapitated because it was lacking a body: Ernst Kantorowicz, *The King's Two Bodies: A Study in Medieval Political Theology* (PUP 1997) 306. One of the first recorded instances of the aphorism that 'corporations have no soul' is attributed to the English jurist Lord Edward Thurlow (1731–1806), who famously said that 'corporations have neither bodies to be punished, nor souls to be condemned' (usually quoted as 'Did you ever expect a corporation to have a conscience, when it has no soul to be damned, and no body to be kicked?'), reproduced in Susan Ratcliffe (ed), *Concise Oxford Dictionary of Quotations* (6th edn, OUP 2011) 379. For a discussion of the ideal of the soulless corporation in law, see Susanna M Kim, 'Characteristics of Soulless Persons: The Applicability of the Character Evidence Rule to Corporations' (2000) 3 University of Illinois Law Review 763.

[14] See eg List and Pettit (n 8) 178ff. For a discussion of the distinction between natural and artificial persons with respect to corporations, see John Dewey, 'The Historic Background of Corporate Legal Personality' (1926) 35 Yale Law Journal 655, 669.

[15] See eg Rönnegard (n 13); Manuel G Velasquez, 'Debunking Corporate Moral Responsibility' (2003) 13(4) Business Ethics Quarterly 531; Wahlberg (n 8) 4961; Gustav Ramström, 'The Analytical Micro–Macro Relationship in Social Science and Its Implications for the Individualism-Holism Debate' (2018) 48 Philosophy of the Social Sciences 474; Seumas Miller and Pekka Makela, 'The Collectivist Approach to Collective Moral Responsibility' (2005) 36 Metaphilosophy 634.

[16] For useful introductions in this respect, see David P Schweikard and Hans B Schmid, 'Collective Intentionality' in Edward N Zalta (ed), *The Stanford Encyclopedia of Philosophy* (2013) <https://plato.stanford.edu/archives/fall2019/entries/identity-per

This makes absolute sense from a philosophy-of-science perspective. Indeed, if one takes an entity to be the truly irreducible fundamental particle of our social ontology, then precisely because it is the *fundamental* building block, everything that refers to it can be potentially described in terms of *it* rather than of a higher-order entity.[17] In this regard, higher-order entities made out of such building blocks will never be 'real' entities over and above their members, *by definition*. If, for example, one axiomatically posits that the basic unit of society is the individual, then it should come as no surprise that everything that entails the behaviour of such individuals, from a reading group to society itself, will be analysable in terms of those individuals and therefore be nothing 'over and above' its members.

Rather than trying to postulate them as real entities, some philosophers working within the 'individual vs organization' frame have tried to show that corporate entities can actually function in a manner that is independent of their members, through the familiar argument of causal discontinuity between member and corporate intentions. However, in contrast to international lawyers, philosophers have essentially abandoned majority-voting-based tests for reasons very similar (in their abstract outline) to those identified in Chapter 3 of this book.[18] The most innovative approaches in this regard have drawn on the theory of judgement aggregation to argue that only a premised-based decision-making procedure could exhibit discontinuity between member and group intentions.[19] But at the end of the day, even the most complex of

---

sonal/> accessed 5 February 2025; David P Schweikard, 'Limiting Reductionism in the Theory of Collective Action' in Hans B Schmid, Katinka Schulte-Ostermann, and Nikos Psarros (eds), *Concepts of Sharedness: Essays on Collective Intentionality* (Ontos Verlag 2008). See also Kirk Ludwig, *From Individual to Plural Agency: Collective Action I* (OUP 2017); Tuomela (n 8).

[17] For an insightful analysis of the problem in this regard, see Ramström (n 15); Julie Zahle, 'The Individualism-Holism Debate on Intertheoretic Reduction and the Argument from Multiple Realization' (2003) 33 Philosophy of the Social Sciences 77. See also Rajeev Bhargava, *Individualism in Social Science: Forms and Limits of a Methodology* (OUP 1992).

[18] For the idea that adopting a majority voting decision-making procedure does not do away with the reductionist challenge surrounding corporate entities, see Ludwig (n 16) 281ff; Rovane (n 11) 1669.

[19] List and Pettit (n 8) 5, 70. For a discussion of the so-called judgment aggregation voting paradox outside of the context of group agency, see Kenneth J Arrow, *Social Choice and Individual Values* (2nd edn, John Wiley & Sons 1963); Lewis A Kornhauser and Lawrence G Sager, 'The One and the Many: Adjudication in Collegial Courts' (1993) 81 California Law Review 1.

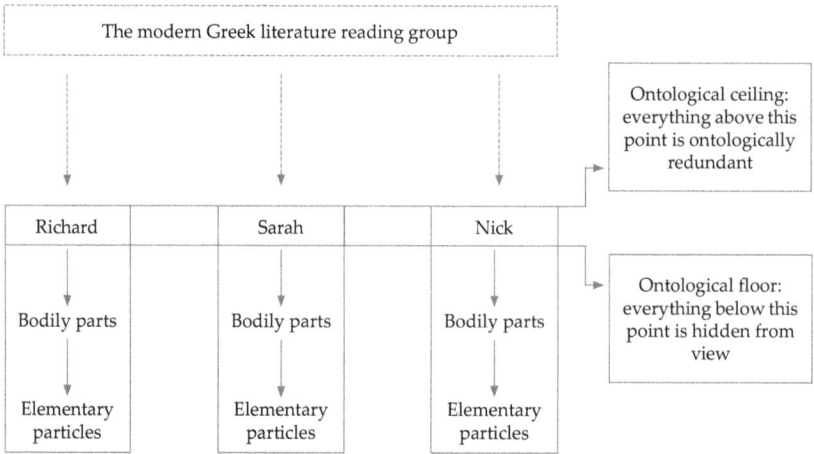

Figure 6.1 An example of the 'individual vs organization' framework for corporate existence

voting patterns do not necessitate the ontological supposition of a corporate entity. As David Rönnegard has put it:

> [A] voting procedure is similar to an algorithm. It is like programming a computer to run an algorithm (with votes as inputs) and then saying that the output is the autonomous choice of the computer. The fact that the procedural choice is discontinuous with member attitudes does not shift any agency ability or moral responsibility onto the procedure.[20]

Thus, according to this line of critique, there would seem to be no 'explanatory gap' that could have only been fulfilled by the postulation of a corporate entity.[21] The respective individuals can be thought of as having, at a certain point, accepted a decision-making procedure, and their intentions can again be analysed based on that decision-making procedure being in place.[22]

All in all, this discussion may give us a glimpse of how the problem of corporate entities is analysed from the 'individual vs organization' viewpoint (Figure 6.1). For most philosophers working with the starting assumption that individuals are themselves irreducible entities, the only

---

[20] Rönnegard (n 13) 54. See also Miller and Makela (n 15) 648–649; Leo Townsend, 'Being and Becoming in Group Agency' (2013) 7 Abstracta 39.
[21] Kurt L Sullivan, 'How to Be a Redundant Realist' (2012) 9 Episteme 271, 280.
[22] Ludwig (n 16) 281.

issue with corporate entities is explanatory, not ontological. It is to explain and analyse the types of relations *between individuals* that may account for the appearance of such entities in the social world. Individuals thus present the non-penetrable ontological floor from which these theories take off from; all reductionist inquiries stop at their level. They form ontological 'boxes' of their own, the system's respective 'billiard balls', making corporate entities by definition ontologically redundant. In turn, this means that individuals form not only the ontological base level but also the ceiling.

6.4 The 'Organization vs Organization' Framework for Corporate Existence

6.4.1 Why Should Individuals Be Thought of as Real in the First Place?

In Section 6.3, I discussed how, from a philosophy-of-science perspective, if one assumes an entity to be fundamental, then by definition all other entities that are made up by it will also be reducible to it. Under the best interpretation of this view, the role that corporate entities play in such a context is to summarize facts about individual beings and their inter-actions. Nevertheless, this conclusion becomes less certain when its key premise is questioned, that is when one asks why individuals should be thought of as non-reducible entities in the first place. In other words, what is the underlying rationale that makes us draw a line that hides from view what happens below the individual level?

Posing this question forms a basis for a series of critiques to the 'individual vs organization' framework. These critiques give rise to competing theories about corporate existence that do not themselves attribute the existence of corporate entities to any kind of metaphysical or organicist theory, as Otto von Gierke's theory arguably did (see Chapter 3), yet they do suggest that corporate entities may exist in a manner that is not reducible to their members. In a broad sense, they do so by arguing that the same rationale that can make individuals rise as entities above and beyond their parts can establish the non-redundant existence of corporate entities.

The 'organization vs organization' is a label behind which lies a vast, complicated, and heterogeneous set of literature. Once more, the purpose here is to illuminate an alternative way of thinking about the problem of corporate existence, not to claim that this is the definitive way of viewing things from an abstract philosophical standpoint. This different viewpoint will prove useful for contextualizing the discussion about international organizations that is to follow. The role of philosophy in this respect is to unveil a new pathway for reasoning our way out of the problem in its current configuration.

We have already discussed how one may think about the existence of any type of entity as a problem of inter-level relationships. The problem of existence then becomes whether one entity exists in relation to the lower-level entities that make it up. For example, in the case of the modern Greek literature-reading group, that would consist of the members of the group. The reductionist view would look at the reading group and see only the participating individuals. In this account, the group itself would just be a shorthand expression for these individuals and their relations. As social ontologist Dave Elder-Vass explains when critiquing this line of argument:

> All versions of this argument implicitly depend on the belief that it is possible to justify the claim for the causal effectiveness of entities at *some* levels of a multi-levelled structure, while rejecting that of entities at other levels. Reductionists, however, often fail to offer any positive argument to justify their belief in the causal effectiveness of the levels they favour. Without such an argument, of course, reductionism is logically incoherent. A coherent reductionism must not only *dismiss* arguments for the causal effectiveness of higher levels, but also *establish* some for the causal effectiveness of lower levels.[23]

In the case of corporate entities and human beings, the 'individual vs organization' view suggests that all the causal powers of the former should be attributed to the respective individuals. In turn, this assumes that individuals are somehow distinct from the lower-level entities that supposedly make them up. However, human beings themselves are composed of bodily parts and organs, which in turn are composed of cells, which in turn are composed of molecules, and so on.[24] If we are reductionist about corporate entities, then why not be reductionist about human beings and individuals as well? This argument suggests that there is no particular problem regarding corporate entities that does not arise when looking at individuals.[25]

---

[23] Elder-Vass (n 8) 55. See also Sheehy (n 8) 22.
[24] Elder-Vass (n 8) 55. See also Sheehy (n 8) 90–91; Epstein (n 8) 36–49; Parfit (n 7) 332; Scruton (n 9) 256.
[25] See eg Gregory S Kavka, 'Is Individual Choice Less Problematic Than Collective Choice?' (1991) 7 *Economics and Philosophy* 143; Schulte-Ostermann (n 9) 191.

The notion that there is such a problem with respect to 'artificial' entities to begin with, including corporate ones, often rests on a particular concept of agency known as the natural account of agency, echoing the Eleatic principle that was discussed in Chapter 5 (in short: 'to be is to be causally active'). The natural account of agency understands agency in terms of a causal pathway that leads to an action. According to this account, action should be understood in terms of intentionality, and intentionality is explained in terms of causation by the agent's mental state and life events, such as her beliefs and desires.[26]

Consider for instance the following example: George is thirsty, so he walks from his room to the kitchen and drinks a glass of water. In this simple scenario, we are inclined to describe George drinking the glass of water as *his* action on the ground that this action was caused by his bodily movements which in turn were caused by his intentions. So far so good, say critics of the natural account of agency. But then the following problem arises. George's intentions also presumably have a prior cause, in this case being thirsty. In turn, being thirsty also has a prior cause, and so on, leading us to question whether George himself has a causal influence in the world. In philosophy, this is known as the problem of the 'disappearing agent'.[27]

The problem of the disappearing agent results from the following observation. If agency can be fully explained in terms of the causality of an appropriate mental step, then the agent essentially vanishes from view, as a non-contributing factor to the course of events, since the mental state that led to the action would invariably also appear to have prior causes.[28] Thus, this critique goes, if we want to explain how a human being itself, and not some outside event, is the initiator of an action, we either have to let go of the axiom that every cause is caused by

---

[26] For the natural account of agency, see Markus Schlosser, 'Agency' in Edward N Zalta (ed), *The Stanford Encyclopedia of Philosophy* (2015) <https://plato.stanford.edu/entries/agency/> accessed 5 February 2025. See also Christine M Korsgaard, 'The Normative Constitution of Agency' in Manuel Vargas and Gideon Vaffe (eds), *Rational and Social Agency: The Philosophy of Michael Bratman* (OUP 2014) 190; Herline Pauer-Studer, 'A Constitutive Account of Group Agency' (2014) 79 Ekrenntnis 1623, 1629.

[27] See in general Schlosser (n 26). For this 'gap' between the agent and his action, see Michael E Bratman, 'Two Problems of Human Agency' in Michael E Bratman (ed), *Structures of Agency: Essays* (OUP 2007) 91; Schulte-Ostermann (n 9) 191; Olle Blomberg, 'Form Simple to Composite Agency: On Kirk Ludwig's *From Individual to Plural Agency*' (2019) 5 Journal of Social Ontology 101.

[28] As Korsgaard suggests, agency is supposed to indicate that the agent intersects herself in the causal chains of the world rather than being a locus of happenings. Korsgaard (n 26) 194.

another cause, or otherwise refine our understanding of what agency really amounts to.[29]

As many philosophers have argued, this problem cannot be solved by postulating a Cartesian immaterial substance or a 'soul' doing all the work.[30] There are two problems with such a Cartesian account. First, it ultimately rests upon a premise that has not been proven and cannot even be disproven, since it seems impossible to prove that such an immaterial substance does not exist.[31] Second, even if such a thing existed, it is difficult to conceptualize how it would connect to the physical world. As philosopher Deborah Tollefsen has put it, '[i]t is a bit like asking a ghost to open a door. Its "hand" would simply pass through the doorknob'.[32]

6.4.2   Going under the Problem: Individuals Too Are Organizations of a Certain Kind

6.4.2.1   The Idea *That* Individuals Themselves Are a Type of Organization

Even as we may accept that a putative 'ghost in the machine' cannot account for our existence as individuals that are causally separated from their environment, the problem remains. Rather than look for such a ghost, a rich philosophical tradition has sought to trace the emergence of individual existence in non-metaphysical sources. Contrary to anthropomorphic analogies for collective entities, this tradition has suggested that individuals themselves also form a kind of (mini-) organization. The difference between corporate and individual entities then becomes one of degree rather one of underlying metaphysical or even biological qualities: both are ways in which human beings can construct themselves, potentially as individuals and potentially as parts of collective entities.

---

[29] David J Velleman, 'What Happens When Someone Acts?' (1992) 101 Mind 461, 467. As Thomas Nagel sums up this problem: '[e]verything I do or that anyone else does is part of a larger course of events that no one does, but that happens, with or without explanation. Everything I do is part of something I don't do, because I am part of the world': Thomas Nagel, *The View from Nowhere* (OUP 1986) 114. One response to this problem may be to distinguish between causes that are 'external' and those that are 'internal' to the agent. Yet the internal/external distinction does not seem to alter the critique to the natural account of agency, given that the 'internal' seems to be subject to the same laws of causality as the 'external'.

[30] Descartes (n 12).

[31] Epstein (n 8) 18.

[32] Tollefsen (n 8) 67.

The idea that *we* are a type of organization is quite old. Famously, Plato sought to explain the unity of the individual by comparing it to the unity of the *polis*.[33] Modern thinkers, such as David Hume, would also compare the individual person with the notion of 'a republic or commonwealth'.[34] Hume's work thus conceived the individual in a disaggregated fashion that could survive changes in its bodily parts for the same reason that forms of political organization could also endure such changes without a shift in their identity. For him, the 'self' was itself a construction of imagination.[35]

Contemporary philosophy has also drawn inspiration from the analogy with corporate entities to illuminate the nature of individual identity. As Roger Scruton would suggest, for example, '[i]t is precisely by studying the case of corporate personality, that we see how to understand the human person. The human being . . . is "naturally" a person, only in that he acquires personality, in the circumstances which cause him to flourish'.[36] Personality then is not understood as a metaphysical preexisting trait but is rather 'gradually wrestled from the world'. In that setup, collective personality is representing just another branch of human development, not an inherently mysterious ontologically proposition.[37]

Present-day philosophers have further mined the analogy between corporate and individual existence in an effort to better understand both. Most prominently, Christine Korsgaard has linked the problems of the 'disappearing agent' to the puzzles surrounding individual and corporate existence. Her key insight is that while unity is possible both at the

---

[33] See Book II of *The Republic*. For a brief discussion, see Ioannis D Evrigenis, 'The Psychology of Politics: The City-Soul Analogy in Plato's *Republic*' (2002) 23 History of Political Thought 590.

[34] David Hume, *A Treatise of Human Nature* (Lewis A Selby-Bigge and Peter H Nidditch (eds), Clarendon Press (1978) 261.

[35] In his earlier work, Hume understood the whole problem of personal identity of human beings as being in principle the same as the one regarding 'plants, and animals, and ships, and houses'. As he explained, '[t]he identity, which we ascribe to the mind of man, is only a fictitious one, and of a like kind with that which we ascribe to vegetables and animal bodies. It cannot, therefore, have a different origin, but must proceed from a like operation of imagination upon like objects', Hume (n 34) 259. For the evolution of Hume's thinking on the matter and the enduring ambiguities of it, see Donald C Ainslie, 'Hume on Personal Identity' in Elizabeth S Radcliffe (ed), *A Companion to Hume* (Willey-Blackwell 2011) 147–156. See also Susan Mendus, 'Personal Identity: The Two Analogies in Hume' (1980) 30 The Philosophical Quarterly 118, 61.

[36] Scruton (n 9) 253.

[37] ibid.

individual and the collective levels, this unity is normative as much as it is analytical. As she writes:

> Why do you think of yourself as one person now? ... Just now you are reading this paper. You may also be sitting in a chair, tapping your foot, and feeling hot or tired or thirsty. But what makes it one person, who is doing and experiencing all this? You have loves, interests, ambitions, virtues, vices and plans. You are a conglomerate of parts, dispositions, activities, and experiences. As Hume says, you are a bundle. What makes you one person even at one time?[38]

As Korsgaard suggests, it is choosing between your conflicting desires rather than waiting to see which one wins that makes you a person instead of a mere bundle. According to her, your conception of yourself as a unified agent instead of a sum of other elements or a 'collection of pebbles' is based neither on some metaphysical quality nor on some externally definable analytical boundary. Korsgaard's fundamental observation is that *individuals themselves represent a type of organization*: human beings have the capacity to 'constitute ourselves' into persons, bringing together these outwardly disparate elements into unity.[39] Just as Hume compared the notion of the person to a 'republic or commonwealth' or Plato analogized an individual's existence to that of the *polis*, Korsgaard argues that the individual person should be understood similarly to the state:

> [a] better comparison [to the notion of the individual person] would be the state. ... A state ... is a moral or formal entity, defined by its constitution and deliberative procedures. A state is not merely a group of citizens living on a shared territory. We have a state only where these citizens have constituted themselves into a single agent. They have, that is, adopted a way of resolving conflicts, making decisions, interacting with other states, and planning together for an ongoing future.[40]

Following this rationale, a person is something that we (can) make of ourselves out of our disaggregated elements by organizing ourselves in a certain way – not something that is destined to happen and is naturally occurring or something that owes its presence to some immaterial substance.

---

[38] Korsgaard (n 6) 109–110.
[39] See generally Christine M Korsgaard, *Self-Constitution: Agency, Identity, and Integrity* (OUP 2009) 42–43.
[40] Korsgaard (n 6) 101, 114–115. See also Korsgaard (n 39) 133ff.

According to Korsgaard, this organization – literally bringing ourselves together as one – consists in adopting a deliberative standpoint.[41] By adopting the deliberative standpoint, we effectively describe the world to ourselves in certain terms, by adopting a certain point of view. We thus render certain causes into *reasons* that we can then weigh against each other.[42] As Korsgaard explains, from a third person perspective outside the deliberative point of view, it may seem as if the strongest of someone's conflicting desires wins when that person makes a choice. Still, she explains, this is not how 'it is for you when you deliberate. When you deliberate it is as if there were something over and above all your desires, something that is *you*, that *chooses* which desire to act on'.[43] Your reflective stance transforms, so to speak, what would otherwise seem as outside biddings into reasons before you can act upon them.[44] So, for example, from *my* deliberative standpoint, being thirsty is *a reason* to drink water, not a desire that causes me to do so.[45] In terms of our previous analysis, it is the deliberative standpoint that can help us distinguish which 'becauses' should be thought of as conveying

---

[41] In that sense, personhood is always a question of becoming, a matter of 'effort and will': Carol Rovane, 'Personal Identity, Ethical, Not Metaphysical' in Cynthia Macdonald and Graham Macdonald (eds), *McDowel and His Critics* (Blackwell Publishing 2006) 95–120.

[42] According to Korsgaard, this can be traced back to the self-reflective nature of the human mind. According to her, '[f]or our capacity to turn our attention onto our own mental activities is also a capacity to distance ourselves from them and to call them into question. . . . The reflective mind cannot settle for perception and desire, not just as such. It needs a *reason*. Otherwise, as long as it reflects, it cannot commit itself or go forward.' Christine M Korsgaard, *The Sources of Normativity* (CUP 1996) 93.

[43] ibid 100.

[44] ibid 94.

[45] As Korsgaard explains:

> [i]n fact, it is only from the practical point of view that actions and choices can be distinguished from mere 'behavior' determined by biological and psychological laws. This does not mean that our existence as agents is asserted as a further fact, or requires a separately existing entity that should be discernible from the theoretical point of view. It is rather that from the practical point of view our relationship to our actions and choices is essentially authorial: from it, we view them as our own (footnotes omitted). (Korsgaard (n 6) 120–121)

See also David Velleman who suggests that '[w]hat makes us agents rather than mere subjects of behavior – in our conception of ourselves, at least, if not in reality – is our perceived capacity to interpose ourselves into the course of events in such a way that the behavioural outcome is traceable directly to us': David J Velleman, 'What Happens When Someone Acts?' in David J Velleman (ed), *The Possibility of Practical Reason* (OUP 2000) 123, 128.

causal relations, and which not. In this regard, Korsgaard argues, agency should be understood as a normative and constructed concept rather than as a causal or natural one: it is to be analysed in terms of justification of action from a specific point of view rather than in terms of explanation or prediction of behaviour from the external point of an objective observer.[46]

Korsgaard's explanation of human agency on normative grounds suggests a deeper connection between individual and collective agency, or rather the absence of any fundamental discontinuity. In the final analysis, she suggests, both are varieties of the same phenomenon. If acting should be understood as acting for a reason, then the origin of the reason and the corresponding deliberative point of view gives us the identity of the agent. Having thus decoupled this deliberative standpoint from any metaphysical or naturalist grounding, Korsgaard suggests that there is no logic limiting agential unification within the conventional boundaries of a single human body. As she explains, 'there are agents of different sizes in the world. Whenever a group wants or needs to act as a unity, it must form itself into a sort of person'.[47] If that is the case, she argues, we do not need to posit a metaphysically mysterious entity to make sense of the notion of agency with respect to corporate entities that would make them non-eliminable in our eyes: it is still human beings doing all the work of thinking and deliberating, but they do it from the perspective of the group, not their individual standpoint.[48]

---

[46] Korsgaard (n 6) 101, 119–120. To the objection that 'the freedom we find in reflection is a delusion', Korsgaard replies:

> [i]t is from within the deliberative perspective that we see our desires as providing suggestions which we may take or leave. You will say that this means that our freedom is not 'real' only if you have deemed the 'real' as what can be identified by scientists looking at things third-personally and from outside. ... The Scientific World View is a description of the world which serves the purposes of explanation and prediction. When its concepts are applied correctly it tells us things that are true. But it is not a substitute for human life. And nothing in human life is more real than the fact we must make our decisions and choices 'under the idea of freedom'. (Korsgaard (n 42) 96–97)

In that sense, it could be argued that there is no natural or abstract hierarchy between the scientific and the first-person point of view: each responds to different needs and serves different purposes.

[47] Korsgaard (n 6) 114.

[48] ibid 114–115.

The idea that we cannot overcome the problem of the ontologically elusive individual without simultaneously accepting the possibility of corporate existence is also present in the work of another contemporary philosopher, Carol Rovane. Rovane too focuses on the notion that both individual and collective existence are constructed rather than natural entities. According to her, agency should not be understood in naturalistic terms but is itself an achievement, 'a product of effort and will'.[49] Inspired by John Locke's distinction between the human being as an animal and the human being as a person,[50] Rovane explains that a human being existing as a biological organism does not necessarily suffice for the existence of a person with agency. In other words, we are not born into the shoes of an individual agent; rather, we have the capacity of becoming one.

Expanding on Locke's notion of the person as a reflective being, Rovane suggests that human beings can become agents when they deliberate from a given point of view, that is, when they think about what the best course of action is instead of simply being moved by their desires.[51] When a human being thus becomes an agent, the result is that they see *reasons* on the basis of which one course of action is preferred over another, where others see only causes playing out their part. Agency, in other words, consists in a normative commitment on behalf of the human being to view the world from a certain deliberative point of view from which reasons take centre stage – nothing more, nothing less.

Again, this non-metaphysical and non-natural account of agency puts the problem of individual and corporate existence on the same pedestal, suggesting that, at the very least, there is no category distinction between the two. Instead, their common thread is the adoption of a specific deliberative point of view. As Rovane explains:

> There must always be reasons for embracing together the many considerations that constitute a single deliberative point of view. These reasons are given by unifying projects whose pursuit requires significant coordination of thought and effort within some boundary or other – whole human lives, or groups of them or parts of them. These different sorts of unifying projects would then give rise to agents of different sizes – agents of human size, or group agents comprising many human lives, or multiple agents within a single human life.[52]

---

[49] Carol Rovane, 'Is Group Agency a Social Phenomenon' (2017) 196 Synthese 4869, 4874.
[50] Locke (n 4) 225.
[51] For Rovane's discussion of Locke's criterion of personal identity, see Rovane (n 7) 3–19.
[52] Rovane (n 49) 4877.

Thus, Rovane suggests that the rational point of view need not be tied to a particular soul, animal, or phenomenological viewpoint. Our capacity to project ourselves into the future is the same one that allows us to pursue goals that are extended not only across time but also across space and beyond our bodily point of view. When the unifying rational point of view is wider than one single human being, this will lead to the creation of a collective agent. In short, both the temporarily extended agency of individuals and the possibility of collective agency would seem to rest on the same basic human capacity to plan and otherwise organize our lives.

Like Korsgaard, Rovane thus posits the possibility of collective agency, without making any metaphysical claim about the nature of group, or indeed individual, personality: all these deliberative viewpoints always reside within a human being's mind, and not within a collective Cartesian immaterial substance or a Gierkian super-mind. It is invariably the human being that thinks and acts, just not always from an individual point of view.[53] Consequently, the human being that is the carrier of these different rational points of view is not merely swapping masks or changing roles. According to Rovane:

> ... this would not aptly be characterized as 'role playing.' It would be better characterized as a fragmentation of the human being into relatively independent spheres of rational activity, so as to generate separate rational points of view that can be separately engaged. ... What is true is that a group person may initially be brought into existence through the individual decisions and actions of smaller persons, typically of human size. But if these initial efforts have been successful, then a group person will have been brought into existence.[54]

---

[53] This is even as bringing a collective agent into existence will typically occur through the individual decisions and actions of smaller persons, as Rovane suggests. Rovane (n 41) 95, 104. In many ways this part of Rovane's work draws inspiration, but also develops and pushes to new directions, Michael Bratman's work on planning agency. For Michael Bratman's engagement with Rovane's work, see *Michael E Bratman, Shared and Institutional Agency Toward a Planning Theory of Human Practical Organization* (OUP 2022) 142–155.

[54] ibid 95, 104–105. See also ibid 106, where Rovane suggests:

> I am certainly not arguing for the possibility of disembodied agency. Indeed, I have expressly assumed that the rational and practical capacities which are necessary for personal agency belong by nature to human beings. But it doesn't follow that the point of view from which a person deliberates and acts is the same thing as the bodily point of view from which an animal perceives and moves. For the point of view from which a person deliberates and acts is a rational point of view. And, for all the reasons I gave above, the

The point is that, ultimately, there is no fundamental discontinuity between individuals and groups. Ultimately, Rovane suggests that

> it is not nature, but intentional activity and undertaking of appropriate projects that transforms a human being into a human-size person. There is no law of nature that precludes a less ambitious transformation into multiple persons instead. To a certain, extent, this happens when human-size persons give over portions of their lives to group endeavors.[55]

Rovane's way of looking at the problem leads her to question the distinction between natural and artificial persons as illusory: '[A]ll agents, no matter what their size, are products of effort and will, and in that sense artificial.'[56] Both individuals and corporate entities rise into unity, and thus existence, through the operation of the same functions as human beings, none being more 'natural' or 'artificial' than the other.[57]

All in all, a strand in contemporary philosophy unties the notion of the individual from both naturalist and metaphysical explanations. Yet the emerging disaggregated picture does not lead these philosophers to conclude, like Epirchamus' debtor, that the individual does not survive from one moment to the next. At the end of the day, these scholars argue, with some variations, that individuals should not be contrasted to organizations; *we are* essentially organizations of a particular kind. Our own existence, as well as potentially that of corporate entities, is not buttressed by interjecting a metaphysical entity in the course of causal events; rather,

> boundaries of a rational point of view are not set by the boundaries of an animal's body, nor of its whole lifespan.

As Rovane further explains:

> [t]his is not to say that there is no sense at all in which separate, human-size points of view would be left intact. All of the human beings involved would still have separate centers of consciousness and, hence, separate *phenomenological* points of view. But it is important not to confuse a phenomenological point of view with the sort of point of view that each individual person has, by virtue of which it can be engaged in distinctively interpersonal relations. The latter is a *rational* point of view. (Carol Rovane, 'A Nonnaturalist Account of Personal Identity' in Mario De Caro and David MacArthur (eds), *Naturalism in Question* (HUP 2004) 243.)

[55] Rovane (n 54) 246.
[56] Rovane (n 49) 4896.
[57] See also Scott J Shapiro, *Legality* (Belknap Press 2011) 194, arguing, specifically with reference to law, that 'political government is continuous with the intimately familiar activities we understand so well. ... [F]ar from being an esoteric activity completely divorced from ordinary experience, the law is simply a sophisticated apparatus for planning in very complex, contentious, and arbitrary communal settings'.

it is arrived at by questioning the descriptive priority that should be accorded to the abstracted, 'scientific', point of view when addressing these questions. Ultimately, individual existence is not a barrier to corporate existence as the standard interpretation 'individual vs organization' framework would have us think; instead, it is an expression of the same logic at a different level of organization.

6.4.2.2   The Idea of a Rule of Re-description Lying at the Foundation of Corporate Existence

Before moving on, it is worth looking at a final account of corporate personhood, developed by Peter French. Contrary to the aforementioned philosophers who wrote primarily on the notions of agency and personal identity and then went on to explain how their accounts translated to corporate entities, French wrote directly with corporate entities in mind. He was specifically concerned with the question of whether corporate entities such as business corporations could be held morally responsible.[58] For this to be the case, French suggested that they would have to be considered 'moral persons', and for that they would at least need to be shown to be non-eliminable intentional actors. He reasoned that this could only be the case if intentions were attributed directly to the corporate entity rather than being attributed to its members.

In a way, French was grappling with many of the same problems that we have encountered so far. For him, the question of whether an action is intentional or not could not be meaningfully posed from an abstracted, third-person point of view. Intentionality, French suggested, cannot be exclusively determined by the action or event itself, but can vary depending on our description of it.[59] A single event can be an intentional action when described in a certain manner and unintentional when described in another: under one description, me drinking water is an intentional action, while under another description, it is just the product of a chain of causes that run through me without the need to posit any intentionality.

Faced with this conundrum, French argued that it is impossible to decide in the abstract which description was true or false. Rather the real question is which one should have priority in a given context. French

---

[58] French (n 8) 38. See also Peter A French, 'Crowds and Corporations' (1982) 19 American Philosophical Quarterly 271; Peter A French, 'The Corporation as a Moral Person' (1979) 16 American Philosophical Quarterly 207.

[59] Peter A French, 'Integrity, Intentions, and Corporations' (1996) 34 American Business Law Journal 141, 148–149, where he explains that intentionality should not be understood in causal terms.

theorized that different descriptions of the same event may be operating on different 'layers'.[60] On some layers, an event may be described as the effect of prior causes, on others it may be described as the effect of reasons. He suggested that events count as actions only if there exists a level at which they could be described as intentional.[61] As he then went on to explain: '[a]t every layer at which it is proper to describe an event as an intentional action, there is a ... person, an actor'.[62] According to French, for a corporate entity to be morally responsible, it need only be the case that some events are describable in a way that makes them intentional for it.

For that to happen, French argued that a corporate entity must feature what he called a 'Corporation's Internal Decision Structure'.[63] This broadly corresponds to Korsgaard's idea of 'adopting a deliberative standpoint'. For French, the corporate entity's internal decision structure provides the 'requisite redescription device that licenses the predication of corporate intentionality'.[64] What happens then is a 'descriptive transformation of events', a 'subordination and synthesis of the intentions and acts of various biological persons into a corporate decision'.[65] Accordingly, an internal decision structure transformatively 'incorporates acts of biological persons'.[66] The result is that actions, such as voting by a corporate entity's governing council, are re-described as the corporate entity's actions.[67] The ensuing picture is one where the corporate entity's decisions are dependent on human beings but they are not 'caused' by them in the counterfactual sense, because, in that scenario, the human beings are viewed as elements of the decision-making process rather than external forces.

But why should things be viewed from the corporate entity's perspective to begin with? Even if we accept that idea that there is no abstract hierarchy between different possible descriptions, this does not mean that we have established a *positive* reason for preferring the corporate entity's perspective from that of the respective individuals, or indeed from the abstracted 'scientific' point of view. Here we may distinguish between an analytical and a contextual reason for doing so. The first pertains to

---

[60] French (n 8) 40.
[61] French's argument in this regard was greatly influenced by Donald Davidson on the theory of action, especially his article 'Actions, Reasons, and Causes': see Donald Davidson 'Actions, Reasons, and Causes' (1963) 60 The Journal of Philosophy 685.
[62] French (n 8) 40.
[63] ibid 39.
[64] ibid.
[65] ibid 41.
[66] ibid 42.
[67] ibid 44.

reasons of internal coherence: if one accepts that the individual person emerges from the human capacity to self-describe rather than some metaphysical substance, then for reasons of consistency alone, one would have to accept the inherent power of this capacity to lead to a collective person, much in the same manner that Korsgaard or Rovane do.[68] The second reason for descriptive priority relates to context. This suggests that even though there may not be an abstract priority between different descriptions, there may well be a socially instituted one. In that sense, a 'rule of redescription' functions as a rule of recognition that puts in place a new level of description wherefrom the corporate entity itself can be seen as an intending and acting being.[69] Crucially, as Chapter 7 explains, this rule of re-description can itself be sourced in social facts – facts about what human beings do – rather than metaphysical notions, much in the same way that other types of social institutions operate.

French's construction of the corporate entity can be visualized as shown in Figure 6.2.

French's account concludes my exposition of the 'organization vs organization' viewpoint for looking at corporate existence. Although French was not much concerned with the distinction between natural and artificial persons, his account is still valuable for pulling together key conceptual threads of what has been discussed so far. These are that, first, a certain event can be described at more than one level. Second, actions can be intentional from one point of view and unintentional from another. Third, there is no inherent or abstract priority or hierarchy between these different descriptions; instead, there may be a socially instituted priority, whereby one level of description is given priority over

---

[68] Indeed, there appears to be empirical evidence to suggest that we are not born as fully developed, self-aware persons. Indeed, it appears that our sense of separation from our environment, including most prominently our caretakers, is a gradually developed rather than an in-built feature of our existence. See indicatively Ross A Thompson, 'The Development of the Person: Social Understanding, Relationships, Conscience, and Self' in Nancy Eisenberg and others (eds), *Handbook of Child Psychology: Volume 3 – Social, Emotional, and Personality Development* (6th edn, Wiley 2006) 24, 77–80.

[69] French (n 8) 52–53; HLA Hart, *The Concept of Law* (3rd edn, OUP 2012) 94. French further explained that his 'internal recognition rule' operates in a very similar manner to what HLA Hart referred to as a 'rule of recognition'. See Hart, ibid, 117. Similar to Hart, French argued that whether such a rule of recognition could perform its role was ultimately a question of social fact. Even though French's terminology of 'constitutive rules' echoes that of John Searle, there are arguably some differences in the way that these two scholars understood collective action: see Seumas Miller, 'Joint Action: The Individual Strikes Back' in Savas L Tsohatzidis (ed), *Intentional Acts and Institutional Facts: Essays on John Searle's Social Ontology* (Springer 2007) 89–90.

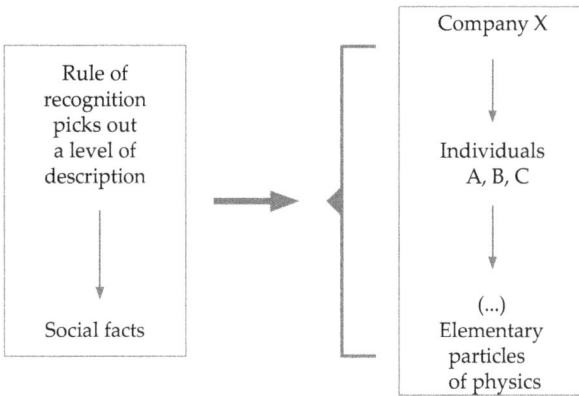

Figure 6.2 A reconstruction of French's account of corporate existence

another (saying that the company decided X instead of A, B, and C and voted for X), thanks to an accepted rule of recognition.

6.5 Conclusion

This chapter discussed how the problem of corporate existence in relation to individual human beings can be looked at within two broader frameworks of starting assumptions. The first assumes that individuals are themselves intrinsically irreducible entities thanks to some immaterial or natural predicate that they possess. The second argues that while individuals may indeed rise to be distinct entities from the lower-level entities that make them up, their unity and identity are not metaphysically or naturalistically given. Rather, individuals are themselves organizations of a certain kind. The two frameworks suggest diametrically opposed approaches to the problem of corporate existence. Following to the best interpretation of the first, the impossibility of genuine corporate entities seems unobjectionable: if one assumes an entity to be a fundamental ontological unit, then entities made up of that unit will always be describable in terms of that unit. In this case, the individual is, so to speak, the ontological floor and the ontological ceiling. According to the second, one cannot just assume that any entity is fundamental, including the individual human being. Instead, this viewpoint suggests we should interrogate our criterion for assuming that individuals themselves can be thought of as real and distinct entities to begin with.

Opening the 'black box' of the individual suggests an altogether different approach to the problem: the distinction between natural and artificial entities is seen as illusory. In its broad outline, this framework suggests that the same forces that can explain individual unity and identity through time can buttress the unity and identity of corporate entities. In this case again, the individual can be the ontological floor, but the foundations entail the possibility of more levels on top.

Institutional Genealogy as the Foundation for Theorizing International Organizations

7.1 Thinking about States as Corporate Entities

7.1.1 A Basic Ontological Account of the State as an Artificial Corporate Entity

So far, this book has suggested that we cannot properly theorize international organizations before ascribing to some theory about the entities that are supposed to make them up, including states. In this respect, much of current scholarship has tended to proceed with an image of the state akin to that of a 'natural' and, in any event, fundamentally irreducible entity. Wherever this premise has been adopted, explicitly or implicitly, it has led down to two problematic paths: international organizations are either merely artificial and 'mechanistic' entities or just as real and 'natural' as states are. By contrast, Chapter 4 suggested that theorizing international organizations should take place in an altogether different context, one where the state itself is conceptualized as a unitary, albeit artificial, corporate entity. Chapters 5 and 6 then outlined the problems surrounding corporate existence from a philosophical perspective. It is now time to unravel in more detail what all this means with regard to states, and eventually international organizations.

Most contemporary doctrinal explorations of statehood revolve around definitional concerns. Simply put, they are mainly preoccupied with figuring out what counts as a state for the purposes of international law. The assumption behind this exercise seems to be that international law features a general customary norm defining statehood. The latter is often associated with familiar criteria such as territory, population, government, or the capacity to enter into relations with other states.[1] Thus

---

[1] Rowan Nicholson, *Statehood and the State-Like in International Law* (OUP 2019) 101. The first three criteria are often attributed to Georg Jellinek: see Stefan Talmon, 'The Constitutive versus the Declaratory Theory of Recognition: *Tertium non datur?*' (2004) 75 BYIL 101, 109–110, discussing Georg Jellinek, *Allgemeine Staatslehre* (O Häring 1900)

defined, the state is often taken to be the non-negotiable, fundamental particle of our doctrinal universe. This outlook does not necessarily preclude the emergence of other entities, yet it makes these ultimately analysable in terms of what states are and do. Non-state entities are processed either as agents of states or as owing their legal personality to a norm created by states.

To understand why this methodological statism is ultimately misleading, we need to revisit how we approach the question of statehood as such. And, to do that, we need to distance ourselves from (perfectly legitimate for their own purposes) efforts to pin down the 'ordinary meaning' of the term 'state' that have dominated discourse.[2] Rather than trying to abstract what states look like once they have already been established, we should instead shift focus on *how* they are possible to begin with. Hence, the purpose here is to provide a bare-bones ontological exegesis of a state's emergence as a form of social organization. Doing so, this chapter seeks to develop a theoretical account from first principles and examine how this corresponds to contemporary practice.[3] The proposed ontological account of the state will then serve to unveil key continuities with the idea of international organization.

Asking the 'how' question about the state presents us with a genuine fork in the road, a juncture that requires the adoption of an analytical starting point. States can be construed either as naturally irreducible entities or as artificially constructed ones. While both these approaches have deep historical roots and varying degrees of explanatory appeal, this book will defend the second. Even as this stance does not present the kind of radical philosophical position that it might have in the past, it is

---

355–393. See also James Crawford, *The Creation of States in International Law* (2nd edn, OUP 2007) 45–95; Thomas D Grant, 'Defining Statehood: The Montevideo Convention and Its Discontents' (1999) 37 CJT L 403.

[2] My intention in shifting focus to the 'how' question is not meant to assess, or take anything away from, the historical context within which international lawyers became preoccupied with defining statehood in the first place. There is, after all, nothing paradoxical with different times calling for different questions. On the history of trying to objectively define statehood as a means of moving away from the standard of civilization and realizing the principle of non-intervention, see Arnulf Becker Lorca, *Mestizo International Law: A Global Intellectual History 1842–1933* (CUP 2015) 327–352. See also Hermann Kantorowicz, 'The Concept of the State' (1931) 35 *Economica* 1.

[3] Consequently, my aim is not to engage with, or rewrite international law's rich intellectual history. On the complex relationship between history, practice, and doctrine, see Anthony Carty, 'Doctrine versus State Practice' in Bardo Fassbender and Anne Peters (eds), *The Oxford Handbook of the History of International Law* (OUP 2012).

still worth explaining for the sake of analytical clarity. This is especially the case as, despite our seemingly more sophisticated contemporary philosophical understandings of the state in conventional terms, rough anthropomorphic analogies and 'billiard ball' conceptions of the state still find their way in our theory making on all sorts of issues.[4]

Why reject the state as a reality conceptualized along naturalist lines? Certainly, it is impossible to prove that any corporate entity, including the state, does *not* have a soul or a super-mind. But given that it is generally impossible to disprove a negative claim with evidence, the burden should lie on anyone making the claim that the state has a soul or a super-mind to prove it. Until then, a conventional understanding of the state remains by comparison the 'best explanation' of that entity's unitary status.[5] However helpful state anthropomorphism may be for pedagogical purposes, if it entails some sort of natural or soulful existence for the state, then it rests on unproved, and probably unprovable, theoretical assumptions. In other words, even if we assume that there is something natural and inherent about human beings emerging as unitary persons – a topic of intense philosophical discussion – there is arguably nothing natural or inherent about states being unitary persons. In the final analysis, the individual human being may or may not be like the state, as Hume or Plato suggested; what seems unobjectionable, however, is that the state is like the state. Unless otherwise shown, it is itself, if anything, an artificial, corporate entity.

A similar retort holds for the 'fiction' version of state anthropomorphism that understands the state only *as if* it had a soul or mind of its own. Granted, the purpose of a fiction is to admit as true legal propositions in conscious recognition that they are not true.[6] Therefore, these propositions actually not being true does not necessarily mitigate against the use of a fiction. However, the question remains: why accept, even as a legal fiction, that the state should be modelled following a particular philosophical take on the individual human being? While there is some explanatory value to be gained here, the assumption that there is a fiction at play to explain something that can be explained in non-fictional terms

---

[4] Text to n 28 in Chapter 4.

[5] Text to n 33 in Chapter 1.

[6] For this understanding of legal fiction, see Douglas Lind, 'The Pragmatic Value of Legal Fictions' in Maksymylian Del Mar and William Twining (eds), *Legal Fictions in Theory and Practice* (Springer 2015) 83, 100. See also *Blackstone's Law Dictionary*, according to which a legal fiction is 'believing or assuming that something not true is true' – *Blackstone's Law Dictionary Free Online Legal Dictionary* (2nd edn) <https://thelawdictionary.org/fiction/> accessed 5 February 2025.

seems analytically redundant. Following Occam's razor alone, the fiction theory should thus be viewed with scepticism.

Equally important, there is a hard limit to how far we can push the fiction theory without lapsing into logical error. If the state itself, and for that matter any kind of collectivity, rests on nothing but a legal fiction, then who is supposed to be the author of that fiction? If one agrees that the law is ultimately sourced in social facts as opposed to metaphysical or purely conceptual ideas, then a theory about how these social facts – meaning facts that escape the orbit of individual dispositions – give rise to the law and its associated institutions seems, in the final analysis, indispensable. This means that the fiction theory cannot settle the problem by itself.

Finally, as the next pages explain, the fiction version of state anthropomorphism along with the related 'billiard ball' metaphor are contradicted as analytical models by non-international-organizations-related practice from within international law. Despite some enticing simplifications that these models may offer, a host of examples suggest that the state is *not* treated by international law as an inherently irreducible entity for all intents and purposes. Most importantly, practice shows that the state may fragment itself through decentralization while maintaining its legal personality. Hence, the state can indeed be conceptualized as closed off and unitary, but only *under certain circumstances*, and not inherently so. Instead, there is a much deeper logic behind the state's construction, both without and within international law, a logic that suggests that there is nothing elementary or monolithic about it.

The following pages uncover this logic and show how it can buttress the emergence of not only states but also international organizations. Zeroing in on the 'how' question regarding the emergence of states as unitary actors, this section argues that the state itself should be construed as an artificial entity. This competing picture traces the ontological, and eventually the analytical, possibility of the state's emergence to two foundational elements: (1) a rule or rules, explicit or implicit, for the transformative description of events; (2) some sort of social convention or acceptance within a community such that the aforementioned rule can be considered to enjoy the status of a social fact.

7.1.2   Descriptive Transformation of Events as the Ontological Foundation of Statehood

Perhaps the most famous aphorism regarding states' existence in international law belongs to James Crawford: '[a] State is not a fact in the sense that a chair is a fact; it is a fact in the sense in which it may be said a treaty is a fact: that is, a legal status attaching to a certain state of affairs by virtue of certain rules or practices'.[7] Leaving for a moment to the side the epithet *legal*, the idea seems premised on a separation between certain things that just exist as such in the physical world and things that can only exist once some status is ascribed to them.

This proposition can be deceptive. It may create the impression that certain entities can somehow emerge in the world in a manner independent of our descriptions.[8] This notion is equally dubious for states as it is for chairs, for neither enjoys an existence that is mind-independent. Indeed, if all creatures with minds were to somehow disappear from existence, there would no longer be states to speak of, but also chairs. All these things would no longer exist, not in the sense that the physical reality that we presently associate with them would cease to exist, but in the sense that the descriptive carve-out that we engage in when employing notions such as 'chair' would now be absent from the world. In other words, while some entities may have seemingly more or less remote connections to so-called physical reality, or even no connection whatsoever, they are all in need of a description before they can be viewed as such. In turn, this need of a description makes them equally mind-dependent at a fundamental level.[9]

Contemporary social ontology often articulates this kind of status-ascribing descriptions in term of 'X counts as Y' propositions, where 'X' denotes the entity to which the status is assigned and 'Y' the status thus assigned. For example: *this piece of paper counts as money*. Such descriptions may be entirely abstract or context-dependent: 'this piece of paper counts as money' versus 'this piece of paper counts as money *in the US*', or 'these pieces of wood count as a chair' versus 'these pieces of wood count as a chair *for the purposes of the International Convention on the*

---

[7] Crawford (n 1) 5.

[8] This does not suggest that these descriptions are somehow inherently arbitrary and thus not worth investigating. As we saw in Chapter 5, many philosophers have been preoccupied with discovering the 'true' nature of things. But this is different than saying that our descriptions of things, whether more or less meaningful, would somehow exist in a manner independent of our cognitive capacities.

[9] See also John Searle's suggestion that 'we need to show the continuous line that goes from molecules and mountains to screwdrivers, levers, and beautiful sunsets, and then to legislatures, money, and nation-states. The central span on the bridge from physics to society is collective intentionality'. John R Searle, *The Construction of Social Reality* (Penguin 1996) 41.

Harmonized Commodity Description and Coding System.[10] Corporate entities too, including states, cannot exist apart from such status-ascriptions. Indeed, from a pure naturalist perspective, 'there are no activities of the state which can be called "its own"'.[11] Instead, the state relies on rules describing reality in a certain way,[12] giving rise to status-ascriptions such as 'human being X counts as the head of state', without which the state literally cannot act.

Social reality can appear immensely complex when viewed in terms of 'X counts as Y' propositions. In practice, however, human communities tend to entrust whole sectors of status-ascriptions to particular subsets of human beings. Thus, for example, Greece's constitution provides that any legislation voted by a majority in Parliament counts as law, as well as who counts as an MP, and so on. In other words, an institutionalized way of generating status-ascriptions has been put in place that may set increasingly context-specific statuses and status-ascription conditions. Facts covered by such status-ascriptions can be called 'institutional' because they can only make sense given the existence of the human institutions in question.[13] For example, being a Greek citizen only makes sense in the context of an institutionalized setting: the relevant laws that define and confer nationality, the authorities entrusted with making such laws, and so on.

---

[10] See International Convention on the Harmonized Commodity Description and Coding System (adopted 14 June 1983, entered into force 1 January 1988) 1503 UNTS 167, annex: Harmonized System Nomenclature, codes 9401.10–9401.90, 9402.10. I owe this observation to Nicholson (n 1) 20–21. The formulation of 'X counts as Y' was famously put forward by Searle (n 9), 43–51, and updated in John R Searle, *Making the Social World: The Structure of Human Civilization* (OUP 2010) 100–102; see also Brian Epstein, *The Ant Trap: Rebuilding the Foundation of the Social Sciences* (OUP 2015) 50–60. This basic formulation could be interpreted to suggest that at the bottom of all social structures lie presumably non-social, purely physical entities. While I do not see why even these supposedly purely physical entities could themselves be anything but equally dependent on description by human beings, I will bypass such issues as they are not essential to the analysis that follows. Generally, see Francesco Guela, 'The Philosophy of Social Science: Metaphysical and Empirical' (2007) 2(6) Philosophy Compass 954, at 961–962.

[11] ILC, 'Third Report on State Responsibility, by Mr. Roberto Ago, Special Rapporteur, the Internationally Wrongful Act of the State, Source of International Responsibility' (1971) UN Doc A/CN.4/246 and Add.1–3) 199, 218, para 58, fn 78.

[12] Searle describes these as constitutive rules: Searle (n 9) 43. David Hume would describe similar phenomena in terms of conventions: see the analysis of Hume's work in Epstein (n 10) 53–55. The analysis that follows does not hinge on adopting one term as opposed to the other.

[13] John R Searle, 'What Is an Institution?' (2005) 1(1) Journal of Institutional Economics 1, 3.

Still, regardless of how complex this system may develop to be, it can always be traced back to more elementary descriptions, such as 'X counts as the constitution of Greece'. The idea here is not that we can source the emergence of a state or the validity of its laws back to a hypothetical fundamental norm in the way that Hans Kelsen suggested.[14] Rather, it is to appreciate how, at the most basic level of the state's existence, lies the *capacity to assign status*, in the sense of crafting and maintaining the descriptive priority of certain versions of events over others as part of social reality (making it the case, for example, that a document counts as a constitution as opposed to another piece of paper).

This capacity may well develop in a nested fashion.[15] When this happens, a fundamental proposition of 'X counts as Y' contemplates the power of Y to further assign statuses by virtue of its institutional role that may then do the same with Z and so on. For example, a constitution may create a parliament that may then create a consumer protection authority that then may pass its own regulations as to what counts as deceptive advertising, and so on.[16] Beginning from the basic level of 'X counts as Y', each anterior step then structurally supports the next steps of the sequence, with no apparent inherent upper analytical limit as to the branching out of this process.

To conclude, in whatever terms states may be abstracted after they have been set up, they can only owe their continued existence to describing certain aspects of physical reality in corresponding institutional terms. From this perspective, what is elementary and non-eliminable is not the ideal-type 'state', but rather the capacity to read this institution into the world. Crucially, this capacity may develop in a nested manner, in practice often branching out in a highly sophisticated and structured series of descriptive transformations.

---

[14] Hans Kelsen, *General Theory of Law and State* (HUP 1945) 110–111.

[15] My inspiration for the nesting metaphor comes from Michael E Bratman, 'Planning and Its Function in Our Lives' (2024) 41(1) Journal of Applied Philosophy 1. See also Scott J Shapiro, *Legality* (Belknap Press 2011) 121–122, drawing from Bratman's earlier work to describe the nested nature of plans, which for Shapiro form a basis for theorizing law as such. Bratman's work on planning, in particular, *Michael E Bratman, Intentions, Plans, and Practical Reason* (CUP 1999) has also had a major influence in first developing core ideas of my account. This includes, most importantly Bratman's connection between diachronic individual agency and shared agency. See also *Michael E Bratman, Shared and Institutional Agency Toward a Planning Theory of Human Practical Organization* (OUP 2022). The nesting metaphor has also been employed by Spyros Blavoukos and Dimitris Bourantonis, 'Nested Institutions' in Rafael Biermann and Joachim A Koops (eds), *Palgrave Handbook of Inter-Organizational Relations in World Politics* (Palgrave Macmillan 2016) to describe inter-organizational relations.

[16] Similarly, Searle, 'What Is an Institution?' (n 13) 16–17.

7.1.3   The Need for a Social Convention Supporting the
Descriptive Transformation of Events

Theorizing the state as an artificial entity means that at the very root of this chain of descriptive transformations lie social facts regarding a community of actual people interacting in certain ways rather than metaphysical or naturalistic notions. Sourcing the state in social reality also signifies that its existence rests on more than mere analytical postulate: it is neither just 'turtles all the way down' nor an endless self-referential loop.[17] Rather, from an ontological point of view, this capacity for status-ascription must be shown to correspond to social facts, meaning facts about how certain human beings relate to each other and the wider world, in the very elementary way in which conferring status to any sort of entity generally operates at a social level through social convention.

This idea encapsulates two basic elements. The first refers to the human beings whose behaviour anchors the existence of a particular status. This goes back to the mind-dependent nature of social facts and the notion that, were all human beings to disappear, there would no longer be states to speak of, or chairs (again, in the sense of their conceptualization as objects that are distinct from the rest of the physical world), and so on. The second element pertains to the way in which facts about these human beings have to interrelate so as lead to the emergence of these social facts.

There are numerous theories as to how transformative re-description actually operates in that regard. Social ontologist John Searle, for example, traced its emergence to 'individuals directly involved and a sufficient number of members of the relevant community' who must 'recognize and accept the existence of such facts'.[18] The question in that sense has also been posed by legal theorists. HLA Hart, for instance, referred to the 'rule of recognition' that establishes the conditions under which legal prescriptions may become valid. Famously, Hart gave a sociological rather than a normative account of what puts this rule in place, itself not too dissimilar from Searle's.[19] He argued that the system's 'officials', meaning legal practitioners such as judges and lawyers, need to hold a convergent set of practices conforming to the rule of recognition. Crucially, they also need

---

[17] Cf Nicholson (n 1) 105.
[18] Searle (n 9) 117.
[19] See Josep M Vilajosana, 'Social Facts and Law: Why the Rule of Recognition Is a Convention' in Lorena Ramírez-Ludeña and Josep M Vilajosana (eds), *Legal Conventionalism* (Springer 2019) 89–107. For the idea of 'governance as an expression of human sociality', see Liesbet Hooghe, Tobias Lenz, and Gary Marks, *A Theory of International Organization* (OUP 2019) 19.

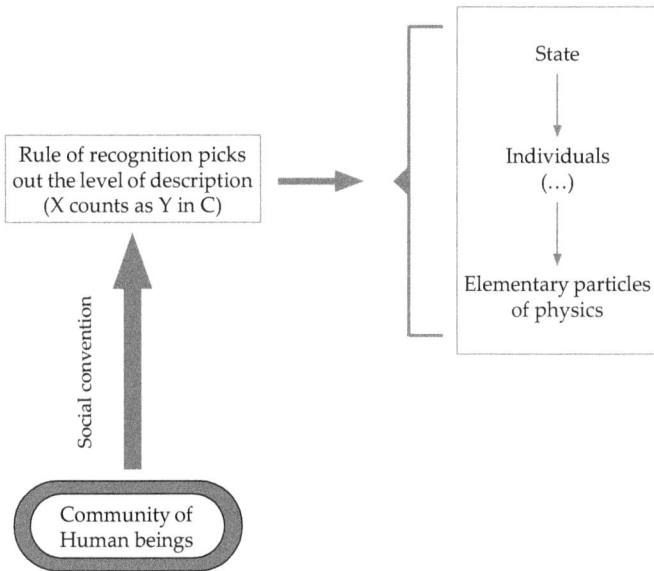

Figure 7.1   A basic ontological account of the state as an artificial entity

to exhibit a practical attitude of rule acceptance, whereby they guide and evaluate conduct in accordance with those rules. Apart from legal officials, ordinary citizens need to manifest their acceptance, in practice evidenced largely by acquiescence in the outcomes of these activities.[20]

While neither Searle's nor Hart's accounts have been left unquestioned,[21] the key here is to grasp the immanent conceptual structure that emerges regardless of individual variations: to the extent that it corresponds to a social reality, a state can only meaningfully exist on the basis of (1) human beings (2) accepting through convention or other means (3) a descriptive transformation of events (Figure 7.1).

This broad account radically departs from how we tend to imagine the state as international lawyers. It puts front and centre a status-generative *relationship* rather than an abstractly defined and hermetically sealed elementary particle. The following pages show how, properly construed, basic

---

[20] HLA Hart, *The Concept of Law* (3rd edn, OUP 2012) 56–65, 100.

[21] For a critique of Searle, see Hans Bernhard Schmid, *Plural Action: Essays in Philosophy and Social Science* (Springer 2009); Leo A Zaibert, 'Collective Intentions and Collective Intentionality' in David Koepsell and Laurence S Moss (eds), *John Searle's Ideas about Social Reality: Extensions, Criticisms and Reconstructions* (Wiley-Blackwell 2003). For another sociological account of the origins of the rule of recognition that is critical of Hart, see Shapiro (n 15) 79–119.

notions of international law correspond to this alternative approach to statehood that is relational rather than atomistic. This relational account will not dislodge the state as a unitary actor but instead explain why international law can inherently admit any and all other actors that emanate from that same relation, including international organizations.

7.2   Theorizing the State for the Purposes of International Law

7.2.1   A Transformative Description of Events Accepted through Convention or Other Means

Re-imagining statehood as a relationship puts front and centre of our legal ontology a descriptive transformation of events that is rooted in social facts. This is a purposive self-description in institutional terms that may then fire off a chain of nested status-ascriptions that encompass the state's apparatus, and potentially other institutions as well.

International law's relationship to this descriptive transformation can be construed in two ways. First, international law can be thought to register directly what happens at the state level.[22] In this scenario, international law does not produce its own descriptions of states' institutional reality but rather relies on those descriptions provided by those states and their adjacent institutions by assigning descriptive priority to them. Alternatively, international law does not register directly a state's own sanctioned descriptions of its institutional reality but instead relies on other actors' acceptance of these descriptions. This would happen most importantly through the notion of recognition, which would, in that case, rightly be called 'constitutive'.[23] Both ways of configuring international law's relationship to the emergence of a state are viable from an analytical perspective, and, as we shall examine in the following pages, both entail the possibility of international organizations by default. Nevertheless, the first one seems to correspond better to current doctrine and practice in relation to statehood itself.[24] It is thus worth explicating in greater detail what it means.

The key notion that I will be employing in this respect is that of a *renvoi*.[25] Better known as a concept of private international law, a renvoi

---

[22]   Cf Nicholson (n 1) 21, arguing that international law 'constructs' all facts with which it deals.

[23]   See generally Crawford (n 1) 37ff; Nicholson (n 1) 113ff.

[24]   Crawford (n 1) 28.

[25]   Similarly, see Jean-Pierre Rougeaux, 'Les renvois du droit international au droit interne' (1977) 81(1) RGDIP 361; Luc Van den Brande, 'The International Legal Position of

originally refers to the doctrine whereby the courts of one state may come to apply the laws of another state in cases involving some international element.[26] The more abstract idea that is relevant here is the notion that a legal system can refer to, and incorporate, elements of another system, while remaining analytically separate from it. This creates a subtle form of dependence between legal norms, whereby they both exist independently from one another, but one only becomes relevant within a given system because the other refers to it.

A good example of this is the relationship between domestic nationality laws and international legal norms on diplomatic protection. Domestic nationality laws are relevant in this respect only because international law refers to them, and in that sense, they are brought within the system of international law.[27] However, this does not mean that domestic nationality laws are formally 'part' of international law, at least not in the same sense that norms of international law are generally thought to be. Thus, a change in domestic nationality law does not signify any change in terms of international legal norms, precisely because these are understood to belong to different legal systems. Accordingly, if the UK changes its domestic law conditions for granting nationality, this does not mean that customary international law on diplomatic protection has changed. Rather, it means that its application will now be different where the UK is concerned. Of course, international law may develop specific norms that restrict the state's freedom to regulate its own nationality.[28] The point is that this will require a separate norm of international law, *a change* in the legal system that departs from the default renvoi rule.

The example of nationality can help illuminate how international law constructs the very existence of the state as a unitary actor. International law relies on what are essentially outside sources, meaning descriptive

Flanders: Some Considerations' in Karel Wellens (ed), *International Law: Theory and Practice: Essays in Honour of Eric Suy* (Martinus Nijhoff 1998) 151.

[26] Michael Sonnentag, 'Renvoi' in Jürgen Basedow and others (eds), *Encyclopedia of Private International Law* (Edward Elgar 2017) 1538; Jean-Pierre Rougeaux defines renvoi in the following terms: '[d'] une manière générale, le terme "renvoi" peut être défini comme une technique par lequel un ordre juridique declare applicable, pur régler une question dont la solution lui incombe, une norme d'un autre ordre juridique et non l'une de ses normes', Rougeaux (n 25) 362.

[27] Nicholson (n 1) 24.

[28] ILC, 'Draft Articles on Diplomatic Protection' (2006) II/2 YILC 24, art 4; Olivier Dörr, 'Nationality', *Max Planck Encyclopedia of Public International Law* (2019) <https://opil .ouplaw.com/display/10.1093/law:epil/9780199231690/law-9780199231690-e852> accessed 9 February 2025.

statements of the type 'X counts as Y', not only for nationality but also for who counts as an organ of the state, including its representatives at the international level. Thus, for example, article 7 of the VCLT 1969 (reflecting customary international law)[29] provides that a person is considered as representing a state if 'he produces appropriate full powers' or 'it appears from the practice of the States concerned or from other circumstances that their intention was to consider that person as representing the State for such purposes and to dispense with full powers'.[30] Similarly, article 7 does not create the office of or otherwise directly confer authority to a head of state, head of government, or minister of foreign affairs. Instead, it only establishes a rule that no evidence of authority is required for these officials, essentially through a renvoi.[31]

It is by a similar renvoi that state organs are defined for the purposes of international responsibility. For example, article 2 of the ASR explains that '[a]n organ includes any person or entity which has that status in accordance with the internal law of the State'.[32] The deference to state-sanctioned descriptions is further exemplified by article 11, which provides that mere acknowledgement and adoption of a certain conduct by a state as its own suffices for it to be considered as such in international law.[33] Again, as with nationality, there might be instances where international law develops rules limiting its reliance on states' self-description – the notion of de facto organs is one such notable case.[34] But this does not change the underlying principle, which is that international law does, as a default rule,

---

[29] Mark E Villiger, *Commentary on the 1969 Vienna Convention on the Law of Treaties* (Brill–Nijhoff, 2008) 146.

[30] Vienna Convention on the Law of Treaties (adopted 23 May 1969, entered into force 27 January 1980) 1155 UNTS 331, art 7.

[31] As Paul Reuter suggests: '[l]e droit international fait renvoi au droit interne pour l' aménagement pratique des compétences nécessaires à la conclusion des accords internationaux': Paul Reuter, *Droit international public* (4th edn, Presses universitaires des France 1973) 82.

[32] See ILC, 'Draft Articles on Responsibility of States for Internationally Wrongful Acts, with Commentaries' (2001) II/2 YILC 31, 40, para 2. This does not mean that formal recognition by internal law of an organ will always be necessary. As the commentary to art 4 explains, '[i]n some systems the status and functions of various entities are determined not only by law but also by practice, and reference exclusively to internal law would be misleading'. Note that the question of who is an organ of a state is different from the question of whose conduct is attributable to that state. International law does not determine who is an organ of the state, even if it may attribute to the state the conduct of some entities that are not its organs. See also the practice regarding the freedom of states to change their names: Crawford (n 1) 680 fn 54.

[33] Crawford (n 1) 52.

[34] ibid 47.

defer to self-descriptions of institutional facts as far as the state is concerned.[35] This is so much so that entities that arguably meet the classic criteria of statehood are not considered states insofar as they do not claim to be.[36]

A similar rationale prevails with the second element of our basic ontological scheme, namely the relationship between self-descriptions and their societal basis. We already saw how this relationship has been theorized by lawyers and non-lawyers alike through notions such as 'acceptance' or 'convention'. In this respect, international law appears to be relatively agnostic, caring more about whether these social facts exist rather than how they are put into place. When it comes to states, this can be exemplified by the notion of 'statehood as effectiveness'.[37] This also corresponds to the widely accepted notion that the continuity of the state is not challenged by changes in its government, regardless of whether these are 'constitutional' or not.[38] Once again, this is only a default rule that can be subject to exceptions whereby international law may withhold deferral to self-descriptions of certain social facts for particular reasons.[39] Still, it showcases how an entity that may initially seem opaque is itself the product of a complex interaction between different moving parts. While what happens with the creation of states could be described in terms of fulfilling the elements of an abstract definition, the 'how' of it must be boiled down to international law taking

---

[35] In that sense indeed, domestic law can be said to consist in 'merely facts which express the will and constitute the activities of States' *Case Concerning Certain German Interests in Polish Upper Silesia* (Merits) (Judgment) [1926] PCIJ Rep Series A No 7, 19. See also *Prosecutor v Tihomir Blaskic* (Judgment on the Request of the Republic of Croatia for Review of the Decision of Trial Chamber II of 18 July 1997) IT-95-14-AR (26 October 1997) para 41 ('[i]t is well known that customary international law ... leaves it to each sovereign State to determine its internal structure and in particular to designate the individuals acting as State agents or organs').

[36] Taiwan is often mentioned as one such example. See Yaël Ronen, 'Entities That Can Be States but Do Not Claim to Be' in Duncan French (ed), *Statehood and Self-Determination: Reconciling Tradition and Modernity in International Law* (CUP 2013) 23.

[37] Crawford (n 1) 37ff (on effectiveness), 150 (questioning whether democracy forms a continuing condition for statehood); Nicholson (n 1) 93ff.

[38] Crawford (n 1) 680.

[39] ibid 97ff; see also *Accordance with International Law of the Unilateral Declaration of Independence in Respect of Kosovo* (Advisory Opinion) [2010] ICJ Rep 403, 437. The most notable examples ordinarily mentioned in that regard, namely the creation of a state following an unlawful use of force or the imposition of a blatantly racist minority regime such as that of Southern Rhodesia, could also be understood as being applications rather than exceptions to the principle developed here, since in these situations the very claim of corresponding to social facts concerning the communities in question can be disputed.

note of this descriptive transformation of events that is sufficiently rooted in social reality. States themselves are intricate non-monolithic entities of an organizational nature *even for the purposes of international law.*

This descriptive transformation constructs the state by incorporating what might otherwise seem as 'outside' causal forces, which it registers as 'internal' workings of the state. From this perspective, it becomes apparent that, even from inside the system of international law, the presumption of the state's unity and agency is sourced neither in its scientifically observable causal effectiveness nor in metaphysics. Rather, the reality of the state is indeed fully and irreducibly 'a *normative* operation'.[40] International law's criterion of individuating states is *not* natural causal powers. Instead, the respective causal powers are recognized in international law only *after* the state has been circumscribed from other entities. Therefore, what matters is not whether there is a causal link between the state and an act but whether this act is connected to the state in a particular way so as to count as its own. In other words, the 'reality' of the state rests on neither naturalistic or metaphysical notions – or somehow on the fiction thereof – but on international law recognizing legal effect to a series of relationships that bind the state together as one by assigning priority to a given description of reality over others.

Crucially, this priority should be understood to refer by default to the state's own descriptions of its institutional reality. In practical terms, this means that the state already has a rule of re-description in place that anchors propositions such as 'X counts as head of state'. International law recognizes the corporate unity of the state by giving effect to propositions such as this one. Therefore, when a head of state signs a treaty, international law does not process this event as the head of state *causing* the state to consent to a treaty; rather, from the perspective of international law, the head of state's signature *counts as* the state's acceptance. There is certainly a dependence relationship between these two events: without the head of state moving her hand, the state cannot sign. However, in the eyes of international law, this relationship is understood as an 'internal', or an 'in virtue of' form of dependence rather than a causal one.[41] Similarly, when a state's government is replaced, international law does not consider that the state has changed, as the

---

[40] Emphasis added. ILC, 'Draft Articles on Responsibility of States' (n 32) 35, para 6 (art 2 and commentary thereto).
[41] See text to n 18 in Chapter 5.

relationship that occurs between the state and any given individuals acting as its officials is not considered to be one of identity.

7.2.2   An Element of Community

Systems of re-description and social convention are not free-floating entities: they have an ontological conditioning that involves actual human beings and cannot meaningfully exist apart from them. Any group of human beings that is capable of creating such institutions owing to some convention or practice, I will refer to as a 'community'. Employing this term, I am not aspiring to define this notion in anthropological or abstract political terms. Rather I am employing it as a placeholder for the idea that there is an irreducibly social element to the creation of institutions.[42] Typically, this community will be seen and interacted with through the institutions it creates. In practice, the most certain evidence that it exists will be the fact that it has been active in setting up such institutions. Still, we should not lose sight of the fact that, at a basic ontological level, the underlying community of human beings enjoys a separate existence from its institutions.[43]

---

[42] Cf the notion that a state must possess a 'permanent population' which forms part of the classic criteria for defining statehood. See Crawford (n 1) 52–55. This notion is not necessarily synonymous to the notion of a 'community' that I am employing here but it does allow for the same inclusive sensibility; as Arnulf Becker Lorca in this respect, the notion of a permanent population represented a move away from substantive criteria, such as the race, religion, or culture of the population, which were often used as a means of restricting claims of statehood, and the associated protections, only to certain polities: Lorca (n 2) 307.

[43] In a way, the very name inter-*national* law as well as its predecessors 'law of *nations*' and 'jus gentium' should serve as standing reminders of this often-overlooked conceptual separateness between states and the human communities that are supposed to underpin them. Famously, the term 'international law' first appeared in Jeremy Bentham, *Introduction to the Principles of Morals and Legislation* (first published in 1789, OUP 1996); depending on the translation, 'gentium' can be understood either as 'nation' or as 'people'. Generally, see Jörg Fisch, 'Peoples and Nations' in Bardo Fassbender and Anne Peters (eds), *The Oxford Handbook of the History of International Law* (OUP 2012). The argument developed here is not premised on the direct recognition by international law of either 'nations' or 'peoples', or indeed any other notion of community, as distinct *legal persons* in the classic sense of them possessing rights and duties of their own. Depending on one's reading of history, as well as one's views as to when modern international law truly emerges, this recognition can be pinned at different points in the field's development and be given different meanings. Instead, the argument about the nature of the state and its ontological foundation, meaning a descriptive transformation of events, a community, and the need for a social convention connecting the two, presents a theory as to

What type of community has the capacity to constitute itself into a state presents a broader problem for international law, and one regarding which the law has not always been inclusive or unambiguous.[44] I will revisit this question at the end of this chapter, where I will explain that it can be bracketed out as a common variable in theorizing both states as well as international organizations. The key point here is to register an analytical understanding of a community as an entity that may lead to the formation of a state but necessarily exists separately to it and may persist regardless of it, being in that sense fundamental in its own regard. Most importantly, at the very least behind already constituted states, there exists a community of interrelated human beings, however the latter is defined, rather than a supra-individual organism or a 'ghost' doing all the work, or the fiction of one.

The 'best explanation' of the state's potential for emergence and persistence through time then is to construe it as a unitary, yet artificial, entity. International law should be thought to construct the state by recognizing the capacity of re-description of the underlying community

---

how an already admitted concept of international law, namely statehood, can be theorized in an abstract sense. This argument could have been advanced and defended at any point in the field's development as the 'best explanation' for the emergence and continuity of states, as well as other related institutions.

[44] Regardless of how one answers this question, the terms in which it is posed, namely asking which communities can create states, betrays the same immanent rationale, namely that whatever they are, states are made up by communities of human beings. Modern international law, and especially self-determination, can be even more instructive in that regard. Consider, for example, the 'continuous' nature of the right of peoples to self-determination that persists regardless of foreign occupation or alien subjugation: Karl Doehring, 'Self-Determination' in Bruno Simma and others (eds), *The Charter of the United Nations: A Commentary* (2nd edn, OUP 2002) 56; Antonio Cassese, *Self-Determination of Peoples: A Legal Reappraisal* (CUP 1995) 284–288. Such communities may, analytically speaking, predate the state. This is the case, for example, of the peoples of non-self-governing and trust territories who have a right of self-determination, including the right to create their own sovereign states as well as a right to the territorial integrity of their territory (on the right to territorial integrity of a non-self-governing territory as a corollary of the right to self-determination, see *Legal Consequences of the Separation of the Chagos Archipelago from Mauritius in 1965* (Advisory Opinion) [2019] ICJ Rep 95, 134). Peoples may also legally exist *without* their own state, when they have not constituted a state but reside in a trust or non-self-governing territory that is dependent on or otherwise associated with a geographically separate state. See Karen Knop, *Diversity and Self-Determination in International Law* (CUP 2002) 52–53. See also Crawford, who argues that self-determination is a genuine collective right of a people as separate from the state; James Crawford, 'The Rights of Peoples: "Peoples" or "Governments"?' (1985) 9 Bulletin of the Australian Society of Legal Philosophy 136, at 138; Crawford (n 1) 618.

which the state 'encapsulates'. Thus, the state is a *unitary* entity because the internal descriptive transformation by which the state views itself as such is admitted by international law. The state can further be called an *artificial* entity because the state's activities and existence are ultimately grounded on suitably related facts involving lower-level entities, and not on the assumption of some metaphysical or organic quality attached to it. Indeed, just as some philosophers suggest that a human being can constitute itself into a person by viewing itself as unitary, a community can constitute itself into a corporate entity when it puts in place rules of re-description – rules that create a new level of description under which the community in question appears as a unitary entity. Therefore, statehood should be understood as another form of organization rather than as an intrinsic quality with quasi-metaphysical import that is somehow breathed into an entity when certain objective criteria are met. What is fundamental is not the state as a platonic form, but the status-ascribing relationship that may lead to its creation and sustain its institutional apparatus.

7.3   Institutional Organization besides or beyond the State

Conceptualizing statehood as a form of organization ultimately founded in a community's exercised capacity to self-describe rather than as a fixed quality suggests that there are no inherent limitations to restrict the exercise of this capacity only to the creation of states.[45] This view reintroduces the state just as *a* potential member of a broader family of entities that are all equally admissible by default within international law. All these entities can be said to form a family not because of any abstract institutional or functional similarities that they may or may not share but due to their common root in the capacity of a community to self-describe, and to the extent that this capacity is recognized by international law.[46] Put simply, international law cares about the shared roots of these institutions rather than how they may come to branch out.

---

[45] See also Jochen von Bernstorff, '*Autorité oblige*: The Rise and Fall of Hans Kelsen's Legal Concept of International Institutions' 31(2) EJIL 2020, 497, 511, attributing to Kelsen an understanding of 'international law as a potentially unrestricted social technique of international relations'.

[46] Whether we call this capacity self-determination or sovereignty – terms with complex historical origins – is less important than appreciating the foundational analytical function that it plays in the way international law constructs its own ontology.

I call this approach 'institutional genealogy'. Through that term I wish to shift focus from a discourse that revolves around trying to define as accurately as possible certain platonic types of institutions (such as statehood or international organizations) back to the continuous line that connects all these entities to a common ontological core, namely the status-generative capacity of certain communities of human beings.[47]

Having already seen how this rooted capacity of communal self-description lies behind international law's construction of the state as a unitary corporate entity, the next step then is to register how this capacity may branch out beyond, or even outside, the state. This will help explain why it is this capacity with its relational underpinning rather than the abstraction of the state that should be thought of as our non-eliminable point of reference and, hence, why the system does not pose any default limits on what forms of social organization may emerge from exercising that capacity.

Apart from deducing it analytically, this foundational primacy and elementary character of communal self-description can also be inferred from practice. As we have seen, at a very basic level, this concerns the state's very identity as a continuous entity at a given point and through time. For the same underlying reason, statehood itself is restricted only to entities that claim to be, and thus self-describe as, states at any given point.[48] Similarly, the foundational primacy of self-description may account for bringing already constituted states to an end: it allows a state to contract itself out of existence by voluntarily dissolving into its component parts or merging with another state. Likewise, a state can partially devolve by granting independence to one of its sub-parts. Arguably, none of these practices need to be authorized or otherwise prescribed by separate norms of customary international law: they are inherent in the very notion of the state itself just being a product of descriptive transformations of events.

Between the extremes of state creation and dissolution lies a myriad of other instances of the creation of sub- or supra-state entities that equally evidence international law's default deferral to self-descriptions of institutional reality by a community.[49]

---

[47] I thus employ the term 'genealogy' inspired by the ordinary sense of the word and not as the form of historical critique that is normally associated with the work of Michel Foucault.

[48] See Ronen (n 36) 23.

[49] See also *Western Sahara* (Advisory Opinion) [1975] ICJ Rep 12, 43–44, for the proposition that 'no rule of international law ... requires the structure of the State to follow any particular pattern, as is evident from the diversity of the forms of State found in the world today'.

A classic case of sub-state entities in that regard is those federal states for which the component states enjoy the capacity to conclude international agreements with third parties directly and in their own name.[50] To the extent to which these entities enjoy legal personality in international law, this is neither to the exclusion of the federal state nor is it identical to it.[51] Instead, 'each level of personality operates within a different network of legal relations'.[52] This approach was echoed in the ILC's earlier work on state responsibility, which noted that:

> [w]here an organ of a component State of a federal State acts in a sphere in which the component State has international obligations that are incumbent on it and not on the federal State, that component State clearly emerges at the international level as a subject of international law separate from the federal State, and not merely as a territorial government entity subordinate to the federal State.[53]

It is also in line with arbitral practice suggesting that components of federal states can be held responsible for the commitments that they have undertaken directly and in their own name.[54]

---

[50] For extensive references to practice, see Duncan B Hollis, 'Why State Consent Still Matters – Non-State Actors, Treaties, and the Changing Sources of International Law' (2005) 23(1) Berkeley Journal of International Law 137, 147; Gleider Hernández, 'Federated Entities in International Law: Disaggregating the Federal State' in Duncan French (ed), *Statehood and Self-Determination: Reconciling Tradition and Modernity in International Law* (CUP 2013) 491.

[51] Hernández (n 50) 509. See also Judge Huber's description of a federal state as one in which 'a jurisdiction is established in order to apply, as need arises, rules of international law to the interstate relations of the States members': *Island of Palmas Case* (1928) 2 RIAA 829, 840.

[52] Hernández (n 50) 509.

[53] ILC, 'Report of the International Law Commission on the Work of Its Twenty-Sixth Session, 6 May – 26 July 1974, Official Records of the General Assembly, Twenty-Ninth Session, Supplement No. 10' (1974) UN Doc A/9610/Rev.1, 157, 281. This approach is not contravened by the final text of article 7, which provides that 'the conduct of an organ of a territorial government within a State shall also be considered as an act of that State under international law, provided that organ was acting in that capacity in the case in question' (emphasis added). ILC, 'Draft Articles on Responsibility of States' (n 32) art 7.

[54] See *Affaire du Montijo (EU v Colombie)* (26 July 1875), 3 Recueil des arbitrages internationaux 675:

> En cas de violation d'une stipulation d'un traité, il est … évident qu'un recours doit être fait auprès de l' entité avec lawquelle l'engagement international a été conclu. La requête ne peut être addressée à personne d'autre. En matière des traités, les États particuliers sont inexistants; ils on renoncé à une certaine partie bien définie de leur souveraineté inhérente et

The opposite, methodologically statist view would have federal components in all circumstances acting merely as agents of the federal state. This position has been summarized by Sir Gerald Fitzmaurice as follows:

> In so far as they are empowered or authorized under the constitution of the union to negotiate or enter into treaties with foreign countries, *even if it is in their own name*, they do so as agents for the union, which, as alone possessing international personality, is necessarily the entity that becomes bound by the treaty and responsible for carrying it out.[55]

> on ne peut traiter avec eux que par l' entremise des représentants ou délégués accrédités du Gouvernement federal ou général.

See also *Cayuga Indians (Great Britain) v United States* (1926) 6 RIAA 173, suggesting that a treaty signed by the state of New York with the Cayuga Indians (whose claim the UK espoused in that case) was not binding on the US federal state; *Rosenstein v Germany*, Arbitral Tribunal (Romania/Germany) 17 January 1927, Annual Digest of Public International Law Cases, 1927–1928, finding that a claim for damages arising out of the cancellation of a contract concluded by a Romanian national with the state of Hamburg could not give rise to the responsibility of Germany. This does not suggest in any way that federal states may not be internationally responsible when their component states act in a manner that is incompatible with the international obligation of the federal state as such. See ILC, 'Draft Articles on Responsibility of States (n 32) art 4 and commentary thereto, 41, para 9.

[55] See ILC, 'Third Report on the Law of Treaties by Mr G.G. Fitzmaurice, Special Rapporteur' (1958) UN Doc A/CN.4/115 and Corr.1, 24 (emphasis added). For another restatement of this idea, see ILC, 'First Report on the Law of Treaties by Sir Humphrey Waldock, Special Rapporteur' (1962) UN Doc A/CN.4/144 and Add.1, 36, art 2:

> In the case of a federation or other union of States, international capacity to be a party to treaties is in principle possessed exclusively by the federal State or by the Union. Accordingly, if the constitution of a federation or Union confers upon its constituent States power to enter into agreements directly with foreign States, the constituent State normally exercises this power in the capacity only of an organ of the federal State or Union, as the case may be.

Hans Kelsen expressed a similar view, albeit in more qualified terms:

> Since the component states have their competence in accordance with the federal constitution, the organs of the component states, in concluding treaties with the competence conferred upon them by the federal constitution, may also be considered as indirect organs of the federal state; hence the international person concluding the treaty may be considered to be the federal state acting, in certain regards, through a component state.

Hans Kelsen, *Principles of International Law* (Rinehart & Co 1952) 172. See also Alf Ross, *A Textbook of International Law: General Part* (Annie I Fausbøll tr, Longmans, Green & Co 1947) 26, arguing that sub-entities of states are not suited to be subject to international duties. The standout here is Hersch Lauterpacht, who accepted international law's default openness to the autonomous international capacity of member states of a

This view takes off from a very different premise than the one employed here. Disregarding practice, it axiomatically assumes that the state's legal personality does not admit gradation, analysing away other entities through concepts such as authorization, consent, or agency. Indeed, as we have seen, if one posits the state as *the* fundamentally irreducible particle, then it is not only possible but also inescapable to then eventually reduce all other such entities, including international organizations, back to it: any one of these entities could be re-described through the fiction of authorization as just another instance of the state acting and being the 'real' actor.[56] But the question remains as to why one should adopt such a view of the state. If one understands the state by reference to social facts through a default renvoi to already established descriptive priorities rather than as a metaphysically fixed point, then there is no reason to restrict the corporate form to the state alone.

Practice supporting this notion goes beyond federal states in ways that may defy neat classification but exhibit the same underlying rationale. Protectorates having their own measure of international legal personality in parallel to the protecting state are a case in point.[57] The same is true for non-self-governing territories whose people have, in their exercise of their right of self-determination, elected to freely associate with an independent state, usually their former administrating power, rather than

---

federation: ILC, 'Report on the Law of Treaties by Mr H Lauterpacht, Special Rapporteur' (1953) UN Doc A/CN.4/63, 138–139.

[56] Both Fitzmaurice and Waldock would resist this logical conclusion in relation to international organizations by admitting a renvoi to the organization's constitution, the operation of which they would not admit in relation to the constitution of a state. Fitzmaurice argued that international organizations had an 'inherent treaty-making capacity within the scope of their purposes and functions, and matters ancillary thereto, and are also subject to any specific limitations arising from the terms of their constitutions': ILC, 'Third Report on the Law of Treaties by Mr. G.G. Fitzmaurice, Special Rapporteur' (n 55) 24. Waldock would also recognize the capacity of international organizations to enter into treaties in their own name 'to the extent that, such treaty-making capacity is expressly created, or necessarily implied, in the instrument or instruments prescribing the constitution and functions of the organization or agency in question': ILC, 'First Report on the Law of Treaties by Sir Humphrey Waldock, Special Rapporteur' (n 55) 36. Nevertheless, the encapsulation of the renvoi in a treaty or in a constitution should not be determinative. This is because either one accepts that new legal entities that exist parallelly to the state can emerge or one does not; whether this materializes through a unilateral act or a treaty should in principle be analytically indifferent.

[57] Crawford (n 1) 314–320; see *Nationality Decrees Issued in Tunis and Morocco* (Advisory Opinion) [1923] PCIJ Series B No 4, 27.

create their own states.[58] Although these arrangements vary in practice, they too reflect the idea of an entity not being legally subsumed by its so-called parent state, without being a state in itself.[59] Thus, for example, associated entities such as Puerto Rico, the Cook Islands, or Niue have been admitted as members to a number of international organizations in their own name.[60]

These instances not only show that the state should not be conceptualized as an inherently closed-off entity but also that international law admits communal self-description giving rise to institutions that do not fit our classic definition of what counts a state.

Another adjacent category of practice showcasing the same ideas has historically concerned certain sub-parts of non-federal states. One prominent such case is Hong Kong, which has the status of a special autonomous region of China. While formally part of China, Hong Kong's Basic Law also gives it the right to make agreements with other states.[61] As Crawford explained in that regard, 'as a matter of international law, these are obligations of Hong Kong, and to that extent Hong Kong may be described as an international legal person'.[62] In fact, Hong Kong has signed a number of such agreements.[63] It has also joined international organizations, including the WTO in its own right – an organization to which, since 2001, China is also a member. Similarly, British dominions such as Australia, Canada, New Zealand, and South Africa were recognized as having the capacity to sign treaties in their own name for some time before they became formally independent states.[64] While not states at the time, these dominions also became members to the League of Nations, along with India when it was still a non-self-governing colony, and thus even further away from statehood.[65] The UN has also featured similar examples of parts of states acting in ways that do not fit the classic 'billiard ball' conception of the state: India, again, as well as the

---

[58] UNGA Res 1541 (XV), 'Principles Which Should Guide Members in Determining Whether or Not an Obligation Exists to Transmit the Information Called for under Article 73e of the Charter' (15 December 1960).

[59] Crawford (n 1) 625.

[60] ibid 633.

[61] The Basic Law of the Hong Kong Special Administrative Region of the People's Republic of China, art 13, para 4.

[62] Crawford (n 1) 250.

[63] See also Hernández (n 50) 508.

[64] Nicholson (n 1) 2.

[65] ibid.

Philippines and the Soviet constituent republics of Belarus and Ukraine became members of the organization without being independent states at the time, *in parallel* to the UK, US, and the USSR being considered fully fledged states in their own regard, and members of the UN.[66]

In sum, all these sub-state or otherwise dependent entities possess an international legal presence that truly exists in parallel to that of their so-called parent state. Leaving to the side theoretical arguments, the very existence of these examples evidences the artificiality of the view that these entities are invariably just acting as agents of some other state: it makes little sense of practice to argue that a state becomes a member to an international organization but also 'delegates' to one of its sub-entities to represent it at the same organization. On the whole, these examples showcase in practice what the previous pages argued through logical deduction: the state should not be understood as an inherently irreducible monolithic entity, including in the eyes of international law.[67] Instead, the state is a constructed entity, neither inherently open nor closed. It can be moulded and remoulded by default and without prescription by a specific rule of international law in a non-pre-defined manner that can give rise to a practically infinite variety of legal institutions and arrangements that may exist in parallel to one another.

Following this rationale, there is nothing that restricts such alternative forms of organization from taking place beyond the state level. And indeed, practice is also replete with instances of supra-state or intrastate arrangements evidencing the same principle at work. Historically, these have ranged from 'condominiums' to 'personal' and 'real' unions, and confederate entities.[68] These too exhibit remarkable diversity, being almost as varied in terms of typology as the historical circumstances that gave birth to them. Admittedly of decreasing importance in the modern world, these examples may too yield deeper insights into how international law constructs the state in a conventional and constructed, rather than essentialist, manner.[69]

---

[66] ibid. See also Edward Dolan, 'The Member-Republics of the U.S.S.R. as Subjects of the Law of Nations' 4(4) ICLQ 1955, 629.

[67] Nicholson (n 1) 204, 119.

[68] For a more detailed discussion of this classification, see Henry Wheaton, *Elements of International Law* (8th edn, Sampson Low, Son & Co 1866) 60–88; Crawford (n 1) 482–492.

[69] As an early scholar of international organizations put it, 'it is undoubtedly a mistake to look upon sovereignty as an irreducible entity' – Paul S Reinsch, 'International Administrative Law and National Sovereignty' (1909) 3 AJIL 1, 10.

Confederations are perhaps the most interesting such case for our purposes. Contrary to federal states, confederations are set up by an international agreement rather than a national constitution.[70] The units that make up the confederation remain states in their own right, retaining their legal personality, while the new entity that emerges – the confederation – is also bestowed with its own separate legal personality.[71] The confederation thus represents a partial decentralization that leaves participating states still standing as legal persons while also giving rise to a new, and legally distinct, entity. Although encompassing only a handful of historical examples,[72] the key here is the underlying idea that the notion of a confederation corresponds to: the capacity of a political community to organize itself at the same time within and beyond national boundaries, leading to the creation of a legal person that exists in parallel to its members in the international legal order. As with the examples of sub-state entities mentioned earlier, here too international law seems to admit by default a legal entity that emerges out of the state, without the need for special rules of incorporation or other 'structural changes' in the system.[73]

7.4   International Organization as a Corollary of the Capacity to Constitute a State

Understanding the state as an artificial yet unitary entity in this manner opens up a different approach to theorizing international organizations than those currently on offer. If at the foundation of international law lies the capacity of a community to self-describe as a unitary entity, and *if*

---

[70] Hersch Lauterpacht and Elihu Lauterpacht, *International Law Vol 3: The Law of Peace, Parts II–VI* (CUP 1977) 11.

[71] See Crawford (n 1) 484; Lauterpacht and Lauterpacht (n 70) 11.

[72] The case of the EU is interesting in this regard. A lot of ink has been spilled on whether the EU is a confederate or a federal entity or something else entirely. See among others: Bruno de Witte, 'The EU as an International Legal Experiment' in Gráinne de Burca and JHH Weiler (eds), *The Worlds of European Constitutionalism* (CUP 2012) 19–56; Armin von Bogdandy, 'Neither an International Organization Nor a Nation State: The EU as a Supranational Federation' in Erik Jones and others (eds), *The Oxford Handbook of the European Union* (OUP 2012) 761–776. The point here is that, even though this may be an important question from the perspective of political science, it is not as much from the perspective of general international law.

[73] See eg Wheaton (n 68) 65–77. See also Fred L Morrison, 'Confederation of States', *Max Planck Encyclopedia of International Law* (2007) <https://opil.ouplaw.com/view/10 .1093/law:epil/9780199231690/law-9780199231690-e1385> accessed 5 February 2025.

states are the products of that capacity being exercised, the question then becomes whether these communities can further organize themselves beneath or beyond the national level. The whole inquiry then turns to whether there is an inherent barrier that prevents the descriptive transformation that 'animates' the state to also give rise to interstate or suprastate entities. This is a markedly different problem from trying to make sense of the differences and similarities of states and international organizations as platonic archetypes, or assuming that there is barrier to entry for the latter and trying to overcome it by positing rules of incorporation or changes in the definition of international law as we saw in Chapters 2–4.

Drawing inspiration from the philosophical exposition of this problem, which also corresponds to practice regarding entities other than international organizations, we should answer this question in the negative: there is no such barrier to begin with. The same capacity can support partial and total corporate unification of a political community within and beyond national boundaries, and the emergence of the respective corporate actors in the eyes of international law. The theory advocated here boils down to this proposition: a community of the type that has the capacity to organize itself as a state can also organize itself beneath and beyond the state level, whether directly or through nested institutions. In other words, if international law recognizes the capacity of a community to set up a state, then, by the same token, it recognizes its capacity to set up other types of corporate entities, and in general to freely delegate, decentralize, or otherwise organize itself.

In a sense, the recognized capacity of a political community to set up a state, and the ensuing capacity of the latter to set up an international organization, operates as a rule of incorporation, since both are supposed to license descriptive transformations of events. However, the argument here differs from positing a general rule of incorporation in the sense of domestic law. It negates pinning that capacity to a new, separate, and ultimately special positive rule of customary international law. Moreover, by tracing international organizations back to the same capacity to constitute the state itself, the theory advanced here negates the notion that there is an intrinsic difference between these institutions and states: they are just variations of the same theme at different scales. International organizations' existence is anchored to the political communities whose capacity to produce authoritative descriptions of events has been at play. This capacity has been presumably already recognized within the system of international law, given how in practice international organizations are normally founded and membered by institutions that are themselves an expression of it, including most commonly states themselves. It is being anchored to this capacity that matters and not whether some sense of 'community' may then emerge within an organization's bureaucratic apparatus.[74] In sum, international law should be thought of as capable of *inherently* accommodating entities with distinct legal personality existing in parallel to the state when these represent the organization of the underlying political communities at a different level.

The case of confederations can be especially instructive for how the emergence of international organizations should be understood in this regard. The takeaway is *not* that international organizations are confederations,[75] much less that they are all-encompassing 'super-states' if that expression means that they somehow absorb the legal orders of their member states.[76] Rather, it is that states may set up a new legal person that is recognized by international law as having its own legal personality *and*

---

[74] Cf David J Bederman, 'The Souls of International Organizations: Legal Personality and the Lighthouse at Cape Spartel' (1996) 36 Vanderbilt Journal of Transnational Law 275, 371.

[75] At the infancy of international organizations law, there was a fervent debate on whether the League of Nations was a confederation of its members. The arguments turned to interpreting the very notion of confederation and whether the League could fall under it. See eg Lassa Oppenheim, 'Le Caractère Essentiel de La Société Des Nations' (1919) 26 Revue Générale de Droit International Public 234, 237, arguing that the League was not a confederation. Cf Percy Corbett, 'What Is the League of Nations? (1924) 5 BYIL 119. Cf ILC, 'First Report on Relations between States and Inter-governmental Organizations, by Mr. Abdullah El-Erian, Special Rapporteur' (1963) UN Doc A/CN.4/ 161 and Add.1, 165, paras 42–45, where El-Erian criticized Kelsen's view that international organizations are essentially confederations of states. As he suggested:

> [a] confederation of States is usually a first step towards the creation of a federal or even unitary State, while an international organization simply provides a framework for international co-operation between States without being necessarily envisaged as a stage towards the establishment of a union of states. . . . [Kelsen's] definition fails to bring forward the distinctive character of international organizations.

[76] See Djura Ninčić, *The Problem of Sovereignty in the Charter and in the Practice of the United Nations* (Martinus Nijhoff 1970). For some historical background to this idea, see Mark Mazower, *Governing the World: The History of an Idea* (Penguin 2012). As is well known, the ICJ dismissed this idea that the UN was some sort of a 'super-state' in its 1949 Advisory Opinion. See *Reparation for Injuries Suffered in the Service of the United Nations* (Advisory Opinion) [1949] ICJ Rep 174, 179. For the idea that international organizations are not states, see also *Jurisdiction of the European Commission of the Danube between Galatz and Braila* (Advisory Opinion) [1927] PCIJ Rep Series B No 14, 64.

retain their individual legal personalities. Accordingly, there is no reason why the same logic cannot sustain the creation of an international organization without the need for arguments concerning changes in the law.

Instead, the correct analysis should be that there is a spectrum of 'public' entities in international law, and that states, confederations, international organizations, as well as any other entity that exists on that spectrum, are part of the same family tree of legal persons.[77] We may call such entities collectively 'public' institutions,[78] because they are ultimately anchored to what international law recognizes as public authority in its most elementary sense, meaning authority that is exercised in the name of one or more communities as a whole rather than the concerned individuals.[79] The conceptual relationship of these actors with states is based on their common root in that capacity having been exercised, not on some abstract similarity that may or may not obtain between them. Thus, international organizations do not acquire their status because they are 'self-governing' or analogous to states (in certain respects they are, in others they are not), and certainly not due to some special provision allowing for it. Rather, they acquire their status because they are themselves expressions of the same capacity that pulls the state together as one in the eyes of international law, operating at a different level of organization.[80]

---

[77] See Kunz's classic observation that 'Les conceptions des différents liaisons d'États ne sont pas conceptions normatives, ne sont pas des conceptions du droit, mais des conceptions de classification fournies par la doctrine': Joseph L Kunz, 'Une Nouvelle Théorie de l'État Fédérale' (1930) 11 Revue de Droit International et de Législation Comparée 835, 849; Paul Reuter, *Organisations européennes* (Presses universitaires de France 1965) 194–195, describing these institutional forms as operating on a spectrum. On how Kelsen's views could be interpreted as aligning with this idea, see von Bernstorff (n 45) 506–507; for some especially relevant parts of Kelsen's work in that regard, see Kelsen (n 55) 161–173.

[78] See also Sandesh Sivakumaran, 'Beyond State and Non-State Actors: The Role of State-Empowered Entities in the Making and Shaping of International Law' (2017) 55 CJTL 344, who speaks of 'State-empowered entities' with respect to international law-making; Richard Collins, 'Non-State, Inter-State or Supra-State? The Peculiar Identity of the Intergovernmental Organization' in Jean d' Aspremont (ed), *Participants in the International Legal System* (Routledge 2011) 1069, suggesting that international organizations occupy a position somewhere between the interstate and the non-state.

[79] For a similar notion of publicness, see Benedict Kingsbury, 'The Concept of "Law" in Global Administrative Law' (2009) 20 EJIL 23, 31.

[80] In this sense, this view is closer to the ICJ's famous dictum that the UN's members 'had the power, in conformity with international law, to bring into being an entity possessing objective international personality, and not merely personality recognized by them alone', *Reparation for Injuries Suffered in the Service of the United Nations* (n 76) 185. It is worth noting at this point that the Court refers to this 'power' without a reference to a legislative

Accordingly, international organizations should not be theorized as associations of domestic law in systems with or without a rule of incorporation.[81] Instead, the more appropriate legal metaphor is that of an artificial entity exercising public power in relation to another artificial entity exercising such power when they both ultimately stem from common underlying social conventions. For example, this is the relationship that normally occurs in public legal persons in domestic law, where a central authority can create decentralized public entities with a separate legal personality. Therefore, if an analogy must be sought in domestic law, this should be with those independent non-territorial public persons of domestic law that enjoy distinct legal personality but still form part of the state's apparatus in the broad sense – consider, for example, the legal set-up of independent competition or consumer-protection authorities in most European jurisdictions.

All in all, the proposed theory replaces the premise of a rule of incorporation or other change in positive law with the premise that the capacity of a community to organize itself into a state can be exercised in tandem with another organized community in a way that creates a non-eliminable legal point of reference in the eyes of international law. This premise, which corresponds to broader international practice instead of just practice in relation to international organizations, is underpinned by the immanent logic of this capacity when it is theorized as the exercise of a recognized power of re-description, as opposed to the expression of a metaphysical quality of a mysterious 'spirit' of the state, or the fiction of one. In other words, it is not only the same type of 'magic', whatever that may be, that animates both states and international organizations in the eyes of international law; it is actually the same force working across different boundaries and levels of organization, ultimately anchored in shared social facts.[82] The distinctiveness of states *in*

---

intervention, in the form of either a rule of incorporation or a structural change in the legal system.

[81] Finn Seyersted, 'Objective International Personality of Intergovernmental Organizations: Do Their Capacities Really Depend upon the Conventions Establishing Them?' (1964) 34 Nordic Journal of International Law 3, 94–95; Fernando Bordin, *The Analogy between States and International Organizations: Legal Reasoning and the Development of the Law of International Organizations* (CUP 2018) 62ff.

[82] Although the account offered here is doctrinal/analytical, it does largely coincide in sensibility with more recent work that has questioned the uniqueness and primacy of the state as a form of governance from a historical perspective. This work has thrown light on the rich dialectic that underpinned the contemporary emergence of both states and international organizations. See Guy Fiti Sinclair, *To Reform the World: International*

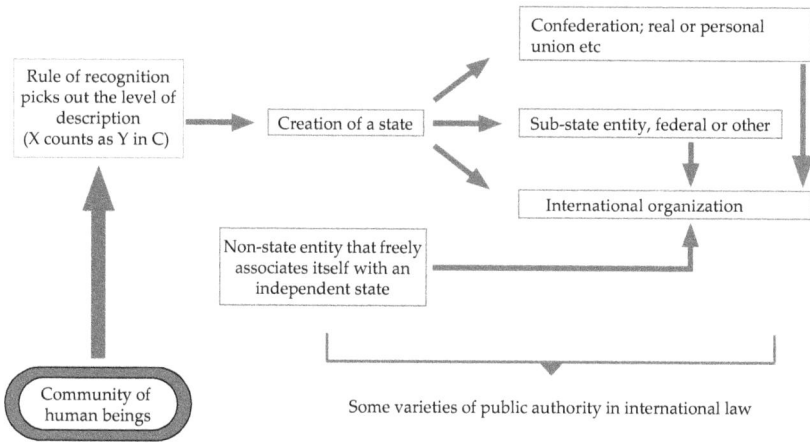

Figure 7.2   Capacity to self-describe and the state as a member of a family of institutions

law creates the conditions for the distinctiveness of international organizations *in law*, to the same extent and with the same effects, rather than being an obstacle to it as the default position implies (Figure 7.2).

This account drastically departs from our classic framework for theorizing international organizations. As Chapter 8 will explore in more detail, the different logic immanent in this alternative account – focusing on continuity in the exercise of public power rather than comparing and contrasting the two actors or analysing international organizations merely as groups of states – yields new insights and more convincing answers to age-old doctrinal problems. Before getting to those, however, it is worth pausing to address two potential ambiguities of what has been suggested so far. These relate to (1) who is the 'self' that engages in self-description through various forms of social organization, including states as well as international organizations; (2) the potential for abuse coupled with the idea of international law's default renvoi to the aforementioned self-descriptions.

Organizations and the Making of Modern States (OUP 2017). For corresponding ideas in international relations, see Hooghe, Lenz, and Marks (n 19) 3–4, who 'conceive domestic and international politics as different contexts for a coherent set of generalizations rather than as two causally unique worlds' and 'governance within states and among states as having a logic that can travel across scale'.

7.5   Addressing Potential Ambiguities of the Present Theory

7.5.1   Who Is the Self That Does the Self-Description?

One of the fundamental elements of the theory advanced here is a community of human beings that exists separately from the state, meaning that it is a constitutive element of the state itself but also in the sense that it continues to exist when a state has been set up, and may also exist regardless of the emergence of the state at a given point in time.[83] This account places this community's capacity for institutionalization at the centre of a radial structure wherefrom the emergence of a state is only one of many possibilities, all equally admissible by default as far as the international legal system is concerned. The question may arise at this point: what type of community has the capacity to engage in self-descriptions such that can lead to the creation of states, as well as these other forms of social organization, in the eyes of international law?

While I will sketch an answer to this question, it is important to appreciate that any answer that is given will apply equally to states and international organizations: if a community has the capacity to organize itself in the form of a state, then it will have ipso facto the capacity to join or form an international organization. In essence, the question of what type of community enjoys this capacity in the eyes of international law is a separate matter that is not peculiar to theorizing international organizations as such and can therefore be bracketed out for the purposes of our analysis. With this in mind, I will now outline my answer.

The question boils down to how one understands international law's relationship to the capacity of a community to self-describe. At a basic level, this capacity can be configured either as a power or as a liberty. In classic Hohfeldian analysis of rights, the term 'power' denotes the capacity to effect a change in legal relations.[84] In turn, this corresponds to another's liability to have their legal relations changed. A classic example of a power in that sense is triggering a unilateral contract extension clause. By contrast, the term 'liberty' denotes a situation whereby one is free to act in a certain way, but this does not correspond to anyone's duty

---

[83] Thus, for example, peoples of trust and non-self-governing territories have an option not only to create their own 'sovereign independent state' but also to choose '[f]ree association with an independent State; or Integration with an independent State': UNGA Res 1541 (XV) (n 58) Principle VI.

[84] Wesley Newcomb Hohfeld, 'Some Fundamental Legal Conceptions as Applied in Judicial Reasoning' (1913) 23 Yale Law Journal 16.

to accommodate them. For example, I am at liberty to pick up an unclaimed five-pound note lying on the pavement, but others do not have a duty not to take it themselves or allow me to take it myself.

Now, consider, for example, a change in a state's head of state. From the perspective of international law, there are two main ways to process such an event. The first is to say that any change in government is an inherent 'power' of a state, that works automatically and with direct legal effect in the field of international relations. It makes sense to describe this as a Hohfeldian power because even such relatively minor changes in self-description impact the entitlements and obligations of other states: for instance, they now must extend head-of-state immunities to that person.

The second way is to describe such changes in self-description only as a 'liberty', meaning that other states do not have a corresponding liability to accommodate these changes in any way. In this scenario, self-descriptions are capable of producing legal effects only to the extent that they meet the recognition or otherwise expressed consent of other states. Here we may further distinguish between the capacity to self-describe as such versus specific instances of exercising that capacity. In the first instance, recognition just offers a longer route to the same outcome as the exercise of a power would. A state recognizes another state and this one-off recognition then admits any and all ensuing self-descriptions, rendering them a Hohfeldian power vis-à-vis this specific recognizing state that becomes liable to accommodate them. In the second and more extreme scenario, recognition needs to attach to individual descriptive transformations and does not create any liability vis-à-vis future changes. This is a world where, for example, the recognition of each new government of a given state would be necessary.

As already mentioned, even though either conception of the capacity to self-describe may analytically entail the emergence of international organizations as an institutional form, configuring it as a Hohfeldian power in the first sense seems to reflect current doctrinal consensus.[85] According to this view, communities of already established states do have the power to effect changes in their legal entitlements, from as minute as changing their government to as profound as partially disaggregating their state or even dissolving it altogether. But this power may extend beyond communities already organized as states. Similarly, for example, a community living in a trust or a non-self-governing territory has a *right*

---

[85] Crawford (n 1) 28. This does not mean that recognition has no role to play even in this scenario: Nicholson (n 1) 127ff.

(in the terms of our analysis better understood as a power) to effect a change in its legal entitlements by pursuing one of the options outlined in GA Res 1541 (XV), including by creating an independent state, while the colonial state has a corresponding liability to have its legal entitlements changed.[86]

What happens beyond these two cases, however, is less clear cut: international law does not seem to pose any abstract requirements on what type of community may eventually lead to the creation of a state or other form of self-government.[87] On the other hand, it does not appear to provide a general legal entitlement to do so in the same sense that it does for example, for peoples living in trust or non-self-governing territories.[88] Yet again, this is a broader problem that cuts across international law and, as such, should not change how we understand the position of international organizations.

7.5.2   Exercise of the Capacity of Self-Description: Limits and the Potential for Abuse

The idea that certain communities have the power to freely change their legal entitlements through self-description may seem strange from a normative point of view. It does not appear to contain any built-in limiting principle or other general guarantee against abuse. Although sensible in origin, such concerns turn out to be mostly speculative. Even though it is theoretically possible that a state names a different head of state every day, grant an ever-increasing number of sub-state entities extensive treaty-making powers, or create an infinite number of international organizations, the realities of political economy severely constrain this freedom in practice. In other words, states seldom try to 'game' the system, because every such change has to abide with considerations of an internal legal and political nature that are by themselves quite restricting.

---

[86] UNGA Res 1541 (XV) (n 58) Principle VI.

[87] Cf *Western Sahara* (n 49) 63, suggesting that some self-identification as a community through 'some forms of common activity, ... common institutions or organs, even of a quite minimal character' may be necessary to that effect.

[88] Generally, see Knop (n 44) 53ff; Crawford (n 1) 124–125, 374ff. See also *Accordance with International Law of the Unilateral Declaration of Independence in Respect of Kosovo* (n 39) 437–438, framing the question of the accordance of declarations of independence as one of non-prohibition under general international law.

This does not mean that the potential for abuse does not exist at all. But here again, we should be reminded that this renvoi to self-description is only the default rule which can be overridden by other norms. This could include a general prohibition of the abuse of rights as part of customary international law[89] or more specific rules restricting this deferral, as, for example, when the emergence of a state is connected 'with the unlawful use of force or other egregious violations of norms of general international law, in particular those of a peremptory character'.[90] Such restricting norms could theoretically develop specifically in relation to international organizations.[91] The fact that there does not seem to be much practice in that regard[92] should, if nothing else, be interpreted as a sign that states generally do not set up or join international organizations with the sole intention of abuse, rather than as an

---

[89] See Alexander Kiss, 'Abuse of Rights', *Max Planck Encyclopedia of International Law* (2006) <https://opil.ouplaw.com/display/10.1093/law:epil/9780199231690/law-9780199231690-e1371> accessed 9 February 2025.

[90] *Accordance with International Law of the Unilateral Declaration of Independence in Respect of Kosovo* (n 39) 437; see also Crawford (n 1) 97ff.

[91] See eg ILC, 'Draft Articles on the Responsibility of International Organizations, with Commentaries' (2011) II/2 YILC 46, 98–99, art 61 and commentary thereto. Titled 'Circumvention of International Obligations of a State Member of an International Organization', article 61(1) provides that

> [a] State member of an international organization incurs international responsibility if, by taking advantage of the fact that the organization has competence in relation to the subject matter of one of the State's international obligations, it circumvents that obligation by causing the organization to commit an act that, if committed by the State, would have constituted a breach of the obligation.

See also *Westland Helicopters Ltd and Arab Organization for Industrialization, United Arab Emirates, Kingdom of Saudi Arabia, State of Qatar, Arab Republic of Egypt, and Arab British Helicopter Company*, International Chamber of Commerce, Court of Arbitration (8 June 1982; 5 March 1984; 25 July 1985) (1989) 80 ILR 595, 612, citing *Case Concerning the Barcelona Traction, Light and Power Company, Limited* (Judgment) [1970] ICJ Rep 3, 39, for the proposition that '[e]quity, in common with the principles of international law, allows the corporate veil to be lifted, in order to protect third parties against an abuse which would be to their detriment'.

[92] Notably, the commentary to draft article 61 cites no practice to substantiate the three conditions posed therein. Rather, it refers to the case law of the ECtHR to reiterate the position that states could still be held responsible for their obligations under the European Convention on Human Rights in a field where they have attributed competence to an international organization. ILC, 'Draft Articles on the Responsibility of International Organizations, with Commentaries' (n 91) 99–100. For a discussion of the ECtHR's case law in that regard, see n 32 in Chapter 8.

inherent conceptual vulnerability of international law.[93] Either way, the point here is that there does not appear to be a special problem with international organizations that is not encountered when thinking about how the state is set up in general.[94]

Finally, the concepts themselves entail certain restrictions. As with states, formal independence is important but not enough for the establishment of an international organization. Just as with states, in extreme cases, the potential lack of factual independence may limit claim to legal distinctiveness.

Formal independence is key in the sense that an entity must at some level be understood as an independent legal entity in the formal sense. As Chapter 8 will further develop, this will remain a question of the intentions of the members concerned, and in absence of a clear statement of intent, subject to an inference regarding these intentions, as the ICJ reasoned in *Reparation for Injuries*.[95] The upshot is not that the intention to create an international organization with international legal personality has to be stated expressly in a treaty. Rather it is that an organization may not possess such personality against the express intentions of the entities that would otherwise count as its members. States' positive declaration that they do not wish to create an entity with international legal personality should be thought as determinative in this respect.[96] Similar treatment should be reserved for when states consciously withhold the description of an entity as an international organization with

---

[93] This is not to say that there is no ambiguity in international law regarding the legal effect of a community's self-descriptions, especially when it comes to questions of state continuity and succession. As Crawford observes in that regard, '[i]n many instances the claim to continuity made by the State concerned will be determinative; other States will be content to defer to the position taken', but there are still outlier cases that are not easy to fit within an overarching framework, most notably those relating the position of Serbia following the dissolution of the Socialist Federal Republic of Yugoslavia: Crawford (n 1) 668–669.

[94] The problem is also mitigated in practice because, as with component members of a federal state with treaty-making capacity, states are free to choose whether they engage with these entities or not. See Van den Brande (n 25) 151.

[95] *Reparation for Injuries Suffered in the Service of the United Nations* (n 76) 178. See also *Case Concerning Pulp Mills on the River Uruguay (Argentina v Uruguay)* (Judgment) [2010] ICJ Rep 14, 53; *Judgment No. 2867 of the Administrative Tribunal of the International Labour Organization upon a Complaint Filed against the International Fund for Agricultural Development* (Advisory Opinion) [2012] ICJ Rep 10, 36.

[96] See eg Agreement Relating to the Establishment of the Functional Airspace Block 'Europe Central' between Germany, Belgium, France, Luxembourg, the Netherlands, and Switzerland (2 December 2010), art 2.2 ('This Agreement does not create an international organization with international legal personality').

legal personality.[97] In such cases, there is no attempted descriptive transformation of events to be given priority by international law to begin with. Likewise, it is hard to see how an international organization can emerge when cooperating states choose to describe an entity solely in domestic law terms.[98]

[97] Arguably this is the case with the OSCE: see Mateja Steinbrück Platise and Anne Peters, 'Transformation of the OSCE Legal Status' in Mateja Steinbrück Platise, Carolyn Moser, and Anne Peters (eds), *The Legal Framework of the OSCE* (CUP 2019) 334. Notably, OSCE itself objected to the fact that the ILC referred to it as an international organization in the context of the Draft Articles on the Responsibility of International Organizations. See Niels M Blokker and Ramses A Wessel, 'Revisiting Questions of Organisationhood, Legal Personality and Membership in the OSCE: The Interplay between Law, Politics and Practice' in Mateja Steinbrück Platise, Carolyn Moser, and Anne Peters (eds), *The Legal Framework of the OSCE* (CUP 2019) 141. Another instance where it can be inferred that states did not originally intend to grant an organization legal personality is when they consciously decide to do so at a later date. For example, the Pacific Islands Forum which is the principal cooperation mechanism for the fourteen independent and self-governing 'small island states' within the Pacific Ocean, as well as Australia and New Zealand, was originally founded in 1971 as the South Pacific Forum without any explicit reference to the organization's legal personality. In 2005, participating states concluded the 2005 Agreement Establishing the Pacific Islands Forum, establishing the forum as an international organization with legal personality. In such circumstances, it is reasonable to infer that until the 2005 agreement enters into force, the forum does not actually count as a legal entity separate from participating states.

[98] This would be the case, for example, with GAVI and the Global Fund to Fight AIDS, Tuberculosis and Malaria, both entities being incorporated associations under Swiss law. On the importance of incorporation under domestic law, see *Dr Horst Reineccius (Claim No 1), First Eagle SoGen Funds, Inc (Claim No 2), Pierre Mathieu and la Société de Concours Hippique de la Châtre (Claim No 3) v Bank for International Settlements (Respondent): Partial Award on the Lawfulness of the Recall of the Privately Held Shares on 8 January 2001 and the Applicable Standards for Valuation of those Shares* (Partial Award), Permanent Court of Arbitration (22 November 2002), 50–51. On the legal status of GAVI and the Global Fund, see Eyal Benvenisti, *The Law of Global Governance* (Brill 2014) 55–56 (for the Global Fund); Gian Luca Burci, 'Public/Private Partnerships in the Public Health Sector' (2009) 6 IOLR 359, at 362 (for GAVI), 363 (for the Global Fund). This is without prejudice to the question of whether it is possible in these cases too to lift the corporate veil of domestic law and thus attribute conduct directly to the participating states. See also mutatis mutandis *Barcelona Traction* (n 91) 39. In any event, nothing prevents the subsequent transformation of an NGO into an international organization. For example, the International Union of Official Travel Organizations, originally founded in 1947 as a non-governmental organization under Swiss law, was subsequently turned into the World Tourism Organization through ratifying a treaty. See Statutes of the World Tourism Organization (adopted 27 September 1970, entered into force 2 January 1975) 985 UNTS 339, art 36. Note that the question of whether an entity is created under the domestic law of a state, as GAVI or the Global Fund, is different from how members choose to name what otherwise constitutes an international organization. Thus, for

Aside from the cases of explicitly withholding such status or of choosing to submit an entity to the domestic jurisdiction of one state, there can also be less direct ways of inferring that participating states did not aim to create an international organization. This will especially be the case where the purported organs of an entity are appointed directly by the respective governments of states as part of their institutional set-up, and the organs' decisions are subject to the subsequent approval of any one of those governments, as was the case with the Administering Authority for Nauru in the respective ICJ case.[99] In all such cases, the resulting absence of international legal personality leads to activities being ultimately attributable to the corresponding cooperating states or other actors, together with any responsibility that may arise under international law for any wrongful conduct carried out.[100]

However, just as with statehood, the intention to create a formally separate legal entity is a necessary but not a sufficient condition for the ascription of the respective legal status.[101] Instead, formal independence creates only a presumption, that may be upturned taking into account other factors, including total factual dependence on another entity.[102] Although it is theoretically possible to imagine such a scenario affecting an international organization, this does not appear to be a real concern in

example, article 1 of the Convention Establishing the Inter-Arab Investment Guarantee Corporation provides that '[t]here is hereby established in accordance with the provisions of this Convention an organization called "The Arab Investment And Export Credit Guarantee Corporation" (hereinafter referred to as "the Corporation")'. While indeed most of the treaty thereafter refers to the organization as 'the Corporation', this alone should not be determinative for what appears to be in every other respect a classic international organization. See Arab League, Convention Establishing the Inter-Arab Investment Guarantee Corporation, 27 May 1971, OXIO 713.

[99] See *Case Concerning Certain Phosphate Lands in Nauru (Nauru v Australia)* (Preliminary Objections – Judgment) [1992] 256–258. This does not mean that no ambiguities may arise in practice. For example, the Agreement on the Privileges and Immunities of the Association of Southeast Asian Nations, 25 October 2009, OXIO 372, indicates that ASEAN members imply the organization possesses an international legal personality, referring in art 2 to the organization's 'legal personality' as well as to its 'capacities under international law'. Still, ASEAN may only act in relation to these capacities 'through its representatives authorised by the Member States'.

[100] Mateja Steinbrück Platise, 'Legitimate Governance as a Privilege and Price for the Autonomy of International Organisations' in Mateja Steinbrück Platise, Carolyn Moser, and Anne Peters (eds), *The Legal Framework of the OSCE* (CUP 2019) 313–314.

[101] See with respect to states, Nicholson (n 1) 98.

[102] See also Crawford (n 1) 76.

practice.[103] Even if it were, it would not fundamentally distinguish international organizations from states, for which the exact same problems could theoretically arise.

7.6 Conclusion

Theorizing states themselves as artificial entities offers a more nuanced way of accounting for the analytical possibility of international organizations with distinct legal personality. In the final analysis, the same capacity that underpins the existence of the state as a distinct legal entity for the purposes of international law can inherently accommodate the notion of international organizations. The state can be conceptualized as a unitarity entity without the need for implausible metaphysical constructions – whether these are employed on an 'as if' basis or not. Once the anthropomorphic premise and the ensuing state's intrinsic ontological status have been dropped, then the space opens to argue that if the state enjoys such status owing to how international law recognizes the capacity of a community to self-organize, then entities that are ultimately anchored in the same capacity also belong to the same family of legal subjects. It is ultimately this deeper connection with the state that defines the legal nature of international organizations rather that an analogy between the two actors or the fulfilment of some abstract criteria of 'self-governing' subjects that international law supposedly adheres to. And, because this connection is a necessary corollary of the state's own legal personality, neither a rule of incorporation nor a structural change in the legal system needs to be assumed before we can make sense of international organizations in positive law.

---

[103] See also ILC, 'Draft Articles on the Responsibility of International Organizations, with Commentaries' (n 91) 97–98, draft arts 59 and 60 and commentaries thereto. This does not mean that the independence of particular individuals working within an organization may not come under threat, a scenario that is more likely in practice. See eg *Bustani v Organisation for the Prohibition of Chemical Weapons* (ILOAT, Judgment No 2232, 16 July 2003) [16]; *Prosecutor v Ngirabatware* (Order to the Government of the Republic of Turkey for the Release of Judge Aydin Sefa Akay) Case no MICT-12-29-R (31 January 2017) paras 11–13. However problematic on their own regard, such interferences with the organization's independent functioning do not by themselves call into question the independent legal existence of the organization as such in the sense contemplated here.

International Organizations as Institutions Distinct from Their Members

8.1 How to Understand the Term 'International Organization'

8.1.1 The (Limited) Analytical Significance of Defining International Organizations

Chapter 7 put forward an alternative way of thinking about international organizations. In the following pages, I outline what this means for more specific doctrinal purposes. I start with considering the relatively limited purposes for which we might need to identify what it means for an entity to be an international organization. I then offer a refined understanding of the term 'international organization'. Following that, I revisit the notion that international organizations can possess a will that is distinct from their members, as well as a legal personality that is opposable towards non-members.

The theory advanced so far is founded on the idea of analytical continuity between international organizations and other forms of communal organization, including states. The logic of this continuity is neither descriptive nor analogical, but 'genealogical'. It is based on a shared basis for institutional emergence between international organizations and their members. This basis is, in essence, a community's capacity to organize at various degrees through self-description – without which not only international organizations cannot be properly accounted for, but also states themselves, both outside as well as within international law. In turn, this shared foundation contains no inherent analytical restriction as to the outputs of this self-description, including any restrictions that correspond to our abstract categories surrounding statehood and its relatives. Thus, international law should be understood to entail, by default, entities that scholars collectively, and somewhat reductively, call 'states' but also 'state-like' entities, as well as supra-state entities, including real and personal unions, confederations, and, finally, international organizations.

Accordingly, it would be misplaced to be looking for any one special customary rule – whether theorized as a rule of incorporation or not – for

Hong Kong, another for confederations, a third for international organizations, and so on, before admitting the existence of any of these as distinct legal entities in international law. Instead, international law should be theorized to possess a single norm that just refers back to the capacity of certain types of communities to organize in a manner that they see fit. A *majore ad minus*, we should not be looking for a customary international law specifically permitting the creation of international organizations of an interstate type, and another one that allows such institutions to be set up by sub-state entities or other international organizations. Consequently, the emergence of international organizations should not be presumed to coincide with any 'radical' change in terms of the actual legal system, even though, undeniably, it came in the wake of significant historical and political developments. This means that we do not need to exhaustively define international organizations as a separate class of entities before they can be allowed into our legal ontology. Instead, the significance of any such definition is limited to applying potential special rules emerging that specifically refer to these institutions.

It is not that differences do not exist between international organizations and other forms of communal organization, or more specifically between international organizations and states. In fact, it is precisely the peculiar needs of the underlying communities that lead to a diversity of form, and also the corresponding openness of the legal system towards it. Indeed, it is hard to imagine how the system would operate, not just with respect to international organizations but also to all the other instances whereby deference is paid to communal self-descriptions, were it not for that openness. Consequently, the present theory is about admitting this diversity of form in law rather than reducing it to one super-category or a series of airtight sub-categories. At the same time, this diversity should not mislead us in analytical terms. Idiosyncrasies in the legal set-up of these actors can make them the legitimate focus of scholarly, and sometimes legislative, concern. However, these differences should be taken to reflect, at least in the first instance, practical concerns rather than deeper analytical distinctions of an essentialist import.

Such practical concerns may at times lead to the elaboration of special norms covering a subset of these institutions, including potentially international organizations. This may legitimately give rise to a corresponding need to come up with a working definition of international organizations to that effect. For example, this could be the case with responsibility for wrongful acts,[1] the law of treaties,[2] or the settlement of disputes.[3] However, the need for such norms lies with working out how more abstract principles apply with respect to certain real or perceived peculiarities of the respective phenomena, rather than with any inherent singularity of the state such that would require new and separate norms every time we move away from the classic 'Montevideo' demarcation. It is not because international organizations are inherently separate as a class of entities that particular norms may need to be elaborated in that regard. It is not as if in the absence of such norms there would be a gap in *lex lata* in the strict sense. Rather, it is because the logic of our default principles may run out of obvious or self-explanatory deductions that we may sometimes have to contemplate more specialized rules that more clearly encompass new factual patterns. Putative specialized norms in these areas may thus require a working definition of these institutions so as to clarify their scope of application *ratione personae*.

Coming up with a definition of international organizations may also be necessary in scenarios that have little to do with the working out how more abstract principles apply in relation to these institutions and extend to classic questions of treaty interpretation. Indeed, nothing precludes international organizations from being handled separately as objects of legislative concern. For instance, art 34§2 of the ICJ Statute provides that the Court 'may request of public international organizations information relevant to cases before it ... '.[4] In this and similar cases, the question inevitably arises as to what counts as an international organization within the given context, in a manner not different in principle from assessing whether an entity counts as a 'state' for the purposes of applying a specific treaty.[5] Excluding cases where a special

---

[1] ILC, 'Draft Articles on the Responsibility of International Organizations, with Commentaries' (2011) II/2 YILC 46.

[2] Vienna Convention on the Law of Treaties between States and International Organizations or between International Organizations (adopted 21 March 1986, not yet in force) UN publication, Sales No E.94.V.5.

[3] In 2022, the ILC decided to include the topic of the 'Settlement of international disputes to which international organizations are parties' to its programme of work (in 2023, the Commission decided to change the title of the topic to 'Settlement of disputes to which international organizations are parties'). See ILC, 'Summaries of the Work of the International Law Commission' (2023) <https://legal.un.org/ilc/summaries/10_3.shtml> accessed 9 February 2025.

[4] See also art 34§3 (referring to the 'constituent instrument of a public international organization') and art 66§2 (referring to any 'international organization considered by the Court').

[5] See eg the question of whether Palestine qualifies as a state for the purposes of establishing the jurisdiction of ICC. For a discussion, see Alain Pellet, 'The Palestinian Declaration and the Jurisdiction of the International Criminal Court' (2010) 8(4) Journal of International

meaning has been established by the parties, this question will turn to the ordinary meaning to be given to the term 'international organization' in its context and in light of the respective treaty's object and purpose.[6] In such cases, we may indeed have to explain what counts as an international organization. While it may seem hard to define international organizations without any ambiguity in this respect, the more important meta-question is to appreciate the limited analytical purpose such a definition serves in each case. In any event, the potential need for a definition in that regard, as well as presumably that definition's divergence from that of other entities, such as states, should not distract us from the underlying default logic of continuity between these actors.

8.1.2 The Ordinary Meaning of the Term 'International Organization'

To the extent that an elucidation of the term 'international organization' may be necessary in the contexts just mentioned, the theory advanced so far allows for the following observations.

First, the notion that international organizations are necessarily 'inter-state' as a definitional requirement (see Chapter 1) should be reconsidered to reflect that the creation of these institutions is not the exclusive providence of states. In reality, the creation of both international organizations and states should be traced back to the capacity of a community to self-describe, with whatever legal consequences and protections international law attaches to the exercise of that capacity, which are, in principle, common across the board. It is thus possible to imagine international organizations who qualify as public institutions in the sense elaborated in Chapter 7 that feature no states among their membership. Indeed, as we have examined, sub-state entities can be, and have been, founding members of international organizations in the past.[7] The same

---

Criminal Justice 981. There is nothing preventing international organizations also counting as states in this context: see e.g. the Convention on the Rights of Persons with Disabilities (adopted 12 December 2006, entered into force 3 May 2008) 2515 UNTS 3, art 44 ('[r]eferences to "States Parties" in the present Convention shall apply to such organizations within the limits of their competence').

[6] This standard formulation comes from the Vienna Convention on the Law of Treaties (adopted 23 May 1969, entered into force 27 January 1980) 1155 UNTS 331, art 31.

[7] Most notably Australia, Canada, New Zealand, India, and South Africa with respect to the League of Nations, and India, Philippines, and the Soviet constituent republics of Belarus and Ukraine. A number of 'associated States' in the sense of UNGA Res 1541

is true for international organizations co-founding other international organizations.[8] Apart from being founders, there is also extensive practice in admitting such non-state entities as members of international organizations.[9] It follows that if an entity has the capacity to co-found or to become a member of an international organization at a later date, this also entails the capacity to do so with or without the presence of any state. We could thus have an international organization made up entirely of international organizations and/or sub-state entities.

Second, regarding the often-quoted 'governmental' nature of international organizations, it is equally entirely possible to have such organizations where no state governments are represented among the membership. This is evidently the case with international organizations made up entirely of other international organizations and/or sub-state entities. But, again following the principle of assigning priority to communal self-descriptions barring any special rules, there is nothing preventing states from creating international organizations whereby membership nominally attaches to some particular agency of the state.[10]

(15 December 1960) have also become members to international organizations, such as with Niue, Puerto Rico, the Cook Islands, and The Commonwealth of Northern Mariana Islands. See James Crawford, *The Creation of States in International Law* (2nd edn, OUP 2007), 633–635.

[8] There appears to be at least one example of an international organization established exclusively by other international organizations. The Centro Internacional de Mejoramiento de Maiz y Trigo (CIMMYT, INT) was established in 1988 through agreement between the International Bank for Reconstruction and Development (part of the World Bank) and the UNDP: see Constitution of the Centro Internacional de Mejoramiento de Maiz y Trigo, annexed to the Agreement between the International Bank for Reconstruction and Development and the UNDP (29 April 1988, amended March 2003 and 20 March 2004) art 5 ('CIMMYT, INT shall be an international organization possessing full juridical personality'). See also the Joint Vienna Institute, established by the IMF, BIS EBRD, IMF, OECD, World Bank, and Austria: Agreement for the Establishment of the Joint Vienna Institute (approved by the Executive Board of the International Monetary Fund on 21 January 1994 (Decision No. 10575-(94/4), 21 January 1994) and came into force on 19 August 1994).

[9] Hong Kong is a member of the WTO; Bermuda, Hong Kong, Macau, and the Netherlands Antilles (until 10 October 2010) are members of the World Customs Organization; the European Investment Bank is a member of the EBRD; the EU is a member to a number of international organizations, including the WTO, FAO, and the EBRD.

[10] This could be the case with INTERPOL, whose constitution provides that '[a]ny country may delegate as a Member to the Organization any official police body whose functions come within the framework of activities of the Organization': Constitution of the International Criminal Police Organization – INTERPOL (13 June 1956) I/CONS/GA/ 1956, art 4. Generally, on the question of INTERPOL's membership, see Rutsel Silvestre J Martha, *The Legal Foundations of INTERPOL* (Hart 2010) 170–172. A similar example

Depending on one's understanding of 'governmental',[11] it could be technically correct to designate some of these organizations as non-governmental. Yet it would be misleading to infer from this a category difference between these institutions and states, or a similarity with classic NGOs, given that the former all represent different expressions of the capacity of a national community to organize, whereas the latter do not (again, in the strict analytical sense employed here).[12] Following the theory developed thus far, all these eventualities – ranging from international organizations with only states as members to others with no state-members at all – are inherent in the system rather than having to rest on a putative new and separate norm of customary international law to that effect.[13] In sum, abstract definitional requirements that international organizations must exhibit an 'interstate' or a

appears to be the Southern African Development Parliamentary Forum, whose membership explicitly encompasses national parliaments: the Constitution of the Southern African Development Parliamentary Forum (SADC PF) (updated as on 15 August 2022), art 7§1.

[11] The term could be taken to denote that an organization has been established by any entity exercising any elements of governmental authority, which would presumably include any organ that exercises 'legislative, judicial, or any other functions' or it could be taken to indicate that an entity has been established by the government of a state in the strict sense. For the first understanding, see ILC, 'Draft Articles on Responsibility of States for Internationally Wrongful Acts, with Commentaries' (2001) II/2 YILC 31, 40–43, art 4–5 and commentaries thereto; for the second, see ILC, 'Draft Articles on the Responsibility of International Organizations, with Commentaries' (n 1) 49, art 2 and commentary thereto.

[12] Conversely, given the foundational role of self-description in this respect, the incorporation of an entity as a private law association will generally be indication enough that it should not be considered 'public' in the sense employed here. This is different to how an international organization may also encompass into its functioning entities that are not themselves expressions of a national community's capacity to self-organize in the sense construed here, such as classic NGOs. The presence of such entities in the functioning of an organization does not by itself change its legal nature (as indeed happens when states incorporate input from NGOs in some elements of their governance structure). Thus, for example, the fact that the World Tourism Organization is open to NGOs becoming non-voting affiliate members does not meaningfully distinguish that institution from other international organizations. See Statutes of the World Tourism Organization (adopted 27 September 1970, entered into force 2 January 1975) 985 UNTS 339, article 7(1): 'Affiliate membership of the Organization shall be open to international bodies, both intergovernmental and non-governmental, concerned with specialized interests in tourism and to commercial bodies and associations whose activities are related to the aims of the Organization or fall within its competence').

[13] Cf the UN Secretariat's view that:

The principle that an international legal person can be created by virtue of a treaty is, after all, nothing more than a rule of customary international law, and it may well be that a new customary rule of international law is emerging under which such a legal person could also be created by an agreement 'governmental'(in the narrow sense) nature can be misleading and should be viewed with much caution.

Third, as already touched upon in Chapter 7, given that the conceptual foundation of international organizations is priority given to a certain description of institutional reality, an element of intentionality is necessary. The underlying intention should concern the creation of an actor that is legally distinct, although no particular form for expressing that intention is required. Such intention need not be encapsulated in an international agreement concluded between states.[14] In fact, it could well be that the intention is inferred from practice, meaning that it reflects a convention among an organizations' members.[15] Moreover, due to the nested nature in which status-ascription via institutions operates in practice, the element of intentionality need not necessarily attach to a state. Theoretically, it could well attach directly to the will of a national community that has not yet constituted itself as a state (and may indeed never do), as, for example, when a non-self-governing territory co-founds or becomes a member to an international organization. Beyond that, it could attach to institutions further created by that national community,

concluded solely by autonomous public entities, such an agreement being governed by international law *pursuant to another new customary rule.*

Legal Opinion of the Secretariat of the UN (1971) United Nations Juridical Yearbook 215, UN Doc ST/LEG/SER.C/9, 218 (emphasis added).

[14] An often-quoted example in this respect is the Nordic Council, established by parallel decisions of the parliaments of Denmark, Iceland, Norway, and Sweden, an arrangement subsequently reflected in the 1962 Treaty of Co-operation between Denmark, Finland, Iceland, Norway, and Sweden, (the Helsinki Treaty), as most recently amended in 1996. See also Henry G Schermers and Niels M Blokker, *International Institutional Law* (5th edn, Martinus Nijhoff 2011) 38; Finn Seyersted, 'Objective International Personality of Intergovernmental Organizations: Do Their Capacities Really Depend upon the Conventions Establishing Them?' (1964) 34 Nordic Journal of International Law 47, 48–55.

[15] This is arguably the case with INTERPOL. See James Sheptycki, 'The Accountability of Transnational Policing Institutions: The Strange Case of Interpol' (2004) 19(1) Canadian Journal of Law & Society/La Revue Canadienne Droit et Société 107, 114–115; see *El Omari v The International Criminal Police Organization*, 21-1458-cv (2d Cir, 24 May 2022); Martha (n 10) 157. See also the analysis regarding the Commonwealth of Nations and the Commonwealth Agricultural Bureaux in Schermers and Blokker (n 14) 38. Note how this deferral to practice in determining institutional descriptions in the absence of expressly stated intentions is also followed by article 7 of the VCLT 1969 (n 6), which suggests that 'full powers' can be dispensed with when 'it appears from the practice of the States concerned or from other circumstances that their intention was to consider that person as representing the State', as well as the respective article 7 of the VCLT 1984 (n 2) with respect to the representatives of international organizations.

including obviously states, but also other sub-state entities that are supposed to be legally distinct from it in the eyes of international law, as well as international organizations themselves.

These three observations may help illuminate the 'ordinary' meaning of the term 'international organization'. However, it should be stressed again that the latter designation does not operate as a gateway to a realm of rights and obligations exclusively reserved for these institutions, as if they would have otherwise been 'blank slates' in the eyes of the law. It is not because certain institutions meet some abstract criteria of 'international organization' (or *mutandis mutandis* 'confederation' or 'personal union of states' or 'condominium') that particular rights, obligations, and capacities can attach to them as a matter of customary international law.[16] Rather, it is due to their common origin as institutions in communal self-description, always within the operating rationale of international law.

Beyond that default affiliation, special rules of custom may develop specifically in relation to a subset of those entities – or even a subset of a subset in the case of regional or bilateral custom. Likewise, treaty provisions may legitimately refer specifically to an arbitrarily narrow set of those entities. In such cases, the previous observations on the concept of international organization will only be suggestive rather than dispositive. Thus, a legal text may legitimately define an international organization as an 'international organization of States'[17] or as an 'intergovernmental organization constituted by States to which its member States have transferred competence over matters governed by this Convention, including the competence to enter into treaties in respect of those matters'.[18] Neither of these understandings is any more right or wrong than the other based on their (non-)correspondence to some more abstract definition of international organizations. Instead, each demands a separate inquiry as to the meaning of the terms employed by the parties. Similarly, a suggestion for the existence of a special customary norm pertaining to 'international organizations', should be followed by

---

[16] Cf Catherine Brölmann, *The Institutional Veil in Public International Law: International Organisations and the Law of Treaties* (Hart Oxford 2007) 84; Rowan Nicholson, *Statehood and the State-Like in International Law* (OUP 2019) 101.

[17] ICJ, Rules of Court (adopted 14 April 1978, entered into force 1 July 1978), art 69(4).

[18] United Nations Convention on the Law of the Sea (adopted 10 December 1982, entered into force 16 November 1994) 1833 UNTS 3 (UNCLOS), art 1, annex IX: Participation by International Organizations.

an account of what sort of international organizations is included in that category and why.

With these caveats in mind, the ordinary meaning of the term 'international organization' should be understood to encompass *any institution created by two or more national communities while exercising their capacity to self-describe, or by institutions already created by these communities while exercising that capacity, and which is intended to be legally distinct from these communities and all other institutions created by them.*

8.2   Letting Go of Causal Markers as Evidence of Distinct Will

8.2.1   No Special Problem Regarding the Distinct Will of International Organizations

Conceptualizing international organizations as corporate entities within a broader family of such institutions can help delineate more clearly their relationship with their members, including their member states. As noted in Chapter 3, a key, if elusive, notion in this respect has been that of an organization's volonté distincte. Scholars have tended to trace this back to the organization featuring some majority decision-making procedure. The core premise of this analysis is that the distinctiveness between the corporate entity and its members must be anchored in some sort of causal discontinuity between the two.

By now it should be apparent that this configuration of the problem corresponds to the 'individual vs organization' framework of looking at corporate existence. As further developed in Chapter 6, this framework takes off from the premise that individuals themselves are irreducible and fundamental entities. Yet, as Chapter 7 argued, what appears as the monolithic 'individual' in this context, namely the state, is anything but that – not only from an abstract ontological perspective, but also in terms of how we should conceptualize it for analytical purposes. Instead, the existence of both states and international organizations, as well as of a variety of different entities, rest on common foundations and are ultimately anchored in the same status-creating capacity of a national community. In other words, there is no mystery of 'distinct' will that is faced by international organizations that is not faced by any of these other institutions, including states: all of them are equally constructed entities. Nor should the state be understood to enjoy a privileged position in that respect as being somehow inherently and irreducibly fundamental. Thus, rather than trying to come up with causal indicia of separateness, we should uncover international law's rationale from individuating one entity from another and apply it to international organizations.

In that regard, as already established, international law follows, in the first instance and barring any special rules, the logic of a renvoi. Following this, it generally accords priority to internally produced descriptions of institutional reality. In practical terms, this means that while both descriptions of 'representatives of states A, B, and C voted for X' and 'international organization Y decided X' are potentially equally true (or equally untrue) from an abstracted perspective, international law gives priority to the second description of events. This is because it is only by this logic of priority that we are allowed to make statements such as '*state* A voted for X' in the first place, as opposed to merely 'a human being raised her hand' or 'signed a piece of paper'. In other words, we cannot construct the state without discounting certain forces as non-causal. It would then be to fall into irreparable contradiction to recognize this capacity to a community up until the construction of one form of institution, namely the state and its associated legal forms, but withhold recognizing the exercise of that capacity specifically when it comes to international organizations. Thus, following this logic, it is as if a provisional 'box' is drawn within this given context around international organization Y. This individuates it from the rest of the world and in relation to the lower-level entities that make it up, namely its members, the members' members, and so on. The relationship that then obtains between the organization and its members is neither one of identity nor one of causation. Rather, it approximates what happens at the internal level between a state and its officials.

This means that, in the eyes of international law, what members A, B, and C vote will *ground*, not cause, what the organization decides. Following this account, the will of the organization is distinct not because it is causally discontinuous from that of its members, but because what counts as an 'internal' space has been effectively created, a space from where the actions of members A, B, and C are transformed from a *cause* that makes something happen to the organization (namely something external), to a *reason* for the organization to act (namely something internal). In that sense, in the eyes of international law, the will of the organization remains dependent on, but not identical with, the will of its members. Those members' wills are also dependent on, but not identical with, the will of the entities that occupy the respective roles of their internal decision-making procedures. The re-description of the latter in terms of the former – the idea that what an official does *counts* as the doing of their state – forms the key idea that also permits the re-description of acts in terms of the organization.[19] In sum, the distinct will of international organizations should be understood as a normative construction employed within a particular context of initial assumptions rather than as reflecting some notion of natural causation, even for in-system purposes. So long as there is a rule of re-description in place that can be traced back to a community of the type that may create a state, that rule will create the space for nesting further formally independent entities in the eyes of international law.[20] Only then will questions of 'real' or 'actual' independence become relevant for international law.[21]

It follows that the existence of a particular decision-making procedure, including one featuring an organ that decides by majority, cannot by itself settle whether an international organization enjoys actual independence from its members. At first, this might seem to take away one safeguard against states potentially colluding and creating international organizations that are just legal shells for their activities. Yet, as already suggested, this would represent an oversimplification of the issue.[22] Because international organizations normally represent hugely complex institutions and some form of political entanglement, their creation is hardly ever 'free' for states. It certainly does not appear to be equivalent to the ease with which individuals can set up corporate entities in certain domestic jurisdictions.

Moreover, equating independence to causal discontinuity between the intentions of the organization and its members may be missing the point.

[19] See also the ICJ's jurisprudence on determining whether the authorship of an act belongs to an international organization: *Certain Expenses of the United Nations (Article 17, paragraph 2, of the Charter)* (Advisory Opinion) [1962] ICJ Rep 151, 168; *Effects of Awards of Compensation Made by the United Nations Administrative Tribunal* (Advisory Opinion) [1954] ICJ Rep 47, 53.

[20] See also Niels M Blokker, 'International Organizations and Their Members' (2004) 1(1) IOLR 139, 154.

[21] For the notion of 'real' or 'actual' independence, see Crawford (n 7) 72–88. Thus, a clear finding of the absence of legal personality makes the examination of whether an institution possesses a distinct will of its own unnecessary. See in this respect *Judgment No. 2867 of the Administrative Tribunal of the International Labour Organization upon a Complaint Filed against the International Fund for Agricultural Development* (Advisory Opinion) [2012] ICJ Rep 10, 35–36. In that case, the Court, after making a negative finding as to whether International Fund for Agricultural Development enjoyed a distinct legal personality, did not go at all into the question whether that entity enjoyed a volonté distincte.

[22] Text to n 92 in Chapter 7.

To revisit our example from Chapter 3, compare a hypothetical organization that unanimously decides to empower its secretariat to set up a new international criminal tribunal with an organization that decides by majority vote what items will appear on the menu of the organization's in-house canteen. Which organization enjoys more independence? Indeed, there can be no straightforward abstract comparison between a power that is granted unanimously but then allows for virtually unfettered discretion and a power that is granted by majority but is only nominal in scope. This suggests that the discipline should disassociate the notion of autonomy from the absence or presence of a specific decision-making procedure, as well as from its more obscure 'somewhat metaphysical character'.[23]

This conclusion aligns with practice. When members expressly confer legal personality to an organization, the ICJ generally treats this as determinative without delving into issues of decision-making.[24] In *Pulp Mills* it did so, even despite the fact that, by definition, the decisions of the organization in question had to be adopted by common accord by its two member states, Argentina and Uruguay. Instead, the Court put weight on whether the organizations' decisions are 'prepared and implemented by a secretariat whose staff enjoy privileges and immunities'.[25] Equally important for the Court was whether an organization's secretariat has the power to 'decentralize its various functions by setting up whatever subsidiary bodies it deems necessary'.[26] In general, the Court seems to defer to explicit conferrals of legal personality.[27] Beyond that,

---

[23] Brölmann (n 16) 21.

[24] See eg *Judgment No. 2867 of the Administrative Tribunal of the International Labour Organization* (n 21) 35, with respect to the International Fund for Agricultural Development and the International Union for the Protection of New Varieties of Plants; *Case Concerning Pulp Mills on the River Uruguay (Argentina v Uruguay)* (Judgment) [2010] ICJ Rep 14, 53, with respect to the Comisión Administradora del Río Uruguay.

[25] *Case Concerning Pulp Mills on the River Uruguay (Argentina v Uruguay)* (n 24) 53. On the importance of immunities granted to the staff of the organization, see also *Judgment No. 2867 of the Administrative Tribunal of the International Labour Organization* (n 21) 35. The Court first established a strong link between an organization's independence and that of its agents in *Reparation for Injuries Suffered in the Service of the United Nations* (Advisory Opinion) [1949] ICJ Rep 174, 183.

[26] See ibid. See also Guglielmo Verdirame, *The UN and Human Rights: Who Guards the Guardians?* (CUP 2011) 33–34; Fernando Bordin, *The Analogy between States and International Organizations: Legal Reasoning and the Development of the Law of International Organizations* (CUP 2018) 77–78.

[27] See also *Judgment No. 2867 of the Administrative Tribunal of the International Labour Organization* (n 21) 35–36.

the discretion that an organization's officials may enjoy in implementing decisions, or whether they are shielded from the exercise of their members' domestic jurisdictions (which is premised on the legal separateness of the institution to which they are attached), seem to provide stronger evidence as to the existence of the organization's separate identity than a particular decision-making procedure.

Whether the substantive aspect of this separate identity is jeopardized because a member 'directs and controls' the organization will remain a distinct factual question.[28] The member in question may incur responsibility, as the law provides, but this will not normally negate the legal personality of the organization.[29] Of course, it is theoretically conceivable that permanent loss of any real or actual independence may undermine an organization's claim to legal personality to begin with. However, states too need to show some ongoing minimum degree of real or actual independence.[30] Again, the takeaway is not that the law is entirely unambiguous at this point, but rather that there is no special puzzle concerning international organizations in that regard.

8.2.2   Members and the Legal Distinctiveness of International Organizations

Construing the distinct legal personality of international organizations in this manner does not absolve members from their responsibility regarding conduct that is incompatible with their own international obligations. As a matter of principle, the priority given to certain descriptions of institutional reality does not foreclose that reality being appraised separately and concurrently under a different rule, thus preventing one description totally 'eclipsing' the other. This is essentially the idea that two entities may legally exist in a parallel yet distinct manner. This is why, for example, individual criminal responsibility for state officials is conceptually and analytically possible as a matter of international law.

---

[28] ILC, 'Draft Articles on the Responsibility of International Organizations, with Commentaries' (n 1) 97–98, art 59 and commentary thereto. See also Nikolaos Voulgaris, *Allocating International Responsibility between Member States and International Organizations* (Hart 2019).

[29] See also Jean d'Aspremont, 'The Multifaceted Concept of the Autonomy of International Organizations and International Legal Discourse' in Richard Collins and Nigel D White (eds), *International Organizations and the Idea of Autonomy: Institutional Independence in the International Legal Order* (Routledge 2011) 69.

[30] See generally Crawford (n 7) 72–88.

Similarly, and especially since members do not forego their own legal personality by joining an international organization, their acts in the context of that organization can constitute internationally wrongful acts on their own terms.[31] Such acts could consist in voting or implementing a particular decision for the organization, potentially triggering member states' international obligations to 'prevent and punish' genocide or 'respect and ensure' certain human rights.[32] Yet, in the final analysis, this too presents a problem of interpreting the respective obligations, not a problem specific to international organizations.

The proposed non-causal account of distinct will allows for further insights regarding the structural relationship between international organizations and their members. The ensuing recognition that a vertical relation of dependence of the type that can obtain between a state and its officials may obtain between an organization and its members means that, while international organizations are still dependent on their members (simply put, if all members disappeared, there would be no international organizations), they should not be thought of as being identical to them.

This non-identity of an organization and its members can support a range of propositions. The first one is a theoretical account of why the membership of international organizations may change and the organization may remain the same without any rule of incorporation to that effect: so long as an international organization is connected to 'a'

---

[31] See in this respect ECtHR's dictum in *Waite and Kennedy*:

> where States establish international organisations in order to pursue or strengthen their cooperation in certain fields of activities, and where they attribute to these organisations certain competences and accord them immunities, there may be implications as to protection of fundamental rights. It would be incompatible with the purpose and object of the [European Convention on Human Rights], however, if the Contracting States were thereby absolved from their responsibility under the Convention in relation to the field of activity covered by such attribution.

Waite and Kennedy v Germany [GC], App no. 26083/94, ECHR 1999-I, 15. See also *Bosphorus Hava Yolları Turizm ve Ticaret Anonim Şirketi v Ireland [GC]*, App no. 45036/98, ECHR 2005-VI. Generally see Voulgaris (n 28); on the related topic of 'piercing the corporate veil', see Odette Murray, 'Piercing the Corporate Veil: The Responsibility of Member States of an International Organization' (2011) 8 IOLR 291.

[32] See also Frederic Naert, *International Law Aspects of the EU's Security and Defence Policy, with a Particular Focus on the Law of Armed Conflict and Human Rights* (1st edn, Intersentia 2010) 361ff; Jennifer Trahan, *Existing Legal Limits to Security Council Veto Power in the Face of Atrocity Crimes* (CUP 2020) 210–215.

community in the sense developed thus far, it will not eclipse as a legal person (even as it may no longer qualify as an *inter*-national organization if it ends up being connected to only one such community). The second is that two organizations can be legally distinct from each other even if they share the same members, not too differently from when two sub-state entities of the same state both enjoy distinct legal personality (a conclusion that is very hard to justify for those who analyse international organizations as groups of states). Finally, this account explains why international organizations cannot be considered to automatically become parties to the treaties of their members.[33] Following the theory developed here, it does not follow ipso facto that international organizations are 'transitively' bound by their members' obligations.[34] This underlying rationale however does not apply when international organizations do

---

[33] See eg *Priorities from India/ASTRAZENECA*, EPO, Decision of the Enlarged Board of Appeal (26 April 2004) G 2/02 and G 3/02 [2004] EPOR 39, para 8.3, where the Enlarged Board of Appeals of the EPO held that:

> The EPO is not itself party to the WTO and the TRIPS Agreement. Thus, the obligations deriving from the TRIPS Agreement do not bind the EPO directly but only such Contracting States of the EPC [European Patent Convention] as are members of the WTO and the TRIPS Agreement. In this connection, it is irrelevant whether some or all of the Contracting States of the EPO are party to the TRIPS Agreement. Even if all of them had become members of the TRIPS Agreement on January 1, 1995, so that no problems of reciprocity under the Indian patent law would have arisen, a notification under Art 87(5) EPC would still have been required.

[34] Cf Pierre Klein who argues that the *nemo plus iuris dat quam ipse habet* is a principle of international law, leading him to conclude that international organizations may be bound transitively by the treaties of their members. Pierre Klein, *La Responsabilité Des Organisations Internationales Dans Les Ordres Juridiques Internes et En Droit Des Gens* (Bruylant 1998) 341–344. For a similar argument, see Henry G Schermers, 'The European Communities Bound by Fundamental Human Rights' (1990) 27(2) Common Market Law Review 249. According to the theory elaborated here, the principle does not come into play, since the proper conceptualization of the membership relation is not one of 'giving' any rights attached to the members' separate legal identity. Taken literally, the alternative would also probably mean that international organizations are bound by all treaty obligations of all their members, regardless of whether these were shared between them. This would seem to radically depart from how the issue is understood in practice. See also Olivier De Schutter, 'Human Rights and the Rise of International Organisations: The Logic of Sliding Scales in the Law of International Responsibility' in Jan Wouters and others (eds), *Accountability for Human Rights Violations by International Organisations* (Intersentia, 2010) 51, 62–63, describing this doctrine as 'unworkable' in practice. What has been said about the non-identity of an organization with its members in legal terms is without prejudice to duties of the members to act in good faith in their treaty relations. On the latter, see Murray (n 32). For the general problematique surrounding an organization's 'institutional veil', see also Brölmann (n 16) 260–272.

not just operate in parallel to its members on the international plane but functionally succeed them with respect to the exercise of some of its competences, as is the case in certain instances with the EU and its members.[35]

8.3 The Legal Personality of International Organizations vis-à-vis Non-members

This way of framing the problem of international organizations' separate identity can also illuminate how we should understand the opposability of their legal personality to non-members. The account advanced here ties this opposability to the more general problem of the objective legal effect of status-ascriptions resulting from communal self-description – including the problem of how states relate to each other in this respect. It thus does away with the persistent idea that tracing the legal personality of an international organization back to a grant by its members somehow makes it opposable only vis-à-vis them.

By virtue of its 'genealogical' account of the problem, the proposed theory also dispenses with the need for a change in positive law that would institute the opposability of international organizations' legal personality vis-à-vis non-members. Instead, what has been said so far suggests that international law does not need a separate rule of customary international law, either conceptualized as a rule of incorporation[36] or something equivalent,[37] nor a 'structural'[38] change or a 'radical extension

---

[35] For this more exceptional scenario, see Robert Schütze 'The "Succession Doctrine" and the European Union' in Robert Schütze (ed), *Foreign Affairs and the EU Constitution* (CUP 2014); Case C-21-24/72 *International Fruit Company NV v Produktschap voor Groenten en Fruit* [1972] ECR 1219, paras 14–18. See also Case T-315/01, *Kadi v Council and Commission* [2005] ECR-II 3659, paras 192–204, referring to case law of the EC courts to support the proposition that 'unlike its Member States, the Community as such is not directly bound by the Charter of the United Nations'. The Court of First Instance then went on to source an obligation to observe the Charter by virtue of the Treaty Establishing the European Community, referring by analogy to the *International Fruit Company Case*. The judgment of the Court of First Instance was later reversed on appeal by the Grand Chamber but on different grounds.

[36] Bordin (n 27) 54, 198.

[37] See eg *ECOWAS v Bank of Credit and Commerce International*, French Court of Appeals, Paris (13 January 1993) 113 ILR 473, referring to a possible rule of customary international law superseding the norms enshrined in art 34 and 35 of the VCLT 1968 on the relative effect of treaties towards third parties.

[38] ILC, 'Third Report on the Question of Treaties Concluded between States and International Organizations or between Two or More International Organizations by

of its definition'[39] before it can accommodate international organizations. Nor does international law need to accompany these institutions' separate identity with a test for independence that is conceptually different from the one that it employs in relation to states. The state's corporate existence is not anchored in some metaphysical substance doing all the work, or the fiction of one, but rather in the effectiveness of a community's capacity to put in place a rule of recognition that prioritizes certain descriptions over others. Thus, as I have argued, the capacity to constitute an international organization should be seen as an in-built option of the system, an extension of the capacity to organize in the form of a state. We cannot accept the latter capacity as producing legal effects in international law without simultaneously allowing for the possibility of the former.

Coupling the problem of international organizations' and states' corporate existence in this manner suggests that international law cares *by default* about the descriptions of institutional reality produced by international organization's own rule of re-description. Doing so, international law thus dissociates the separate identity of international organizations from a structural change taking place in the law or a rule of incorporation becoming part of positive law. Moreover, it does so in a way that dispels the notion that international organizations are free-floating or even self-anchored rules of recognition that are competitors to states – a plausible but ultimately counterintuitive construction of some arguments from analogy.[40] According to the theory advanced here, international organizations are not, and should not be, theorized as self-crowned legal persons, even if that is only so that they can then be compared with states. Instead, their foundation emanates from a reshuffling and reorganization of the same capacity that constitutes their members, most prominently states, at a different level. It is this quality rather than any analogy that allows states and international organizations

---

Mr. Paul Reuter, Special Rapporteur – Draft Articles with Commentaries' (1974) UN Doc A/CN.4/279 and Corr.1 (E. only) 135, 150, para 20.

[39] Seyersted (n 14) 93. See also Jan Klabbers, 'On Seyersted and His Common Law of International Organizations' (2008) 5 IOLR 381–382.

[40] Klabbers explains this conceptualization of the problem very well in Jan Klabbers, 'The Emergence of Functionalism in International Institutional Law: Colonial Inspirations' (2014) 25 EJIL 645, 666. See also Guy Fiti Sinclair, *To Reform the World: International Organizations and the Making of Modern States* (OUP 2017) 295, echoing some of the same sensibilities but in a less doctrinal context.

to be thought of as belonging to a common class of entities in international law.

This account adds nuance to the theoretical justification for international organizations having a legal personality that is opposable to non-members. If the emergence of states and international organizations as corporate entities can be traced back to the same mechanism, then the legal effects of the descriptions produced by this mechanism should be thought of in the same terms: if the former are thought capable of producing in-system 'objective' – meaning opposable erga omnes – descriptions of institutional reality, so should the latter. Thus, the legal personality of international organizations should not be thought of as being objective because there is something inherently 'odd' about the notion of relative subjects, as some authors have suggested. Rather, it should be thought of as being objective for the same reason that the legal personality of their members, including most prominently their member states, is recognized as objective in international law.[41] If a rule of recognition can yield descriptions of events at the state level which are valid erga omnes in the eyes of international law (that is, without the need for ad hoc recognition by other states), so can a rule of recognition of an international organization which is nested by it. Both yield descriptions of events that are by default valid erga omnes because both are offspring of international law's admission of the same capacity for institutionalization through self-description.

Conversely put, there is no special problem regarding the objective legal personality of international organizations that is not encountered by states. This means that even if we accept the constitutive theory of recognition as it is generally construed,[42] a state that recognized states A and B would not need to extend separate recognition to a putative international organization C created by A and B, because it would have had already recognized the descriptive power of the underlying communities of states A and B to constitute themselves as unitary legal persons, which would in turn lie at the foundation of international organization C.[43] This understanding of the problem may explain why, despite the

---

[41] See eg James D Fry, 'Rights, Functions, and International Legal Personality of International Organizations' (2018) 36 Boston University International Law Journal 221, 233; Bordin (n 27) 61–62.

[42] For a discussion of the constitutive theory, see Crawford (n 7) 19–22.

[43] This is just a hypothetical employed to exhibit the logic behind what is being advocated here. The theory developed herein is inclined to follow the majority view regarding state recognition, namely that it has only a declaratory effect. See text to n 24 in Chapter 7.

fierce theoretical debate, there has never been a significant practice of recognition or non-recognition regarding international organizations.[44]

In sum, the capacity to create international institutions with objective legal personality should be understood to be inherent in international law, since the latter already admits the capacity of a community to organize itself by constituting a state as a unitary corporate actor. To subject this to the emergence of a rule of incorporation or a structural shift in the system of international law would be inconsistent with our rationale for recognizing the state's objective legal existence in the first place. Instead, if exercising this capacity can create actors that are recognized as objective by international law, the same effect should be recognized when that capacity is exercised to create corporate actors beyond national boundaries. Consequently, international law should not be theorized to possess a separate checklist of conditions for recognizing the legal personality of international organizations.[45]

8.4   Conclusion

Once we understand states and international organizations as part of a continuous genealogy of legal entities, we can start reappraising key doctrinal puzzles surrounding the structural relationship that may obtain between these two institutions. This has implications for the very definition of international organizations. It properly accounts for their founding and membership involving entities other than states, rather than just registering this heterogeneity as an empirical observation with uncertain analytical import. It also unveils the rather limited analytical value that such a definition may have in practice. This value is mostly confined to conventional efforts to pin down the ordinary meaning of the term 'international organization'. At the same time, the conceptual continuity with states suggests that international organizations' distinct will no longer needs to be established through the existence of a specific decision-making procedure that would supposedly allow international organizations to escape the ontological orbit of their members. Rather, distinct will should be understood in conventional terms, much in the same terms that happens with states as well as all the other state-like

---

[44] See Chittharanjan F Amerasinghe, *Principles of the Institutional Law of International Organizations* (2nd edn, CUP 2005) 87. Cf the practice regarding the Soviet Union when it denied the objective legal existence of the EU: Brölmann (n 16) 85.
[45] Cf Brölmann (n 16) 84.

entities that have been discussed. Similarly, the opposability of inter-national organizations' legal personality may rest on the same basis as that of their members. If international law recognizes that the capacity of a community to create institutions operates in an objective manner, then there is no reason to distinguish between that capacity being exercised within and beyond the confines of a state.

International Organizations and Customary International Law

9.1 International Organizations and the Formation of Customary International Law

9.1.1 General Theory behind the Capacity of International Organizations to Contribute to the Formation of Customary International Law

The insight that, despite their differences, there is no analytically hard-wired category distinction between states and international organizations as species of legal entities (always barring the potential emergence of special rules) should inform how we appraise the practice of these institutions with respect to the formation of customary international law. Once we let go of anthropomorphic understandings of the state, this problem becomes one of understanding international law's deeper logic rather than trying to compare and contrast international organizations with states or reduce the former to the latter. In turn, this can help illuminate the adjacent problem of the extent to which customary international law applies to international organizations.

The guiding idea here too is that international law should be understood to be in principle indifferent to the particular forms that the self-organization of a community may take. Not only is there no numerus clausus of such institutions, but precisely because international law does not dwell on form in that sense, the operating logic should be construed in terms of what I have called these institutions' 'genealogy': their common root back to community-sanctioned self-descriptions. Thus, what should matter for the formation of customary international law is whether the practice in question attaches to an organ that can ultimately source its authority back to a national community.

This reorientation of the problem calls out as artificial any respective blanket distinction between states and international organizations with respect to the formation of customary international law. It firmly admits international organizations as well as other institutional variations that communal organization may take as perfectly legitimate contributors to the formation of international custom.

At the same time, because this theory is founded on continuity in the exercise of power rather than analogy, a more intuitive account of the weight to be attached to this practice becomes possible. While the practice of international organizations should count towards the formation of custom, it should not be appraised separately in terms of its representativeness: if an organization with three member states and those three members all concurrently engage in the same practice, this only yields three national communities' worth of practice, even as the practice of all four institutions should be taken into account. By extension, if an organization with three member states engages in some practice that any or all its members do not engage in, then its practice should still be taken into account.

To understand the contribution of the theory advanced here, we have to first consider how the analogy between states and natural persons imposes an 'all or nothing' approach to this problem. Indeed, if the state is modelled as a natural entity, then international organizations can either be theorized as artificial entities, and thus incapable of contributing anything on their own to international customary law-making, or they can themselves be theorized in rough anthropomorphic terms, whose contributions should thus in principle be thought of as equally valuable as that of any other subject of the system, meaning, in this case, states. Followed consistently, the second approach suggests that international organizations and states are each entitled to 'one vote' when it comes to international law-making.

While there are no elections in international law to test this theory,[1] the formation of customary international law, with all its flaws and

---

[1] It is worth noting that according to procedural rules of the drafting conference of the Vienna Convention on the Law of Treaties between States and International Organizations or between International Organizations (adopted 21 March 1986, not yet in force) UN publication, Sales No E.94.V.5 (VCLT 1986), international organizations had the right to submit procedural proposals as well as substantive proposals, but they did not themselves have the right to vote, and their proposals could not be put into a vote unless formally supported by a state. For the text of the draft rules of procedure, see UNGA Res 40/76 (11 December 1985) UN Doc A/RES/40/76 Annex I: Draft rules of procedure. For a discussion, see Catherine Brölmann, *The Institutional Veil in Public International Law: International Organisations and the Law of Treaties* (Hart Oxford 2007) 189–190; Fernando Bordin, *The Analogy between States and International Organizations: Legal Reasoning and the Development of the Law of International Organizations* (CUP 2018) 127–128.

ambiguities, is still thought to reflect a practice that is followed by a sense of legal obligation that is sufficiently 'widespread' and 'representative'.[2] If international organizations truly represented separate communities of their own, the second approach would imply that practice should be widespread and representative among states *and* international organizations. This could present a dubious proposition in terms of custom's development, given that international organizations currently outnumber states in the international legal order. It also does not reflect how the identification of customary international law tends to proceed in practice.

There are other examples apart from the formation of custom which strongly suggest that a logic other than an analogy between international organizations and states is at work. For example, as we have seen, it is generally agreed that the emergence of jus cogens norms rests upon the recognition and acceptance by 'the international community of *states* as a whole'.[3] Echoing a similar rationale, the VCLT 1986 counts only ratification or accession by states for the purposes of that treaty entering into force while not counting the respective confirmation or accession by international organizations.[4] All in all, neither doctrine nor practice appears to unreservedly count international organizations as just another state with respect to the formation of international custom, as well as other fundamental aspects of international law-making.

Contrary to this analogy, or its negation, the theory advanced here suggests that it is equally misplaced to view international organizations as mindless corporate entities as it is to view them as soulful individuals. Instead it is crucial to appreciate that both international organizations and states represent different institutional forms that emanate from the exercise of the same capacity at different levels of organization. Moving away from the aforementioned 'all or nothing' approach, this suggests

---

[2] See eg ILC, 'Draft Conclusions on the Identification of Customary International Law, with Commentaries' (2018) UN Doc A/73/10, 135 (Draft Conclusion 8); Committee on Formation of Customary (General) International Law, 'Statement of Principles Applicable to the Formation of General Customary International Law' in International Law Association London Conference Final Report of the Committee (International Law Association, London 2000) 1.

[3] See Vienna Convention on the Law of Treaties (adopted 23 May 1969, entered into force 27 January 1980) 1155 UNTS 331 (VCLT 1969) art 53; see also VCLT 1986 (n 1) art 53. See also ILC, 'Second Report on *jus cogens* by Dire Tladi, Special Rapporteur' (2017) UN Doc A/CN.4/706, pp. 30–39.

[4] See VCLT 1986 (n 1) art 85 (including Namibia as a non-state entity which was at the time represented by the UN Council for Namibia).

that international organizations can contribute to the formation of customary international law directly and in their own name but their practice is not to be weighed separately to that of their members in terms of its representativeness.[5]

Imagine for instance that states A and B create an organization X, and then A, B, and X each engage in a certain practice. According to the theory advocated here, X's practice would constitute admissible evidence for the formation of a new customary norm. However, between them, A, B, and X would only produce two national communities' worth of practice, regardless of how the production of the evidence pointing to that practice is distributed among the institutions that these communities have created. Thus, when assessed for whether it is sufficiently representative and widespread, the practice of X would not count as if it was that of one extra state. Crucially, however, it would still count as practice even if only one or none of its members engaged in that practice at all.

The rationale behind this is similar to the following scenario. Imagine that 200 organs from a single state engage in a certain practice.[6] Now compare this with the case of a single organ from 200 different states engaging in a certain practice. In both instances there are 200 organs engaging in a practice. In both, their practice contributes to the formation of customary international law. Yet in the first case, the practice of 200 organs is not weighed separately: it still counts as that of one state

---

[5] For the notion that the practice of international organizations can contribute to the formation of customary international law 'in certain cases', see ILC, 'Draft Conclusions on the Identification of Customary International Law, with Commentaries' (n 2) 130–131 (Draft Conclusion 4 and commentary thereto). The commentary suggests that the practice of international organizations will normally be relevant in two scenarios: where member states have transferred exclusive competences to an international organization and where they have transferred competences to an organization that are functionally equivalent to those exercised by states.

[6] Following standard doctrine, the practice of any organ of the state counts towards the formation of new norms of customary international law. See ILC, 'Draft Conclusions on the Identification of Customary International Law, with Commentaries' (n 2) 132–133 (Draft Conclusion 5 and commentary thereto). As the commentary to conclusion 5 explains:

> . . . State practice consists of any conduct of the State, whatever the branch concerned and functions at issue. In accordance with the principle of the unity of the State, this includes the conduct of any organ of the State forming part of the State's organization and acting in that capacity, whether in exercise of executive, legislative, judicial or 'other' functions, such as commercial activities or the giving of administrative guidance to the private sector.

(even if due to the volume of evidence we may more easily characterize it as consistent). In the second, it is weighed for each state individually and is counted accordingly. Similarly, because international organizations are genuine collective institutions, the practice of their organs should count towards the formation of international custom, even though when weighing this practice's evidentiary value, regard must be had for the underlying base of the respective national communities (most frequently organized through states) that ultimately ground the organization.

This goes back to our philosophical discussion of identity, composition, and constitution: we may conceptually separate an entity from the lower-level entities that make it up without hiding the underlying dependence relations from view.[7] Thus, we may conceptualize a wall as being distinct from its individual bricks, meaning, for example, that we may replace a brick and still have the same wall. However, in whatever manner we describe the wall – as an aggregate of bricks or as a separate entity – we are bound to assess its weight at a given time in the same manner. Simply put, even if the wall is thought to be non-identical to the individual bricks, it is still dependent upon bricks. In the same manner that weight is a derivative property dependent on the wall's bricks, the weight of an organization's practice can be thought of as a derivative property and needs to be weighed accordingly. This means that the practice of an organization with two members should be weighed differently than that of one with 200 members, even though both practices should count. Thus, both the distinct legal existence of international organizations and the desideratum of representativeness in the identification of customary norms are safeguarded. The latter especially would indeed be threatened if we allowed for the practice of each international organization to be weighed separately, coupled with states' inherent capacity to create a practically infinite number of legal persons (both sub-state and supra-state).

This logic can also help explain the idea that peremptory norms have to be accepted by 'the international community *of States* as a whole'[8] or why a universal treaty, such as the VCLT 1986, does not take into account accession by international organizations for the purposes of it entering into force.[9] In these cases, international law seems to be

---

[7] Text to n 26 in Chapter 5.

[8] Emphasis added. VCLT 1969 (n 3) art 53; VCLT 1986 (n 1) art 53. See also ILC, 'Yearbook of the International Law Commission 1982 Volume II Part Two: Report of the Commission to the General Assembly on the Work of the Thirty-Fourth Session' (1982) UN Doc A/CN.4/SER.A/1982/Add.1 (Part 2), 56, para 3 on the ILC's rationale for excluding international organizations from the wording of art 53 of the VCLT 1986 (n 1).

[9] VCLT 1986 (n 1) art 85.

concerned with the fact that a sufficient threshold of representation among the international community is achieved. The way in which both cases are dealt with suggests that international organizations do not indeed themselves weigh as separate political communities, but they rather represent a reorganization of existing ones at a different level.

Not counting international organizations in these circumstances should be understood to rest on logically derived principles rather than some essentialist rationale. Recognizing that a wall is distinct from its individual bricks introduces a 'new' entity into the world but it does not add new matter to it. If we have a stack of individual bricks weighing 1,000 kg and then we re-describe those bricks as a wall, we still have only 1,000 kg of material, not 1,000 kg + 1,000 kg = 2,000 kg. Accordingly, if a rule sets out to guarantee maximum representation, it should count bricks, not bricks *and* walls. This makes sense: not every state is necessarily a member of an international organization, and some states may be part of more than one international organization; at the same time, every state can be thought to correspond, at least analytically, to a distinct national community. In line with this logic, international law does not count international organizations as just another state in this instance not because they do not have a proverbial soul, but because this is the likeliest way to achieve the widest possible representation of the underlying political communities in practice, always following the operating rationale of international law. Thus, while actors such as states, international organizations, and confederations all belong to the same class of legal actors, the state typically forms the first institutional step in this ladder of organization, and thus occupies de facto a special systemic position in certain aspects of international law-making. Singling out the state among the broader family of what have been described here as 'public' entities is only because it is generally thought to be, at least by comparison, the most representative form of political organization among national communities – not due to some obscure metaphysical difference among them.[10]

---

[10] Whether this systemic assumption about states being the most representative form of organization is accurate in its entirety or it presents an oversimplification motivated by practical considerations is up for debate. Even though normally thought only as a temporary phase until the achievement of statehood or association with another state, the possibility of national communities not represented through states certainly seems to exist in international law, most notably with non-self-governing territories. Formulations such as 'a norm accepted and recognized by the international community *of States* as a whole' do not reflect this nuance, perhaps because not being a state and at the same time not being associated with any state was thought of as somewhat exceptional and, in any

This means that the old subject/object dichotomy does not capture the conceptual relationship between states and international organizations, if we associate the distinction with the capacity to participate in international law-making.[11] In certain respects, most notably the formation of customary international law, international organizations can themselves contribute to international law-making and in this sense be considered subjects of international law. However, the state will in practice remain a unique point of reference in matters such as the identification of peremptory norms. Yet the reason for this is not that the state somehow represents a more real or natural entity than international organizations, but rather because it is presumed to reflect more accurately the tally of the underlying political communities.[12] Certainly, this soft presumption should be overturned when it does not correspond to the overarching principle at work. Most notably this would be the case in domains where international organizations do not just exist in parallel with their members but functionally succeed them, as with the EU and its members with respect to certain of its competences.[13] Excluding such international organizations from the pool of entities whose 'acceptance and recognition' needs to be taken into account in the identification of peremptory norms imposes an arbitrary distinction that unjustifiably disadvantages those political communities that have chosen to organize in this manner.

With that caveat in mind, there appears to be no inconsistency between recognizing the role that international organizations play in the formation of customary international law and them not normally being taken into account when assessing the acceptance and recognition

---

event, transitional status. Still, this scenario is not unheard of in practice. For example, from 1967 until it became an independent state in 1990, Namibia was represented by the United Nations Council for Namibia. Although clearly not a state, nor associated with one, Namibia was institutionally represented, and even concluded a number of international agreements during that period, including the VCLT 1986 (n 1). While the VCLT 1986 describes the United Nations Council for Namibia apart from states and international organizations, in contradistinction to the latter, art 84 does count its ratification for the entry into force of the convention.

[11] For this distinction, see Robert Jennings and Arthur Watts KCMG QC, *Oppenheim's International Law: Volume 1 Peace* (9th edn, OUP 2008) 117, 561.

[12] See also James Crawford, *The Creation of States in International Law* (2nd edn, OUP 2007) 127, linking statehood to the notion of 'established and recognized separate political units . . . excluding for the purposes of the self-determination rule those parts of States which are themselves self-determination units as defined'.

[13] Generally, on functional succession, see Robert Schütze, 'The "Succession Doctrine" and the European Union' in Robert Schütze (ed), *Foreign Affairs and the EU Constitution* (CUP 2014) 91–119.

of a norm of peremptory character by the international community of states as a whole, as a view based on the analogy between states and international organizations would suggest.[14] Similarly, it is not necessarily paradoxical that international organizations are not to be taken into account when counting accessions for the purpose of a treaty entering into force, as the VCLT 1986 does.[15] In both cases, the omission of international organizations should not be taken to reflect some obscure exception. Instead, it should be seen as a faithful application of an overarching logic of accurate representativeness among national political communities that international law seems to aspire to in that regard (always within the system's parameters and assumptions). In turn, so long as this underlying logic is preserved, international organizations should be thought to enjoy the capacity to contribute to the formation of customary international law in parallel to states.

9.1.2   The Forms That the Practice of International Organizations May Take

This practice of international organizations in that regard should be understood to include (1) acts that are the direct result of members' input, such as resolutions, as well as (2) acts carried out by organs as part of the organizations' independent functioning.

Although the distinction between the two categories of practice may seem somewhat artificial, the matter has caused some confusion in the past and thus warrants explicit treatment. For example, the 2000 ILA Report on the identification of customary law considered that the independence of an organization's organs meant that their practice could not be considered when identifying customary norms.[16] The same report admitted the resolutions adopted by states within international organizations as 'state practice' because they were 'best regarded as a series of verbal acts by the individual member States participating in that organ'.[17]

---

[14] Cf Bordin (n 1) 125, who laments the ILC for its 'regrettable inconsistency' on this matter.

[15] VCLT 1986 (n 1) art 85.

[16] 'Statement of Principles Applicable to the Formation of General Customary International Law' (n 2); see also eg ILC, 'Draft Conclusions on the Identification of Customary International Law, with Commentaries' (n 2) 149 (Commentary to Conclusion 13), implying that only the practice of national courts may serve as practice.

[17] 'Statement of Principles Applicable to the Formation of General Customary International Law' (n 2) 19 (Principle 11 and commentary thereto).

By contrast, the present account includes the practice of organs that cannot be directly traced back to an organization's members, including that of secretariats or courts: the independence from state input does not disqualify the practice in question from reflecting public authority in the sense developed here, and thus from counting towards the formation of customary norms. As far as members' direct input in the organization's functioning is concerned, this can indeed be appraised independently. But while voting may be construed as member conduct for the purposes of applying certain rules, the output of the decision-making should be thought of as practice of the organization itself (with the caveats expressed previously regarding the weight and representativeness assigned to that practice, as well as avoiding in this case double counting).[18]

9.1.3   The Types of Norms to Whose Formation the Practice of International Organizations May Contribute

The practice of international organizations thus construed can help identify norms of customary international law.[19] The content, including the field of application of these norms, is an altogether different matter, which Section 9.2 will cover in more detail. It is, however, worth noting at this point that the absence of a hardwired category distinction between states and international organizations at a general level implies that, by default, customary norms too operate at a level of abstraction that does

---

[18] This account aligns with the approach of the ICJ that does not seem to draw a distinction in principle between the different UN organs when identifying norms of customary law. For example, in *Chagos*, the Court considered ICJ looked at the practice of 'the General Assembly or any other organ of the United Nations' when investigating the status of the right to territorial integrity of a non-self-governing territory in customary international law: *Legal Consequences of the Separation of the Chagos Archipelago from Mauritius in 1965* (Advisory Opinion) [2019] ICJ Rep 95, 134; see also *Case Concerning East Timor (Portugal v Australia)* (Judgment) [1995] ICJ Rep 90, 102, referring to UN practice for the proposition that the right of self-determination enjoys an erga omnes character.

[19] Care must be taken to distinguish between the so-called internal practice of an organ and practice that contributes to the formation of norms of customary international law. Often, the practice of an organ will be relevant only within the context of the organization, as was exemplified by the practice of the Security Council with respect to the practice of voluntary abstention by a permanent member as not constituting a bar to the adoption of resolution. See *Legal Consequences for States of the Continued Presence of South Africa in Namibia (South West Africa) Notwithstanding Security Council Resolution 276 (1970)* (Advisory Opinion) [1971] ICJ Rep 16, 22. See also Jan Klabbers, 'The Cheshire Cat That Is International Law' (2020) 31 EJIL, 269, 280.

not dwell on the form that public power has taken in each instance. According to what is advocated here, there is no specific customary prohibition of the use of force for states, another one for unions of states or confederations, another one for sub-state entities, and so on: there is just one norm covering public power regardless of the way in which it has been organized. Correspondingly, the practice of each type of those entities contributes in the first instance to the formation of general norms. For example, UN practice with regard to international humanitarian law influences the formation of the latter body of norms as such, and not only in relation to activities undertaken by international organizations (always paying due attention to the actual terms of that practice). Thus, for example, the ICRC is correct to refer to the practice of international organizations with respect to general norms of customary international law that are also applicable to states.[20] Conversely, the practice of states in the field of international humanitarian law should also inform what norms armed forces deployed by international organizations should abide by.

Beyond these general norms, it is theoretically possible that special customary norms may develop. In this respect, we can distinguish between (1) norms that may refer to international organizations as a putative class of entities, for example, potential norms regarding specifically their immunities, and (2) norms that may refer to certain specific institutions within that class, much in the way that norms of particular

---

[20] Consider eg the ICRC's inclusion of the practice of the UN Interim Administration Mission in Kosovo (UNMIK) in the Customary International Humanitarian Law Database, in the study on customary international humanitarian law: see International Committee of the Red Cross International Humanitarian Law Database, 'Rule 44: Due Regard for the Natural Environment in Military Operations – Section B: The Precautionary Principle' <https://ihl-databases.icrc.org/en/customary-ihl/v1/rule44> accessed 9 February 2025; the inclusion of the practice of the UN Transitional Administration for Eastern Slavonia, Baranja and Western Sirmium (UNTAES) on the issue of the return of displaced persons: see International Committee of the Red Cross International Humanitarian Law Database, 'Rule 132: Return of Displaced Persons' <https://ihl-databases.icrc.org/en/customary-ihl/v1/rule132> accessed 9 February 2025. The ICRC has also cited extensively the practice of the UN Transitional Administration for East Timor (UNTAET) with respect to the prosecution of crimes: see Jean-Marie Henckaerts and Louise Doswald-Beck, *International Committee of the Red Cross – Customary International Humanitarian Law: Volume 1: Rules* (CUP 2005), 346, 554, 556, 558, 566–568, 616 (respectively citing UNTAET Regulation 2000/ 15, §§ 6(1)(a)(vii), 14, 49(2), 14(3), 14(3) and 16, 21, 21, 6(1), and 17(1)).

customary law may refer only to a limited number of states.[21] Presumably, in the first case these are generally applicable customary norms that just happen to have a more limited scope *ratione materiae*. Being general customary norms, such norms could in theory also be identified through the practice of states and not just international organizations (meaning, for example, that a potential customary norm regarding international organizations' immunities could be identified also through the practice of national courts). The second case is one of particular custom, and the relevant pool of practice to be consulted should only include the international organizations concerned, just as it happens with particular custom in the case of states.[22]

Still, these theoretical possibilities should not be employed to arbitrarily insert into legal reasoning artificial distinctions between international organizations and states, or between international organizations themselves. Just as the possibility to have a regional or bilateral state custom always operates in the background of more general norms that are applicable by default, so too with international organizations the burden of identifying such norms should lie with those advocating a departure from the general norms. The same goes for arguing that otherwise generally applicable customary norms are somehow not applicable because international organizations are involved. In both cases, the denomination 'international organization' should not by itself create the impression that a 'special' practice is entered into. For example, armed forces do not create a new stream of practice corresponding to new particular norms just because they happen to attach to an international organization. Where novel problems arise in applying the relevant norms due to international organizations' peculiar set-up (problems that are often much less idiosyncratic to these institutions than commonly thought), these should be solved in the first instance through interpretation of the relevant norms, rather than be taken as a sign that general norms

---

[21] See Anthony A D'Amato, 'The Concept of Special Custom in International Law' (1969) 63 AJIL 211. Cf ILC, 'Draft Conclusions on the Identification of Customary International Law, with Commentaries' (n 2), 154 (Conclusion 16 and Commentary thereto), referring to the possibility of 'regional, local, or other' particular norms of customary international law that develop between a limited number of states.

[22] See ILC, 'Draft Conclusions on the Identification of Customary International Law, with Commentaries' (n 2) 154 (Conclusion 16) suggesting that '[t]o determine the existence and content of a rule of particular customary international law, it is necessary to ascertain whether there is a general practice among the States concerned that is accepted by them as law (*opinio juris*) among themselves'.

somehow do not apply at all due to the lack of more specific practice and opinio juris on the part of international organizations.[23]

9.2 The Extent to Which International Organizations Are Bound by Customary International Law

9.2.1 General Theory behind the Application of Customary International Law to International Organizations

The foregoing analysis also illuminates the applicability of customary international law to international organizations. At this point, it should be kept in mind that this problem pertains to the extent to which custom is binding, not whether it can bind international organizations in the first place.[24] In this respect, the analytical continuity between these institutions and states suggests that the same norms of customary international law that govern the relations between states are by default equally applicable, *as a whole*, to international organizations. Consequently, no separate pool of practice and opinio juris that refer specifically to international organizations needs to be identified each time the question of which norms apply to them arises.

These two propositions have been out of reach of current theoretical constructions. Chapter 4 explained how rough anthropomorphic conceptions of the state have influenced theorizing on this issue. Three popular approaches were discussed in this respect.

The first essentially admits states as comprising of a closed class of legal persons, routinely analogized to the position that natural persons enjoy in domestic law. In this scenario, there is a category distinction between states and international organizations. Therefore, to the extent that the international legal order may accommodate other types of legal persons, including international organizations, this is achieved by the development of special norms. International organizations come into this picture as 'blank slates', waiting for some kind of legislative intervention

---

[23] See also Orfeas Chasapis Tassinis, 'Customary International Law: Interpretation from Beginning to End' (2020) 31 EJIL 235.

[24] As already noted in Chapter 3, the often-quoted *WHO-Egypt* Advisory Opinion dictum that '[i]nternational organizations are subjects of international law and, as such, are bound by any obligations incumbent upon them under general rules of international law' does not by itself settle the debate around which obligations under customary international law are actually 'incumbent upon' those institutions. *Interpretation of the Agreement of 25 March 1951 between the WHO and Egypt* (Advisory Opinion) [1980] ICJ Rep 73, 89–90.

before propositions about the content of their rights and obligations can be safely articulated. International organizations are admitted in the legal system, but what happens after is left up to introducing *new and separate norms that are specifically addressed to this new class of legal subjects.*

The second approach draws on analogy to suggest that international organizations can be treated, in certain ways, in the same manner as states. While intuitive in certain respects, this approach faces limitations when considered against the background of the problems discussed here. As already mentioned, the analogy rests on dubious grounds when considered as a matter of *lege lata.* The argument, in its many variations, is often analytically tied to a radical redefinition of international law, or the emergence of a customary rule of incorporation, both propositions being ultimately difficult to prove in positive law. Furthermore, when analogy is upheld based on pure abstract reasoning, it tends to devolve into an inductive line of reasoning that does not necessarily yield true propositions (of the type: states are legal persons/international organizations are legal persons; states are bound by human rights → international organizations are bound by human rights).[25]

A third approach would analyse international organizations as being another name for groups of states acting together and thus have them be transitively bound by their members' obligations. The flaws of this view have already been discussed in Chapter 2. In essence, this view finds itself in tension with the very idea that international organizations possess a distinct legal identity. It also contains no built-in limiting principle that would confine this transitive effect only to customary, as opposed to treaty law. Yet the transitive effect of treaties is a much more complicated proposition, both because of the generally presumed relative effect of treaties as well as of what it would mean in practice in view of the fluctuating membership of these institutions.[26] Finally, and crucially

---

[25] One way of limiting this uncertainty is to better contextualize the analogy within specific, and usually quite abstract, areas of the law (for example, international responsibility). Cf José Alvarez, 'Book Review: "International Organizations and Their Exercise of Sovereign Powers" by Dan Sarooshi' (2007) 101(3) AJIL 674, who argues that 'since custom and other state-centric sources of international obligation historically stem from the actions of states and were largely intended to address the actions of states, it may be that many of these obligations do not apply, or apply only with considerable modification, to the actions of international organizations'. In any event, arguments from analogy produce diminishing returns when persuasive comparisons start to run out, as for example with respect to notions such as territory or nationality.

[26] See VCLT 1986 (n 1) art 34 ('A treaty does not create either obligations or rights for a third State or a third organization without the consent of that State or that organization.').

from a theoretical standpoint, this approach wrongly assumes that the membership of international organizations is confined to states, again misleadingly placing states at the epicentre of international law's ontology.[27]

The theory advanced here suggests an alternative approach. Rather than viewing international organizations as sui generis entities, or as analogous to states, or merely as groups of states, this account is based on the foundational continuity between these institutions and states. International organizations are not bound by customary international law because some specific norms have developed to this effect, nor because they are, to some extent, similar to states or just another name for states acting together. They are bound because the distinction between them and states is a practical distinction that should not be taken ipso facto to reflect the deeper structure of customary norms.

Customary norms do not distinguish between the different forms that communal organization may assume in this respect. This is the mirror image of international law's reliance on communal self-description for the construction of the state in the first place, whose logical corollary is that there is no a priori numerus clausus of the different forms that this construction may take. It would be odd to match this freedom to self-organize with arbitrary distinctions suggesting that different norms apply depending on whether an entity is a federal state, a union of states, a sub-state entity, a condominium, a confederation, an international organization, and so on. Thus, while international organizations are indeed 'definitely not states',[28] this is not a difference that matters for the application of general norms of customary international law that are typically associated with states in practice. At the same time, international organizations differ from familiar non-state actors such as corporations or NGOs. In contrast to international organizations, corporations and NGOs do not derive their authority from, and represent, some institutional aspect of one or more national communities as a

---

Cf Pierre Klein, *La Responsabilité Des Organisations Internationales Dans Les Ordres Juridiques Internes et En Droit Des Gens* (Bruylant 1998) 341–344. For a discussion, see text to n 34 in Chapter 8.

[27] On the varied membership of international organizations, see text to n 7 in Chapter 8.

[28] Allain Pellet, 'International Organizations Are Definitely Not States' in Maurizio Ragazzi (ed), *Responsibility of International Organizations: Essays in Memory of Sir Ian Brownlie* (Martinus Nijhoff 2013).

whole. Consequently, the same customary norms cannot be thought to apply automatically to them by virtue of the theory advanced here.[29]

To summarize: *if* international law does not anticipate the various forms that communal self-organization may take, it would be baseless to presume that it separates between them for the purposes of applying its customary norms. Therefore, in principle, the same customary norms that apply to states are equally binding on international organizations without the need to present new evidence of practice and opinio juris that relates specifically to international organizations or arguments from analogy. As already mentioned, this does not mean that international organizations cannot be distinct objects of legislative concern, and that, potentially, more specific norms may evolve with respect to them. Yet in the absence of such norms, the default position should be that the same norms that are binding on states are also binding on them.

The logic of continuity rather than analogy can also help overcome a lingering ambiguity concerning *the extent* to which customary international law applies to international organizations. Rather than perennially pondering on the relative importance of these institutions' similarities or differences when compared to states, the logic of continuity explains why the totality of norms is ipso facto applicable to both, regardless of any comparison.

In this respect, a distinction must be drawn between the general applicability of a branch of law to an entity and the application of a norm in a given instance following the fulfilment of certain factual circumstances. Take for example customary law governing the continental shelf. From the point of view of general applicability, this part of the law is binding on all states, whether they have a coastline or they are landlocked. Still, a landlocked state will not derive in casu any rights to a continental shelf due to the factual circumstances in which it finds itself, namely the absence of a coastline.[30]

This distinction between general applicability and application in a specific case carries considerable analytical weight. First, general applicability preserves, in a sense, the rights of the landlocked state in case the

---

[29] See in that sense *Accordance with International Law of the Unilateral Declaration of Independence in Respect of Kosovo* (Advisory Opinion) [2010] ICJ Rep 403, 437, suggesting that the principle of territorial integrity does not produce legal obligations for human beings acting in their capacity as individuals.

[30] This example was inspired by Kristina Daugirdas, 'How and Why International Law Binds International Organizations' (2016) 57 Harvard International Law Journal 325, 367.

circumstances change. If a landlocked state somehow manages to acquire a coastline, then it will have the same rights as other coastal states. Second, general applicability produces legal effects regardless of whether the factual situation changes. Even though a landlocked state does not derive any right from customary law on the continental self, it derives obligations from it. For instance, it has an obligation to respect the rights of states that do feature a continental shelf. It may also incur responsibility in relation to the acts of other states violating those rights when it aids or assists these other states in committing such violations.[31]

The distinction between general applicability and application in a given instance should inform how the application of customary international law to international organizations is to be understood. According to the theory proposed here, customary law extends equally to states and international organizations in terms of its general applicability. Whether international organizations will derive the same claim-rights and duties from it in a specific instance will remain a question of interpreting the relevant norms and examining the factual as well as the legal circumstances that these institutions find themselves in, including their constituent instruments.[32] Constituent instruments in particular may put in place specific rules that derogate from general customary international law as far as the relationship between an organization and its members is concerned. In principle this matter is not too different from where a state or state-like entity's capacity to act internationally is constrained through international agreement.[33] Nevertheless, in all these cases of treaties potentially serving as leges speciales, the presumption should remain that whatever customary law was applicable has not been derogated from, absent a clearly expressed intention to the contrary.[34]

---

[31] On the notion that a state may be responsible in connection to the act of another state, see UNGA Res 56/83 (28 January 2002) UN Doc A/RES/56/83, Annex I: Responsibility of States for Internationally Wrongful Acts, arts 16–19.

[32] As Bordin convincingly argues, 'restrictions laid down by their constitutional instruments cannot without more be taken to legally affect or govern their relations with third parties' (Bordin (n 1) 131). The present analysis is concerned with customary law and does not cover the question of which powers an international organization enjoys vis-à-vis its member states as a matter of its constituent instrument.

[33] See Crawford (n 12) 236 (on the Free City of Danzig), 303 (on the legal effects of protectorate arrangements).

[34] *Case Concerning Elettronica Sicula S.p.A. (ELSI) (United States of America v Italy)* (Judgment) [1989] ICJ Rep 15, 42. The ICJ will also employ customary international law as part of 'any relevant rules of international law applicable in the relations between the parties' to be taken into account when interpreting a treaty, pursuant to VCLT 1969

In sum, the patent differences that often exist between states and international organizations do not affect the default general applicability of customary international law to these institutions. Furthermore, this general applicability does not lapse due to norms enshrined in an organization's constituent instrument, unless a clear and specific intent to the contrary is evident.

These nuances about the general applicability of customary international law to international organizations are sometimes lost in the literature. For example, Felice Morgenstern argued in quite general terms that 'international law is between states and large areas of international law remain patently inapplicable to international organizations which have no territory, confer no nationality and do not exercise jurisdiction in the same way as states'.[35] In a similar vein, Fernando Bordin dwells on certain 'structural differences' between states and international organizations. He argues that these differences limit the ambit of certain customary norms only to states.[36] As he suggests, 'when it comes to territorial matters, the analogy between States and international organizations is defeated by the fact that the two categories of legal subjects present a crucial structural difference'.[37] Bordin reserves a similar verdict with respect to rules that are 'premised upon the political bond of nationality', that will not be extended to international organizations by analogy.[38] This view could be interpreted to suggest that there are certain areas of the law that do not apply by definition to international organizations, unless they somehow become more like states, for example, by acquiring territorial rights or developing relations similar to the bond of

---

(n 3) art 31(3)(c): see *Case Concerning Oil Platforms (Islamic Republic of Iran v United States of America)* (Judgment) [2003] ICJ Rep 161, 182.

[35] Felice Morgenstern, *Legal Problems of International Organizations* (Grotius 1986) 32. See also William T Worster, 'Relative International Legal Personality of Non-State Actors' (2016) 42 Brooklyn Journal of International Law 207, 220, who argues that 'under the functional approach, one can understand an entity as having international legal personality to the extent necessary to execute its tasks'; Noëlle Quénivet, 'Binding the United Nations to Customary (Human Rights) Law' (2020) 17 IOLR 379, 401–402. An early version of this idea can be traced back to Kelsen, who argued that the extent to which general international law applied to an international organization depended on the powers conferred to it by its member states. Hans Kelsen, *Principles of International Law* (Rinehart & Co 1952) 173.

[36] Bordin (n 1) 104.

[37] ibid 92.

[38] ibid.

nationality.[39] Concerns such as these echo the notion that as corporations in domestic law 'cannot marry', there are therefore some relations for which international organizations are not, by default, legally susceptible to.[40]

By contrast, the theory advanced here suggests that the dissimilarities between states and international organizations are entirely irrelevant in terms of the general applicability of the same norms of customary international law to both types of entities. This is not just because international organizations may, whether intra or ultra vires, assume functions that we would typically associate with states.[41] International organizations do not have to gradually evolve into states before the same law can apply to them. While the differences listed in the literature are real, they should not limit the general applicability of relevant norms only to states. Instead, they may become relevant when it comes to the question of whether a norm that is generally applicable to international organizations produces rights or duties for them in a particular set of circumstances.

Take for instance the principle of territorial integrity. International organizations may be non-territorial entities and still be bound by this principle in the sense that they have to respect it vis-à-vis states by not directly infringing upon it. Furthermore, if, for example, they 'aid or assist' or 'direct and control' states to breach that norm, they will also bear responsibility, as the act is internationally wrongful for them as well.[42] Still, they will not derive the same rights as states from the principle: they will typically not enjoy a right to territorial integrity – not because that part of the law is not binding on them, but because they do not possess territory of their own. The same holds true for the obligation of international organizations to respect the right of peoples to self-determination.[43] Likewise, for nationality. If a state attempts to

---

[39] ibid 92, 95.

[40] Ignaz Seidl-Hohenveldern, *Corporations in and under International Law* (Grotius 1987) 74.

[41] See Daugirdas (n 30) 367, providing the hypothetical of 'overzealous WIPO officials started patrolling the territorial seas of coastal states that, in their view, were too lax in enforcing laws protecting intellectual property'.

[42] See ILC, 'Draft Articles on the Responsibility of International Organizations, with Commentaries' (2011) II/2 YILC 46, 66–70 (arts 14–19 and commentaries thereto).

[43] See eg Case C-104/16 P *Council v Front Polisario* [2016] ECR 973, paras 88–89, where the European Court of Justice concluded that 'that principle [self-determination] forms part of the rules of international law applicable to relations between the European Union and the Kingdom of Morocco'.

withdraw the nationality of one of its citizens in contravention of customary human rights norms, international organizations are bound to not recognize the effects of that withdrawal – a proposition confirmed in practice.[44] The relevant customary norms continue to apply, even though no international organization has, technically speaking, 'nationals' of its own.

9.2.2   Applying the Theory to Practice: International Organizations and Human Rights

The example of nationality can provide further insights into how customary human rights law in general applies to international organizations.[45] Following the theory advanced here, human rights law is equally binding as a whole on international organizations as it is on states.[46] Still, this does not mean that human rights law will always produce the same

---

[44] See *In re Pilowsky*, Judgment 848 (ILOAT, 10 December 1987), where the Tribunal held that '[t]he Organization is bound to recognise that "everyone has the right to a nationality" and that "no one shall be arbitrarily deprived of his nationality", as stated in the Universal Declaration of Human Rights approved on 10 December 1948'.

[45] For the idea that at least some human rights are part of customary international law, see Theodor Meron, *Human Rights and Humanitarian Norms as Customary Law* (OUP 1989) 80ff; Hurst Hannum, 'The Status of the Universal Declaration of Human Rights in National and International Law' (1996) 25(1) Georgia Journal of International and Comparative Law 289, 317–352; William A Schabas, *The Customary International Law of Human Rights* (OUP 2021). Specifically regarding the human rights obligations of international financial institutions, such as the IMF, under customary international law, see ECOSOC, Committee on Economic, Social and Cultural Rights 'Public Debt, Austerity Measures and the International Covenant on Economic, Social and Cultural Rights' (22 July 2016) UN Doc E/C.12/2016/1, para 7; Markus Krajewski, 'Human Rights and Austerity Programmes' in Thomas Cottier and others (eds), *The Rule of Law in Monetary Affairs: World Trade Forum* (CUP 2014) 502.

[46] This proposition has been accepted for some time in the literature, albeit with different lines of reasoning: either assuming that international organizations are bound by the human rights treaties signed by their members, or by assuming that human rights obligations follow just by the characterisation of international organizations as international legal persons, or, finally, by interpreting human rights obligations in organizations' constituent instruments: see eg Philippe Sands and Pierre Klein, *Bowett's Law of International Institutions* (6th edn, Sweet & Maxwell 2009) 766–767; Guglielmo Verdirame, *The UN and Human Rights: Who Guards the Guardians?* (CUP 2011) 70–71; Eyal Benvenisti, *The Law of Global Governance* (Brill 2014) 119–121; *The Prosecutor v André Rwamakuba* (Decision) ICTR-98-44C-T (31 January 2007), [48]. On why international organizations cannot automatically be considered parties to the human rights treaties of their members, see text to n 34 in Chapter 8; on why designating international organizations as international legal persons or subjects cannot resolve this problem, see text to n 36 in Chapter 2. Constituent instruments remain a viable alternative

duties for both types of entities. In practice, international organizations will have at a bare minimum the negative 'duty to respect', meaning a duty to refrain from interfering with the human rights of persons within their jurisdiction.[47] Whether they will also have the positive duty to protect and fulfil those rights will depend on the position that they actually find themselves in.[48]

The position of international organizations in that regard should not be appraised differently from that of states, for whom the existence of positive human rights duties is linked to the exercise of effective control.[49] If one takes the very fact of an interference with said human rights as creating a presumption for the existence of effective control in the first place, it follows that the baseline obligation to respect human rights follows international organizations whatever they do, including when they adopt decisions or suggest policies to their members. Whether their additional obligations to protect and to fulfil human rights are also triggered will depend on the particular circumstances. For example, an organization administering territory will presumably also have some obligations to protect and maybe even to fulfil certain human rights.

for holding international organizations bound to certain human rights. This type of argument has to be followed by a case-by-case analysis of the respective instruments.

[47] For the notion that states must protect human rights 'within their jurisdiction', see eg International Covenant on Civil and Political Rights (adopted 16 December 1966, entered into force 23 March 1976) 999 UNTS 171 (ICCPR), art 2 (1); Convention for the Protection of Human Rights and Fundamental Freedoms (European Convention on Human Rights, as amended) (ECHR), art 1; Convention on the Rights of the Child (adopted 20 November 1989 entered into force 2 September 1990) 1577 UNTS 3 (CRC), art 2 (1). Note, however, that the International Covenant on Economic, Social and Cultural Rights (adopted 16 December 1966, entered into force 3 January 1976) 993 UNTS 3 (ICESCR), lacks a general clause on the scope of its application, comparable to that of art 2(1) ICCPR. In any event, the term 'jurisdiction' is generally interpreted to extend beyond the notion of territorial jurisdiction. As Marko Milanovic puts it, 'the notion of jurisdiction in human rights treaties relates essentially to a question of fact, of actual authority and control that a state has over a given territory or persons. "Jurisdiction", in this context, simply means actual power, whether exercised lawfully or not. See Marko Milanovic, *Extraterritorial Application of Human Rights Treaties* (OUP 2011) 41. If the term jurisdiction is somehow interpreted to include only the notion of territorial jurisdiction, international organizations that do not exercise such jurisdiction could still incur responsibility in relation to the acts of other states or international organizations violating those rights.

[48] On the distinction between the duty to respect, protect, and fulfil, see Manfred Nowak, *UN Covenant on Civil and Political Rights: CCPR Commentary* (2nd edn, Engel 2005) xxi; See also Milanovic (n 47) 18.

[49] Milanovic (n 47) 18.

Finally, assuming that an international organization's conduct does not already constitute a breach on its own terms, the organization may still incur responsibility for its conduct in connection with an act that violates human rights.[50] This may be especially relevant for international financial institutions' involvement in the adoption of policies by their member states that infringe upon socio-economic rights.[51] This makes sense on a more abstract level as well. The human rights protections against the exercise of public power that individuals enjoy, they enjoy regardless of how this power is legally configured, meaning whether it is exercised by a state or a nested institution.

9.2.3   Applying the Theory to Practice: International Organizations and Immunities

Immunities under customary international law is another area that can benefit from clarifying the conceptual relationship between states and international organizations as species of legal actors. As we saw in Chapter 2, the issue has caused some confusion in practice, with certain

---

[50] See ILC, 'Draft Articles on the Responsibility of International Organizations, with Commentaries' (n 42) 66–70 (arts 14–19 and commentaries thereto).

[51] Whether such institutions do in fact exercise direction and control over the acts of one of their members in a given instance will be a question of evidence. The Draft Articles on the Responsibility of International Organizations suggest that 'the term "controls" refers to cases of domination over the commission of wrongful conduct and not simply the exercise of oversight, still less mere influence or concern', while 'the word "directs" does not encompass mere incitement or suggestion but rather connotes actual direction of an operative kind' (footnotes omitted). See ILC, 'Draft Articles on the Responsibility of International Organizations, with Commentaries' (n 42) 67 (art 15 and commentary thereto). It is entirely plausible that an international financial institution may be thought to exercise 'domination' and 'direction of the operative kind' over states. See, for example, the Supplemental Memorandum of Understanding that was agreed between Greece and the ESM, the IMF, and the European Commission (the Troika) in June 2016. This memorandum mandated extremely detailed prescriptions for Greece regarding the deregulation of its labour market and the 'reform' of the healthcare sector. At the same time, the Memorandum stipulated that the Troika had to agree *beforehand* to any action by the Greek government that was relevant to the achievement of the objectives of the goals set out in the Memorandum. See 'Supplemental Memorandum of Understanding' (16 June 2016) <https://economy-finance.ec.europa.eu/system/files/2017-11/ecfin_smou_en1.pdf> accessed 9 February 2025. The question of direction and control is without prejudice to whether the organization may also be directly responsible for its own conduct if this is found to constitute a breach of human rights on its own terms. For a similar problem regarding state behaviour and human rights, see Frederik Naert, *International Law Aspects of the EU's Security and Defence Policy, with a Particular Focus on the Law of Armed Conflict and Human Rights* (1st edn, Intersentia 2010) 361ff.

scholars suggesting that special norms need to be identified before international organizations can enjoy immunities in customary international law.[52] The opposite issue has arisen with respect to whether immunities enjoyed by state officials can be invoked vis-à-vis international organizations, most prominently in the *Al Bashir* case before the ICC.[53]

With respect to the first issue, the theory advanced here suggests that no separate practice and opinio juris needs to be identified specifically in relation to international organizations before they can enjoy the same immunities as states before third jurisdictions.[54] Just as states, international organizations should be thought to enjoy immunity from adjudicative and enforcement jurisdiction under customary international law vis-à-vis non-members, subject to the same potential exceptions, including those regarding acts of a commercial nature.[55] Non-members should respect the institutional organization that international organizations represent on the same basis that they are bound to do so for states. As for members, they should extend immunity insofar as this is provided

---

[52] Michael Wood, 'Do International Organizations Enjoy Immunity under Customary International Law?' (2013) 10 IOLR 287.

[53] *The Prosecutor v Omar Hassan Ahmad Al Bashir* (Judgment) ICC-02/05-01/09 OA2 (6 May 2019) [1]–[2], [114]–[117].

[54] The case law on this matter is mixed. In favour of international organizations' immunities under customary international law, see indicatively, *Cristiani v Istituto italo-latino-americano*, Italy, Corte di Cassazione (Sezione Unite), 23 November 1985, no. 5819, 87 ILR 21; *Spaans v Iran-US Claims Tribunal*, Netherlands, Supreme Court, 20 December 1985, 94 ILR 321, (1987) 18 NYIL 357, 360. Cf *Amaratunga v Northwest Atlantic Fisheries Organization*, Supreme Court of Canada, 29 November 2013, 2013 SCC 66; *International Tin Council v Amalgamet Inc* (1988) 524 NYS2d 971. On the whole, the relevant case law needs to be read with caution, as many decisions may be applying domestic law provisions on immunities or be otherwise subject to considerations peculiar to their own legal systems. Cases also tend to not address the problem of international organizations' legal nature as such. Generally, see August Reinisch, 'Transnational Judicial Conversations on the Personality, Privileges, and Immunities of International Organizations – An Introduction' in August Reinisch (ed), *The Privileges and Immunities of International Organizations in Domestic Courts* (OUP 2013) 7–8; Cedric Ryngaert, 'The Immunity of International Organizations before Domestic Courts: Recent Trends' (2010) 7 IOLR 121.

[55] On this exception, see generally James Crawford, *Brownlie's Principles of Public International Law* (9th edn, OUP 2019) 480. What is developed in the following pages with regard to immunities is without prejudice to how these might interact with human rights norms, including the right of access to a tribunal or equivalent form of dispute resolution mechanism.

by special agreement, normally enshrined in the constituent instrument of an international organization or in a separate treaty.[56]

The reason often invoked for reserving separate treatment for international organizations vis-à-vis third states is that the principle of sovereign equality – regularly identified as the key rationale justifying immunity – is inoperable in relation to these institutions.[57] Yet this represents a somewhat reductive view of the notion: equality in that sense should be thought to obtain between those communities that have, at least as far as international law is concerned, the same recognized capacity to self-organize as they see fit, regardless of how they exercise that prerogative. Equality signifies that the protection of immunity, granted by international law to the exercise of that capacity, should be taken by default to extend all the way to any institutions nested by it vis-à-vis foreign exercises of jurisdiction.[58] It should therefore extend to international organizations in their relations with non-members.

The same should hold for international organizations' personnel for conduct performed in their official capacity. They should enjoy the same protections that they would have enjoyed had they been acting for a

---

[56] In practice, many international organizations do enjoy certain privileges and immunities pursuant to their constituent instruments and/or some other treaty to that effect. For an overview, see Niels M Blokker, 'International Organizations: The Untouchables?' in Niels M Blokker and Nico J Schrijver (eds), *Immunity of International Organizations* (Brill–Nijhoff, 2015) 10–11.

[57] Hazel Fox, QC and Philippa Webb, *The Law of State Immunity* (3rd edn, OUP 2015) 578; see also Edward Chukwuemeke Okeke, *Jurisdictional Immunities of States and International Organizations* (OUP 2018) 239. On the close relationship between sovereign equality and state immunity, see *Jurisdictional Immunities of the State (Germany v Italy: Greece intervening)* (Judgment) [2012] ICJ Rep 99, 123.

[58] It is worth noting that a very similar problem arises more generally with entities that are not states but belong to family of 'public' institutions in the sense employed here, such as component units of federal states with an international legal presence of their own. Although the subject is not free of ambiguity, such entities arguably enjoy said immunities in customary international law. See Fox and Webb (n 57) 343, 353 (suggesting that 'The general principle ... seems to be that immunity is to be applied only to an entity which pursuant to the internal constitutional distribution of powers enjoys a personality of its own in its foreign relations with other countries'). On Hong Kong's immunities under general international law, see Roda Mushkat, 'Hong Kong as an International Legal Person' (1992) 6 Emory International Law Review 105, 163. On the immunities of dependent entities in general, see Crawford (n 12) 633. Cf Xiaodong Yang, *State Immunity in International Law* (CUP 2012) 230, who rationalizes such instances in terms of these entities ultimately acting on behalf of a state.

state.[59] If, when it comes to states, such immunities apply regardless of the level of the officials' post and just by virtue of performing official functions,[60] then the same rationale should extend by the same measure to all the 'organs, agencies or instrumentalities'[61] of international organizations. Conversely, if, as it has been argued, certain categories of personnel, such as teachers or medical workers, should be excluded from these protections, then the same would apply to international organizations.[62] The point here is not to resolve the ongoing debate on the scope of these immunities but rather that there appears to be no reason for differentiating based on whether the official in question serves for a state or an international organization.

By contrast, the immanent rationale of state immunity does not seem to automatically extend to international organizations vis-à-vis their members.[63] The need for immunities comes into play only after an organization has been created as a distinct legal entity in international law. The ensuing relations between an organization and its members as distinct legal persons can be construed in a sense as 'international' (and

---

[59] Note that the ICJ could be interpreted to equate, or at least not differentiate, between functional immunity and the immunity of the State itself. For example, in *Certain Questions of Mutual Assistance in Criminal Matters (Djibouti v. France)* (Judgment) [2008] ICJ Rep 177, 242, the Court reasoned that Djibouti's claim that its *procureur de la République* and its head of national security were entitled to functional immunity was 'in essence, a claim of immunity for the Djiboutian State, from which the procureur de la République and the Head of National Security would be said to benefit'.

[60] This was the position taken by the ILC's Special Rapporteur Roman Kolodkin: ILC, 'Preliminary Report on Immunity of State Officials from Foreign Criminal Jurisdiction, by Roman Anatolevich Kolodkin, Special Rapporteur' (2008) UN Doc A/CN.4/601, 177, para 80.

[61] *Certain Questions of Mutual Assistance in Criminal Matters* (n 59) 244. Cf n 27 in Chapter 2 for a potential exception regarding violations of international criminal law.

[62] Some members of the ILC have expressed this view: ILC, 'Report of the International Law Commission on the Work of Its Sixtieth Session, 5 May–6 June 2008, Official Records of the General Assembly, Sixty-Third Session, Supplement No. 10' (1974) UN Doc A/63/10 333, para 288. See also Riccardo Pisillo Mazzeschi, 'The Functional Immunity of State Officials from Foreign Jurisdiction: A Critique of the Traditional Theories' (2015) 17 *QIL, Zoom out* 3.

[63] Text to n 57 in this chapter. Note that so-called functional immunities of certain state officials can be thought to rest on a complementary rationale of ensuring these officials' 'effective performance of their functions on behalf of their respective states'. *Case Concerning the Arrest Warrant of 11 April 2000 (Democratic Republic of the Congo v Belgium)* (Judgment) [2002] ICJ Rep 3, 22. It is not inconceivable that this rationale may find application in the relations between an organization and its members. See also n 67, n 71 in this chapter.

in any event as occurring beyond the level of the state).[64] Yet the organization's creation is only possible because, and to the extent, it is an expression of 'two or more national communities exercising their capacity to self-describe, or by institutions already created by these communities while exercising that capacity'(see Chapter 8). It would thus seem odd for an organization to claim immunity from a jurisdiction as 'foreign', when both it and the institution exercising that jurisdiction are expressions of the same community's capacity to self-describe.[65] In any event, this prima facie freedom to exercise jurisdiction may be restricted on account of obligations that members have undertaken. In practice, this will often be the case through headquarters agreements, agreements on privileges and immunities, as well as international organizations' constituent instruments themselves.[66]

Conversely, being branches to the same institutional tree as states, international organizations cannot ignore the immunities of states and their officials because somehow these would only apply in relations between 'sovereign' states. As this book has argued, international organizations are neither blank slates nor simply groups of states. They are, however, exercising authority that is, in the final analysis, equally

---

[64] Cf Christiane Ahlborn, 'The Rules of International Organizations and the Law of International Responsibility' (2012) 8 IOLR 397 (on the nature of the relation between an organization and its members). Cf also Lorenzo Gasbarri, 'The Dual Legality of the Rules of International Organizations' (2017) 14 IOLR 87 (on the nature of the 'internal' law of an international organization).

[65] See also Ignaz Seidl-Hohenveldern, 'L'immunité de juridiction des Communautés européennes' (1990) 338 Revue du Marché Commun 475–476. For cases where national courts exercise jurisdiction in the absence of a grant of immunities by the organization's members, see August Reinisch, *International Organizations before National Courts* (CUP 2000) 180–185; Jakob Wurm, 'Asking National Courts to Correct the Over-flight Charges of Eurocontrol', in August Reinisch (ed), *Challenging Acts of International Organizations before National Courts* (OUP 2011).

[66] Blokker (n 56) 10–11; Okeke (n 57) 351. The rationale of these immunities can indeed be called 'functional', since it is supposed to guarantee that international organizations can perform their mandate unobstructed by their members. The number of such conventions could serve as indication that states deem that such immunities would not cover the organization under customary international law. This is irrespectively of the notion that according immunities to an institution creates a strong presumption that it was indeed intended to be legally distinct from its members: see *Case Concerning Pulp Mills on the River Uruguay (Argentina v Uruguay)* (Judgment) [2010] ICJ Rep 14, 53. Regardless of any explicit mention of immunities, a further argument can be made that some amount of protection for certain activities of the organization may be inferred from the nature of the membership relation itself as this has been circumscribed in the respective constituent instrument.

founded on the capacity of certain national communities to self-describe and, to that extent, should themselves be thought obligated to afford the same protections to other institutions that are expressions of that capacity, including states. This means that the ICC in *Al Bashir* erred to the extent that it sought to identify a separate customary norm extending head-of-state immunity vis-à-vis 'international courts' specifically.[67] Instead, the only avenue for it to reach the conclusion regarding the non-application of head-of-state immunity in that case would have been to find some exception to the currently established general customary norms on immunity. In turn, such an exception would have had to be buttressed by specific practice and opinio juris to that effect.

Apart from being analytically cogent, dissociating the protections, such as immunities, to be afforded to institutions from the specific form that the latter may take makes systemic sense. The opposite view would arbitrarily leave communities experimenting with forms of organization other than the state vulnerable to third-party interference that they would not have suffered had they chosen to restrict their organization to the institution of the state. It would also leave defenceless all those institutions, including states, against the interference by any other institutions such as international organizations, that, by a small or a wide margin, do not meet our classic definition of statehood. In both cases, insisting on drawing artificial distinctions between states and international organizations would contradict the system's underlying principles (and normative balance) in a rather counterintuitive manner.

9.2.4   The Default Applicability of Custom Is No Substitute for Properly Assessing the Content of Its Norms

All that being said, the default general applicability of customary international law in the manner suggested here does not constitute licence to dispense with proper analysis as to the content of these norms in a given case. This includes identifying the rationale of these norms and the possibility that special norms may develop, but also correctly applying

---

[67] *The Prosecutor v Omar Hassan Ahmad Al-Bashir* (n 53) [114]–[115]. The rationale developed earlier with respect to international organizations not enjoying immunities vis-à-vis their members under customary law (see text to n 66) does not apply here in reverse. Because an international organization will typically represent the capacity of more than one community to organize, the exercise of jurisdiction by the organization vis-à-vis one of its members would seem to necessarily entail a 'foreign' element that will trigger the application of immunities under customary international law.

special concepts that may be found in otherwise generally applicable norms.[68] As already hinted at, this may encompass concepts such as territory or nationality. Even though international organizations may incur obligations in that regard, this should not in any way imply that we can ipso facto extrapolate the entirety of the legal relations envisaged by the norm. For example, despite the close legal bond that may exist between an international organization and its agents, it would be erroneous to equate that to the bond of nationality.[69] Similarly, it should not be accepted without further analysis that some agent of an organization counts as a 'head of state' or as a 'minister of foreign affairs' for the purposes of international customary law on immunities. Instead, the focus should be on what is the exact scope and rationale of the relevant norms before examining whether they can accommodate the factual patterns in question.[70]

To generalize: when some customary right or obligation that is typically associated with states is *not* tied to some special rationale or technical element which international organizations are lacking, then it should be thought to apply by default to them as well in its entirety. If applying the relevant norm *is* tied to some special rationale or technical element that international organizations are lacking, then they will not derive the same rights and obligations as states in a given situation, even though they will still both be bound by the norm in terms of its general

---

[68] On the notion that customary international law can be the object of interpretation, see Chasapis Tassinis (n 23).

[69] See *Reparation for Injuries Suffered in the Service of the United Nations* (Advisory Opinion) [1949] ICJ Rep 174, 182 ('It is not possible, by a strained use of the concept of allegiance, to assimilate the legal bond which exists, under Article 100 of the Charter, between the Organization on the one hand, and the Secretary-General and the staff on the other, to the bond of nationality existing between a State and its Nationals.').

[70] For example, in the *Arrest Warrant* case, the ICJ found that ministers of foreign affairs enjoy personal immunity under customary international law after considering all the functions exercised by them, such as the need to take part in 'international negotiations and intergovernmental meetings' but also referring to the Minister of Foreign affairs as having 'Ambassadors and other diplomatic agents carry out their duties under his or her authority' and being able to bind her state 'by virtue of her office', while needing to be 'in constant communication with the Government, and with its diplomatic missions around the world, and be capable at any time of communicating with representatives of other States'. *Case Concerning the Arrest Warrant of 11 April 2000* (n 63) 22–23. See also *Certain Questions of Mutual Assistance in Criminal Matters* (n 59) 237–238. Given the apparent non-correspondence of this rationale to most agents of international organizations, it remains uncertain to which officials, if any, the Court would ever be inclined to extend such immunity under customary law.

applicability.[71] In both cases, this will present a problem of interpreting and applying the relevant norms – in principle not different from what we should be doing in a variety of other contexts – rather than pinning down some essentialist difference between states and international organizations. At the end of the day, even though they are not themselves states, international organizations exercise the same kind of authority, emanating from the same source and anchored in the same social facts. Customary international law is applicable neither by virtue of an abstract comparison between international organizations and states, nor because the former can be reduced to the latter, but by the logic of continuity in the exercise of what international law constructs as public power.

9.3   Conclusion

Breaking with anthropomorphic conceptions of the state can help theorize the relationship between international organizations and customary international law on a more solid basis. International organizations are neither soulless mechanistic entities that are unable to contribute to the formation of customary law nor should their practice count as if they were another state. Rather, international organizations' practice should be taken into account, bearing in mind to not overstate its impact in terms of its representativeness when the members also parallelly engage in the same practice. A similar rationale obtains with respect to applying customary international law to these institutions. The absence of a category gap between them and states suggests that the same norms are in principle applicable to both, even though the specific rights and duties that they each one derive from them in a particular instance may vary considerably.

---

[71] In that sense, the ICJ was correct to suggest in the *Reparation* Advisory Opinion that the rights and duties of international organizations may not be necessarily identical to those of states: see *Reparation for Injuries Suffered in the Service of the United Nations* (n 69) 178–179.

~

Conclusion

There has always been something paradoxical with mainstream theories of international organizations in public international law. Yet the source of the field's many perplexities has remained somewhat elusive. Instead of adding another layer on top of existing constructions, this book has argued that the real problem lies right at the bottom. It pertains to how international lawyers have generally tended to theorize the state for analytical purposes, explicitly or implicitly, literally or fictionally. So long as we leave these assumptions about the state uninterrogated, our theories are bound to push themselves into the same analytical corner.

Imagining the state as a 'soulful' or 'organic' individual has certain explanatory appeal but does not withstand scrutiny. It can also seriously mislead when theorizing international organizations. Crucially, it pins down the theorizing effort between equally unappealing analytical opposites: assuming that international organizations are not mere contractual arrangements between their members, they have to be theorized either as organic entities and competitors to states or as their purely artificial and mechanistic creations.

Apart from this dubious metaphysical baggage, the analytical image of the state as an inherently closed-off and irreducible entity leads to a quite uncompromising legal ontology. It suggests that the state enjoys the status of an elementary particle in our doctrinal universe, almost naturally paving the way for methodological statism – ultimately conceiving, in one form or another, anything international-law-related in terms of the state. Following that, the default position for international organizations is bound to be eliminative, suggesting that these institutions are by default 'nothing over and above' their members. In this set-up of the problem, international organizations can only rise as entities greater than the sum of their parts through some state-sanctioned change in positive law that institutes their non-eliminable legal existence.

Thankfully, however, we can set all that aside. In the equation of corporate existence, states are not constants. They are themselves variables, no less so than international organizations. Both entities are, if anything, constructed out of the behaviour of human beings interacting in certain ways. Rather than trying to selectively deconstruct one as opposed to the other, or pin down each one's separate perceived qualities, we should instead appreciate the genealogical continuity between them – how they both emerge on account of the same capacity of a community to self-describe. Ultimately, it is this analytical connection that solves the puzzle: whatever states and international organizations may or may not be, they can only be analysed together as part of the same phenomenon, both in an abstract sense as well as for the purposes of international law. Whatever states and international organizations may or may not be, they are institutions that grow out of the same root.

At this root lies a suitably interrelated community of human beings. This is a community that organizes aspects of its life through soliciting transformative re-descriptions of events. At the same time, international law itself is at its core a system of soliciting and prioritizing certain descriptions of reality over others. It constructs the state through recognizing this capacity of transformative self-description to a certain type of human community. For those communities that it does recognize this capacity, international law should be thought to admit by the same token the creation of a potentially infinite number of entities that are ultimately also expressions of this capacity, including international organizations. Thus, international organizations exhibit their legal features not because they are similar or analogous to states, nor because they are merely groups of states, but because the capacity to constitute an international organization is itself inherent in, and an expression of, the capacity of a community to self-organize, including by constituting a state.

This conclusion is supported by pure deductive reasoning but also by practice from other areas of international law. Throughout history, human communities and the institutions they create have led to the emergence of a myriad of more or less idiosyncratic arrangements. From confederations to personal unions, from federal states to sub-parts of states with their own international legal personality, the same overarching principle has been at work. We risk losing sight of this if we overly focus on defining statehood on the basis of certain abstract criteria. Instead we should account for how the corporate organization that states represent is possible to begin with. The conclusion is not that international organizations, confederations, or indeed any other entity is literally a state. It is rather that this is not the type of comparison we should be making in the first place. Instead, what matters is that all these entities belong by default to a common class that matches international law's corresponding inherent openness to institutional form. Special rules and exceptions may develop, but these will have to be identified separately as opposed to be assumed in advance.

This alternative approach breathes fresh air into old doctrinal puzzles. It accounts for the objective legal personality of these institutions without positing a 'radical extension' of the definition of international law or a rule of incorporation emerging in the system. At the same time, it explains why international lawyers can leave behind unsatisfying causal tests regarding the distinct will of international organizations. Such tests not only set the bar unnecessarily high but also rehearse troublesome assumptions about the nature of the state, making them miss the mark altogether. Moreover, the theory advanced explains why the practice of international organizations should be thought of as capable of contributing to the formation of customary international law. It does so without falling into the pitfalls of considering these institutions either as fully fledged subjects on par with states or as spiritless mechanisms. The practice of international organizations can contribute to the formation of customary international law directly, with the important caveat that this practice should not be weighed separately from that of their members in terms of its representativeness: what international organizations do matters, but not at the expense of other forms of communal organization, including states. Finally, the theory advanced here suggests that even as international organizations may not be formally bound by the treaties of their members, they are still bound by the same norms of customary international law that bind states. They are bound because they are both expressions of the same capacity at different degrees of centralization, not because of any differences or similarities they might exhibit.

Zeroing in on these particular problems, I have focused on what I have thought to be the more foundational issues or the ones that have seemed to me, perhaps to some extent arbitrarily, more puzzling from an analytical perspective. My hope is that by providing clarifications on these matters, this book can provide inspiration on other fronts as well, where that is called for.

Concluding this study, I would like to take a step back and reflect on this book's own epistemological assumptions. In that regard, it may seem that I have sought to rid us of crude anthropomorphic conceptions of the state only to replace them with humanlike accounts of two other notions: (1) the communities that have the capacity to self-describe, thus leading to the emergence of states as well as international organizations, and (2) international law itself.

Throughout this book I have put international law in the syntactic position of a subject. In Chapters 1–9, international law supposedly 'does' all sorts of things: it 'admits', 'recognizes', 'precludes', 'constructs', and so on. In my mind this has always been an entirely provisional shorthand for referring to the content of certain norms. Yet at this point the question may legitimately arise: where do these norms come from? Do they not presuppose 'states', and, if so, are we not lapsing back to a legal ontology where the state is somehow pre-existing and fundamental rather than constructed? I think both of these questions should be answered in the negative. To explain why, let me turn to the first potential charge of anthropomorphism, concerning the community that has the capacity to self-describe, and which, in doing so, may lead to the creation of states as well as international organizations.

This charge of anthropomorphism I will happily accept. Not in the sense, hopefully clearly refuted by now, that these communities somehow enjoy a soul or a super-mind. Rather, in the sense that at the end of the day there is nothing more humanlike than people coming together to organize and plan their communal life. This is not to imply that this is an easy process or one that is somehow destined to take place. Instead it is to suggest that whatever human organization represents, it is *human*, no more, no less. The construction of complex norms, including systems of re-description and rules of recognition, should not be approached as some deep mystery but as the most reasonable exegesis for the emergence of institutions. These may succeed for a while and then collapse or fail to take off altogether. But when they succeed, they do create social facts, that is, relational facts that escape the orbit of individual dispositions. At the same time, institutions and social facts always remain grounded on what human beings do. International law is such a fact. In the final analysis, its existence matters only insofar as it can be ultimately anchored, directly or indirectly, in social convention.

To thus go back to the popular paradox about international law creating the state that then creates international law, this disappears once we put everything in the correct order and assign it its proper name. International law is created by institutions that are themselves created by certain communities that are capable in fact of creating those institutions and have historically actually done so. The possibility of international law existing is not only premised on certain communities having that capacity but also is an expression of it. There is nothing paradoxical with the notion that, once the socially embedded system of re-description that we have come to call international law has been put in place, it may then abstract, conceptually refine, and accommodate any institution emanating from the same foundation. By contrast, it is when we substitute the word 'institution' for the word 'state' that we end up obscuring from view the social grounding of states as well as their historical variance and trajectory. That those who make this substitution then end up with the curious proposition that 'states create international law which in turn creates states' should come as no surprise. But the perplexing nature of things when viewed from this vantage point should give pause to those subscribing to this view and not the other way around.

Finally, I feel the need to turn, even briefly, to the bigger normative arc. It is common, especially for earlier works on international organizations, to conclude with an inspiring statement on the future and significance of these institutions. My study has taken a more cautious tone throughout. Romanticised views of international organizations hardly seem tenable anymore, even if the field is so vast that it is always possible to find redeeming examples. The idea that international organizations cannot by their nature commit internationally wrongful acts sounds today as out of touch with reality as it has ever been. From peacekeeping to international financial and debt governance, the bureaucracies of international organizations are constantly implicated in scenarios where they affect the rights of others. The upshot is not that international organizations are demons or, of course, angels. Instead, it is that they may not be so special after all. Rather than mysterious corporate persons that linger between their counterintuitive equation with states and the counterproductive blanket categorization as non-state actors, international organizations should be thought of – normatively as well as analytically – as what they most truly are: forms of exercising public power.

BIBLIOGRAPHY

United Nations

International Law Commission

ILC, 'Report on the Law of Treaties by Mr H Lauterpacht, Special Rapporteur' (1953) UN Doc A/CN.4/63

ILC, 'Third Report on the Law of Treaties by Mr. G.G. Fitzmaurice, Special Rapporteur' (1958) UN Doc A/CN.4/115 and Corr.1

ILC, 'First Report on the Law of Treaties by Sir Humphrey Waldock, Special Rapporteur' (1962) UN Doc A/CN.4/144 and Add.1

ILC, 'First Report on Relations between States and Inter-governmental Organizations, by Mr. Abdullah El-Erian, Special Rapporteur' (1963) UN Doc A/CN.4/161 and Add.1, 166

ILC, 'Report by Mr. R. Ago, Chairman of the Sub-Committee on State Responsibility' (1963) UN Doc A/CN.4/152

ILC, 'Third Report on State Responsibility, by Mr. Roberto Ago, Special Rapporteur, the Internationally Wrongful Act of the State, Source of International Responsibility' (1971) UN Doc A/CN.4/246 and Add.1-3) 199

ILC, 'Report of the International Law Commission on the Work of Its Twenty-Sixth Session, 6 May–26 July 1974, Official Records of the General Assembly, Twenty-Ninth session, Supplement No. 10' (1974) UN Doc A/9610/Rev.1

ILC, 'Report of the International Law Commission on the Work of Its Sixtieth Session, 5 May–6 June 2008, Official Records of the General Assembly, Sixty-Third Session, Supplement No. 10' (1974) UN Doc A/63/10

ILC, 'Third Report on the Question of Treaties Concluded between States and International Organizations or between Two or More International Organizations by Mr. Paul Reuter, Special Rapporteur – Draft Articles with Commentaries' (1974) UN Doc A/CN.4/279 and Corr.1 (E. only)

ILC, 'Sixth Report on the Question of Treaties Concluded between States and International Organizations or between Two or More International Organizations by Mr. Paul Reuter, Special Rapporteur – Draft Articles with Commentaries (continued)' (1977) UN Doc A/CN.4/298

ILC, 'Yearbook of the International Law Commission 1979 Volume 1: Summary Records of the Meetings of the Thirty-First Session 14 May–3 August 1979' (1979) UN Doc A/CN.4/SER.A/1979

ILC, 'Yearbook of the International Law Commission 1980 Volume 1: Summary Records of the Meetings of the Thirty-Second Session 5 May–15 July 1980' (1980) UN Doc A/CN.4/SER.A/1980

ILC, 'Draft Articles on the Law of Treaties between States and International Organizations or between International Organizations, with Commentaries' (1982) II/2 YILC 17

ILC, 'Yearbook of the International Law Commission 1982 Volume II Part Two: Report of the Commission to the General Assembly on the Work of the Thirty-Fourth Session' (1982) UN Doc A/CN.4/SER.A/1982/Add.1 (Part 2), 56

ILC, 'Yearbook of the International Law Commission 1985 Volume 1: Summary Records of the Meetings of the Thirty-Seventh Session 6 May–26 July 1985' (1985) UN Doc A/CN.4/SER.A/1985

ILC, 'Draft Articles on Responsibility of States for Internationally Wrongful Acts, with Commentaries' (2001) II/2 YILC 31

ILC, 'Draft Articles on Diplomatic Protection' (2006) II/2 YILC 24

ILC 'Fourth Report on Responsibility of International Organizations, by Mr. Giorgio Gaja, Special Rapporteur' (2006) UN Doc A/CN.4/564 and Add. 1-2

ILC, 'Yearbook of the International Law Commission 2006 Volume 1: Summary Records of the Meetings of the Fifty-Eighth Session 1 May–9 June and 3 July–11 August 2006' (2006) UN Doc A/CN.4/SER.A/2006

ILC, 'Preliminary Report on Immunity of State Officials from Foreign Criminal Jurisdiction, by Roman Anatolevich Kolodkin, Special Rapporteur' (2008) UN Doc A/CN.4/601

ILC, 'Yearbook of the International Law Commission 2009 Volume 1: Summary Records of the Meetings of the Sixty-First Session 4 May–5 June and 6 July–7 August 2009' (2009) UN Doc A/CN.4/SER.A/2009

ILC, 'Draft Articles on the Responsibility of International Organizations' (2011) II/2 YILC 2

ILC, 'Draft Articles on the Responsibility of International Organizations, with Commentaries' (2011) II/2 YILC 46

ILC, 'Second Report on *jus cogens* by Dire Tladi, Special Rapporteur' (2017) UN Doc A/CN.4/706

ILC, 'Draft Conclusions on the Identification of Customary International Law, with Commentaries' (2018) UN Doc A/73/10

ILC, 'Summaries of the Work of the International Law Commission' (2023) <https://legal.un.org/ilc/summaries/10_3.shtml> accessed 9 February 2024

General Assembly

UNGA 'Annual Report of the Secretary-General on the Work of the Organization' (1 July 1949–30 June 1950) UN Doc A/1287

UNGA Res 1541 (XV), 'Principles Which Should Guide Members in Determining Whether or Not an Obligation Exists to Transmit the Information Called for under Article 73e of the Charter' (15 December 1960)

UNGA Res 3314 (14 December 1974) annex, Definition of Aggression FN 89 Chapter 2

UNGA Res 40/76 (11 December 1985) UN Doc A/RES/40/76 Annex I: Draft Rules of Procedure

UNGA Res 56/83 (28 January 2002) UN Doc A/RES/56/83, Annex I: Responsibility of States for Internationally Wrongful Acts

Other Organs

Legal Opinion of the Secretariat of the UN (1971) United Nations Juridical Yearbook 215, UN Doc ST/LEG/SER.C/9

ECOSOC, Committee on Economic, Social and Cultural Rights, 'Public Debt, Austerity Measures and the International Covenant on Economic, Social and Cultural Rights' (22 July 2016) UN Doc E/C.12/2016/1

Other International Sources

Committee on Formation of Customary (General) International Law, 'Statement of Principles Applicable to the Formation of General Customary International Law' in *International Law Association London Conference Final Report of the Committee* (International Law Association, London 2000) 1

European Data Protection Board, 'Guidelines 2/2020 on Articles 46 (2) (a) and 46 (3) (b) of Regulation 2016/679 for Transfers of Personal Data between EEA and non-EEA Public Authorities and Bodies' (15 December 2020) <https://www.edpb.europa.eu/our-work-tools/our-documents/guidelines/guidelines-22020-articles-46-2-and-46-3-b-regulation_en> accessed 9 February 2025

International Committee of the Red Cross International Humanitarian Law Database, 'Rule 44: Due Regard for the Natural Environment in Military Operations – Section B: The Precautionary Principle' < https://ihl-databases.icrc.org/en/customary-ihl/v1/rule44> accessed 9 February 2024

International Committee of the Red Cross International Humanitarian Law Database, 'Rule 132: Return of Displaced Persons' <https://ihl-databases.icrc.org/en/customary-ihl/v1/rule132> accessed 9 February 2024

'Supplemental Memorandum of Understanding' (16 June 2016) <https://econ omy-finance.ec.europa.eu/system/files/2017-11/ecfin_smou_en1.pdf> accessed 9 February 2025

Literature

Aarnio A, 'Paradigms in Legal Dogmatics: Toward a Theory of Change and Progress in Legal Science' in Aleksander Peczenik, Lars Lindahl and Bert Van Roermund (eds), *Theory of Legal Science* (Lund 1983)

Ahlborn C, 'The Rules of International Organizations and the Law of International Responsibility' (2012) 8 *International Organizations Law Review* 397

'The Use of Analogies in Drafting the Articles on the Responsibility of International Organizations – An Appraisal of the "Copy-Paste Approach"' (2012) 9 *International Organizations Law Review* 53

Ahrne G and Brunsson N, *Meta-organizations* (Edward Elgar 2011)

Ainslie DC, 'Hume on Personal Identity' in Elizabeth S Radcliffe (ed), *A Companion to Hume* (Wiley-Blackwell 2011)

Alexy R and Peczenik A, 'The Concept of Coherence and Its Significance for Discursive Rationality' (1990) 3 *Ratio Juris* 130

Alston P, 'The "Not-a-Cat" Syndrome: Can the International Human Rights Regime Accommodate Non-State Actors?' in Philip Alston (ed), *Non-State Actors and Human Rights* (OUP 2005)

Alvarez J, *International Organizations as Law-Makers* (OUP 2005)

'Book Review: "International Organizations and Their Exercise of Sovereign Powers" by Dan Sarooshi' (2007) 101(3) *AJIL* 674

Amerasinghe CF, *Principles of the Institutional Law of International Organizations* (2nd edn, CUP 2005)

Anghie A, 'Time Present and Time Past: Globalization, International Financial Institutions, and the Third World' (2000) 32 *New York University Journal of International Law and Politics* 243

Aniche ET, 'Beyond Neo-functionalism: Africa in Search of a New Theory of Regrional Integration' in Ernest Toochi Aniche, Ikenna Mike Alumona and Inocent Moyo (eds), *Regionalism, Security and Development in Africa* (Routledge 2021)

Armstrong DM, *A Theory of Universals: Universals and Scientific Realism*, vol II (CUP 1978)

A World of States of Affairs (CUP 1997)

Arrow KJ, *Social Choice and Individual Values* (2nd edn, John Wiley & Sons 1963)

Arsanjani MH, 'Claims against International Organizations: Quis Custodiet Ipsos Custodes' (1981) 7 *Yale Journal of World Public Order* 131

d'Aspremont J, 'The Multifaceted Concept of the Autonomy of International Organizations and International Legal Discourse' in Richard Collins and

Nigel D White (eds), *International Organizations and the Idea of Autonomy: Institutional Independence in the International Legal Order* (Routledge 2011)

'The International Law of Statehood: Craftmanship for the Elucidation and Regulation of Births and Deaths in International Law' (2014) 29 *Connecticut Journal of International Law* 201

'The Law of International Organizations and the Art of Reconciliation: From Dichotomies to Dialectics' (2014) 11 *International Organizations Law Review* 428

'The International Law of Statehood and Recognition: A Post-Colonial Invention' in Thierry Garcia (ed), *La Reconnaissance du Statut d'Etat à des Entités Contestées* (Pedone 2018)

Audi P, 'A Clarification and Defense of the Notion of Grounding' in Fabrice Correia and Benjamin Schneider (eds), *Metaphysical Grounding: Understanding the Structure of Reality* (CUP 2012)

'Grounding: Toward a Theory of the *In-Virtue-Of* Relation' (2012) 12 *The Journal of Philosophy* 685

Aufricht H, 'Personality in International Law' in Fleur Johns (ed), *International Legal Personality* (Routledge 2010)

Austin J, *The Providence of Jurisprudence Determined* (Wilfrid Rumble ed, first published 1832, CUP 2009)

Bankowski Z, Summers RS and MacCormick N, 'On Method and Methodology' in Neil MacCormick and Robert S Summers (eds), *Interpreting Statutes: A Comparative Study* (Ashgate 1991)

Barclift JZ, 'Fuzzy Logic and Corporate Governance Theories' (2007) 6 *Pierce Law Review* 177

Barnett M and Finnemore M, *Rules for the World: International Organizations in Global Politics* (CUP 2004)

Bederman DJ, 'The Souls of International Organizations: Legal Personality and the Lighthouse at Cape Spartel' (1996) 36 *Vanderbilt Journal of Transnational Law* 275

Bekker PH, *The Legal Position of Intergovernmental Organizations: A Functional Necessity of Their Legal Status and Immunities* (Brill 1994)

Belof J and Smythies JR (eds), *The Case for Dualism* (University of Virginia Press 1989)

Bentham J, *Introduction to the Principles of Morals and Legislation* (first published in 1789, OUP 1996).

Benvenisti E, *The Law of Global Governance* (Brill 2014)

von Bernstorff J, '*Autorité oblige*: The Rise and Fall of Hans Kelsen's Legal Concept of International Institutions' (2020) 31(2) *EJIL* 497

Bhargave R, *Individualism in Social Science: Forms and Limits of a Methodology* (OUP 1992)

Bhaskar R, *The Possibility of Naturalism: A Philosophical Critique of the Contemporary Human Sciences* (3rd edn, Routledge 1998)

Bhuta N, 'State Theory, State Order, State System – Jus Gentium and the Constitution of Public Power' in Stefan Kadelbach, Thomas Kleinlein and David Roth-Isgkeit (eds), *System, Order, and International Law: The Early History of International Legal Thought from Machiavelli to Hegel* (OUP 2017)

Bianchi A (ed), *Non-State Actors and International Law* (Ashgate 2009)

'The Fight for Inclusion: Non-State Actors and International Law' in Ulrich Fastenrath and and others (eds), *From Bilateralism to Community Interest: Essays in Honour of Bruno Simma* (OUP 2011)

Blake DJ and Lockwood Payton A, 'Balancing Design Objectives: Analyzing New Data on Voting Rules in Intergovernmental Organization' (2015) 10 *Review of International Organization* 377

Blavoukos S and Bourantonis D, 'Nested Institutions' in Rafael Biermann and Joachim A Koops (eds) *Palgrave Handbook of Inter-Organizational Relations in World Politics* (Palgrave Macmillan 2016)

Bliss R and Trogdon K, 'Metaphysical Grounding' in Edward N Zalta (ed), *The Stanford Encyclopedia of Philosophy* (2016) <https://plato.stanford.edu/entries/grounding/> accessed 9 February 2024

Blokker NM, 'International Organizations and Their Members' (2004) 1(1) *International Organizations Law Review* 139

'International Organizations: The Untouchables?' in Niels M Blokker and Nico J Schrijver (eds), *Immunity of International Organizations* (Brill–Nijhoff, 2015)

Blokker NM and Wessel RA, 'Revisiting Questions of Organisationhood, Legal Personality and Membership in the OSCE: The Interplay between Law, Politics and Practice' in Mateja Steinbrück Platise, Carolyn Moser and Anne Peters (eds), *The Legal Framework of the OSCE* (CUP 2019)

Blomberg O, 'Form Simple to Composite Agency: On Kirk Ludwig's *From Individual to Plural Agency*' (2019) 5 *Journal of Social Ontology* 101

Bluntschili JC, *The Theory of the State* (Batoche Books 2000)

Bogdandy A von, 'Neither an International Organization Nor a Nation State: The EU as a Supranational Federation' in Erik Jones and others (eds), *The Oxford Handbook of the European Union* (OUP 2012)

Bogdandy A von and others (eds), *The Exercise of Public Authority by International Institutions: Advancing International Institutional Law* (Springer 2010)

Bordin F, *The Analogy between States and International Organizations: Legal Reasoning and the Development of the Law of International Organizations* (CUP 2018)

Bratman ME, *Intentions, Plans, and Practical Reason* (CUP 1999)

'Two Problems of Human Agency' in Michael E Bratman (ed), *Structures of Agency: Essays* (OUP 2007)

Shared and Institutional Agency Toward a Planning Theory of Human Practical Organization (OUP 2022).

'Planning and Its Function in Our Lives' (2024) 41(1) *Journal of Applied Philosophy* 1

Brölmann C, 'A Flat Earth? International Organizations in the System of International Law' (2001) 70 *Nordic Journal of International Law* 319

The Institutional Veil in Public International Law: International Organisations and the Law of Treaties (Hart Oxford 2007)

'Capturing the Juridical Will of International Organisations' in Jean d' Aspremont and Droubi Sufyan (eds), *International Organizations and Non-State Actors in the Formation of Customary International Law* (Manchester University Press 2020)

Brölmann C and Nijman JE, 'Personality' in Sahib Singh and Jean d' Aspremont (eds), *Concepts for International Law: Contributions to Disciplinary Thought* (Edward Elgar 2019)

Brownlie I, *Principles of Public International Law* (7th edn, OUP 2008)

Burci GL, 'Public/Private Partnerships in the Public Health Sector' (2009) 6 *IOLR* 359

Butler J and Perry J, 'Of Personal Identity' in John Perry (ed), *Personal Identity* (2nd edn, University of California Press 2008)

Campbell K, 'Selective Realism in the Philosophy of Physics' (1994) 77 *The Monist* 27

Canale D, 'Looking for the Nature of Law: On Shapiro's Challenge' (2012) 31 *Law and Philosophy* 409

Carter AJ, 'Global Relativism' in Adam J Carter (ed), *Metaepistemology and Relativism* (Palgrave MacMillan 2016)

Carty A, 'Doctrine versus State Practice' in Bardo Fassbender and Anne Peters (eds), *The Oxford Handbook of the History of International Law* (OUP 2012)

Cassese A, *Self-Determination of Peoples: A Legal Reappraisal* (CUP 1995)

Chasapis Tassinis O, 'Customary International Law: Interpretation from Beginning to End' (2020) 31 *EJIL* 235

Chen Y, 'International Institutions as Forms and Fora: Rao Geping and the Law of International Organizations in China' 2023 34(4) *EJIL* 855

Chimni BS, 'International Institutions Today: An Imperial Global State in the Making' (2004) 15 *EJIL* 1

'International Organizations: 1945–Present', in Jacob Katz Cogan and others (eds), *The Oxford Handbook of International Organizations* (OUP 2016)

Clapham A, *Human Rights Obligations of Non-State Actors* (OUP 2006)

Churchill R and Ulfstein G, 'Autonomous and Institutional Arrangements in Multilateral Environmental Agreements: A Little-Noticed Phenomenon in International Law' (2000) 94 *AJIL* 623

Collins R, 'Non-State Actors in International Institutional Law' in Jean d' Aspremont (ed), *Participants in the International Legal System* (Routledge 2011)

'Non-State, Inter-State or Supra-State? The Peculiar Identity of the Intergovernmental Organization' in Jean d' Aspremont (ed), *Participants in the International Legal System* (Routledge 2011)

'The League of Nations and the Emergence of International Administration: Finding the Origins of International Institutional Law' (2019) 71 *Revista Española de Derecho Internacional* 285

Colyvan M, *The Indispensability of Mathematics* (OUP 2001)

Copp D, 'What Collectives Are: Agency, Individualism and Legal Theory' (1984) 23 *Dialogue* 249

Corbett P, 'What Is the League of Nations?' (1924) 5 *BYIL* 119

Coyle S, 'Two Concepts of Legal Analysis' in Sean Coyle and George Pavlakos (eds), *Jurisprudence of Legal Science: A Debate about the Nature of Legal Theory* (Hart 2005)

Crawford J, 'The Rights of Peoples: "Peoples" or "Governments"?' (1985) 9 *Bulletin of the Australian Society of Legal Philosophy* 136

  The Creation of States in International Law (2nd edn OUP 2007)

  Brownlie's Principles of Public International Law (9th edn, OUP 2019)

D'Amato AA 'The Concept of Special Custom in International Law' (1969) 63 *AJIL* 211

Daugirdas K, 'How and Why International Law Binds International Organizations' (2016) 57 *Harvard International Law Journal* 325

  'International Organizations and the Creation of Customary International Law' (2018) 31 *EJIL* 201

Davidson D, 'Actions, Reasons, and Causes' (1963) 60 *The Journal of Philosophy* 685

De Schutter O, 'Human Rights and the Rise of International Organisations: The Logic of Sliding Scales in the Law of International Responsibility' in Jan Wouters and others (eds), *Accountability for Human Rights Violations by International Organisations* (Intersentia, 2010)

De Witt Dickinson E, 'The Analogy between Natural Persons and International Persons in the Law of Nations' [1917] *Yale Law Journal* 564

Descartes R, *Meditations on First Philosophy* (John Cottingham tr, CUP 1996)

Descombes V, *Puzzling Identities* (Harvard University Press 2016)

Dewey J, 'The Historic Background of Corporate Legal Personality' (1926) 35 *Yale Law Journal* 655

Dickson J, *Legal Theory Today* (Hart 2001)

Doehring K, 'Self-Determination' in Bruno Simma and others (eds), *The Charter of the United Nations: A Commentary* (2nd edn, OUP 2002)

Dolan E, 'The Member-Republics of the U.S.S.R. as Subjects of the Law of Nations' 4(4) *ICLQ* 1955

Dominicé C, 'La Société Internationale à La Recherché de Son Équilibre' (2006) 370 *Collected Courses of International Law* 144

Dörr O, 'Nationality', *Max Planck Encyclopedia of Public International Law* (2019) <https://opil.ouplaw.com/view/10.1093/law:epil/9780199231690/law-9780199231690-e852> accessed 9 February 2024.

Douglas Z, *The International Law of Investment Claims* (CUP 2009)

Dumberry P and Labelle-Eastaugh E, 'Non-State Actors in International Investment Law: The Legal Personality of Corporations and NGOs in the Context of Investor-State Arbitration' in Jean d' Aspremont (ed), *Multiple Perspectives on Non-State Actors in International Law* (Routledge-Cavendish 2011)

Dworkin R, *Law's Empire* (Fontana Press 1986)

Effingham N, 'The Metaphysics of Groups' (2010) 149 *Philosophical Studies* 251

Ehring D, 'Causal Relata' in Helen Beebee, Christopher Hitchcock and Peter Menzies (eds), *The Oxford Handbook of Causation* (OUP 2009)

Elder-Vass D, *The Causal Power of Social Structures: Emergence, Structure and Agency* (CUP 2010)

Ellis BD, *Truth and Objectivity* (Blackwell 1990)

Ellis DC, 'Theorizing International Organizations: The Organizational Turn in International Organization Theory' (2010) 1 *Journal of International Organizations Studies* 11

Epstein B, *The Ant Trap: Rebuilding the Foundation of the Social Sciences* (OUP 2015)

'A Framework for Social Ontology' (2016) 46 *Philosophy of the Social Sciences* 147

Evnine SJ, 'Constitution and Composition: Three Approaches to Their Relation' (2011) 27 *Protosociology* 212

Evrigenis ID, 'The Psychology of Politics: The City-Soul Analogy in Plato's *Republic*' (2002) 23 *History of Political Thought* 590

Fine K, 'Things and Their Parts' (1999) 23 *Midwest Studies in Philosophy* 61

'Guide to Ground' in Fabrice Correia and Benjamin Schneider (eds), *Metaphysical Grounding: Understanding the Structure of Reality* (CUP 2012)

Fiore P, *International Law Codified and Its Legal Sanction* (E Borchard tr, Baker Voorhis 1918)

Fisch J, 'Peoples and Nations' in Bardo Fassbender and Anne Peters (eds), *The Oxford Handbook of the History of International Law* (OUP 2012)

Fitzmaurice M, Muchlinski P and Szuniewicz M, 'From the Editors' (2001) 1 *Non-State Actors and International Law* 1

Fortin K, The Accountability of Armed Groups under Human Rights Law (OUP 2017)

Fox H QC, and Webb P, *The Law of State Immunity* (3rd edn, OUP 2015)

French PA, 'The Corporation as a Moral Person' (1979) 16 *American Philosophical Law Quarterly* 207

'Crowds and Corporations' (1982) 19 *American Philosophical Quarterly* 271

Collective and Corporate Responsibility (Columbia University Press 1984)

'Integrity, Intentions, and Corporations' (1996) 34 *American Business Law Journal* 141

Fry JD, 'Rights, Functions, and International Legal Personality of International Organizations' (2018) 36 *Boston University International Law Journal* 221

Gallois A, 'Identity over Time' in Edward N Zalta (ed), *The Stanford Encyclopedia of Philosophy* (2016) <https://plato.stanford.edu/entries/identity-time/> accessed 9 February 2024

Gardner J, 'Legal Positivism: Five and a Half Myths' (2001) 46 *The American Journal of Jurisprudence* 199

Gasbarri L, 'The Dual Legality of the Rules of International Organizations' (2017) 14 *International Organizations Law Review* 87

 'Beyond the Either/Or Paradigm in the Formation of Customary International Law by International Organizations' in Jean d' Aspremont and Sufyan Droubi (eds), *International Organizations and the Formation of Customary International Law* (Manchester University Press 2020)

 The Concept of an International Organization in Public International Law (OUP 2021)

Gazzini T, 'Personality of International Organizations' in Jan Klabbers and Asa Wallendahl (eds), *Research Handbook on the Law of International Organizations* (Edward Elgar 2011)

 'The Relationship between International Legal Personality and the Autonomy of International Organizations' in Richard Collins and Nigel D White (eds), *International Organizations and the Idea of Autonomy: Institutional Independence in the International Legal Order* (Routledge 2011)

Gierke O von, *Political Theories of the Middle Age* (Frederic W Maitland tr, CUP 1900)

 'The Nature of Human Associations' in John D Lewis (ed), *The Genossenschaft-theory of Otto Von Gierke* (CUP 1932)

 Community in Historical Perspective (Antony Black ed, Mary Fisher tr, CUP 1990)

Gilbert M, *On Social Facts* (PUP 1989)

Golia A and Peters A, 'The Concept of International Organization' in Jan Klabbers (ed), *The Cambridge Companion to International Organizations Law* (CUP 2022)

Gött H, *The Law of Interaction between International Organizations* (Springer 2020)

Grant TD, 'Defining Statehood: The Montevideo Convention and Its Discontents' (1999) 37 *Columbia Journal of Transnational Law* 403

Grant TD and Nicholson R, 'The Early United Nations Advisory Opinions (1948–62)' in Eirik Bjorge and Cameron Miles (eds), *Landmark Cases in Public International Law* (Hart 2017)

Green F, 'Fragmentation in Two Dimensions: The ICJ's Flawed Approach to Non-State Actors and International Legal Personality' (2008) 9 *Melbourne Journal of International Law* 47

Greimann D, '"No Entity without Identity": A Reductionist Dogma?' (2000) 60 *Grazer Philosophische Studien* 13

Guela F, 'The Philosophy of Social Science: Metaphysical and Empirical' (2007) 2(6) *Philosophy Compass* 954

Guzman A, 'International Organizations and the Frankenstein Problem' (2013) 24 *EJIL* 999

Hager MM, 'Bodies Politic: The Progressive History of Organizational "Real Entity" Theory' (1988) 50 *University of Pittsburgh Law Review* 575

Hahn HJ, 'Euratom: The Conception of an International Personality' (1958) 71 *Harvard Law Review* 1001

Hannum H, 'The Status of the Universal Declaration of Human Rights in National and International Law' (1996) 25(1) *Georgia Journal of International and Comparative Law* 289

Harman GH, 'The Inference to the Best Explanation' (1965) 74 *The Philosophical Review* 88

Harris R, 'The Transplantation of the Legal Discourse on Corporate Personality Theories: From German Codification to English Pluralism and American Big Business' (2006) 63 *Washington and Lee Law Review* 1421

Hart HLA, *The Concept of Law* (3rd edn, OUP 2012)

Hart HLA and Honoré T, *Causation in the Law* (2nd edn, OUP 1985)

Heath J, 'Methodological Individualism' in Edward N Zalta (ed), *Stanford Encyclopedia of Philosophy* (2020) <https://plato.stanford.edu/cgi-bin/encyclopedia/archinfo.cgi?entry=methodological-individualism>

Henckaerts J-M and Doswald-Beck L, *International Committee of the Red Cross – Customary International Humanitarian Law: Volume 1: Rules* (CUP 2005)

Hernández G, 'Federated Entities in International Law: Disaggregating the Federal State' in Duncan French (ed), *Statehood and Self-Determination: Reconciling Tradition and Modernity in International Law* (CUP 2013)

Higgins R, *Problems and Process: International Law and How We Use It* (OUP 1994) 'The Legal Consequences for Member States of the Non-Fulfilment by International Organizations of Their Obligations toward Third Parties' (1995) 66 *Yearbook of the Institute of International Law* 251

Hindriks F, 'The Status Account of Corporate Agents' in Hans B Schmid, Katinka Schulte-Ostermann and Nikos Psarros (eds), *Concepts of Sharedness: Essays on Collective Intentionality* (Ontos Verlag 2008)

Hobbes T, *Elements of Philosophy: The First Section, Concerning Body* (R&W Leybourn 1656)

Hofweber T, 'Logic and Ontology' in Edward N Zalta (ed), *Stanford Encyclopedia of Philosophy* (2017) <https://plato.stanford.edu/entries/logic-ontology/#DifConOnt> accessed 9 February 2024

Hohfeld WN, 'Some Fundamental Legal Conceptions as Applied in Judicial Reasoning' (1913) 23 *Yale Law Journal* 16

Hollis DB, 'Why State Consent Still Matters – Non-State Actors, Treaties, and the Changing Sources of International Law' (2005) 23(1) *Berkeley Journal of International Law* 137

Hooghe L, Lenz T and Marks G, *A Theory of International Organization* (OUP 2019)

Hume D, *A Treatise of Human Nature* (Lewis A Selby-Bigge and Peter H Nidditch eds, Clarendon Press 1978)

Hylton P and Kemp G, 'Willard Van Orman Quine' in Edward N Zalta (ed), *Stanford Encyclopedia of Philosophy* (2020) <https://plato.stanford.edu/archives/spr2020/entries/quine/>, accessed 9 February 2024

van Inwagen P, 'Materialism and the Psychological-Continuity Account of Personal Identity' (1997) 11 *Philosophical Perspectives* 305

Jellinek G, *Allgemeine Staatslehre* (O Häring 1900)

Jenks CW, 'The Legal Personality of International Organizations' (1945) 22 *BYIL* 267

Jennings R, 'Foreword' in Peter Bekker, *The Legal Position of Intergovernmental Organizations: A Functional Necessity of Their Legal Status and Immunities* (Brill 1994)

Jennings R and Watts A KCMG QC, *Oppenheim's International Law: Volume 1 Peace* (9th edn, OUP 2008)

Johns F, 'Critical International Legal Theory' in Jeffrey L Dunnoff and Mark A Pollack (eds), *International Legal Theory* (CUP 2022)

Kantorowicz E, *The King's Two Bodies: A Study in Medieval Political Theology* (PUP 1997)

Kantorowicz H, 'The Concept of the State' (1931) 35 *Economica* 1

Kavka GS, 'Is Individual Choice Less Problematic Than Collective Choice?' (1991) 7 *Economics and Philosophy* 143

Kelsen H, *General Theory of Law and State* (Harvard University Press 1945)
    Principles of International Law (Rinehart & Co 1952)
    General Principles of International Law (2nd edn, Holt Reinhart & Winston 1966)
    Pure Theory of Law (Max Knight tr, The Law Book Exchange Ltd 2005)

Keohane R, *After Hegemony: Cooperation and Discord in the World Political Economy* (PUP 1984)

Kim J, 'Causation, Nomic Subsumption, and the Concept of Event' (1973) 70 *The Journal of Philosophy* 217

Kim SM, 'Characteristics of Soulless Persons: The Applicability of the Character Evidence Rule to Corporations' (2003) 3 *University of Illinois Law Review* 763

Kingsbury B, 'The Concept of "Law" in Global Administrative Law' (2009) 20 *EJIL* 23

Kingsbury B and Casini L, 'Global Administrative Law Dimensions of International Organizations Law' (2009) 6 *International Organizations Law Review* 319

Kingsbury B, Krisch N and Stewart RB, 'The Emergence of Global Administrative Law' (2005) 68 *Law and Contemporary Problems* 15

Kiss A, 'Abuse of Rights', *Max Planck Encyclopedia of International Law* (2006) <https://opil.ouplaw.com/display/10.1093/law:epil/9780199231690/law-9780199231690-e1371> accessed 9 February 2024

Klabbers J, 'Presumptive Personality: The European Union in International Law' in Martti Koskenniemi (ed), *International Law Aspects of the European Union* (Brill 1997)

'Constitutionalism Lite' (2004) 1 *International Organizations Law Review* 31

'The Concept of Legal Personality' (2005) 11 *Jus Gentium* 35

'The Paradox of International Institutional Law' (2008) 5 *International Organizations Law Review* 1

'On Seyersted and His Common Law of International Organizations' (2008) 5 *International Organizations Law Review* 381

An Introduction to International Institutional Law (2nd edn, CUP 2009)

'Autonomy, Constitutionalism and Virtue in International Institutional Law' in Richard Collins and Nigel D White (eds), *International Organizations and the Idea of Autonomy: Institutional Independence in the International Legal Order* (Routledge 2011)

'The Emergence of Functionalism in International Institutional Law: Colonial Inspirations' (2014) 25 *EJIL* 645

Advanced Introduction to the Law of International Organizations (Edward Elgar 2015)

'The EJIL Foreword: The Transformation of International Organizations Law' (2015) 26 *EJIL* 9

'Theorizing International Organizations' in Anne Orford and Florian Hoffmann (eds), *The Oxford Handbook of the Theory of International Law* (OUP 2016)

'Sources of International Organizations' Law' in Jean d' Aspremont and Samantha Besson (eds), *The Oxford Handbook of the Sources of International Law* (OUP 2017)

'The Cheshire Cat That Is International Law' (2020) 31 *EJIL* 269

An Introduction to International Organizations Law (4th edn, CUP 2022)

Klabbers J and Fiti Sinclair G, 'On Theorizing International Organizations Law: Editors' Introduction' 31(2) *EJIL* 2020, 489

Klein P, *La Responsabilité Des Organisations Internationales Dans Les Ordres Juridiques Internes et En Droit Des Gens* (Bruylant 1998)

Knop K, *Diversity and Self-Determination in International Law* (CUP 2002)

Kolb R, 'History of International Organizations or Institutions', *Max Planck Encyclopedia of International Law* (2011) <https://opil.ouplaw.com/view/10.1093/law:epil/9780199231690/law-9780199231690-e501> accessed 9 February 2024

Theory of International Law (Hart 2016)

Koremenos B, Lipson C and Snidal D. 'The Rational Design of International Institutions' (2001) 55(4) *International Organization* 761

Kornhauser LA and Sager LG, 'The One and the Many: Adjudication in Collegial Courts' (1993) 81 *California Law Review* 1

Korsgaard CM, 'Personal Identity and the Unity of Agency: A Kantian Response to Parfit' (1981) 18 *Philosophy and Public Affairs* 101

The Sources of Normativity (CUP 1996)

Self-Constitution: Agency, Identity, and Integrity (OUP 2009)

'The Normative Constitution of Agency' in Manuel Vargas and Vaffe Gideon (eds), *Rational and Social Agency: The Philosophy of Michael Bratman* (OUP 2014)

Koslicki K, 'Constitution and Similarity' (2004) 117 *Philosophical Studies* 327

Krajewski M, 'Human Rights and Austerity Programmes' in Thomas Cottier and others (eds), *The Rule of Law in Monetary Affairs World Trade Forum* (CUP 2014)

Kreß C, Frank P and Barthe C, 'Functional Immunity of Foreign State Officials before National Courts: A Legal Opinion by Germany's Federal Public Prosecutor General' (2021) 19(3) *JICJ* 697

Kribbe H, 'Corporate Personality: A Theory of Political Association' (Doctoral dissertation, London School of Economics 2014)

Kunz JL, 'Une Nouvelle Théorie de l'État Fédérale' (1930) 11 *Revue de Droit International et de Législation Comparée* 835

Kusch M, 'The Metaphysics and Politics of Corporate Personhood' (2014) 79 *Erkenntnis* 1587

L'Abate L (ed), *Paradigms in Theory Construction* (Springer 2012)

Laertius D, *Lives of the Eminent Philosophers*, vol I (Drew Hicks tr, Harvard University Press 1925)

Lagrange E, *Functionalism according to Paul Reuter* (2020) 31(2) *EJIL* 543

Lauterpacht H, *Private Law Sources and Analogies in International Law* (Longmans, Green & Co 1927)

'The Subjects of the Law of Nations' in Fleur Johns (ed), *International Legal Personality* (Routledge 2010)

Lauterpacht H and Lauterpacht E, *International Law Vol 3: The Law of Peace, Parts II–VI* (CUP 1977)

Lewis D, 'Causation' (1973) 70 *Journal of Philosophy* 556

'Events' in David Lewis (ed), *Philosophical Papers: Volume II* (OUP 1986)

Liang Y, 'Notes on Legal Questions concerning the United Nations Reparation for Injuries Suffered in the Service of the United Nations' (1949) 43 *AJIL* 460

Lind D, 'The Pragmatic Value of Legal Fictions' in Maksymylian Del Mar and William Twining (eds), *Legal Fictions in Theory and Practice* (Springer 2015)

Lipton P, *Inference to the Best Explanation* (2nd edn, Routledge 2004)

List C and Pettit P, *Group Agency: The Possibility, Design, and Status of Corporate Agents* (OUP 2011)

Locke J, *An Essay Concerning Human Understanding* (Tegg & Son 1836)

Long T and Schultz CA, 'Republican Internationalism: The Nineteenth-Century Roots of Latin American Contributions to International Order' (2022) 35(5) *CRIA* 639

Lorca AB, *Mestizo International Law: A Global Intellectual History 1842–1933* (CUP 2015)

Lowe EJ, 'Individuation' in Michael J Loux and Dean W Zimmerman (eds), *The Oxford Handbook of Metaphysics* (OUP 2005)

Ludwig K, *From Individual to Plural Agency: Collective Action I* (OUP 2017)
  From Individual to Plural Agency: Collective Action II (OUP 2017)

Mace G, 'Regional Integration in Latin America: A Long and Winding Road' 1988 43(3) *International Journal* 404

Marchegiano G, 'The Juristic Character of the International Commission of Cape Spartel Lighthouse' (1931) 25 *AJIL* 339

Martha RSJ, *The Legal Foundations of INTERPOL* (Hart 2010)

Matthews GB, 'Aristotelian Essentialism' (1990) 50 *Philosophy and Phenomenological Research: Supplement* 251

Mazower M, *Governing the World: The History of an Idea* (Penguin 2012)

Mazzeschi RP, 'The Functional Immunity of State Officials from Foreign Jurisdiction: A Critique of the Traditional Theories' (2015) 17 *QIL, Zoom out* 3

McNair AD, 'The Functions and Differing Legal Character of Treaties' (1930) 11 *BYIL* 100

Mendus S, 'Personal Identity: The Two Analogies in Hume' (1980) 30 *The Philosophical Quarterly* 118, 61

Menzies P, 'A Unified Account of Causal Relata' (1989) 67 *Australasian Journal of Philosophy* 59

Menzies P and Beebee H, 'Counterfactual Theories of Causation' in Edward N Zalta (ed), *The Stanford Encyclopedia of Philosophy* (2019) <https://plato.stanford.edu/archives/win2019/entries/causation-counterfactual/> accessed 9 February 2024

Meron T, *Human Rights and Humanitarian Norms as Customary Law* (OUP 1989)

Micheler E, *Company Law: A Real Entity Theory* (OUP 2021)

Milanovic M, *Extraterritorial Application of Human Rights Treaties* (OUP 2011)
  'Revisiting Coercion as an Element of Prohibited Intervention in International Law' (2023) 117(1) *AJIL* 601

Miller S, 'Joint Action: The Individual Strikes Back' in Savas L Tsohatzidis (ed), *Intentional Acts and Institutional Facts* (Springer 2007)

Miller S and Makela P, 'The Collectivist Approach to Collective Moral Responsibility' (2005) 36 *Metaphilosophy* 634

Moore M, *Corporate Governance in the Shadow of the State* (Hart 2013)

Morgenstern F, *Legal Problems of International Organizations* (Grotius 1986)

Morrison FL, 'Confederation of States', *Max Planck Encyclopedia of International Law* (2007) <https://opil.ouplaw.com/view/10.1093/law:epil/9780199231690/law-9780199231690-e1385> accessed 9 February 2024

Morss JR, 'The International Legal Status of the Vatican/Holy See Complex' (2015) 26(4) *EJIL* 927

Morton PA, *A Historical Introduction to the Philosophy of Mind: Readings with Commentary* (Broadview Press 1997)

Murphy SD, 'Identification of Customary International Law and Other Topics: The Sixty-Seventh Session of the International Law Commission' (2015) 109 *AJI L* 822

Murray O, 'Piercing the Corporate Veil: The Responsibility of Member States of an International Organization' (2011) 8 *International Organizations Law Review* 291

Mushkat R, 'Hong Kong as an International Legal Person' (1992) 6 *Emory International Law Review* 105

Naert F, *International Law Aspects of the EU's Security and Defence Policy, with a Particular Focus on the Law of Armed Conflict and Human Rights* (1st edn, Intersentia 2010)

Nagel T, *The View from Nowhere* (OUP 1986)

Nicholson R, *Statehood and the State-Like in International Law* (OUP 2019)

Nijman JE, *The Concept of International Legal Personality: An Inquiry into the History and Theory of International Law* (TMC Asser Press 2004)

'Paul Ricoeur and International Law: Beyond "The End of the Subject". Towards a Reconceptualization of International Legal Personality' in Andrea Bianchi (ed), *Non-State Actors and International Law* (Ashgate 2009)

'Non-State Actors and the International Rule of Law' in Cedric Ryngaert and Math Noortmann (eds), *Non-State Actor Dynamics in International Law* (Routledge 2016)

Ninčić D, *The Problem of Sovereignty in the Charter and in the Practice of the United Nations* (Martinus Nijhoff 1970)

Noonan HW, *Personal Identity* (2nd edn, Routledge 2003)

Nowak M, *Toward a Theology of the Corporation* (The AEI Press 1981)

UN Covenant on Civil and Political Rights: CCPR Commentary (2nd edn, Engel 2005)

O' Connell DP, *State Succession in Municipal Law and International Law, Vol II: International Relations* (CUP 1967)

Oddie G, 'Armstrong on the Eleatic Principle and Abstract Entities' (1982) 41 *Philosophical Studies: An International Journal for Philosophy in the Analytic Tradition* 285

Odello M and Seatzu F (eds), *Latin American and Caribbean International Institutional Law* (Springer 2015)

Odobo SO, 'Conceptualising and Historicising African Regionalism in the Context of Pan-Africanism' in Ernest Toochi Aniche, Ikenna Mike Alumona and Inocent Moyo (eds), *Regionalism, Security and Development in Africa* (Routledge 2021)

Okeke EC, *Jurisdictional Immunities of States and International Organizations* (OUP 2018)

Olaoye KF, 'Samuel Kwadwo Boaten Asante and the United Nations Centre on Transnational Corporations (1975–1992)' (2023) 34(2) *EJIL* 291

Olsen J and McCormick J, *The European Union: Politics and Policies* (6th edn, Taulor & Francis 2017)

Olson ET, *The Human Animal: Personal Identity without Psychology* (OUP 1997)

'Personal Identity' in Edward N Zalta (ed), *Stanford Encyclopedia of Philosophy* (2019) <https://plato.stanford.edu/archives/fall2019/entries/identity-personal/> accessed 9 February 2024

Oppenheim L, 'Le Caractère Essentiel de La Société Des Nations' (1919) 26 *Revue Générale de Droit International Public* 234

International Law: A Treatise, vol 1 (3rd edn, Longmans, Green & Co 1920)

Overton WF, 'Evolving Scientific Paradigms: Retrospective and Prospective', in Luciano L'Abate (ed), *Paradigms in Theory Construction* (Springer 2012)

Paddeu F, *Justification and Excuse in International Law* (CUP 2018)

Parfit D, *Reasons and Persons* (OUP 1984)

Pauer-Studer H, 'A Constitutive Account of Group Agency' (2014) 79 *Erkenntnis* 1623

Paul LA, 'Counterfactual Theories' in Helen Beebee, Christopher Hitchcock and Peter Menzies (eds), *The Oxford Handbook of Causation* (OUP 2009)

Paul R, 'Principes de Droit Internationale Public' (1961) 103 *Collected Courses of International Law* 424

Peczenik A, *The Basis of Legal Justification* (Lund [A Peczenik] 1983)

Scienta Juris, Legal Doctrine as Knowledge of Law and as a Source of Law (Springer 2005)

Pellet A, 'The Palestinian Declaration and the Jurisdiction of the International Criminal Court' (2010) 8(4) *JICJ* 981

'International Organizations Are Definitely Not States' in Maurizio Ragazzi (ed), *Responsibility of International Organizations: Essays in Memory of Sir Ian Brownlie* (Martinus Nijhoff 2013)

Peters A, 'International Organizations and International Law', in Jacob Katz Cogan, Ian Hurd, and Ian Johnstone (eds), *The Oxford Handbook of International Organizations* (OUP 2017)

'Constitutionalisation', in Jean d'Aspremont and Sahib Singh (eds), *Concepts for International Law: Contributions to Disciplinary Thought* (Edward Elgar, 2019)

'Constitutional Theories of International Organisations: Beyond the West' (2021) 20(4) *CJIL* 649

Pettit P, 'Groups with Minds of Their Own' in Frederik F Schmitt (ed), *Socializing Metaphysics* (Rowman & Littlefield Publishers 2003)

Philpott D, 'Sovereignty' in Edward N Zalta (ed), *The Stanford Encyclopedia of Philosophy* (2016) <https://plato.stanford.edu/entries/sovereignty/> accessed 9 February 2024

Pieth M and Radha I (eds), *Corporate Criminal Liability: Emergence, Convergence, and Risk* (Springer 2011)

Pitson T, *Hume's Philosophy of the Self* (Routledge 2002)

Plutarch, *Lives: Theseus and Romulus, Lycurgus and Numa, Solon and Publicola* (Bernadotte Perrin tr, Harvard University Press 1967)

Portmann R, *Legal Personality in International Law* (CUP 2010)

Quénivet N, 'Binding the United Nations to Customary (Human Rights) Law' (2020) 17 *International Organizations Law Review* 379

Quine WV, *Ontological Relativity and Other Essays* (Columbia University Press 1969)

Quinton A, 'The Soul' in John Perry (ed), *Personal Identity* (University of California Press 1975)

Rama-Montaldo M, 'International Legal Personality and Implied Powers of International Organizations' (1970) 44 *BYIL* 111

Ramström G, 'The Analytical Micro–Macro Relationship in Social Science and Its Implications for the Individualism-Holism Debate' (2018) 48 *Philosophy of the Social Sciences* 474

Rapisardi-Mirabelli A, 'La Théorie Générale Des Unions Internationales' (1925) 7 *Collected Courses of the Hague Academy of International Law, The Hague Academy of International Law* 345

Ratcliffe S (ed), *Concise Oxford Dictionary of Quotations* (6th edn, OUP 2011)

Raz J, 'Can There Be a Theory of Law?' in Martin Golding and William Edmundson (eds), *Blackwell Guide to Philosophy of Law and Legal Theory* (Blackwell 2004)

  Between Authority and Interpretation: On the Theory of Law and Practical Reason (OUP 2009)

Rea MC, 'The Problem of Material Constitution' (1995) 104 *The Philosophical Review* 525

Reid T, 'Of Mr Locke's Account of Our Personal Identity' in John Perry (ed), *Personal Identity* (2nd edn, University of California Press 2008)

Reinisch A, 'Transnational Judicial Conversations on the Personality, Privileges, and Immunities of International Organizations – An Introduction' in August Reinisch (ed), *The Privileges and Immunities of International Organizations in Domestic Courts* (OUP 2013)

  International Organizations before National Courts (CUP 2000)

Reinsch PS, 'International Administrative Law and National Sovereignty' (1909) 3 *AJIL* 1

Reuter P, *Organisations européennes* (Presses universitaires de France 1965)
  Droit international public (4th edn, Presses universitaires des France 1973)

Reuterswärd R, 'The Legal Nature of International Organizations' (1980) 49 *Nordic Journal of International Law* 14

Ritchie K, 'The Metaphysics of Social Groups' (2015) 10 *Philosophical Compass* 316

Ronen Y, 'Entities That Can Be States but Do Not Claim to Be' in Duncan French (ed), *Statehood and Self-Determination: Reconciling Tradition and Modernity in International Law* (CUP 2013)

Rönnegard D, *The Fallacy of Corporate Moral Agency* (Springer 2015)

Rooney MT, 'Maitland and the Corporate Revolution' (1951) 26 *New York University Law Review* 24

Rosen G, 'Metaphysical Dependence: Grounding and Reduction' in Bob Hale and Aviv Hoffmann (eds), *Modality: Metaphysics, Logic, and Epistemology* (OUP 2010)

Ross A, *A Textbook of International Law: General Part* (Annie I Fausbøll tr, Longmans, Green & Co 1947)

Roucounas E, 'The Users of International Law' in Mahnoush H Arsanjani and others (eds), *Looking to the Future: Essays on International Law in Honor of W. Michael Reisman* (Brill–Nijhoff 2011)

Rougeaux J-P, 'Les renvois du droit international au droit interne' (1977) 81(1) *RGDIP* 361

Rovane C, *The Bounds of Agency: An Essay in Revisionary Metaphysics* (PUP 1998)
  'A Nonnaturalist Account of Personal Identity' in Mario De Caro and David MacArthur (eds), *Naturalism in Question* (Harvard University Press 2004)
  'Personal Identity, Ethical, Not Metaphysical' in Cynthia Macdonald and Graham Macdonald (eds), *McDowel and His Critics* (Blackwell Publishing Ltd 2006)
  'Group Agency and Individualism' (2014) 79 *Erkenntnis* 1663
  'Is Group Agency a Social Phenomenon' (2017) 196 *Synthese* 4869

Rozemond M, 'Real Distinction, Separability, and Corporeal Substance in Descartes' (2011) 35 *Midwest Studies in Philosophy* 240

Runciman D, *Pluralism and the Personality of the State* (CUP 1997)

Ryngaert C, 'The Immunity of International Organizations before Domestic Courts: Recent Trends' (2010) 7 *IOLR* 121

Sands P and Klein P, *Bowett's Law of International Institutions* (6th edn, Sweet & Maxwell 2009)

Sarooshi D, *International Organisations and Their Exercise of Sovereign Powers* (OUP 2005)
  'The Role of Domestic Public Law Analogies in the Law of International Organizations' (2008) 5 *International Organizations Law Review* 237

Scelle G, *Précis de Droit Des Gens: Principes et Systématique*, vol II (CNRS 1932)

Schabas WA, *The Customary International Law of Human Rights* (OUP 2021)

Schaffer J, 'Is There a Fundamental Level?' (2003) 37 *Noûs* 498

—— 'On What Grounds What' in David J Chalmers, David Manley and Ryan Wasserman (eds), *Metaphysics: New Essays on the Foundation of Ontology* (OUP 2009)

—— 'Grounding, Transitivity, and Contrastivity' in Fabrice Correia and Benjamin Schneider (eds), *Metaphysical Grounding: Understanding the Structure of Reality* (CUP 2012)

—— 'Grounding in the Image of Causation' (2016) 173 *Philosophical Studies* 94

—— 'The Metaphysics of Causation' in Edward N Zalta (ed), *Stanford Encyclopedia of Philosophy* (2016) <https://plato.stanford.edu/archives/fall2016/entries/causation-metaphysics/> accessed 9 February 2024

Schermers HG, 'The Legal Bases of International Organization Action' in René-Jean Dupuy (ed), *A Handbook on International Organizations* (2nd edn, Martinus Nijhof 1998)

—— 'The European Communities Bound by Fundamental Human Rights' (1990) 27(2) *Common Market Law Review* 249

Schermers HG and Blokker NM, *International Institutional Law* (5th edn, Martinus Nijhoff 2011)

Schlemmer-Schulte S, 'International Bank for Reconstruction and Development (IBRD)' *Max Planck Encyclopedia of International Law* (OUP 2011)

Schlosser M, 'Agency' in Edward N Zalta (ed), *Stanford Encyclopedia of Philosophy* (2015) <https://plato.stanford.edu/entries/agency/> accessed 9 February 2024

Schmid HB, *Plural Action: Essays in Philosophy and Social Science* (Springer 2009)

Schulte-Ostermann K, 'Agent Causation and Collective Agency' in Hans B Schmid, Katinka Schulte-Ostermann and Nikos Psarros (eds), *Concepts of Sharedness: Essays on Collective Intentionality* (Ontos Verlag 2008)

Schütze R, 'The "Succession Doctrine" and the European Union' in Robert Schütze (ed), *Foreign Affairs and the EU Constitution* (CUP 2014)

Schweikard DP, 'Limiting Reductionism in the Theory of Collective Action' in Hans B Schmid, Katinka Schulte-Ostermann and Nikos Psarros (eds), *Concepts of Sharedness: Essays on Collective Intentionality* (Ontos Verlag 2008)

Schweikard DP and Schmid HB, 'Collective Intentionality' in Edward N Zalta (ed), *The Stanford Encyclopedia of Philosophy* (2013) <https://plato.stanford.edu/archives/sum2013/entries/collective-intentionality/> accessed 9 February 2024

Scruton R, 'Corporate Persons' (1989) 63 *Proceedings of the Aristotelian Society*, Supplementary Volumes 239

Seabright MA and Kurke LB, 'Organizational Ontology and the Moral Status of the Corporation' (1997) 7 *Business Ethics Quarterly* 91

Searle JR, *The Construction of Social Reality* (Penguin 1996)

'What Is an Institution?' (2005) 1(1) *Journal of Institutional Economics* 1

Making the Social World: The Structure of Human Civilization (OUP 2010)

Sedley D, 'The Stoic Criterion of Identity' (1982) 27 *Phronesis* 255

Seidl-Hohenveldern I, *Corporations in and under International Law* (Grotius 1987)

'L'immunité de juridiction des Communautés européennes' (1990) 338 *Revue du Marché Commun* 475.

Seligman P, *On Being and Not-Being: An Introduction to Plato's Sophist* (Martinus Nijhoff 1974)

Seyersted F, 'Objective International Personality of Intergovernmental Organizations: Do Their Capacities Really Depend upon the Conventions Establishing Them' (1964) 34 *Nordic Journal of International Law* 3

'The Legal Nature of International Organizations' (1982) 51 *Nordisk Tidsskrift International Ret* 203

Common Law of International Organizations (Brill 2008)

Shapiro SJ, *Legality* (Belknap Press 2011)

Sheehy P, *The Reality of Social Groups* (Ashgate 2006)

Sheptycki J, 'The Accountability of Transnational Policing Institutions: The Strange Case of Interpol' (2004) 19(1) *Canadian Journal of Law & Society/ La Revue Canadienne Droit et Société* 107

Sinclair GF, *To Reform the World: International Organizations and the Making of Modern States* (OUP 2017)

Sivakumaran S, 'Beyond State and Non-State Actors: The Role of State-Empowered Entities in the Making and Shaping of International Law' (2017) 55 *CJTL* 344

Slowik E, 'Descartes and Individual Corporeal Substance' (2001) 9 *British Journal of the History of Philosophy* 1

Smit Duijzentkunst BL, 'The Concept of Rights in International Law' (Cambridge University Dissertation, 2015)

Snowdon PF, *Persons, Animals, Ourselves* (OUP 2014)

Sonnentag M, 'Renvoi' in Jürgen Basedow and others (eds), *Encyclopedia of Private International Law* (Edward Elgar 2017)

Sparks T, 'State' in Sahib Singh and Jean d' Aspremont (eds), *Concepts for International Law: Contributions to Disciplinary Thought* (Edward Elgar 2019)

Stapleton J, 'Causation in the Law' in Helen Beebee, Christopher Hitchcock and Peter Menzies (eds), *The Oxford Handbook of Causation* (OUP 2009)

Steinbrück Platise M, 'Legitimate Governance as a Privilege and Price for the Autonomy of International organisations' in Mateja Steinbrück Platise, Carolyn Moser and Anne Peters (eds), *The Legal Framework of the OSCE* (CUP 2019)

Steinbrück Platise M and Peters A, 'Transformation of the OSCE Legal Status' in Mateja Steinbrück Platise, Carolyn Moser, and Anne Peters (eds), *The Legal Framework of the OSCE* (CUP 2019)

Sullivan KL, 'How to Be a Redundant Realist' (2012) 9 *Episteme* 271

Swinburne R, *The Evolution of the Soul* (Clarendon Press 1997)

Talmon S, 'The Constitutive versus the Declaratory Theory of Recognition: *Tertium Non Datur?*' (2004) 75(1) *BYIL* 101

Thatcher M, 'Interview for *Woman's Own*', 23 September 1987, at <www .margaretthatcher.org/document/106689>, accessed 9 February 2024

Thompson RA, 'The Development of the Person: Social Understanding, Relationships, Conscience, and Self' in N Eisenberg and others (eds), *Handbook of Child Psychology: Volume 3 – Social, Emotional, and Personality Development* (6th edn, Wiley 2006)

Tollefsen DP, *Groups as Agents* (Polity 2015)

Tomuschat C, 'International Law: Ensuring the Survival of Mankind on the Eve of a New Century: General Course on Public International Law (Volume 281)' in *Collected Courses of the Hague Academy of International Law* (Brill 1999)

Townsend L, 'Being and Becoming in Group Agency' (2013) 7 *Abstracta* 39

Trahan J, *Existing Legal Limits to Security Council Veto Power in the Face of Atrocity Crimes* (CUP 2020)

Tuomela R, *The Philosophy of Sociality: The Shared Point of View* (OUP 2007)

Udehn L, *Methodological Individualism: Background, History and Meaning* (Routledge 2011)

Uzquiano G, 'Groups towards a Theory of Plural Embodiment' (2019) 115 *The Journal of Philosophy* 423

Van den Brande L, 'The International Legal Position of Flanders: Some Considerations' in Karel Wellens (ed), *International Law: Theory and Practice: Essays in Honour of Eric Suy* (Martinus Nijhoff 1998)

Velasquez MG, 'Debunking Corporate Moral Responsibility' (2003) 13 *Business Ethics Quarterly* 531

Velleman DJ, 'What Happens When Someone Acts?' (1992) 101 *Mind* 461
— 'What Happens When Someone Acts?' in David J Velleman (ed), *The Possibility of Practical Reason* (OUP 2000)

Verdirame G, *The UN and Human Rights: Who Guards the Guardians?* (CUP 2011)

Vilajosana JM, 'Social Facts and Law: Why the Rule of Recognition Is a Convention' in Lorena Ramírez-Ludeña and Josep M Vilajosana (eds), *Legal Conventionalism* (Springer 2019)

Villiger ME, *Commentary on the 1969 Vienna Convention on the Law of Treaties* (Brill–Nijhoff, 2008)

Virally M, 'Definition and Classification of International Organizations: A Legal Approach' in Georges Abi-Saab (ed), *The Concept of International Organization* (UNESCO 1981)

Virally M and Bastid S, 'La Notion de Fonction Dans La Théorie de l'organisation Internationale', in S Bastid and others (eds), *Mélanges offerts à Charles Rousseau: La communauté internationale* (Pédone 1974)

Voulgaris N, *Allocating International Responsibility between Member States and International Organizations* (Hart 2019)

Wahlberg TH, 'Why the Social Sciences Are Irreducible' (2019) 196 *Synthese* 4961

Waldron J, 'Planning for Legality' (2011) 109 *Michigan Law Review* 883

Walter C, 'Subjects of International Law', *Max Planck Encyclopedia of International Law* (2007) <https://opil.ouplaw.com/view/10.1093/law:epil/9780199231690/law-9780199231690-e1476> accessed 9 February 2024

Warriner CK, 'Groups Are Real: A Reaffirmation' (1956) 21 *American Sociological Review* 549

Wasserman R, 'Material Constitution' in Edward N Zalta (ed), *Stanford Encyclopedia of Philosophy* (2018) <https://plato.stanford.edu/archives/fall2018/entries/material-constitution/> accessed 9 February 2024

Wheaton H, *Elements of International Law* (8th edn, Sampson Low, Son & Co 1866)

White ND, 'Discerning Separate Will' in Wybo Heere (ed), *From Government to Governance: The Growing Impact of Non-State Actors on the International and European Legal System* (CUP 2004)

The Law of International Organisations (3rd edn, Manchester University Press 2016)

Williams JF, 'The Status of the League of Nations in International Law' (1926) 34 *ILA Report Conferences* 675

de Witte B, 'The EU as an International Legal Experiment' in Gráinne de Burca and JHH Weiler (eds), *The Worlds of European Constitutionalism* (CUP 2012)

Wolfers A, *Discord and Collaboration: Essays on International Politics* (Johns Hopkins Press 1962)

Wood M, 'Do International Organizations Enjoy Immunity under Customary International Law?' (2013) 10 *International Organizations Law Review* 287

Worster WT, 'Relative International Legal Personality of Non-State Actors' (2016) 42 *Brooklyn Journal of International Law* 207

Wurm J, 'Asking National Courts to Correct the Over-flight Charges of Eurocontrol', in August Reinisch (ed), *Challenging Acts of International Organizations before National Courts* (OUP 2011)

Yang X, *State Immunity in International Law* (CUP 2012)

Zahle J, 'The Individualism-Holism Debate on Intertheoretic Reduction and the Argument from Multiple Realization' (2003) 33 *Philosophy of the Social Sciences* 77

Zaibert L, 'Collective Intentions and Collective Intentionality' in David Koepsell and Laurence S Moss (eds), *John Searle's Ideas about Social Reality: Extensions, Criticisms and Reconstructions* (Wiley-Blackwell 2003)

Zürn M, *A Theory of Global Governance: Authority, Legitimacy & Contestation* (OUP 2018)

INDEX

CAMBRIDGE STUDIES IN INTERNATIONAL AND COMPARATIVE LAW

Books in the Series

For EU product safety concerns, contact us at Calle de José Abascal, 56–1°,
28003 Madrid, Spain or eugpsr@cambridge.org.

www.ingramcontent.com/pod-product-compliance
Ingram Content Group UK Ltd.
Pitfield, Milton Keynes, MK11 3LW, UK
UKHW021946101025
463821UK00008B/130